Soviet and Post-Soviet Politics and So...
ISSN 1614-3515

General Editor: Andreas Umland,
Institute for Euro-Atlantic Cooperation, Kyiv, umland@stanfordalumni.org

EDITORIAL COMMITTEE*

DOMESTIC & COMPARATIVE POLITICS
Prof. **Ellen Bos**, *Andrássy University of Budapest*
Dr. **Ingmar Bredies**, *FH Bund, Brühl*
Dr. **Andrey Kazantsev**, *MGIMO (U) MID RF, Moscow*
Prof. **Heiko Pleines**, *University of Bremen*
Prof. **Richard Sakwa**, *University of Kent at Canterbury*
Dr. **Sarah Whitmore**, *Oxford Brookes University*
Dr. **Harald Wydra**, *University of Cambridge*
SOCIETY, CLASS & ETHNICITY
Col. **David Glantz**, *"Journal of Slavic Military Studies"*
Dr. **Marlène Laruelle**, *George Washington University*
Dr. **Stephen Shulman**, *Southern Illinois University*
Prof. **Stefan Troebst**, *University of Leipzig*
POLITICAL ECONOMY & PUBLIC POLICY
Prof. em. **Marshall Goldman**, *Wellesley College, Mass.*
Dr. **Andreas Goldthau**, *Central European University*
Dr. **Robert Kravchuk**, *University of North Carolina*
Dr. **David Lane**, *University of Cambridge*
Dr. **Carol Leonard**, *Higher School of Economics, Moscow*
Dr. **Maria Popova**, *McGill University, Montreal*

FOREIGN POLICY & INTERNATIONAL AFFAIRS
Dr. **Peter Duncan**, *University College London*
Prof. **Andreas Heinemann-Grüder**, *University of Bonn*
Dr. **Taras Kuzio**, *Johns Hopkins University*
Prof. **Gerhard Mangott**, *University of Innsbruck*
Dr. **Diana Schmidt-Pfister**, *University of Konstanz*
Dr. **Lisbeth Tarlow**, *Harvard University, Cambridge*
Dr. **Christian Wipperfürth**, *N-Ost Network, Berlin*
Dr. **William Zimmerman**, *University of Michigan*
HISTORY, CULTURE & THOUGHT
Dr. **Catherine Andreyev**, *University of Oxford*
Prof. **Mark Bassin**, *Södertörn University*
Prof. **Karsten Brüggemann**, *Tallinn University*
Dr. **Alexander Etkind**, *University of Cambridge*
Dr. **Gasan Gusejnov**, *Moscow State University*
Prof. em. **Walter Laqueur**, *Georgetown University*
Prof. **Leonid Luks**, *Catholic University of Eichstaett*
Dr. **Olga Malinova**, *Russian Academy of Sciences*
Prof. **Andrei Rogatchevski**, *University of Tromsø*
Dr. **Mark Tauger**, *West Virginia University*

ADVISORY BOARD*
Prof. **Dominique Arel**, *University of Ottawa*
Prof. **Jörg Baberowski**, *Humboldt University of Berlin*
Prof. **Margarita Balmaceda**, *Seton Hall University*
Dr. **John Barber**, *University of Cambridge*
Prof. **Timm Beichelt**, *European University Viadrina*
Dr. **Katrin Boeckh**, *University of Munich*
Prof. em. **Archie Brown**, *University of Oxford*
Dr. **Vyacheslav Bryukhovetsky**, *Kyiv-Mohyla Academy*
Prof. **Timothy Colton**, *Harvard University, Cambridge*
Prof. **Paul D'Anieri**, *University of Florida*
Dr. **Heike Dörrenbächer**, *Friedrich Naumann Foundation*
Dr. **John Dunlop**, *Hoover Institution, Stanford, California*
Dr. **Sabine Fischer**, *SWP, Berlin*
Dr. **Geir Flikke**, *NUPI, Oslo*
Prof. **David Galbreath**, *University of Aberdeen*
Prof. **Alexander Galkin**, *Russian Academy of Sciences*
Prof. **Frank Golczewski**, *University of Hamburg*
Dr. **Nikolas Gvosdev**, *Naval War College, Newport, RI*
Prof. **Mark von Hagen**, *Arizona State University*
Dr. **Guido Hausmann**, *University of Munich*
Prof. **Dale Herspring**, *Kansas State University*
Dr. **Stefani Hoffman**, *Hebrew University of Jerusalem*
Prof. **Mikhail Ilyin**, *MGIMO (U) MID RF, Moscow*
Prof. **Vladimir Kantor**, *Higher School of Economics*
Dr. **Ivan Katchanovski**, *University of Ottawa*
Prof. em. **Andrzej Korbonski**, *University of California*
Dr. **Iris Kempe**, *"Caucasus Analytical Digest"*
Prof. **Herbert Küpper**, *Institut für Ostrecht Regensburg*
Dr. **Rainer Lindner**, *CEEER, Berlin*
Dr. **Vladimir Malakhov**, *Russian Academy of Sciences*

Dr. **Luke March**, *University of Edinburgh*
Prof. **Michael McFaul**, *Stanford University, Palo Alto*
Prof. **Birgit Menzel**, *University of Mainz-Germersheim*
Prof. **Valery Mikhailenko**, *The Urals State University*
Prof. **Emil Pain**, *Higher School of Economics, Moscow*
Dr. **Oleg Podvintsev**, *Russian Academy of Sciences*
Prof. **Olga Popova**, *St. Petersburg State University*
Dr. **Alex Pravda**, *University of Oxford*
Dr. **Erik van Ree**, *University of Amsterdam*
Dr. **Joachim Rogall**, *Robert Bosch Foundation Stuttgart*
Prof. **Peter Rutland**, *Wesleyan University, Middletown*
Prof. **Marat Salikov**, *The Urals State Law Academy*
Dr. **Gwendolyn Sasse**, *University of Oxford*
Prof. **Jutta Scherrer**, *EHESS, Paris*
Prof. **Robert Service**, *University of Oxford*
Mr. **James Sherr**, *RIIA Chatham House London*
Dr. **Oxana Shevel**, *Tufts University, Medford*
Prof. **Eberhard Schneider**, *University of Siegen*
Prof. **Olexander Shnyrkov**, *Shevchenko University, Kyiv*
Prof. **Hans-Henning Schröder**, *SWP, Berlin*
Prof. **Yuri Shapoval**, *Ukrainian Academy of Sciences*
Prof. **Viktor Shnirelman**, *Russian Academy of Sciences*
Dr. **Lisa Sundstrom**, *University of British Columbia*
Dr. **Philip Walters**, *"Religion, State and Society", Oxford*
Prof. **Zenon Wasyliw**, *Ithaca College, New York State*
Dr. **Lucan Way**, *University of Toronto*
Dr. **Markus Wehner**, *"Frankfurter Allgemeine Zeitung"*
Dr. **Andrew Wilson**, *University College London*
Dr. **Jan Zielonka**, *University of Oxford*
Prof. **Andrei Zorin**, *University of Oxford*

* While the Editorial Committee and Advisory Board support the General Editor in the choice and improvement of manuscripts for publication, responsibility for remaining errors and misinterpretations in the series' volumes lies with the books' authors.

Soviet and Post-Soviet Politics and Society (SPPS)
ISSN 1614-3515

Founded in 2004 and refereed since 2007, SPPS makes available affordable English-, German-, and Russian-language studies on the history of the countries of the former Soviet bloc from the late Tsarist period to today. It publishes between 5 and 20 volumes per year and focuses on issues in transitions to and from democracy such as economic crisis, identity formation, civil society development, and constitutional reform in CEE and the NIS. SPPS also aims to highlight so far understudied themes in East European studies such as right-wing radicalism, religious life, higher education, or human rights protection. The authors and titles of all previously published volumes are listed at the end of this book. For a full description of the series and reviews of its books, see www.ibidem-verlag.de/red/spps.

Editorial correspondence & manuscripts should be sent to: Dr. Andreas Umland, c/o DAAD, German Embassy, vul. Bohdana Khmelnitskoho 25, UA-01901 Kyiv, Ukraine. e-mail: umland@stanfordalumni.org

Business correspondence & review copy requests should be sent to: *ibidem* Press, Leuschnerstr. 40, 30457 Hannover, Germany; tel.: +49 511 2622200; fax: +49 511 2622201; spps@ibidem.eu.

Authors, reviewers, referees, and editors for (as well as all other persons sympathetic to) SPPS are invited to join its networks at www.facebook.com/group.php?gid=52638198614 www.linkedin.com/groups?about=&gid=103012 www.xing.com/net/spps-ibidem-verlag/

Recent Volumes

134 Nikolay Mitrokhin
Die "Russische Partei"
Die Bewegung der russischen Nationalisten in der UdSSR 1953-1985
Aus dem Russischen übertragen von einem Übersetzerteam unter der Leitung von Larisa Schippel
ISBN 978-3-8382-0024-8

135 Manja Hussner, Rainer Arnold (Hgg.)
Verfassungsgerichtsbarkeit in Zentralasien II
Sammlung von Verfassungstexten
ISBN 978-3-8382-0597-7

136 Manfred Zeller
Das sowjetische Fieber
Fußballfans im poststalinistischen Vielvölkerreich
Mit einem Vorwort von Nikolaus Katzer
ISBN 978-3-8382-0757-5

137 Kristin Schreiter
Stellung und Entwicklungspotential zivilgesellschaftlicher Gruppen in Russland
Menschenrechtsorganisationen im Vergleich
ISBN 978-3-8382-0673-8

138 David R. Marples, Frederick V. Mills (eds.)
Ukraine's Euromaidan
Analyses of a Civil Revolution
ISBN 978-3-8382-0660-8

139 Bernd Kappenberg
Setting Signs for Europe
Why Diacritics Matter for European Integration
With a foreword by Peter Schlobinski
ISBN 978-3-8382-0663-9

140 René Lenz
Internationalisierung, Kooperation und Transfer
Externe bildungspolitische Akteure in der Russischen Föderation
Mit einem Vorwort von Frank Ettrich
ISBN 978-3-8382-0751-3

141 Juri Plusnin, Yana Zausaeva, Natalia Zhidkevich, Artemy Pozanenko
Wandering Workers
Mores, Behavior, Way of Life, and Political Status of Domestic Russian Labor Migrants
Translated by Julia Kazantseva
ISBN 978-3-8382-0653-0

David J. Smith (Ed.)

LATVIA—A WORK IN PROGRESS?

100 Years of State- and Nation-Building

ibidem-Verlag
Stuttgart

Bibliografische Information der Deutschen Nationalbibliothek
Die Deutsche Nationalbibliothek verzeichnet diese Publikation in der Deutschen Nationalbibliografie; detaillierte bibliografische Daten sind im Internet über http://dnb.d-nb.de abrufbar.

Bibliographic information published by the Deutsche Nationalbibliothek
Die Deutsche Nationalbibliothek lists this publication in the Deutsche Nationalbibliografie; detailed bibliographic data are available in the Internet at http://dnb.d-nb.de.

Cover picture: #35102589 | © Schlierner - Fotolia.com

∞

Gedruckt auf alterungsbeständigem, säurefreien Papier
Printed on acid-free paper

ISSN: 1614-3515

ISBN-13: 978-3-8382-0648-6

© *ibidem*-Verlag
Stuttgart 2017

Alle Rechte vorbehalten

Das Werk einschließlich aller seiner Teile ist urheberrechtlich geschützt. Jede Verwertung außerhalb der engen Grenzen des Urheberrechtsgesetzes ist ohne Zustimmung des Verlages unzulässig und strafbar. Dies gilt insbesondere für Vervielfältigungen, Übersetzungen, Mikroverfilmungen und elektronische Speicherformen sowie die Einspeicherung und Verarbeitung in elektronischen Systemen.

All rights part of this publication may be reproduced, stored in or introduced into a retrieval system, or transmitted, in any form, or by any means (electronical, mechanical, photocopying, recording or otherwise) without the prior written permission of the publisher. Any person who does any unauthorized act in relation to this publication may be liable to criminal prosecution and civil claims for damages.

Printed in the EU

In Memory of Alfs Vanags, 1942-2016

Contents

David J Smith
State, Nation and Sovereignty amidst Uncertainty and Change: Turning Points and Continuities in Latvian Society and Polity 11

Part One

Andrejs Plakans
Death and Transfiguration: Reflections on World War I and the Birth of the Latvian State 29

Marina Germane
Latvians as a Civic Nation: The Interwar Experiment 55

David J Smith
Why Remember Paul Schiemann? 71

Part Two

Deniss Hanovs and Valdis Tēraudkalns
The Return of the Gods? Authoritarian Culture and Neo-Paganism in Interwar Latvia, 1934–1940 91

Geoffrey Swain
"Come on Latvians, Join the Party—We'll Forgive You Everything": Ideological Struggle during the National Communist Affair, Summer 1959 107

Irēna Saleniece
"At First We Missed Our Latvia...": Attitudes towards Latvian State during the Soviet Period 123

Part Three

Ieva Zake
Latvians in Exile and the Idea of the Latvian State 141

Una Bergmane
International Reactions to the Independence of the Baltic States: The French Example, 1989–1991 155

Li Bennich-Björkman
"You Are Not the People": Revisiting Citizenship and Geopolitics 175

Part Four

Geoffrey Pridham
Post-Soviet Latvia: A Consolidated Democracy in the Third Decade of Independence? 189

Pēteris Timofejevs Henriksson
The Europeanisation of Latvia's Public Policy: The Case of Foreign Aid Policy 2004–2010 205

Daina S. Eglitis
Paradoxes of Power: Gender, Work, and Family in the New Europe ... 225

Part Five

Alfs Vanags
Reflections on the Political Economy of the Latvian State since 1991: The Role of External Goals. What to do now that Externally Defined Goals have been Realised? 243

Aldis Purs
The Unbearable Myth of Convergence: Episodes in the Economic Development of Latvia 261

Matthew Kott
The Roots of Radicalism: Persistent Problems of Class and Ethnicity in Latvia's Politics 279

Index 315

State, Nation and Sovereignty in a Century of Uncertainty and Change: Turning Points and Continuities in Latvian Society and Polity

David J Smith, University of Glasgow

In a world where memorialisation of the past is increasingly ubiquitous, the period 2013–2016 in Latvia was replete with significant anniversaries. In May 2014, the country could take stock of 10 years as a member of the European Union (EU) and NATO, having just joined the Eurozone while looking ahead to assuming the EU Presidency at the start of 2015. The same period also marked 25 years since the set of events that began with the establishment of the Popular Front of Latvia (1988) and led to a newly-elected parliament declaring (on 4 May 1990) an end to Soviet rule and the start of a transitional period to independence, finally confirmed 16 months later following the final collapse of central Soviet authority in Moscow.

Legally speaking, at least, the Latvia that emerged in August 1991 was not a new state, for it was proclaimed and internationally recognised on the basis of unbroken continuity of the Republic of Latvia declared in November 1918. Seen from this perspective, Latvia celebrated the 90th anniversary of its independence in 2008, and will soon be marking its centenary.[1] In the meantime, the current wave of commemorations surrounding World War I is giving cause for fresh reflection on the events that swept away the pre-existing political, social and economic order of the Baltic Provinces and—in the space of only four years—transformed nascent calls for Latvian national autonomy into demands (actualised in November 1918 and internationally confirmed over the following four years) for a Latvian nation-state.

The experience of the ensuing two decades of sovereign statehood is, however, still overshadowed in official narratives by the events of 1939–1945. In this respect, the period since 2013 has seen a further set of anniversaries connected with (to paraphrase Aldis Purs in his contribution to the current volume)

---

1   David J. Smith, David J. Galbreath and Geoffrey Swain, Eds., *From Recognition to Restoration: Latvia's History as a Nation-State* (Amsterdam, New York: Rodopi, 2010).

Latvia's "loss of agency" as a state. Thus, 23 August 2014 marked 75 years since the signature of the Molotov-Ribbentrop Pact, which consigned Latvia to a Soviet sphere of influence and paved the way for military occupation and forcible incorporation into the USSR. With this, the country and its inhabitants were drawn into what Timothy Snyder has famously termed the "Bloodlands" of Central and Eastern Europe.[2] The transformation (*de facto* if not *de jure*) of the Latvian Republic into the Latvian Soviet Socialist Republic under Stalinist auspices was accompanied by arrests, executions and mass deportations during 1940–1941. This was followed by three years of Nazi German occupation, which saw the systematic killing of almost the entire Jewish population. In today's Latvia, the subsequent expulsion of the German forces by the Soviet Army and the end of World War II is officially remembered not as liberation, but as the replacement of one occupying regime by another: independent statehood was not restored, and the resumption of Soviet rule (preceded during 1944–1945 by a large-scale exodus of Latvians to the West) brought a further wave of arrests and deportations, as well as several years of bitter partisan warfare in the Latvian countryside. The official version of events is, however, still widely questioned amongst the large population of Soviet settlers and their descendants which was established in Latvia during the post-war decades, in a wave of migration that radically transformed the ethno-demographic make-up of the territory.

The cluster of significant anniversaries outlined above provided the original inspiration for this collection of articles reflecting on the historical processes that have shaped present-day Latvia and which continue to inform its development as the country looks ahead to 2018 and the 100th anniversary of the original Declaration of Independence. As Geoffrey Pridham notes in his contribution to this volume, on 21 March 2013 Latvia recorded the 7,884th day since the restoration of its independence in 1991—one day more than the duration of the first period of sovereign statehood from 18 November 1918 to 17 June 1940. Entry to NATO and the EU in 2004 was widely portrayed in official discourse (both Latvian and European) as setting the seal on the reconstruction of a liberal democratic and market-oriented nation-state, by having drawn a line under

---

2   Timothy Snyder, *Bloodlands: Europe between Hitler and Stalin* (London: Bodley Head, 2010).

the events of World War II and its aftermath and returned Latvia to the state of European "normality" it had attained during 1918–1940. However, a quarter of a century on from the restoration of independence, processes of state and nation-building in Latvia are still ongoing. Issues such as citizenship, language policy, minority rights, legitimacy of democratic institutions, economic stability and security all remain the object of public discussion, as does public commemoration of events in Latvia's past. The current situation reflects in turn longer-standing debates over the course of the past century concerning the relationship between state, nation and sovereignty in the context of Latvian society and polity. By examining different aspects of this relationship this book seeks to reveal both key turning points and continuities in its development and thereby help to inform current debates.

The collection incorporates contributions by established and early career scholars drawn from a range of countries and disciplines, who first came together at a workshop held in Uppsala in December 2013.[3] It addresses the key questions outlined above, whilst also focusing on some hitherto largely unexplored aspects and dimensions of state and nation-building over the past 100 years.

In the opening contribution to the volume, Andrejs Plakans illustrates how the constant upheavals during the past century have made it difficult to craft the kind of coherent "master narrative" of the past that is generally seen as a crucial component of the modern national state. Reflecting on the independence proclamation of 18 November 1918, Plakans argues that the circumstances in which it was adopted and the state of uncertainty and flux which surrounded it make the event difficult to situate within a linear narrative painting independence as the preordained endpoint of the 19th-century National Awakening. While the vision set out by the state founders did ultimately provide a platform for victory over the Bolsheviks and the attainment of international recognition, "18 November in itself was not a transfigurative moment but the start of a transfigurative process" marking the start of a "relatively slow diffusion of the idea of a Latvian state." In this sense, Plakans argues, "the Republic of Latvia remained a 'work in progress' well into the 1920s even though it had already acquired a *de jure* existence."

---

3 The editor and authors gratefully acknowledge the financial support for this event provided by the Uppsala Centre for Russian and Eurasian Studies (UCRS) and the Centre for Russian and Central and East European Studies (CRCEES) of the University of Glasgow.

The first and most essential step in any modern state-building process is to define the *demos* (or *demoi*) which constitutes the basis of the political community.[4] While the founding Declaration of 1918 referred to sovereignty within united ethnographic boundaries, fully one quarter of the inhabitants of the new state were non-Latvian by ethnicity. As Marina Germane demonstrates in the first contribution dealing with interwar Latvia, the need to accommodate the ethnic diversity of the local population had been acknowledged already prior to World War I, in the treatises on Latvian nationhood published by Marġers Skujenieks and Miķelis Valters in 1913 and 1914 respectively. A civic understanding of nationhood was carried over into the early post-independence period, contributing to a 1922 constitution adopted in the name of a political "nation of Latvia" as well as to broad rights of cultural self-government offered to national minorities as part of an ambitious (and by the European standards of the day largely unique) experiment in pluralist democracy.

The next contribution, by David J. Smith, develops Germane's central point by revisiting the life and ideas of one of the key participants in this interwar "experiment"—the German Latvian politician, journalist, lawyer and "Thinker of the European Minorities Movement" Paul Schiemann. Born into the ruling elite of the late tsarist period, Schiemann lived through the creation and subsequent vicissitudes of the independent Latvian state during the first half of the 20th century, dying in 1944 in Nazi-occupied Rīga. Clearly a figure of international stature during the 1920s, he was a prominent minority rights activist, but also a strong patriot of Latvia and passionate advocate of European peace and unity, as outlined in the acclaimed biography published by John Hiden in 2004. The appearance of this biography in Latvian- and Russian-language translation in 2016—the result of an initiative lasting several years and bringing together many prominent figures within society and politics—suggests a continued resonance for Schiemann's ideas in today's Latvia. Smith uses this contemporary initiative as a point of departure for analysing Schiemann's thinking on state- and nation-building and his wide-ranging contribution to the life of the interwar

---

4   Juan J. Linz and Alfred Stepan, *Problems of Democratic Transition and Consolidation: Southern Europe, South America, and Post-Communist Europe* (Baltimore, Md., London: Johns Hopkins University Press,1996), 16.

Republic, during an era which can be seen to offer many lessons both for present-day Latvia and for Europe as a whole.

As Germane shows in her analysis of 1920s debates on language use and citizenship, the Latvian state created after World War I was ultimately ill-equipped to sustain its founding vision. In a vulnerable position internationally and faced with growing pressure from nationalist political forces that called for a "more Latvian Latvia", it ultimately rejected parliamentary democracy in favour of stability and strong leadership. These ideological currents were translated into practice following the *coup* of May 1934, though—as Deniss Hanovs and Valdis Tēraudkalns outline in the third chapter on the interwar period—Kārlis Ulmanis' regime embodied a conservative and person-centred authoritarianism with an emphasis on "traditional values" which distinguished it from the more radical nationalism propounded by the extra-parliamentary *Pērkonkrusts* movement. In their chapter, Hanovs and Tēraudkalns illustrate the main lines of this ideology through an analysis of the authorities' attitude to the neo-pagan *Dievturi* movement, whose ideas were seen as potentially disruptive to the state's relationship with established religious denominations.

While the two decades of interwar independence provide an obvious exercise in contrasts when it comes to the nature of the political regime, there seems much to be said for Artis Pabriks and Aldis Purs' claim that "the accomplishments of the state [during this period] ... were very real and palpable to its citizens."[5] In this regard, the two authors describe as "prophetic" the reported claim by Ulmanis that "the ultimate defence of the Latvian state in the face of Nazi or Soviet aggression would be the memory of the independence era."[6] That the state did much to instil a basic identification on the part of most of its residents is one of the key conclusions that can be drawn from Irēna Saleniece's contribution to the present volume, which uses oral history as a means of exploring popular attitudes to the half century of foreign rule between 1940 and 1990. Following the Soviet takeover, any public expression of identification with the interwar Republic was denounced as "bourgeois nationalism" and expressly prohibited. Privately, however, the period of independence remained a

---

5   Artis Pabriks and Aldis Purs, *Latvia: The Challenges of Change* (London, New York: Routledge, 2001), 22.
6   Pabriks and Aldis Purs, *Latvia*, 23.

reference point for the generation born in Latvia during 1910–1935. In Saleniece's view, the surviving members of this group (while often ambivalent towards post-1991 realities) played a crucial role in the restoration of statehood, by acting as a "bridge" between two periods of independent Latvia and transmitting concrete knowledge about state order, traditions and symbols to their children and grandchildren. A similar "bridging" function can of course be discerned in the case of the large exile communities that were established by those who fled Latvia ahead of the reconquest by the Soviets in 1944. Not least, these became the guardians of the legal continuity ideal which emerged during 1988–1991 as the cornerstone of the movement for independence. This role is explored by Ieva Zake in her wide-ranging contribution on Latvians in the United States, which explores the idea of the Latvian state held by both post- and pre-1940 exile communities.

The independence movement that took shape from 1988 did not, however, emerge as the result of some kind of primordial national reawakening. Rather, it was shaped and led by leaders that had been socialised under Soviet rule and which in most cases had formed part of what could be termed the Soviet Latvian establishment. As scholarship on neighbouring Lithuania has now begun to acknowledge, this invites deeper reflection on the nature of Soviet nationalities policy and a recognition that state- and nation-building were not simply suspended during a Soviet period which carried its own formative legacies for what came after 1991.[7] According to the official ideology of the Soviet regime, 1940 was a popular revolution that overthrew an "unnatural" interlude of bourgeois dictatorship, marking a resumption of the Soviet rule briefly declared in 1918–1919 and making Latvia part of a voluntary federation of sovereign republics. The LSSR was not in fact sovereign in any politically meaningful sense, at least not until Gorbachev's liberalisation in the late 1980s allowed its institutions to acquire a life of their own. However, by casting the LSSR as the territorial homeland of a Latvian nation defined in narrowly ethnic terms, Soviet ideology exhibited a "paradoxical continuity" (to borrow a phrase used by

---

7 On the Lithuanian case, see Violeta Davoliūtė, *The Making and Breaking of Soviet Lithuania: Memory and Modernity in the Wake of War* (Abingdon, Oxon: Routledge, 2013).

Davoliūtė with regard to Lithuania) with the policies of the Ulmanis regime during the 1930s, airbrushing out interwar minority communities like the Germans and Jews from the history of Latvia.[8]

Apparent elements of similarity with the 1930s are, however, significantly outweighed by those of difference when one considers the ultimate aims of Soviet policy and the economic and ethno-demographic changes it wrought in Latvia over the course of half a century. While one can speak of genuine cultural autonomy in the form of Latvian-language schooling, media and other institutions that helped to sustain a Latvian ethnonational identity, the Soviet authorities saw this identity as strictly subordinate to identification with the overall USSR and the top-down project of a building a single "Soviet people" (*Sovetskii narod*). From the 1920s, the Soviet regime had deliberately nurtured the particular identities of non-Russian ethnic groups as a means of promoting their "development" (and—more importantly—of consolidating Soviet power). Yet, the doctrine of "national in form, socialist in content" attached no intrinsic value to the longer-term reproduction of these identities within its overall understanding of socio-economic modernisation. Increasingly denuded of its original Marxist-Leninist ideological content from the 1940s onwards, the construction of *Sovetskii narod* became more and more akin to a standard, culturally-based project of national integration, within which Russian was accorded growing importance as a state language and the Russian people cast as the core, state-bearing nation.

From the perspective of non-Russian ethnic groups living in their "own" republics, what was officially termed "Sovietisation" thus became synonymous with Russification. Such feelings were especially apparent in Latvia, where centrally-dictated Soviet policies of industrialisation brought large numbers of Russian-speaking settlers to the Republic from the 1940s onwards. In the course of 1944–1989, the proportion of ethnic Latvians within the overall population fell from 75% to 52%, and use of Russian became ever prevalent within the public sphere. One can, therefore, point to inherent contradictions within a Soviet nationality policy that, in the words of Ronald Suny, "nourished cultural

---

8   Quotation from Davoliūtė 2014, 3.

uniqueness but denied its expression."[9] Or, put another way, "[institutionalised] both territorial nationhood and ethno-cultural nationality" as well as the tensions between them.[10]

These tensions and contradictions are explored in Geoffrey Swain's contribution ("Come on Latvians, Join the Party") which revisits Latvia's National Communist "Affair" of 1959. Latvian communists had seen socialism as something to be built within a national frame of reference. They now attempted to graft this onto a society that had experienced "an alternative, non-Soviet and self-determined national existence"[11] for fully two decades prior to 1940 and in which individual citizens had experienced a variety of fates and experiences during 1939–45. Some of those who founded the LSSR genuinely adhered to the Leninist dictum of "national in form, socialist in content" which seemed to be making a comeback post-Stalin and was indeed seen as a necessity if hearts and minds were to be won for Soviet power. They were, however, soon disabused of this notion by more conservative elements of the local and all-union party-state bureaucracy.

The basic tension, however, remained unresolved and fed into mounting discontent over the next three decades, which was quickly articulated once Gorbachev initiated political liberalisation during the late 1980s. This gave rise to a mass national movement which quickly adopted the legal continuity of pre-war independence (and consequent illegality of Soviet rule) as its defining argument. The government elected in 1990 took the first steps in post-communist state-building, but could only do so much without the achievement of full sovereignty, which in turn rested on formal external recognition of statehood. This international dimension to the independence struggle is explored by Una Bergmane in her chapter, which (drawing on previously unseen classified documents) focuses on the until now largely unexplored question of France's policy towards the "Baltic Question." As Bergmane demonstrates, the demands for restored independence of Latvia and the other two Baltic countries placed

---

9 Ronald Suny, "Incomplete Revolution: National Movements and the Collapse of the Soviet Empire," *New Left Review* 189 (1992): 113.
10 Rogers Brubaker, *Nationalism Reframed: Nationhood and the National Question in the New Europe* (Cambridge, New York: Cambridge University Press, 1996), 8.
11 V. Stanley Vardys, "Modernisation and Baltic Nationalism," *Problems of Communism* September–October (1975): 36.

Western leaders in a quandary. They could not publicly renounce the legal continuity principle which had guided their interactions for half a century, especially given the need to acknowledge growing support for the Baltic cause amongst their own publics. The restoration of sovereignty to Moscow's satellites in Central Europe and the pending reunification of Germany (marking the end of the Yalta system) also further reinforced the moral case for the restoration of independence. Generally, however, legal continuity was secondary to *Realpolitik* in the thinking of François Mitterand and other Western leaders, whose eyes were firmly on the bigger picture of the USSR and who were reluctant to undermine the position of a Soviet leader who rejected any talk of Soviet occupation and viewed the Baltic territories as an integral part of the USSR. With the elected Baltic governments in a state of limbo, final realisation of independence had to await developments at the Soviet centre and the dramatic collapse of Soviet power following the abortive Moscow *putsch* of August 1991. The Baltic parliaments seized the initiative and declared immediate and unconditional restoration of their independence on the basis of legal continuity. Smaller countries took the bold step of recognising this. The larger powers only did so following the decision by Russia to extend recognition on 24 August. In this sense, Latvia owes much to Yeltsin's Russia.

For all of the positive cooperation evident during 1990–1991, the Baltic and Russian governments were on a different page when it came to the legal foundations governing Baltic independence. The Yeltsin government made it clear that it saw Estonia, Latvia and Lithuania not as pre-existing states restored *de facto* on the basis of legal continuity, but rather as newly-created entitites which should accept the legacies bequeathed by Sovietisation and whose relations with Russia should be governed by treaties signed in January 1991 prior to the fall of the USSR. This brought into focus the question of the large population of Soviet citizens that had settled in Latvia over the previous 50 years and which now made up around a third of the population. The size of this community gave pause for thought and explains why (as Bergmane highlights in her chapter), Latvia followed a more gradual, cautious approach to the question of independence from the USSR. In the course of 1989–1991 the ruling Popular Front had worked pragmatically to unite all residents behind the cause of independence. Among other things it gave assurances that anyone who applied for Latvian citizenship would be granted it unconditionally. This had had some success, though there was an undoubted ambivalence on the part of a large section of the settler population. August 1991 brought a dramatic change in the political situation. Initiative passed to the parties of the Right, which advocated a more restrictive policy of granting citizenship only to those who had held citizenship between the wars or who were descendants of interwar citizens.

In the first of the contributions dealing with post-1991 state- and nation-building, Li Bennich-Björkman revisits the question of why this more restrictive policy was adopted. A common tendency, she observes, has been to attribute this turn of events to a process of nationalist outbidding in which nationalist parties were able to harness a deeply-held but hitherto repressed desire on the part of the Latvian majority for retributive justice and for the restoration of a nation-state as the only viable means of ensuring the longer-term survival of the Latvian language and ethnonational identity. There can be little doubt that the parties of the Right effectively mobilized such feelings in support of a state-building approach that ensured their ascendancy in the elections of 1993 and paved the way for their subsequent dominance within the political system. In so doing they could point to the sanction given to legal continuity by Western governments, which had set no conditions for recognition of independence and had in many cases simply re-established formal diplomatic links severed following the Soviet takeover of 1940.

In Bennich-Björkman's view, however, the approach to citizenship can more plausibly explained by reference to geopolitical motives—namely, the argument that most Russian-speakers (even if they supported independence) retained strong historical and cultural ties to the Russian and Slavic cultural sphere and, had they obtained citizenship immediately and unconditionally, would have pressed for continued political and economic affiliation with the former Soviet space as opposed to the course of integration with the West advocated by Latvia's independence movement. This argument, one can add, was given further weight by reference to the continued presence in Latvia of former Soviet troops as well as Russia's own vision at a time when it was manifestly struggling to define a national identity not linked to the Soviet and longer-term imperial past.

By this interpretation, the citizenship law was dictated by *Realpolitik* and (on the part of many former Popular Front activists) a perceived need for consensus that could unite a majority of the state's population. One can of course only speculate what might have been transpired had citizenship been made immediately available to all residents back in 1991. Nevertheless, citing the contrasting examples of other post-Soviet states such as Moldova and (to use a currently topical example) Ukraine, Bennich-Björkman suggests that the design of the citizenship law—and its consequent exclusion of a prospective "eastward-leaning" electorate—likely served to facilitate Latvia's remarkably fast and smooth association with the West and its membership in NATO and the EU, as well as making it easier to enact reform policies in support of this goal.

As Bennich-Björkman also observes, however, this approach can be seen as a departure from the democratic principles that were regarded as being of symbolically central importance in the repudiation of the former authoritarian regime. Democracy, she writes, "is inescapably rule not for, but by the people who are affected by decisions." By this understanding, Soviet-era settlers and their descendants did not immediately become part of a *demos* or community of citizens with the right to participate in processes of state- and nation-building. Instead, they were recategorised as a Soviet "immigrant minority" which, in order to join the political community, first had to undergo naturalisation on terms set by representatives of (a now predominantly ethnic Latvian) citizenry. The naturalisation paradigm was adopted partly in response to external pressure from the Western democracies and international organisations with which the newly-sovereign Latvia was now seeking to engage. While these endorsed the principle of legal continuity as a basis for state-building, they were not willing to lend their support to the discourse of "decolonisation" propounded by the more radically nationalist parties that emerged from Latvia's independence movement. They therefore insisted that Latvia should do its utmost to facilitate the rapid naturalisation of the large non-citizen population created in 1991.

The right-of-centre political parties that gained ascendancy in Latvia from 1993 struggled to reconcile these external demands with their own agenda of rebuilding a nation-state around a Latvian ethnocultural core, as well as with the associated discourse that deemed post-war Russian-speaking settlers "illegal occupants". The resultant tension was reflected in initially restrictive naturalisation provisions—adopted only in 1995—that set annual quotas on the number of people who could apply for citizenship. Ultimately, however, the geopolitical logic of integration proved most compelling, and Latvia subsequently liberalised provisions for acquisition of citizenship as one of the conditions for entry to the European Union in 2004. On the back of these changes, substantial numbers of non-citizens underwent naturalisation during 1998–2004, while further changes to legislation mean that anyone born to non-citizen parents after 1992 can now obtain Latvian citizenship without fulfilling the naturalisation requirements, provided their parents request this when registering the birth. This means that access to citizenship is set to become increasingly moot as time goes on. The period since 1991 has also seen a marked growth in knowledge of the Latvian language amongst Russian-speakers, especially those of the younger generation.

Despite these encouraging trends, societal integration in Latvia still remains in many respects "a work-in-progress" when seen from the standpoint of 2016. The legal categorisation of Soviet-era settlers as an "immigrant minority" following independence obviously disregarded the complex institutional legacies bequeathed by Soviet rule: these mean that many Russian-speakers living in Latvia have maintained a strong attachment to their particular ethnocultural identity, and this has underpinned political mobilisation along party lines and around a range of issues, not least the longer-term maintenance of publically-funded education in the Russian language and the often diametrically opposed interpretations of World War II and the Soviet past that still predominate within the two ethno-linguistic communities. For the now politically dominant Latvian majority, meanwhile, the ethnic boundaries inherited from the Soviet period raise the question of whether the political community can be reconfigured along more culturally pluralistic lines, and those naturalised after 1991 accepted as full and equal members of this community.

This question is one of several addressed in the next chapter by Geoffrey Pridham, who offers a wide-ranging assessment of the extent to which, more than two decades on from the restoration of independence and a decade on from EU accession, Latvia can be considered a fully consolidated democracy. Here, Pridham focuses on different levels (state and institutions; intermediary actors (parties, NGOs, media); civil society and economy; external actors) and dimensions (structural, attitudinal and behavioural) of consolidation, setting these against the formidable challenges arising from the Soviet legacy and the need to effect what Claus Offe has elsewhere termed a "triple transition" entailing concurrent political liberalisation, economic marketisation and (re)construction of a sovereign nation-state.[12] Overall, Pridham sees evidence of considerable progress, especially as regards the routinisation and institutionalisation of democracy. EU accession and subsequent membership have had a significant impact in particular areas, while contributing to an international environment far more benign than the one with which Latvia was constructed between the wars. It remains to be seen whether the multiple crises currently besetting Europe (over Russia's actions in Ukraine, the Eurozone and refugees) will mutate into the kind of "drastic international circumstances" that could shake the foundations put in place since 1991. Barring this, however, Pridham considers that democracy "has far stronger prospects of survival" than it did during the period of the interwar republic. Key challenges nevertheless remain, not least in the form of the still limited legitimation attained by democracy over the past two decades, as well as weaknesses in the internalisation of new rules and procedures. Continued ethnic divisions are also highlighted as a factor undermining participation, which, as already pointed out by Bennich-Björkman, can be considered a key hallmark of any democratic system.

Pridham's analysis also leads him to conclude that adaptations made during Latvia's accession to the EU had an opportunistic quality, which can be seen by some degree of backsliding since 2004. This issue is explored more fully in the chapter by Pēteris Timofejevs Henriksson, who uses the case of Latvia's post-2004 foreign aid policy as a lens for revisiting and moving beyond the long-standing "rationalist" versus "constructivist" dichotomy that exists within the literature on "Europeanisation East." In the case of foreign aid, Timofejevs Henriksson finds that Latvia (one of the poorest of the new member states) did not in fact comply with standard rationalist expectations of policy backsliding

---

12 Claus Offe, "Capitalism by Democratic Design? Democratic Theory facing the Triple Transition in East Central Europe," in Claus Offe, ed., *Varieties of Transition* (Cambridge: Polity Press, 1996), 29–49.

during the post-accession period, as aid volumes continued to increase in absolute terms and policy continued to evolve, even following the severe financial crisis that set in after 2008. His findings suggest that this can be attributed in large part to the fact that domestic decision-makers perceived peer pressure from governments of other EU member states and feared the opprobrium that might result should they fail to comply with the expectation that they provide aid to developing countries. This sensitivity, he argues, should be linked not to any measure of EU conditionality. Rather—adopting a constructivist perspective—he sees it as arising from a continued deeply-felt need for ontological security. This drives policymakers to present and act according to a coherent narrative of state identity capable of appealing to both a domestic and an external audience, and of sustaining a sense of coherent "Self" that would ensure Latvia's credibility and predictability within the wider international community.

Alfs Vanags' chapter on political economy further underscores the importance of EU and also NATO accession as "external anchors" for state and nation-building. The goal of entry to these two organisations, Vanags argues, served to depoliticise key issues and greatly assisted in "creating at least the infrastructure of a modern democratic state—if not always the substance." A similar anchoring role is apparent in the case of entry to the Eurozone, which was used to justify austerity measures adopted in response to a 2008 economic slump exacerbated by fiscal irresponsibility during the boom years of the pre- and immediate post-accession period. The strategy of "internal devaluation" used to combat the crisis has since enabled Latvia to redress the steep decline in GDP during 2008–2010, but has further exacerbated levels of poverty and social inequality that are amongst the highest in the European Union.

The social costs of post-Soviet economic transition provide the focus for the contribution by Daina Eglitis, which uses the case of Latvia to illustrate a "new crisis of men" across the countries that have emerged from behind the former Iron Curtain. To talk of such a crisis is paradoxical, given the continued dominance (with some notable exceptions such as Vaira Vīķe-Freiberga) of men within the Latvian elite and, more broadly, the persistence of a societal context that privileges male actors and masculinity. This structural context, however, has seen the emergence of a population of marginal men characterised by poor health and increased mortality, as well as low educational attainment and labour market participation (in the latter case, Eglitis points to a further paradox whereby women's apparent advantage in the labour market is in part built on a foundation of disadvantage—namely, a concentration within the lower-wage areas of the economy). Statistics also show that during the crisis years of 2009–2010, men were disproportionately represented amongst those leaving Latvia, in a flow of outward labour migration that has become arguably the most pressing issue facing the state following accession to the European Union. As Aldis Purs reminds us in the penultimate contribution to the volume, the scale of this phenomenon provided a key argument for former President Andris Bērziņš' alarming assertion in 2013 that "unless Latvia achieves the average income level of the EU in 10 years' time, it will cease to exist as a politically viable state."

While Purs characterises Bērziņš' statement as exaggerated and ill-informed, he nevertheless sees little prospect that Latvia will achieve convergence with the leading modern, industrial economies of Western Europe anytime soon. In this regard, he cites an analysis suggesting that in order to attain EU average GDP per capita by 2023, Latvia's growth rate would have to outstrip that of the Union as a whole by 5% annually over the entire period in question. Expectations that Latvia would quickly catch up economically with its Western neighbours were widespread in 1991, and perhaps even more so immediately after entry to the EU in 2004. Underpinning such hopes was a prevalent historical narrative which held that the three Baltic States had attained parity with their Scandinavian neighbours during the interwar period and, had it not been for the ensuing Soviet occupation, would today enjoy comparable living standards. For Purs, however, this claim is unfounded, and part of a wider long-standing "myth of convergence" with the West. In so far as it had not been entirely decimated or dismantled during World War I, the economic infrastructure inherited by the interwar Republic of Latvia had been largely geared to the requirements of a large empire rather than to local needs. The post-war situation meant that there was no prospect of reviving the industrial base established in the late tsarist period. In its place came a system largely based on early-stage small market agriculture, which (while vital in undergirding the political legitimacy of the new state) was ill-placed to attract the capital and technical investment necessary to achieve rapid economic modernisation. With the Soviet takeover came a reversion to patterns of development characteristic of the tsarist era, creating an economic base which again all but collapsed with the demise of the USSR.

In short, Purs argues that the longer term economic development of Latvia over the past century has to be "measured against a backdrop of near constant change and frequent ruin." Having reattained "agency" as a state in 1991, Latvia has linked its economic fate to that of the European Union, but still faces the challenge of how to access capital and expertise while maintaining a degree of local control over development. This challenge, moreover, should be viewed not simply in terms of attaining parity with the EU in per capita GDP terms, but also as one of eradicating pronounced levels of inequality and poverty within society. In his earlier chapter, Alf Vanags attributes the high degree of inequality in Latvia to the very modest redistribution generated by the current tax-benefit system, and advances concrete recommendations such as tapering of the withdrawal of benefits as earnings grow above currently very low minimum income thresholds. Vanags also offers further prescriptions for tackling key challenges such as strengthening education, eradicating the shadow economy and increasing accountability of elected representatives as a means of improving policymaking now that the previous external constraints are no longer in place.

Vanags' key question—what to do now that all externally defined goals have been realised?—is of course one that has broader relevance beyond the economic realm. EU and NATO membership may have been hailed as marking an end to "transition" and a return to "normality", but what does it in fact mean to be a "normal" (or "proper", to use Timofejevs Henriksson's term) European country amid the crises and political divisions currently besetting the European Union over monetary union, the response to Russia's actions in Ukraine and, now, "Brexit"? During 2012–2016, the issue of European norms has also been thrown into especially sharp relief by the question of how to respond to the arrival in Europe of hundreds of thousands of refugees displaced by the ongoing conflicts in Syria and Iraq. In a much earlier work on neighbouring Estonia, published in 1993, Rein Taagepera hailed that country's return to independence, but underlined the scale of the challenges posed by independence in an increasingly *inter*dependent world.[13] Nearly a quarter of a century on from the fall of the Soviet Union, Latvia and the other Baltic countries are still coming to terms with this state of affairs. As several the contributions to this volume underline, much still needs to be done to deliver on the initial promise of restored independence and to consolidate a democratic nation-state. At the same time, the nation-state model *per se* often appears ill-placed to contend with the challenges of the contemporary world.

These challenges are alluded to in the concluding chapter to the volume by Matthew Kott, who strikes a cautionary note in a further wide-ranging historical overview spanning the period from the 1905 Revolution right up to the present day. Taking as his central focus the intersection of class and ethnicity in Latvia's politics, Kott highlights a persistent trend towards the securitisation of ethnicity and the "ethnification" of social issues, the result being a vicious circle of radicalisation that has consistently hindered the consolidation of an open, pluralistic, and inclusive polity. The experience of the past 100 years, Kott claims, has given rise to a nation "constructed to view itself as constantly under threat" and to a continued tension between ethnic and civic nationalism that appears to have grown sharper since 2010. While the current international context means that security—as more conventionally understood—remains a real issue for the restored Latvian state, history shows that ethnification and securitisation of social issues offers no long-term perspective. Only by breaking the cycle so often repeated in the past can Latvia hope to move towards the situation of human security that has proved so elusive over the past century.

---

13 Rein Taagepera, *Estonia: Return to Independence* (Boulder: Westview Press), 217–220.

Death and Transfiguration: Reflections on World War I and the Birth of the Latvian State

Andrejs Plakans, Iowa State University

1. Short-Lived "Master Narratives"

In contemporary historical research the concept of "master narrative" has had considerable success in becoming a component in descriptions of modern nation-states. It is widely believed that nation-states generate from within their cultures a dominant interpretation of their long-term history, bordering on the mythical or at least containing mythical elements. In time, the interpretation takes on hegemonic characteristics because it is reiterated over generations, appears in the textbooks of primary and secondary schools, and speads widely throughout popular culture. A "master narrative" is taken to reflect a collectivity's sense of self—its identity—and often serves as an overall justification for domestic or foreign policies and for conceptually separating "us" from "them," the members of the national collective from those who do not belong to it.[1] The term "master narrative" is sometimes used interchangably with an analogous phrase—"official history"—the latter suggesting that the "master narrative" has been produced, directly or indirectly, at the behest of the central government in order to legitimise existing power arrangements.[2] Critical assessments of "master narratives" and "official histories" have for a long time taken both to task for not having insufficient distance from Power—meaning State Power—and for subordinating the investigation of a country's past to the interests of those in power. Other critics tend to be less condemnatory because they recognise that the origins of a society's understanding of its own past emerges through far more complicated processes than simply on "orders from above." Also, most historians will admit that the desconstruction of established "master narratives" is not self-justifying but can be a power-play in disguise, aiming to substitute a

---

1   David Carr, *Time, Narrative, and History* (Bloomington, Ind.: Indiana University Press, 1986)
2   A discussion of this "official history" genre can be found in Robin Higham, *Official Histories: Essays and Bibliographies from around the World* (Manhattan, Kansas: Kansas State University Press, 1970) and Jeffrey Grey, *The Last Word? Essays on Official History in the United States and British Commonwealth* (Westport: Praeger, 2003).

new "master narrative" for a prevailing one because the new narrative better serves the political purposes of its proponents.

With respect to Latvian-language history writing in the 20th century—the century in which it became a continuous activity—it can be said that various proposed "master narratives" have had little luck in living a long life. Latvia has not been an hospitable context for the development of all-inclusive historical accounts of the kind that frequently characterise the writing of history in nation-states with relatively stable borders, stable governments, a stable population, and institutional continuity among the professional researchers who call themselves historians. At the end of the 19th century, Jānis Krodznieks (1851–1924), who is understood to be the "founder" of modern Latvian historiography, sought to depose what he believed to be the "master narratives" about the Baltic littoral in the history writing of Baltic German scholars.[3] Yet, even as Krodznieks was writing, he was already finding himself in competition with the Marxist-inspired general history of Kārlis Landers (1883–1937), who sought to dethrone both the Baltic German and the early Latvian nationalist historical discourses.[4] In the meantime, a "popular" narrative of the Latvian past, accumulating in the pseudo-historical writings of Latvian nationalist activists, was constructing a long-term story about the centuries-long travails of the Latvian *tauta* (Engl. nation) that, according to this version, had been blocked from normal historical nation development by the arrival in the 13th century of German merchants and crusaders who in due course established themselves as regional overlords. How firmly any of these competing "master narratives" seized the imagination of the Latvian-speaking population of the Russian Baltic Provinces remains an open question. But they probably were more appealing than those being written by Imperial *Russian* historians, who conceptualised the Baltic region as a borderland and tied its story to that of the rise of the Russian state.[5]

---

3   See the compilation of his shorter writings in Jānis Krodznieks, *Iz Baltijas vētures* (Rīga: Rīgas Latviešu Biedrības Derīgu Grahmatu Nodaļas Izdevums, 1913).
4   Kārlis Landers, *Latvijas wehsture: kultur-wehstursiki apzerejumi*, I (Peterburga: A. Gulbis, 1908).
5   Karsten Brüggemann, "The Baltic Provinces and Russian Perceptions in Late Imperial Russia." In Karsten Brüggemann and Bradley D. Woodworth, eds., *Russland an der Ostsee: Imperiale Strategien der Macht und kulturelle Wahrnehmungsmuster* (16. bis 20. Jahrhundert) (Vienna: Böhlau Verlag, 2012), 111–141.

The "competition of narratives" before World War I was temporarily rendered moot by the founding of the Latvian state in 1918 and the gradual entrenchment of a self-referential national historical narrative with the Latvian *tauta* as the central actor.[6] Historical developments over the centuries were evaluated in terms of how they affected Latvians, and judgements were made about other peoples in terms how helpful they had been in the emergence of Latvians as a distinct and self-conscious people. As it happened, the interwar Latvian historians—numbering no more than perhaps a dozen—were opening themes that elsewhere in Western history writing became popular some 30 years later: the focus on Latvians was certainly "history from below" (in the Baltic context), and because details of their everyday lives in the past were now at center stage, it was also "social history" and *Alltagsgeschichte* simultaneously. This thrust was was inevitable if one was to highlight the bottom layer of Baltic society—the peasant estate, *Bauernstand*—to which most Latvians had either belonged for centuries or from which they had become in recent decades only one or two generation removed. The new master narrative that struggled to emerge from these "national" studies meant to link centuries of subordination to the 19th-century "National Awakening" and eventually to the appearance of the Latvian state in 1918, the latter—a relatively recent event—being portrayed as the culmination toward which long-term historical change was pointing. In these re-conceptualisations, Latvian academic history moved closer to the "popular" version of the same story, since both were *tauta*-centred.

The two interwar decades turned out to be too short for a "national narrative" to be consolidated. Two occupations—the Soviet (1940–1941) and the Nazi-German (1941–1944)—rendered impossible for a half-decade any written version of Latvian history that was not Communist Party-approved during the first and did not fit with Nazi ideology during the second.

To the Communist Party, the interwar Republic meant domination of the "Latvian working people" by a "bourgeois clique" and after 1934 by a "fascist dictatorship"; Nazi propaganda foresaw Latvians—a racially somewhat inferior population—either being expelled from the Baltic region or Germanised if continuing to live there. The imperfectly formulated "master narrrative" of the interwar

---

6 A. Tentelis, "Lasītājiem," *Latvijas Vēstures Institūta Žurnāls* 1 (1937): 3–7.

decades, however, lived on in the work of a handful of Latvian historians who in 1944–1945 fled Latvia and after the late 1940s came to settle in such new homelands as Sweden, the United States, the Federal Republic of Germany, and Canada.[7] In exile, no organisation of Latvian historians existed, however, and individual professionals were on their own. Some of those who had been trained as historians in the late 1930s entered other lines of work and continued to write Latvian history in their spare time. Given their very small number, their efforts hardly constituted a "master narrative" in the normal sense, i.e. an agreed-upon version accepted by hundreds of professionals, the consensus view of an entire field. Generally, the first generation of Latvian émigré historians (with some exceptions) continued to have weak institutional anchors in their new homelands; those who did, did not seek to launch a new narrative but continued to work within the general framework of interwar national history.[8] In the course of time, the first and second exile generations had to yield the stage to younger professional historians of Latvian background whose approaches to the Latvian past were influenced far more by interests and research directions in the Western historical professions than by the formulations of their senior Latvian colleagues.

In the meantime, during the decades of the Cold War the historians of the Latvian SSR produced several successive editions of Party-approved "master narratives," of which the most recent (1986) replaced an earlier Stalinist-era version.[9] Ironically, this last work appeared just at the start of the internal upheavals that eventually destroyed the USSR and returned state sovereignty to Latvia, so that for all intents and purposes the 1986 "master narrative" of the Soviet era was stillborn. Latvia entered a new phase of its history without a "master narrative" other than the rather sketchy variant on offer from the émigré Latvian historians. Convinced that a "master narrative" was needed, however, the researchers of the post-1991 Latvian Intitute of History and the Faculty of History (both entities eventually at the University of Latvia) set out to create one dealing

---

7   Edgars Andersons, "Latviešu vēsturnieku darbs" *Arhīvs* 21 (1980): 57–76.
8   Andrejs Plakans, "Remaining Loyal: Latvian Historians in Exile 1945–1991," in Maria Zadencka, Andrejs Plakans, and Andreas Lawaty, eds, *East and Central European History Writing in Exile 1939–1989* (Amsterdam: Brill, 2015).
9   A. Drīzulis, ed. *Latvijas PSR Vēsture: no viduslaikiem līdz mūsdienām* (Rīga: Zinatne, 1986).

with the history of of the Latvian *tauta* (people) and state during the 19th and 20th centuries. As of this writing, three volumes have been produced by this effort but the intended series remains unconcluded.[10] The intent of the series was to lay out the interpretation of the past that Latvian historians could produce after being freed of ideological contraints. Unfortunately, during the first decade after renewed independence, the reading public remained deeply suspicious of the entire historical profession in Latvia. Pre-1991 historical writings had for decades formed a kind of easily recognised congealed orthodoxy that demanded repeated demonstrations of loyalty from researchers and from several generations of secondary school pupils and university students. The suspicion was extended to all manner of official-sounding and official-looking historical publications, even though they were being produced in the total absence of a "Party line."

Unsurprisingly, the further development of the Latvian historical profession during the past two decades has not brought into prominence a new commanding version of Latvian history in the long term—i.e. no "master narrative." Nearly every component of previous "master narratives"—especially of the Marxist-Leninist variant but also of the interwar era and of the writings of the *émigré* historians—has been evaluated, reexamined, deconstructed and if necesary disagreed with.[11] The period since 1991 has thus been an era of contestation, but not—it should be noted—of ringing condemnation of earlier Latvian historical writing. Some descriptions of short streches of the Latvian past have been accepted, possibly becoming candidates for a later "master narrative," if one appears. Some have been closely reexamined (Kārlis Ulmanis' authoritarian rule, for example) and new interpretations offered, while entirely new research

---

10 For the 19th century: Jānis Bērziņš, ed., *Latvija 19. gadsimtā: vēstures apceres* (Rīga: Latvijas Vēstures Institūta apgāds, 2000). For the 20th century: Valdis Bērziņš, ed., *20. gadsimta Latvijas vēsture*: Vol. I, 1900–1918 (Rīga: Latvijas Vēstures Institūta apgāds, 2000); Vol. II, 1918–1940 (Rīga: Latvijas Vēstures Institūta apgāds, 2003).

11 This revisionism has taken many forms, one of which is exemplified by Kaspars Zellis, ed., *Mīti Latvijas vēsturē* (Rīga: "Latvijas Vēsture" fonds, 2006), a collective work published in contemporary Latvia and examining various "myths" in Latvian history writing. Such uncovering of "myths" and "legends" was also evident in the *émigré* literary journal *Jaunā Gaita*: see Jānis Krēsliņš, "Mīti par latviešu un Latvijas vēsturi in piezīmes par tā dēvēto Latvijas tēla jautājumu," *Jaunā Gaita* 213 (1998): 18–25; and by the same author, "Rosinājums likvidēt dažas plaši izplatītas leģendas par Latvijas vēsturi," *Jaunā Gaita*, 214 (1998): 37–38.

domains have been opened and as of this writing are in the process of gaining currency.[12] New versions of monographs published in the Soviet decades have been produced, with their empirically-based sections preserved and the Soviet-era theoretical framework discarded. Headway has been made in new fields of historical work—oral history, the workings of historical memory, cultural history—but the products of these still remain discrete and unmerged into an all encompassing long-term story. The role of Baltic Germans and other minority populations of historic Latvian geographic space is seldom treated any longer as involving "outsiders", but is described respectfully or at least without the assumption that non-Latvians in the Baltic littoral were always oppressors.

This process of change in the historical profession has not been accompanied, however, by a diminution in the sharpness of contrasting viewpoints. This is especially so in the realm of media-generated historical narratives in which collisions continue between the perception in the Russophone and Lettophone populations of the country, especially with respect to World War II and the decades following it.[13] There also remains a fairly substantial cleavage between the careful and fine-grained investigations of academic history and the overall mega-visions often preferred by a Latvian-using general readership. The latter has continued to insist that there is already a usable long-term narrative in place—as exemplified by such perennialy popular works as Uldis Ģērmanis' *Latviešu tautas piedzīvojumi* (The Adventures of the Latvian People)[14]—and has repeatedly charged that the painstaking investigations of academic historians are too specialised and too hesitant to assist in the "patriotic" education of young Latvians. Finally, due to severe resource shortages, research areas falling outside the time frame of about 1850 to 2014 remain short of specialists

---

12 See, for example: Valters Ščerbinskis and Ēriks Jēkabsons, eds., *Apvērsums: 1934. gada 15.maija notikumi avotos un pētījumos* (Rīga: Latvijas Nacionālais Arhīvs, 2012); Vita Zelče, *Nezināmā: Latvijas sieviete 19.gadsimta otrā pusē* (Rīga: Latvijas Arhīvistu biedrība, 2002); Ineta Lipša, *Seksualitāte und sociālā kontrole Latvijā 1914–1939* (Rīga: Zinātne, 2014).

13 See, for example: Mārtiņš Kaprāns and Vita Zelče, eds., *Pēdējais karš: atmiņa un traumas komunikācija* (Rīga: Mansards, 2011). See also Viktors Makarovs, "Pretrunīgā Latvijas vēsture: ko un kāpēc par to domā latviešu un krievu skolēni?," in Deniss Hanovs, ed., *Atcerēties, aizmirst, izdomāt: kultūru un identitāšu biogrāfijas 18.–21.gs. Latvijā* (Rīga: SIA Drukātava, 2009), 93–103.

14 Uldis Ģērmanis, *Latviešu tautas piedzīvojumi* (Rīga: Jāņa sēta, 1990).

and funded projects, which ultimately means that very long stretches of Latvian history will remain unrevised, unsupplemented and unprepared to be included into a new "master narrative" if and when one comes into being. Though one can find consensus about this or that phenomenon in the Latvian past, an overall generally accepted interpretation—a "master narrative" in the usual sense—is therefore as of this writing not close to having formed itself.

2. The Place of the 1918 Independence Proclamation

It is highly likely that a new "master narrative" will assign an important role to the independence proclamation of 18 November 1918, but what that role will be is not yet clear. One meaning that will probably not be resusciated in full would come from the orthodox Marxist-Leninist contention that the 1918 Republic was a "bourgeois" structure. This understanding relied heavily on the idea of historical inevitability and pictured the 1918 state as a product of developments that unfolded according to "historic laws" (Latv. *likumsakarīgi*). The "national" school—the interwar historians and the first generation of *émigrés*— also flirted with inevitability, but its historical references referred to different phenomena. In both of these interpretations the persons on the stage of the building that is now the National Theatre on 18 November 1918 were acting out roles prepared for them by "historical change" over which neither they nor any other human beings had full control.

There is a strong possibility, however, that fragments of the two dominant interpretations will make their way into a new "master narrative." For the national historians, the Republic of Latvia proclaimed on that date represented the culmination of the final phase of a process that had started in the mid-19th century with the activists of the "National Awakening" and perhaps even earlier. The motor of this process of change was the emergence and growth of a national consciousness (not "class conflict"), at first in the minds of a handful of young educated Latvians and in time in the minds of tens of thousands of other Latvian-speakers of the Russian Baltic Provinces. This psychological alteration reflected a very different sense of belonging: a new mentality that differentiated and united simultaneously. The new way of thinking brought Latvia-using individuals to the realisation that in their very beings they were different from other peasants in a particular locality and region in which they were living but also that they were the same as other persons living elsewhere who spoke the same language. Activists believed that they were neither creating nor inventing a new consciousness but rather were uncovering it: its components already existed and had to be "awakened" and "brought into the light." Ultimately, the goal of the "national awakeners" was to show Latvian-speakers that in the depth of their being they were a *tauta* entitled to self-determination. Everywhere on the European continent similar "awakening" activities were going on, especially among the long-subordinated peoples of the multi-national empires; and the Latvian "awakeners" felt themselves to be participants in a great historical trend that would produce a new Europe consisting of a large array of self-conscious peoples each making a contribution to a composite European civilisation.[15] The task of "awakening" would be long and hard but it would inevitably reach its culmination when the Latvian *tauta* reached the highest stage of self-awareness. The "national" narrative would eventually tie together disparate elements of this long story to suggest that no other outcome than the 1918 Republic was possible. The distinction between ineluctability and inevitability was seldom preserved in these later interpretations.

For Marxists-Leninists, on the other hand, the 1918 Republic was only the penultimate step of a much more binding process that was taking the proletariat toward its inevitable triumph. The "laws" of historical development required there to be a period of time when the "bourgeoisie" were dominant, and the interwar period served this ideological purpose. The real turning point in this scheme was to come in 1940–1941 when, with the help of the USSR, the Latvian masses finally rid themselves of the oppressive bourgeoisie as a class and cleared the way for the true revolution. The reason this had not taken place earlier, in the World War I period, had to do with the armed interference in Latvian affairs of the capitalist and imperialist countries. This understanding of Latvian history reduced considerably the importance of the 1918 proclamation, seeing it as creating a temporary state structure that was fated to disappear.

The Marxist-Leninist interpretation of Latvian events of course had virtually no currency in Latvia during the interwar decades. For the national historians the important struggle was between *tautas* (peoples), not classes, which led them

---

15 Andrejs Plakans, *A Concise History of the Baltic States* (Cambridge: Cambridge University Press, 2011), 223–241.

to the medieval era, when the "normal" evolution of the Baltic region had been derailed. The pre-13th century tribal societies had been in the process of becoming states and would have done so had it not been for the invasion of the Baltic crusaders and the subjugation of the native population.[16] It was strongly suggested that throughout the next "700 years of slavery" the desire for political independence lay just outside the reach of the Latvian-speaking population. Certain stylistic mannerisms became charateristic of this discourse, such as the projection of the term *Latvija* (Latvia) backwards in time and its use as a kind of shorthand to refer to the territory of the Baltic littoral inhabited by speakers of the Latvian language. The name of the political entity that had been proclaimed on 18 November 1918 was used in place of clumsier but more accurate territorial descriptions such as "the territory of the 20th century Latvian state" or "the sector of the Baltic Provinces inhabited by Latvian speakers" or "the territory of the two adjacent Baltic Provinces of Livland and Courland, plus several districts of Vitebsk." At the same time, similar usage of collective nouns such as "Latvians" (*latvieši*) in the description of earlier centuries suggested that the littoral sub-population that spoke the Latvian language (and its precursors) already possessed a proto-consciousness of commonality that was standing by in the realm of the spirit and just waiting to enter historical reality. These usages were present even in the writings of historians who understood perfectly well that they were anachronistic, but the desire to rush into existence the Latvian state and and its supportive consciousness appears to have been irresistible. It was a way of "nationalising" the earlier history of the territory that became the state in the 20th century. "*Latvija*" was an *implied* reality throughout the complicated history of the Baltic littoral, until in 1918 it was finally made an *explicit* reality. These usages were an endorsement of the belief widespread among the "national awakeners" of the 19th century that they were simply working to bring to the surface a mentality that was already present among those who spoke the Latvian language—nothing new, in other words, was being created or invented, the 1918 state itself having being always present in the shadows, as it were.

---

16 The *émigré* historian Edgars Dunsdorfs in his *Latvijas vēstures atlants* (Melbourne: Goppera fonds, 1969), 19, describes these tribal societies as containing "peoples who lived in separate states."

The effort to produce a truly "Latvian" history of the territory that was now a Latvian state came to an abrupt end in 1940 when, as mentioned earlier, the country was occupied and annexed by the USSR and the Marxist-Leninist historical framework became mandatory for nearly a half-century. Most of the leading national historians went into exile in 1944–1945 and, as best they could, continued their work in new homelands. The merger of the efforts of the first and second generation of exile Latvian historians produced a formidable body of work with the so-called *"Daugava* series"—entitled "The History of Latvia" (*Latvijas vēsture*)—eventually becoming emblematic of this effort.[17] The series title implied that even if the pre-1918 volumes were about the *territory* in which Latvians lived, historical change was preparing the resident population for the appearance of the Latvian state. The individual volumes of the series that were sent to friends or colleagues in the Latvian SSR were confiscated by customs officials, redirected to *specfondi*, or simply consigned to the flames. Though on library shelves the *Daugava* series physically resembled what a "master narrative" might look like—a row of eleven volumes each some 600 pages long, handsomely bound, all in the Latvian language—it was able to have only a limited impact outside Latvian-reading population in the West and virtually none at all on potential readers in the Latvian SSR.

For understandable reasons, the 20th-century Latvian state has subsequently had a mesmerising effect on Latvian history-writing, which also means that political history—the emergence, disappearance, dependence, reemergence, and inner workings of the state—have been somewhat privileged. How political events have interacted with those in other domains of life—social, economic, cultural—has not received as much attention, but a certain kind of revisionism has been coming to the fore in recent years as a result of the desire to reexamine the impact on Latvian life of the two 20th-century World Wars. Researchers of the workings of historical memory in Latvia have recently published a series of volumes dealing with World War II, and several conferences in Rīga about World War I have produced papers concluding that we simply do

---

17 The reference is to the *émigré* publishing firm *Daugava* in Stockholm, which, starting in 1959, published the first ten volumes of the series, while the last volume was published in 2002 by the Latvian Institute of History in Rīga.

not know as much as we should about this complicated earlier period.[18] These developments may turn out to be the first steps toward the recognition that the *political* dimension of fundamentally important episodes in the history of the Latvian *tauta* are not necessarily deserving of greater primacy than other aspects of the past. An inclusive survey of the details of the World War I period (1914–1920) does suggest that the relationship between the political events in it and other phenomena is very complicated indeed. There existed sub-state processes that were directly or indirectly changing the *mentalité* (in the French *Annales* sense) of the residents of the Baltic Provinces through alterations in the cultural and intellectual environment of their everyday lives, their *habitus*, and in this sense were reshaping the ground in which the idea of the independent Latvian state had to be realised once it was proclaimed. In other words, the Independence Declaration of 1918 may need to be problematised more than it has been so far. The interplay between the idea of a Latvian state and the social, cultural, and economic history of the territory in which it was to be anchored needs further explication.[19] As an illustration of what is needed, the following sections take up two such elements and their complicated interplay. Borrowing the dramatic terminology in the title of well-known piece of music, these elements will be referred to as "Death" and "Transfiguration."

3. "Death" and "Transfiguration"

These terms, of course, come from the title of Richard Strauss' famous 1888 tone poem of the same name—"Death and Transfiguration" (*Tod und Verklärung*)—in which the composer, pondering the death of a friend, sought to describe musically the experience of dying and the moment of "transfiguration", when, in the Christian understanding of death, the soul is transported to

---

18 See, for example, Nīls Muižnieks and Vita Zelče, eds., *Karojošā piemiņa: 16. marts un 9. maijs* (Rīga: Zinatne, 2011) and Uldis Neiburgs and Vita Zelče, eds., *(Divas) puses: Latviešu kara stāsti* (Rīga: Mansards, 2011). Conferences in 2014 were held on the subjects of "War, Library, and Cathedral: The First World War in European Culture" (June) and "Society, War, and History: The Military, Political, and Social Developments of the First World War in the Baltic Region 1914–1918"(August).

19 An important theme needing further research is the sucessful maintenance of Latvian-language cultural life outside the political framework of the Latvian state, as, for example, in the long decades before 1918 and, again, among Latvian *émigrés* in western countries after World War II.

heaven.[20] The listener is asked to allow the music to bring to the imagination a prolonged period of suffering and decline, as bodily functions slow down, consciousness dims, and the end draws near. The soul prepares to leave the body. The process begs to be described in figurative language since this is a Christian mystery: the cessation of measurable bodily functions is only the middle of the story. "Death" is followed by a moment of "transfiguration", when earthly material is miraculously transformed into eternal substance and the soul is lifted to a higher sphere of being. This terminology goes far beyond the normal language used to describe on-the-ground historical change and asks the reader to consider the realm of the less documentable: emotion, perception, spirituality, the non-material. On reflection, the two terms do not seem inappropriate for the psychological dynamic operative in the World War I years, when the "normal" socio-economic and political environment in which Latvians were living began, in a sense, to "die," only to experience a seemingly miracuous "transfiguration" on 18 November 1918, when the Latvian state was proclaimed.

As in the late afternoon on that date a company of some 60 people stood on the stage of the Russian Theatre (later, the "National Theatre") in Rīga and joined in the Declaration (some rather unwillingly), most were fully aware that the terrritory they had proclaimed to be a state had been in the process of expiring for some four years. Since the start of World War I in 1914, the eastern Baltic littoral had been living with "death" in both the literal and figurative sense. The diminution of the territory's human, industrial, and institutional resources had started early in the war as thousands of young Latvian men enlisted in the Imperial Army and began to die in the unsuccessful Russian-German military confrontations on the eastern front. But the 18 November participants were also hopeful that this process of expiration—a slow death—might be arrested by a dramatic gesture that just might bring the continuation of life at a "higher" plane. In this case the "higher plane" of being meant the continuation of life within the framework of an independent Latvian state. All the wartime misery that was leading Latvians down the road of despair and hopelessness could be given new meaning if they could be persuaded that the earlier destructive processes had been purposeful and could be understood as necessary for them to become masters of their own fate. The 1918 proclamation thus became a

---

20 http://en.wikipedia.org/wiki/Death_and_Transfiguration (accessed August 30, 2014).

transfiguratory act that was supposed to invest the immediate and distant future with new meaning.

The realists among the 18 November assembly understood that among the thousands of the persons whose thinking the Declaration was meant to affect—the human content of the new state—there were many who had not yet experienced in their personal identities the emergence of a new consciousness of group belonging and would not immediately comprehend what membership in a Latvian state was. Their sense of "belonging" to the Russian Empire was fading—or dying—but it had not yet been replaced with the feeling of belonging to a national entity or even with the feeling that a something like a new state was possible or even desirable. These facets of everyday life—comprising a pervasive sense that the old context was ceasing to hold but that there was nothing that pointed to the return of stability or normality—were common enough features of the Latvian territories and are described in detail by autobiographical accounts of those who lived through and survived the World War I period.[21] But, in these retrospective descriptions their psychological destructiveness is rendered less harmful by the writer's knowledge that eventually the transfiguratory act—the Declaration—did bear fruit. The declaration did not cause ongoing destruction to cease; nor was there an immediate mass conversion to the idea of Latvian statehood as a result of the Declaration. The next year—1919—brought the short-lived Stučka Bolshevik regime and the War of Independence—that is, more death and destruction—but now these events could be perceived as having a different meaning and could be interpreted as possibly leading to a new life at a "higher" level. These interconnected phenomena are in need of a depiction that is more than linear single-level history: the situation entails understanding of how the interplay of material, social, political and psychological elements produced the outcomes that subsequently become "the historical record" about the founding of the Latvian state.

"Death" before 18 November

The men who met on 18 November 1918 to proclaim the existence of a Latvian state were not riding a wave of triumphant accomplishments. No foe had been

---

21 See, for example: Fēlikss Cielēns, *Laikmetu maiņā: atmiņas un atziņas.* (Stockholm: Memento, 1963), II, 16–33.

vanquished and no inner doubts fully overcome. In fact, just the opposite was the case. Latvians continued to be surrounded by "death" in all its forms, literal and figurative. From the very beginning of the war, the number of people living on the historic Latvian territory of the Baltic littoral—those who could become the human capital of the future Latvian state—was being reduced steadily. Between 1913 and 1920 the territory lost about a third of its population, which dropped from from 2.5 million to 1.5 million; the future capital of Latvia, Rīga, shrank from 520,000 inhabitants in 1913, to 212,000 in 1917.[22] Thousands had been mobilised in the tsarist army at the start of the war, and hundreds had been killed in battle in the first two years. Some 12,000–14,000 rairoad cars were used to evacuate Rīga's industrial enterprises to inner Russia, and the same fate befell secondary schools and specialised institutes.[23] In 1915, after the German army occupied Courland, an estimated 850,000 refugees began stream northward and eastward from the countryside, abandoning their farms and livestock and bringing with them not much more than could be carried in a horse-drawn cart.[24] This wave of refugees carried many thousands into Livland and the Russian interior and created an ongoing problem for the Imperial government, which was unpepared for a population displacement of this magnitude. A number of ethnic groups—Germans, Jews—were evacuated to the Russian interior by the government as potentially too unreliable to be allowed to live near the front, which had stabilised on the Daugava River. Fighting continued and the front moved back and forth on Latvian soil, material destruction grew: by the armistice of 1918 some 80,000 buildings had been destroyed, 66,000 horses had been killed, 184,000 cows, 385,000 small farm animals, 228,000 farmbirds, and 44,000 bee colonies had been scattered. The rural areas of Latvian territory had lost some 883,000 pieces of farm machinery, 631,000 hectares of arable land had been rendered unusable by trenches and barbed wire, 133,000 hectares of forest had been destroyed, as well as 1.4

---

22 M. Skujenieks, *Latvija: zeme un iedzīvotāji* (Rīga: Valsts Statistiska Pārvalde, 1922), 192, 207; T. Līventāls and V. Sadovska, eds., *Rīga kā Latvijas galvas pilsēta* (Rīga: Pilsētas Valde, 1932), 176.
23 Arnolds Aizsilnieks, *Latvijas saimniecības vēsture* (Stockholm: Daugava, 1968), 31–32.
24 Estimate from Skujenieks, *Latvija: zeme un iedzīvotāji*, 294–295.

million fruit trees and berry bushes.[25] These ravages had taken place concurrently, and from the point of view of the civilian population as well as in the eyes of the literary intelligentsia, they seemed chaotic and random, without any trajectory or meaning. Very little of Latvian-language writing of these war years portrayed the destruction as happening in a glorious cause, or on behalf of a beloved homeland, or in the name of some greater good. The brief period of celebratory writing in the early months of the war had given way to a new sensibility that accepted destruction, chaos, and directionlessness as a new normality; and some saw the continuing presence of the Imperial German army units on Latvian territory as a harbinger of the victory of the "traditional enemy"—the Baltic German landowning aristocracy. Perhaps the most demeaning symbol of *de facto* Latvian powerlessness was the fact that by November of 1918 the German military contingents had established control of the metropolis of Rīga, so that in order to hold the 18 November gathering the Latvian independence proclaimers had to negotiate with the German military authorities, who evidently perceived it as a harmless sideshow.

In neither the population of the Latvian territories nor in the Latvian population at large was the response to wartime destruction a uniform one. As already mentioned, in terms of numbers flight was the most common response, sometimes to faraway places and sometimes to only adjacent Russian provinces. More than likely, most people expected to return when the war ended, even if at the moment of departure it was not clear what they would be returning to. A substantial number of Latvians (estimated at about 12%) had already been living and working outside Latvian territory before the war[26], and among these the question of returning remained problematic. The civilians who chose not to flee from the Latvian territory had to put up with the demands of an occupation army in Courland, and the increasingly strained circumstances of daily life elsewhere. The wartime shortages that affected everyone began to turn public opinion toward questioning the central government and its apparent inability to take care of the home front. Among political activists, responses depended on the ultimate goals of activism. On the left, socialists began to think of the war as as

---

25 All statistics from Valdis Bērziņš, ed., *20. gs. Latvijas vēsture, II*, 371–372.
26 Skujenieks, *Latvija: zeme un iedzīvotāji*, 292.

opportunity to finally end the autocratic regime and introduce democratised institutions; the Bolsheviks among them looked forward to revolution and the arrival of a dictatorship of the proletariat. Those who had come to believe in parliamentarism called for political reforms that would enlarge the role of the Imperial *Duma* in decision-making and continued to think in terms of a Western-style parlimanetary monarchy. Among politically active Latvian moderates the most commonly held belief well into the wartime period foresaw a "free Latvia in a reformed Russia," i.e. parliamentary monarchy presiding over a multi-national empire that granted autonomy of action to its component provinces and regions. Among Latvians, the only formally organised party was the Social Democratic Workers Party, but as the war continued, other groupings showed a willingness to overcome internal differences and establish parties in the formal sense. The impulse to organise became increasingly stronger as the image of the central government lost its attractiveness and no one could predict in which direction power would continue to devolve.

Among Latvian enlistees in the tsarist army, the earlier enthusiasm had turned by 1915 to recalcitrance, as personal experience with and stories about the front reported incompetence of Russian officers and the general staff. In August of 1915, the General Staff finally accepted the idea that Latvians should be permitted to form their own military units that, of course, would remain part of the Imperial Army. As it turned out, this essentially military decision resulted in the creation of what many Latvian civilians quickly began to think of as their "own" soldiers, because this kind of engagement contrasted sharply with the earlier dispersal of Latvian enlistees and draftees throughout the tsarist forces. The visual image of units of "Latvian" Riflemen (*strēlnieki*) was a powerful one to Latvian civilians, but as time passed the ranks of the *strēlnieki* came to reflect the same divisions of political opinion that existed in the civilian population. For many, Latvian autonomy was a worthy goal, but for increasingly larger numbers the agitation by Bolshevik activists communicated a decisiveness that was also very attractive. One organisational decision that gave the *strēlnieki* units considerable visibility among Latvian civilians created special subunits of artists, writers, and journalists who, though their members wore the *strēlnieki* uniform, were not used in combat but were assigned to morale building, i.e. reporting on the "heroic" deeds of the Riflemen and creating a written and visual record of their military prowess. This, of course, enhanced the image of the Latvian *strēlnieki* as "our heroes" (*mūsu varoņi*) among Latvian civilians; in a sense, a small section of the vast Imperial army had become "nationalised" even without the existence of a Latvian state.[27]

The February 1917 Revolution had contributed heavily to the disorientation of the Latvian civilian population: another form of "death" had claimed an ancient institution that older Latvians remembered as venerating from their childhood, just as their parents and their grandparents had done. Political activists at all points of the spectrum received new energy from the March Revolution, in spite of the fact that the attitudes of the Kerensky's Provisional Government for the time being did not point clearly at any special outcome for the western borderlands. The geographical dispersion of the Latvian population continued, as did the German military presence on Latvian territory. The November 1917 Bolshevik *coup* in Petrograd did produce an outcome of sorts on which radically inclined Latvians, including those in the *strēlnieki*, could now focus their attention. The new society promised by the Bolsheviks appealed to many, but at the same time the idea was forming in the minds of others that an independent Latvian state might just be possible. But on Latvian territory there was no peace discernible in the short run. The later Allied decision to permit German military units to remain active in the Baltic littoral as a buffer against Bolshevism, the full-scale reorientation of many of the *strēlnieki* battalions and in the civilian population toward support of the Bolshevik cause, and the nascent belief among the "bourgeois" Latvian political activists that the idea of political independence could be manoeuvered into reality all merged and rendered the immediate future even less clear. In all the activist camps it was also quite evident that the particular outcome each wanted would not be achieved without violence. "Death" in the Baltic littoral therefore continued in a different form, but now without the overarching framework of the Imperial government or, later, of a World War. In such a context there were no reassurances for the civilian population—either in the Baltic region itself or outside of it—that peace and

---

27 By far the best-researched monograph on the Latvian *strēlnieki* is Valdis Bērziņs, *Latviešu strēlnieki: drāma un traģēdija* (Rīga: Latvijas Vēstures Institūta apgāds, 1995). Another important monograph, dealing in geater detail with the services rendered by the *strēlnieki* to the Bolshevik cause is Andrew Ezergailis, *The Latvian Impact on the Bolshevik Reovlution* (Boulder: East European Monographs, 1983).

normality would return anytime soon or that any one of the regional combatants would emerge triumphant. Doubt and uncertainty remained as the dominant mood, joined now by continually deteriorating material circumstances for the civilians who had not fled. There were no perceivable developments in this given moment that could be "read" as harbingers of what the Baltic region would look like when hostilities ceased, and the continuing hostilities themselves seemed likely in the near term to require additional costs in human lives. Strategies of individual survival, accompanied by considerable cynicism about the future among the refugees, came to seem to many as a much more realistic way to deal with the situation than unquestioning commitment to one or another ideology.

The 1918 Proclamation: Reality and Symbolism

Within the continuing atmosphere of "death" (people and institutions dying and disappearing), the 18 November 1918 proclamation announced the existence of a new political entity—the Republic of Latvia. The language of the news used the present and not the future tense, thus implying that this entity had already become objective reality: "United in its ethnographic territory (Kurzeme, Vidzeme, Latgale), Latvia *is* an independent, sovereign, and democratic republican state ... (italics added)."[28] The oratory accompanying the announcement assured the listener and reader that what was being described as real was the political form of the imagined community that had many decades of successful culture-building behind it,[29] as evidenced by the existence of a people (*tauta*) that used the Latvian language—the most important sign of that people's uniqueness. In actuality, of course, this new state remained invisible: for the time being it "existed" only in the anouncements, the organising meetings surrounding the announcement, and in the titles of the group of men who had been

---

28 Cited from Spricis Paegle, *Kā Latvijas valsts tapa* (Riga: published by author; republished in 1985 by the Latviešu Natcionālais Fonds, Stockholm), 222.

29 A recent history of Latvian culture described the creation of the Republic of Latvia in 1918 as the realization of an "ancient dream" (*senais sapnis*): see Andris Vilsons, ed., *Latvijas kultūras vēsture* (Rīga: Zvaignze ABC, 2003), 220. The actual age of this "dream" is ably discussed in Uldis Ģērmanis, "The Idea of Independent Latvia and its Development in 1917," in Adolf Sprudzs and Armins Rusis, ed., *Res Balticsa: A Collection of Essays in Honor of the Memory of Dr. Alfreds Bīlmanis (1887–1948)* (Leyden: A. W. Sitjhoff, 1968), 27–87.

chosed to be the first government (cabinet) of the Republic. The well-regarded and active lawyer, Jānis Čakste, who had been voted by the gathering to be the first president of the Republic, was not in attendance due, apparently, to a conflict in scheduling. The distribution of positions in the new government among the participating political parties and groupings had been decided upon, after considerable discussion, during a meeting the previous day (17 November) of the National Council of Latvia (*Latvijas Tautas Padome*).[30] It was the 18 November meeting, however, that produced the iconic photograph that was later to be found in every schoolbook and historical account about the "birth of the state." The photograph of the crowded stage became the first visible image testifying to the existence of a new political leadership for the Latvian territory; this image was assurance that a public act had taken taken place. The new reality embodied in the figures in the photograph, nonetheless, still remained at this juncture a statement of intentions. Shortly after the proclamation, the new government withdrew from Rīga to Liepāja (Libau), the port city of the Baltic Sea, because the capture of Rīga by the Bolshevik army was imminent. The political entity that on 18 November had finally been elevated into public view continued to be obscured by circumstances. It was not even a fully imagined community in the minds of all of its declarers, because Social Democratic members made it clear that the proclaimed Republic for them was not an end in itself but a means to an end.[31] Among those who felt the proclamation as having the nature of a "transfiguration"—of the elevation of all Latvian affairs and activities to a higher, "national" level—the moment was, however, decidedly a turning point. It focused the imagination and changed the meaning of the term "public." If before the proclamation, activism was referenced to what benefitted the *tauta*, now it could be referenced to what benefited the *tauta* located in its own *valsts* (state). Even so, the proclaimers, being men of affairs, understood that the job of establishing a new state in the Baltic littoral required more than simply an announcement of intentions. The state had to have a government capable of exercising executive, legislative, and judicial functions; a

---

30 The 18 November gathering was thus formally the second meeting of the Council.
31 Bruno Kalniņš, *Latvijas sociāl-demokrātijas 50.g. gadi* (Stockholm: Memento, 1993), 136–140.

bureaucratic apparatus large enough to deal with the details of governing; an army capable of defending the state's territory;[32] and a citizenry willing to remain loyal to the state in the long term.

The 18 November proclamation thus inserted into Latvian affairs an entirely new variable with which Latvians themselves and others living on Latvian territory somehow had to reckon. The claim of statehood could not be shrugged aside or ignored, because, if successfully implemented, the new state could permanently alter power relationships and demand that the alterations be recognised as legitimate by other states. But the emergence of the new state could be opposed before its institutions received the full backing of its titular population—the Latvians—and this opposition played out over approximately the next 12 months, a period that would later receive the designation of the War of Independence (*Brīvības cīņas; Neatkarības cīņas*). Opposition to the new state (headed by the Prime Minister Kārlis Ulmanis) and to the structures the 1918 proclamation said were coming came from a composite "enemy" that changed its nature as time passed: the Bolshevik forces—the Red Army and the communist government headed by Pēteris Stučka—that initially had considerable support among the local population but lost much of it during its bloody stay in power from January to March 1919; the various units of the Imperial German army that had been permitted to stay in the Baltic region, sometimes with and sometimes without the support of the armed units of the Baltic German population; and elements of the Latvian population (the Niedra "government") who were convinced that a clean break with the heretofore dominant Baltic German population was a serious mistake. Because of its initial weaknesses, the November 1918 Latvian government had to form an uneasy alliance with the second of these elements for the purpose of armed conflict with the first. The Bolshevik forces having been weakened and defeated by the fall of 1919, the Latvian government had then to focus on its former German "allies" who had their

---

[32] In view of the presence of "foreign" military units on the soil of the territory the announced state was claiming, the question of a "national army" was supremely important. The first efforts to recruit an army quickly were disappointing (P. Bērziņš, *Latvijas brīvības cīņas 1918–1910* (Rīga: A. Gulbis, 1928), 12–16. Somewhat later, however, the results improved substantially, even to the extent that one early important account of the Independence War maintained that "the true creator of the Latvian state is the Latvian army" (Pēteris Radziņš, *Latvijas atbrīvošanas karš* (Rīga: Avots, 1990), 5.

own agenda for the Baltic region. The internal opposition—the popular writer and Lutheran clergyman Andrievs Niedra and his handful of supporters—never became a serious rival for power, receiving virtually no support within the Latvian population at large. Concurrently, the Ulmanis government had to create a "national" army capable of fighting on its own, an apparatus for governing, and a consciousness among the civilian population (on the Latvian territory and outside of it) that the new state and its new government were viable.

In terms of the figurative language being used thus far, the year 1919 turned out to be a period during which "death" overlapped with "transfiguration." However, the 1918 proclamation meant that "death" had now been infused with a new meaning, even though the general population remained to be convinced, at the individual and collective level, that a "miracle" had occurred. Just as Christian belief had invested the "transfiguration of the soul" with reality, so now a transformatory faith in the new nation-state fed the belief systems of increasingly larger numbers of Latvian-speakers, in a process that lasted throughout 1919 and well beyond that year. Continuing death and destruction during 1919 could be portrayed as having a new significance by reference to the symbolic 18 November Act preceding. The death of young Latvian men during the military conflicts with the Bolsheviks and the German forces could be described as having a higher purpose—a "national" purpose. This investiture of "death" with meaning could also have retroactive force: the thousands who had died before November 1918 in the Imperial Army were heroes who had prepared the way for the 1918 proclamation and for the heroic deaths taking place in the "national army" during the independence struggles. All the fallen could become symbols of Latvian bravery and therefore an example for other young persons who might be asked to enlist in the "national" cause when needed. Military and civilian losses in the continuing struggle against the Bolsheviks and the German forces on Latvian soil during 1919 could be protrayed generically as part of a long-term "national struggle" that had started with the "National Awakening" in the 19th century and had finally borne the inevitable fruit in the form of a Latvian nation-state. Regardless of how rocky the road to meaningful statehood, the 1918 proclamation became the point of reference for all subsequent activities and indeed allowed them to be infused with an enhanced purpose: defending the national state. If before November 1918, the term "patriotism" had been ambiguous since it could refer only to the *tauta* and not the state, after November 1918 it could be linked to a political entity that was in the process of claiming a place in the sun. Earlier, when the term *Latvija* was used in writing or conversation, it had involved wishful thinking. Now, however, the term had taken on a living form: *Latvija* was generating flesh-and-blood leaders, institutions of governance, even a military force, and could be a focus for dedication, self-sacrifice, and loss. There was a new framework in existence within which everyday events assumed a purpose, a trajectory, and a goal.

4. Identity Change in the Long Term

The argument being made here is that the November proclamation affected Latvian affairs in ways that are hard to describe with linear political history in a conventional narrative. In the immediate aftermath of the various meeetings and discussions surrounding the 18 November Declaration, the event itself was scarcely discernable to those who had not actually been present. Its effects emerged slowly because the pre-state *mentalité*—the Latvian consciousness in which a Latvian state was at best an imagined structure—proved to be a hardy survivor. As far as current research has been able to determine, large segments of even the ethnic Latvian population in the early wartime years before the 1918 Declaration and for a time after it was agnostic and remained so on the question of political independence.[33] In part, there was a communications problem. As one author of a popular account of the event observed much later:

> The [18 November] proclamation was heard about in Rīga the morning after, and for many Rigans it was a surprise—there was no national press, no radio, an no other instrument of communication or propaganda that could have prepared the masses of the Latvian inhabitants for this step.[34]

---

33 An important new direction in research on subpopulations that remain removed from efforts to create nation-states is suggested by Tara Zahra, "Imagined Non-communities: National Indeifference as a Category of Analysis," *Slavic Review* 69 (2010): 93–119.

34 Pāvils Klāns, *Karsta dzelzs: Latvija tautu likteņu kaltuvē* (New York: Grāmatu Draugs, 1968), 276. See also the Latvian research reported in Ineta Lipša, "Vārgā vilkme. Latviešu valstsgriba Pirmā pasaules kara dūmos." *Rīgas Laiks* (September, 2016). Pp. 24-33, 59.

Clear evidence suggesting that something momentous had happened was hard to find, and many thousands of ethnic Latvians who were not in Rīga or on Latvian territory in November 1918 first heard about these events in the form of rumours that left much room for speculation about what the proclamation might mean. On the face of it, the idea as such was pleasing to the nationalistically inclined; yet, an independent state still remained hard to conceptualise. Well into the next year, the new state seemed to be embodied in only the persons (the Ulmanis government) who claimed to be its officials and its defenders. It would take a number of years until public consciousness became fully accepting of the need to restructure the feeling of political belonging so that it would fit what was rapidly becoming an irreversible political reality. Some— Latvians and non-Latvians—continued to view their new collective identity with ambiguous feeling well into the 1920s, and even then could not convince themselves that it had permanence. The memoirs of the thoughtful Latvians who lived through these years frequently contain variants of the following 1923 observations by one participant of the November 1918 event—Spricis Paegle, a minister of trade in the Ulmanis government:

> It has to be admitted that in the larger masses of the *tauta* there was lacking the enthusiasm and the self-sacrifice that was needed for the building of a new state in difficult circumstances. The citizens of Latvia, who had been under a variety of regimes for centuries and in a state of material and spiritual dependency on foreigners, were unable to immediately appreciate the profound meaning of independence... The consciousness of the necessity for and the possibility of a Latvian state grew far too slowly in the Latvian citizenry ... The difficult tasks [of the provisional Latvian government] were supported enthusiastically and with conviction by the narrow enlightened segment of society, but in the large masses of the *tauta* such support was not strong and had little general resonance.[35]

By the end of 1919 and the sucessful conclusion of the independence struggles, "transfiguration"—in the sense the word is being used here—was well on its way: the idea of an independent Latvia was manifesting itself in the form of a national army, national symbols, a constitutional convention, an administrative apparatus capable to enforcing "the people's will," and international recog-

---

35 Paegle, *Kā Latvijas valsts tapa*, 227.

nition of Latvia's existence. All post-1918 events on Latvian soil were now taking place, as it were, on a different, and more importantly, higher plane of being—that of the nation-state. Activities that had earlier seemed disjointed and leading nowhere took on a communal meaning and generated the will to work hard in "nationalising" the Latvian part of the Baltic Provinces (to use a concept proposed for this phenomenon by the theorist of nationalism, Rogers Brubaker).[36] "Nationalisation" in this new context is to be understood as an active verb, describing not what governments did by taking possession of private property, but what all putative citizens of the new state did in whatever walks of life they found themselves. "Nationalisation" in this sense among Latvians has been ably described recently, for instance, by Per Bolin in his 2012 book *Between National and Academic Agendas,* in which he explains how the old Rīga Polytechnic (founded in 1862) was gradually converted—"nationalised" – into "the University of Latvia"; and by Suzanne Pourchier-Plasseraud in her 2013 book *Les Arts de la nation*, in which she describes how visual culture being created by Latvians came to be viewed as "national" art.[37]

If a new "master narrative" about this crucial period finally coalesces, it will have to find a way to describe how the November 1918 proclamation came to mean something more than a group of men making a public statement. Recognition will have to be accorded to the documentable fact that 18 November in itself was not a transfigurative moment but the start of a transfigurative process: there was, in other words, no immediate mass conversion but rather the relatively slow diffusion of the idea of a Latvian state. The Republic of Latvia remained a "work in progress" well into the 1920s even though it had already acquired a *de jure* existence. The history of these years is not wholly captured in the image of a series of inevitable events following each other in linear progression and leading to a foreordained result. The social component of this history should lead the historian to investigate further the interplay between

---

36 Rogers Brubaker, "Nationalising States in the Old 'New Europe' and the New," *Ethnic and Racial Studies* 19,2 (1996).
37 Per Bolin, Betweeen *National and Academic Agendas: Ethnic Policies and 'National Disciplines' at the University of Latvia, 1919–1940* (Södertörn: Södertörns högskola, 2012); Suzanne Pourchier-Plasseraud, *Les Arts de la nation: construction nationale et arts visuels en Lettonie 1905–1934* (Rennes: Presses Universistaires de Rennes, 2012), expanded English translation published by Brill/Rodopi in 2015..

responses to massive wartime destruction, an almost furtive symbolic political proclamation, the reshaping of consciousness, and the transformation of individual and collective identity that by the mid-1920s finally confirmed the existence of a new political entity on the European map.

Latvians as a Civic Nation—The Interwar Experiment

Marina Germane, University of Glasgow

1. Civic Nationalism

The concept of civic nationalism in Latvia—better known in the Latvian language as a distinction between the ethnic and political nation; or, in its latest incarnation, as the concept of a *unified* (*vienota*) nation—has a long-standing history. This is an issue that was ardently debated at the onset of Latvian statehood in the early 20th century and during the 16 democratic years of the interwar republic (1918–1934). In the 1990s, when Latvia regained independence, the idea of a civic nation promptly came back (in 1997, the Friedrich Naumann Foundation, together with the political party *Latvijas Ceļš* (Latvia's Way), organised a series of roundtable discussions on the subject), only to be dismissed by the wider society, mistakenly, as an idea alien to Latvian public discourse. In April 2013, after almost two decades of being confined to the narrow circles of social scientists, the civic vs. ethnic debate made a spectacular comeback when a discussion on the viability of a unified nation was hosted by the Social Cohesion Parliamentary Committee—an event where social scientists mingled with MPs and journalists, and which received wide coverage in the press.[1]

Admittedly, the civic *vs.* ethnic dichotomy has largely fallen out of favour with political scientists; it has been repeatedly attacked (one may even say vilified) on the grounds of being normatively laden, analytically problematic due to ambiguity of terms, simplistically dual, not accounting sufficiently for the role of national communities, and not suitable for post-communist studies.[2] This author, however, believes that, used strictly as an ideal type, the civic vs. ethnic

---

1   A video recording of the event is available on the *Saeima's* homepage, see http://www.saeima.lv/en/news/saeima-news/20915-vai-ir-iespejama-vienota-nacija-dis kusija-saeima-29-aprili .
2   See, for example: Will Kymlicka, *Multicultural Citizenship*. Oxford : Clarendon Press, 1995); Rogers Brubaker, "Nationalising States in the Old 'New Europe'—and the New," *Ethnic and Racial Studies*, 19,2 (1996); Rogers Brubaker, *Nationalism Reframed. Nationhood and the National Question in the New Europe* (Cambridge: Cambridge Univer-

dichotomy remains a perfectly valid analytical tool; especially so when one deals with historical cases. For example, the civic v. ethnic dichotomy is indispensable if we want to study Latvian nationalism of the early 20th century. Apart from the fact that all interwar debates on nationalism in Latvia used that particular frame of reference, more recent developments, like the heated debates surrounding the adoption of the new Preamble of the Constitution of Latvia, indicate that, unlike some other nations who at least claim the opposite, Latvians are far from being done with the civic/ethnic distinction.[3] Quite possibly, Latvia's tragically interrupted statehood is one of the causes of this delay. And in this light, re-examining the civic nationalism experiment of the interwar years seems to be particularly important: as a famous British liberal thinker once observed, "the follies of our own times are easier to bear when they are seen against the background of past follies."[4]

2. From Cultural to State-Building Nationalism

If, during the first five decades of its existence, the Latvian nationalist movement centred on the preservation of Latvian ethnocultural heritage, the Russian Revolution of 1905 transformed it into a state-oriented and independence-

---

sity Press, 1996); Bernard Yack, "The Myth of the Civic Nation," in: R. Beiner, ed., *Theorising Nationalism* (Albany: State University of New York Press, 1999), 103–118; K. Nielsen, "Cultural Nationalism, Neither Ethnic nor Civic", in Beiner, ed., *Theorizing Nationalism*, 119–130; Taras Kuzio, "'Nationalising states' or 'Nation Building'? A Critical Review of the Theoretical Literature and Empirical Evidence," *Nations and Nationalism*, 7,2 (2001): 135–154.

3 The Preamble to the Constitution, authored by the Head of the President's Commission on Constitutional Law E. Levits, was first presented to the Saeima's Legal Committee in September 2013. The original text contained the term "state nation" (*valstsnācija*), which became the centre of the ensuing contention—the draft was unequivocally supported by the nationalist union All for Latvia/FF-LNIM, but drew sharp criticisms from ethnic minorities and constitutional experts alike. In the final draft, adopted by the *Saeima* on 19th June 2014, the term "ethnic Latvian nation" was substituted for the "state nation"; however, as shrewdly observed by the Head of the *Saeima*'s Legal Committee Ilma Čepāne, "the meaning remains the same. Although the term 'state nation' is not used, its essence is revealed better." (See "Valstnācijas jēdziens no Staversmes preambulas nav pazudis. Saruna ar Ilmu Čepāni," *Latvijas Avīze*, 27 January 2014, Also available at: http://mod.la.lv/main1.php?id=13907612031390761203.9465, accessed on 23 July 2014. All translations by the author, unless indicated otherwise.

4 Bertrand Russell, "An Outline of Intellectual Rubbish," in *Bertrand Russell. Unpopular Essays*, (London and New York: Routledge Classics, 2009), 69.

seeking movement. And although for the next 12 years, until the February Revolution of 1917, most Latvian nationalists would be content with the idea of an autonomous Latvia within a new democratic Russia, they nevertheless had to address the issue of the multiethnic and multilingual nature of the Baltic territories as soon as their movement expanded beyond purely cultural demands.[5]

In terms of ethnic diversity, Latvia was not different from the rest of Eastern Europe during the interwar period. In 1920, Latvians comprised 72.8% of the population, the rest being made up of the six largest ethnic minorities, i.e., Russians (12.6%), Jews (5%), Germans (3.6%), Poles (3.4%), Lithuanians (1.6%), and Estonians (0.6%).[6] In fact, Latvia's percentage of ethnic minorities, far from being exceptional, at 27-28% stood slightly lower than the average percentage of 29.2 for all Eastern European states.[7]

Latvian Social Democrats, who were at the vanguard of the independence-seeking movement, were well aware of the latest developments in the field of political theory. Above all, they were greatly influenced by the ideas of the Austro-Marxists. Indeed, Otto Bauer's book *The Question of Nationalities and Social Democracy*, published in 1907, inspired two significant works by Latvian nationalist thinkers: *The National Question in Latvia* by Marģers Skujenieks, published 1913, and *The Question of Our Nationality* by Miķelis Valters, published a year later.

Skujenieks defined the purpose of his book as follows: "to discuss national relations in Latvia and therefore, at least to some measure, to clarify the question of how the common life of people belonging to different ethnicities can be organised." This is important, claimed Skujenieks, "because the central question of the national problem is how to arrange the common life of different peoples within one state or region."[8] Thus, making the co-existence of different ethnic

---

5   According to the census of 1897, Latvians comprised 68.2% of the population, Russians—12.2%, Germans—7.1%, Jews—6.2%, Poles—3.3%, Lithuanians—1.3%, and Estonians—0.9%. (Source: Skujeneeks, M. (1913) Nazionalais jautajums Latwijā. Peterburgā).
6   Source: Marģers Skujenieks, *Latvija. Zeme un iedzīvotaji* (Rīga: A. Gulbja apgādniecība, 1927).
7   Raymond Pearson, *National Minorities in Eastern Europe. 1848–1945* (London and Basingstoke: The Macmillan Press Ltd, 1983), 148.
8   Marģers Skujenieks, *Nazionalais jautajums Latwijā* (Pēterburgā, A. Gulbja apgahdibā, 1913), 10.

groups within one political unit central to the national project, Skujenieks laid a theoretical foundation for the Latvian *civic* nation.

Miķelis Valters dedicated a whole chapter to the same question, with the telling title *Latvians' association with other ethnic groups, especially Germans*, where, in a somewhat more practical vein than Skujenieks, he evaluated Latvians' potential allies and foes "from within." Valters remained adamant that political unity was a precondition for Latvia's existence:

> "Constant fighting against attempts to destroy our nation makes us consider not only how to reinforce our position through our own means, but also where to look for support among other forces nearby, who, in their own turn, are forced to draw closer to us for their own protection."[9]

The goal of unity, wrote Valters, could be achieved only through solidarity with others rather than in isolation. He spoke both of "peoples with whom we live together" and of "those who are our neighbours" and argued that it would be a political mistake to deny any association outright:

> "While deciding which peoples we should be cooperating with, we should try to look at our mutual relationships from a strictly political point of view, suppressing all emotions...We should, as much as possible, liberate our political life from past memories and recognise that in politics such memories often prevent us from considering the future path calmly."[10]

As for the practical implementation of these tenets expressed by two of the early Latvian national ideologists, all available historical evidence suggests that in 1918, the founders of the Latvian state perceived national unity and ethnic harmony to be integral parts of the future political system, and were firmly committed to the principles of equality and inclusiveness. This willingness to include all ethnic groups living in Latvia in the process of building the new state was manifested both in the first legislative acts and in politicians' speeches, and was widely echoed by the Latvian liberal press.

---

9 Miķelis Valters, *Mūsu tautības jautājums. Domas par Latvijas tagadni un nakotni* (Brisele: Jaunu Rakstu apgādeens, Generalkomisijā pee A. Waltera, J. Rapas u. Beedr, 1914), 120.
10 Valters, *Mūsu tautības jautājums*, 121.

The Latvian Constitution of 1922 famously placed power in the hands of the "People of Latvia" (*Latvijas tauta*), not the "Latvian People" (*latviešu tauta*). The newly appointed Prime Minister Kārlis Ulmanis emphasised in his speech that:

> All citizens, regardless of their ethnicity, are invited to help out [in building the new state], as the rights of all ethnic groups will be guaranteed by the Latvian state. It will be a state of democratic fairness, where there will be no place for oppression and injustice.[11]

The newspaper *Jaunākās Ziņas* enthusiastically greeted the newly born state:

> "The main manifestation of this state's genius is national unity! With a wise and far-sighted vision, different classes and circles represented in the National Council have united around common state tasks. Similarly, the whole Latvian nation without any exception, including our minority fellow-citizens, should with common effort support the building of the new state and all its supreme power institutions!"[12]

Max Laserson, a former Latvian MP representing the Jewish Socialist party *Zeirei Zion*, also recalled that:

> "At its first meeting the National Council gave expression through the speeches of its members to its firm desire to bring minority groups into the structure of the new state. This desire found expression on the part of both right-wing and left-wing circles."[13]

Thus, the newly created democratic Latvian Republic guaranteed cultural rights to the ethnic minorities living on its territory; from the very start the founders of the state assured the minorities of their intention to build a united civic Latvian nation, where people of all ethnic backgrounds were welcome. These principles were enshrined in the National Council Platform; Article 4 of the Platform, which was dedicated to minority rights, declared that national minorities could send their representatives to the Constitutional Assembly and to legislative bodies on a proportional representation basis, that minorities could participate in the Provisional Government on a coalition basis, and that the national and cultural rights of ethnic minorities were protected by constitutional law.

---

11 *Jaunākās Ziņas*, 4, 19 November 1918.
12 *Jaunākās Ziņas*, 4, 19 November 1918.
13 Max Laserson, "The Jews and the Latvian Parliament, 1918–1940," in Mendel Bobe, ed., *The Jews in Latvia* (Tel Aviv: Association of Latvian and Estonian Jews in Israel, 1971), 95.

Notably, all these events took place two months before the Paris Peace Conference began on 18th January 1919, therefore seven months ahead of the Polish Minority Treaty (the first in the series of treaties aimed at the protection of the newly created national minorities) being signed on 28th June 1919, without any direct pressure from the outside world, and of ethnic Latvians' own accord.

Later, in December 1919, the National Council passed two laws. A Law on Latvian Educational Institutions stipulated that all compulsory school studies were to be conducted in the pupil's "family language" and obliged state and municipal institutions to maintain as many schools for each ethnic group as were necessary for their children's compulsory education.[14] A Law on Minority Schools in Latvia established Minority Departments within the Ministry of Education to represent

> "their respective ethnic group in all cultural affairs, with the right to liaise with all departments of the Ministry of Education, as well as to participate, in an advisory capacity, in the sessions of the Cabinet of Ministers related to any aspects of the cultural life of their respective ethnic group."[15]

This remarkable piece of legislation, which was the most liberal law on minority education in Europe at the time (the even more advanced Estonian Law on Cultural Autonomy would not be passed until 1925), did not give rise to any substantial objections from among the delegates, and was passed unanimously, with only 18 abstaining votes.

3. Debates on Language and Citizenship

However, it would be misleading to think of this initial period of Latvia's independence as of a kind of a multicultural idyll. Just four months previously, another minority-related piece of legislation ran into serious trouble, exposing the early underlying tensions between the majority and minority representatives. In August 1919, the National Council reviewed, in two readings, the draft Law on

---

14 "1919. g. 8. Decembra sehdē peenemtais Likums par Latwijas izglihtibas eestahdem," *Waldibas Wehstnesis*, 88, 17 December 1919.
15 "1919.g. 8. decembra sehdē peenemtais Likums par mazakuma tautibu skolu eekahrtu Latwijā," *Waldibas Wehstnesis*, 89, 18 December 1919.

Language Rights. The draft was prepared by the Commission on National Affairs headed by the Baltic German Paul Schiemann; it gave every Latvian citizen the right to use his or her native language in private and public life, and gave ethnic minorities, in those districts where a certain ethnic minority exceeded 20% of the population, the right to communicate in their own language with the local administration and courts.

It is hard to imagine the practical implications of such a law had it been passed (it was not), and it makes one wonder about the precision of its legal definitions. But it is very characteristic of the political climate in Latvia at the time that the Social Democrat Marģers Skujenieks (the very same Skujenieks who later would drift first towards the centre-right, and then towards the right of the political spectrum, ultimately lending his unequivocal support to the authoritarian regime of 1934), who presented the draft to the Council, stated that there were no objections to this "basic request to ensure the use of each minority language." The heated debates that followed concentrated not so much on the minorities' linguistic demands as on the almost complete absence of references to the Latvian language, which some delegates from the centre-right parties interpreted as an insufficiently respectful attitude towards the State language on the part of minorities. Skujenieks retorted that the opponents' judgement was clouded by prejudice, and that they "see ghosts where there are none", and insisted that although it was possible that the draft needed an amendment introducing a definition of the State language, its main points were correct (at this point, the German part of the audience broke into applause).[16]

The draft was returned to the committees for redrafting, and never resurfaced again. And actually, the state language in Latvia remained legally undefined until the adoption of the Regulations on the State Language on 18 February 1932, which established the Latvian language as the state language of the Latvian Republic and made its usage compulsory in the army, navy and all state and municipal offices and enterprises, with a caveat that the use of language in the parliament was regulated by its Rules of procedure—thus, implicitly allowing the use of German and Russian there. Footnote 2 allowed, until the next municipal elections in 1935, the use of the German and Russian languages,

---

16 "Tautas Padomes sēde 27.08.1919," *Jaunākās Ziņas*, 28 August 1919.

with the permission of the chairman, or at least by demand of one-third of members, during the sessions of municipal administrative offices.[17] The State Language Law of 5 January 1935, largely based upon the Regulations of 1932, dropped those clauses and footnotes that referred to language usage in the *Saeima* and during municipal elections, and thus officially excluded the German and Russian languages from the public sphere henceforth.

"Citizenship Wars"

The year 1919 also saw the start of the years-long saga of the Citizenship Law, which was adopted, on its first draft, by the National Council on 23 August. The Citizenship Law would become the most troubled piece of Latvian legislation of the interwar period—it would be returned to the lawmakers on numerous occasions, would be amended several times, and would become a trump card frequently played by both the majority and the minorities in their political game. The legislation would be amended in 1921 (three times), in 1927, 1930, 1932, 1938, and in 1940 (three times; the last amendment of 30 July 1940 was signed by the Soviet appointee President Augusts Kirhenšteins).

It is important to keep in mind that in 1918, when the National Council started debating the issue of Latvian citizenship, there were still no international legal norms regulating the issue in place, apart from the general *de facto* recognition that succession states were expected to grant citizenship to those habitually residing in their territories in order to avoid mass statelessness.[18] But during what has become known as "the great unmixing of people", practically all of the countries of Central and Eastern Europe faced a particular predicament: as a result of the upheavals of the Great War, many of their original, *antebellum* residents were scattered abroad, while refugees from neighbouring countries were still present in great numbers.

In 1914, there were 2.6 million residents in Latvia, whereas in 1918 there were no more than 1.6 million; approximately 730,000–760,000 of Latvia's residents had been uprooted and had fled to Russia, Finland and the unoccupied Baltic

---

17 "Noteikumi par valsts valodu," *Valdības Vēstnesis*, 19 February 1932.
18 There would be no such international norm in place until 1930, when Article 1 of The Hague Convention stipulated that "It is for each State to determine under its own law who are its nationals."

territories.[19] Immediately after the war, the refugees, accompanied by displaced people (including prisoners of war from both sides), started to arrive in Latvia from the east. The culmination was reached in 1921, when 95,000 refugees, *optants* (those exercising their right to option in nationality) and displaced persons entered Latvia.[20] Until 1922, there were also people travelling in the opposite direction, like Russian emigrants returning to their homeland from Europe and the United States to personally witness the greatness of the Bolshevik revolution—in 1921 alone, 135,000 people travelled through Latvia to Russia.[21] But as early as spring 1922, Latvia started witnessing a constant stream of people escaping from Soviet Russia into Western Europe and across the Atlantic. According to the data of the Ministry of the Interior, in the period from November 1918 until September 1928, a total of 236,229 refugees, displaced persons and *optants* arrived in Latvia. Another 248,743 (including 65,000 refugees from Soviet Russia) proceeded via Latvia to other destinations; many of them were stranded in Latvia for months and even years awaiting the necessary travel documents and financial assistance from the Red Cross and other international organisations.[22]

In this mayhem, separating those who had historical ties with Latvia from those who ended up in Latvia by accident was a formidable task. The Citizenship Law of 1919, which established permanent residence in Latvian territories prior to August 1914 as a necessary criterion for eligibility for Latvian citizenship, and the accompanying directives of the Ministry of the Interior, were primarily centred upon this task.

---

19 A. Aizsilnieks, *Latvijas saimniecības vēsture. 1914–1945* (Syndbyberg: Daugava, 1968), 20, 164; Ā. Šilde, *Latvijas vēsture 1914–1945* (Stokholma: Daugava, 1976), 42. Skujenieks estimates the number of wartime refugees from Latvia at 850,000, with a caveat that the census of 1917 in Rīga was not carried out thoroughly. Skujenieks, *Latvija*, 294.

20 This figure is provided by J. Ozols, the editor of the *Iekšlietu Ministrijas Vēstnesis*, in the jubilee edition *Latvija desmit gados* (1928). Skujenieks (*Latvija*, 210) mentions an even larger figure—according to him, 197,114 refugees returned to Latvia from Russia in 1921 and 1922.

21 J. Ozols, "Pārskats par Iekšlietu ministrijas darbību," in M. Ārons, ed., *Latvija desmit gados. Latvijas valsts nodibināšanas un viņas pirmo 10 gadu darbības vēsture.* (Rīga: Jubilejas komisijas izdevums, 1928).

22 Ozols, "Pārskats par Iekšlietu ministrijas darbību."

The first draft of the Law, reviewed by the National Council in August 1919, envisaged granting Latvian citizenship to "all persons, irrespective of their ethnicity, belonging to the Latvian territories prior to August 1914", which was a generous provision for its time, and arguably much more generous than the subsequent Latvian Citizenship Law of 1994. However, its insufficiently precise wording put one particular ethnic group in a disadvantaged position. After the assassination of Alexander II in 1881, the legal status of the Jews had deteriorated, and those outside the Pale of Settlement (which included the Jews of Rīga, Jelgava and Liepāja) were not allowed to stay there unless they were employed in their registered profession.[23] This regulation, which remained in force until February 1917, was not always enforced thoroughly by the Russian authorities, who often turned a blind eye, but it nevertheless kept many Jews off the official registers, thus making them unable to prove that they "belonged" as required by the draft law.

The Jewish Deputy F. Lackijs (United Jewish Socialist Party) proposed an amendment to the draft to read "who *resided in*" the Latvian territories instead of "who *belonged to*" the Latvian territories. This proposal gained only 18 votes in favour, among them those of Paul Schiemann (who also circulated a letter explaining the necessity of the amendment to the Council's members) and A. Bočagovs (Russian National Democratic Party). The law was passed with its original wording.

This was the start of a years-long saga in Latvian interwar politics. The Citizenship Law would be repeatedly amended, in response to internal and external, real and imagined threats, and for various bureaucratic and administrative reasons. Each of the four Latvian interwar parliaments would review the Citizenship Law several times; it would inevitably come up during budget hearings, and in conjunction with government declarations, becoming a subject of elaborate epithets and tropes: "a chronic issue of Latvian politics", "the most controversial issue in Latvian parliamentary life", "the Jewish Law", and the *Van'ka-Vstan'ka*[24] of Latvian legislation. The Citizenship Law would become a trump card in the political game which would be used by all players, majority and

---

23 Leo Dribins, *Ebreji Latvijā* (Rīga: Elpa, 2002).
24 *Van'ka-vstan'ka*—a Russian tilting doll, which springs back upright immediately after being brought down.

minority parties alike, when it suited their interests—which very often had little, or nothing at all, to do with the citizenship issue *per se*.

In May 1927, the "citizenship wars", as the struggle was christened by the MPs, ended with the victory of the minorities—the amendments were finally passed. Ironically, they were passed under the left-wing government of M. Skujenieks, who, in his previous capacity of the Head of the State Department of Statistics, had warned in a previously published article that if the residence requirement were reduced to 10 years, Latvia would be flooded with 230,000 foreigners.[25]

The history of the Citizenship Law of 1919 and its subsequent amendments is vital to understanding the dynamics of majority-minority relations in interwar Latvia. This generally liberal piece of legislation was in line with the citizenship legislation in other Central and Eastern European countries at the time; it was somewhat stricter than the Estonian law of 27 October 1922 (which granted citizenship to all Russian subjects residing in Estonia up until 24 February 1918), but arguably more relaxed than the Lithuanian provisional law of 9 January 1919 (which bestowed citizenship on the descendants of those whose "parents and ancestors had lived in Lithuania since ancient times", or otherwise on those who had been residing in Lithuania for least 10 years up until 1914 as long as they possessed real estate or were permanently employed).

The Law of 1919 granted citizenship to 1,504,308[26] people out of the total population of 1,596,131[27], or 94.25%. By 1925, this number had grown to encompass 1,779,593[28] people, or 96.46% of the total population. In 1925, there were 31,668 foreigners, or 1.72% of the total population, residing in Latvia, and 33,544 stateless persons, or 1.82%.[29] Moreover, ethnic Latvians constituted only 76% of all citizens, while ethnic minorities made up the remaining 24%. The biggest discrepancy between the number of residents and number of citizens can be observed among the Jews—they constituted 5.2% of the whole population, but only 4.5% of citizens.

---

25 See *Darba Balss*, 27 October 1922.
26 M. Skujeneeks, *Latvija. Zeme un eedzīvotāji. Trešais pārstrādatais un papildinatais izdevums* (Rigā: A. Gulbja apgadneecība, 1927), 329.
27 Skujeneeks, *Latvija,* 214.
28 Skujeneeks, *Latvija,* 328.
29 Skujeneeks, *Latvija,* 328.

Civic Identity and Ethnic Bargaining

In short, neither the content of the legal provisions, nor the actual situation with citizenship in the interwar republic can be used as plausible explanations for the notoriety of the Citizenship Law of 1919, for the upheavals it caused and the polemics it sparked.

Incredibly, after nine years of bitter battles in the Parliament and in the press (and not just between the majority and ethnic minorities, but among the ethnic Latvian parties as well), only about 4,000 Jews acquired Latvian citizenship post-1927, a far cry from Skujenieks' predicted 250,000.[30] What made the Citizenship Law into the crux of Latvian political life in between the wars? I would like to offer a two-fold explanation to this question. The first has to do with the huge symbolic importance that Latvian ethnic minorities, who had taken both President Wilson's Fourteen Points and the promises of equality contained in the National Platform of 1918 at face value, assigned to the issue of citizenship. The second explanation is rooted in the theory of ethnic bargaining.

It seems that the founders of the Latvian state in 1918 guaranteed equal rights to ethnic minorities in earnest, at a moment when the sentiments of coming into nationhood, of becoming a part of the new Eastern Europe—liberated from its imperial past—or better still, a part of Old Europe, where Latvians believed their country rightfully belonged (and as a matter of fact, Baltic Germans fully shared this conviction), were running high. When the time came to define the country's citizenry, an effort was made to observe the existing, *de facto,* international norms which aimed to avoid creating large numbers of stateless persons (and indeed no large numbers of such persons were created in Latvia). At the same time, the provisions of the law were "ethnicity-blind." And one may speculate that although the unfortunate wording of Article 1, requiring proof of "belonging" to Latvian territories, in practice excluded a part of the Jewish population from the citizenry, it should have been clear to all interested parties at the time that the potential numbers involved were inherently small. So how did it all escalate into a full-blown inter-ethnic conflict and prolonged struggle among political parties from such a seemingly benign beginning?

---

30 Dribins, *Ebreji Latvijā*, 70.

But if ethnic Latvians earnestly believed back in 1918 that a new era had dawned in Europe, and that in Woodrow Wilson's words "all well-defined national aspirations should be accorded the utmost satisfaction", so did Latvia's ethnic minorities. Latvia freed from imperial Russia's yoke was going to be a paragon of democracy, fairness, and equality—of which the institution of Latvian citizenship was going to be the embodiment. So, when the draft citizenship law excluded a part, albeit a very small one, of the Jewish population from the body of citizens, the Jews were not prepared to swallow the pill. As the most discriminated-against ethnic group in Latvia under the previous Russian domination, they felt that in democratic Latvia, proper justice must be served, and were not willing to taint their participation in the life of the new state with an unfair compromise. As M. Laserson wrote in *Segodnia*,

> "There can be no harmony while one of the interested parties, which is in a stronger position, is trying to convince the other party that it actually does not possess any rights, and can therefore only count on the moral uprightness of the stronger party."[31]

One can only ponder why the Jewish minority, supported by the Baltic Germans (above all, by Paul Schiemann) and the Russians (on this issue, despite numerous disagreements on other matters, the minorities stood united) chose to make the debates on the Citizenship Law into the crucible of Latvian democracy. Why did they not, for example, do this with the laws on cultural autonomy, or the minority language laws—which they also attempted to pass, but with not even half the same fervour; these would arguably have benefitted a much greater number of people? There are at least two possible answers to this question. One, as already mentioned above, is that the minorities—perfectly reasonably—perceived citizenship as a cornerstone of their admission to the life of the state on a par with everyone else, in right and in fact. With this cornerstone missing, no matter what else they attempted to build, it would be based on quicksand. The Law on Citizenship was for Latvian minorities, above all, a matter of principle.

The second possible answer is that the ethnic Latvian side came to regard the Citizenship Law either as the "last bastion" of Latvian national sovereignty, or as a test of Latvian "national character" (which would be belittled by yielding to

---

31 "Liga natsii i men'shinstva," *Segodnia*, 6 April 1922.

the pushy minorities), or both. Even the *crème de la crème* of the Latvian intelligentsia, like Marģers Skujenieks and Kārlis Dišlers, fell prey to these preconceptions, and on many occasions uncharacteristically abandoned any common sense. Skujenieks' obsessive preoccupation with the potential numbers of new immigrants that an amended Citizenship law would allegedly bring into Latvia, endangering its core population, is indeed, to use a definition given by Horowitz, an example of "census games", a "splendid example of the blending of group anxiety with political domination."[32] In short, in no time the citizenship question became a matter of the utmost importance to both opposing parties. This made the Citizenship Law into a trump card of Latvian interwar politics, into a universal bargaining tool unabashedly used by both sides for their own ends.

In one of the latest studies of the theory of ethnic bargaining, Erin Jenne introduces the integrationist versus the segregationist dichotomy, i.e. "the rights of groups to integrate into majority society versus their rights to self-rule (usually on a territorial basis)." She then defines *integrationist rights* as "the rights of minorities to equal standing in the majority-dominated society", which are used "to justify demands ranging from non-discrimination to affirmative action to cultural or linguistic autonomy."[33] Jenne therefore firmly puts cultural autonomy within the sphere of integrationist rights. Not everybody takes such a benign view of the integrational potential of non-territorial cultural autonomy.[34] But the fact that Latvian ethnic minorities made the Citizenship Law, and not the laws on cultural autonomy, or the laws on minority languages' status, into a prime object of their aspirations and political struggle during the interwar period,

---

32 Donald Horowitz, *Ethnic Groups in Conflict* (Berkeley, Los Angeles and London: University of California Press, 2000), 194.
33 Erin K. Jenne, *Ethnic Bargaining. The Paradox of Minority Empowerment.* (Ithaca and London: Cornell University Press, 2007), 205, fn. 1 & 4.
34 See, for example: Genevieve Nootens, "Nations, States and the Sovereign Territorial Ideal," in Ephraim Nimni, ed., *National Cultural Autonomy and its Contemporary Critics* (London and New York: Routledge, 2005), 51–62; B. Barry, *Culture and Equality. An Egalitarian Critique of Multiculturalism* (Cambridge: Polity Press, 2001); Rainer Bauböck, "Political Autonomy or Cultural Minority Rights? A Conceptual Critique of Renner's Model," in Nimni, *National Cultural Autonomy and its Contemporary Critics,* 97–111.

proves that the main tendency displayed by minorities during that period was an integrationist one.

The successful passing of the amendments in 1927 under the left-wing government of M. Skujenieks, to which minorities lent their not-unconditional support, proved to be a Pyrrhic victory for them. Although one may say that justice was served, the practical results, expressed in the number of new citizens resulting from the amendments, were negligible. Skujenieks, who allegedly struck a bargain with the leader of the Religious Zionist party *Mizrahi*, Marcus Nurock, and others in order to have his government confirmed, suffered political humiliation when repeatedly accused by fellow-Latvians of inconsistency in his views on citizenship and a lack of political integrity.[35] Arguably, that sped up Skujenieks' radicalisation, and prompted him to adopt a harsher stance towards minorities, which resulted in restrictive policies on language and education during his second, right-wing government, just a few years later. The minorities themselves got caught up in coalition games and inadvertently aided the authoritarian *coup* of 1934 by giving their votes to the last democratic government under Kārlis Ulmanis, thus conveniently putting him in a favourable position for a power grab. So, all points considered, one may say that, in the end, the Citizenship Law truly became the crux of the matter.

4. Conclusion

To summarise, the civic nationalism experiment in interwar Latvia was short-lived and ultimately a failure, as Latvia's civic nation does not exist to this day. Nevertheless, civic nationalism is not an extravagant foreign invention being artificially planted in Latvian soil, as is often claimed by its opponents: Latvia

---

35 Skujenieks' first, left-wing government (December 1926–January 1928) was dubbed "Nurock's cabinet" by A. Klīve of the Agrarian Union (see *Latvijas Republikas II. Saeimas IV. sesijas 21. sēde 1926. gada 17. decembrī*, 999)—a trope that stuck. As for the alleged inconsistency of Skujenieks' views on the citizenship issue, his opponents did have a good point, as he repeatedly spoke against the amendments in the Parliament, like, for example, on 3 December 1926, when he claimed that: "The first article of the amendments...opens Latvia's doors to an absolutely unpredictable number of people; and it is a big open question whether they are useful for our country economically, culturally or politically." (See *Latvijas Republikas II. Saeimas IV. sesijas 17. sēde 1926. gada 3. decembrī*, 612).

has its own theoretical base of civic nationalism, and its own history of implementing it. This history is not overly long, and it may be full of mistakes, both on the part of the eponymous nation, and on the part of ethnic minorities. But, to quote Lord Acton, "the world gains by its failures, and there is as much to learn from the experience of the nations that have failed as from the discoveries of truth."[36] Besides, as was pointed out to the author by a member of the audience at the International Conference "Latvia—A Work in Progress? 100 Years of State and Nation-building" (5–6 December 2013, Uppsala University), where an earlier version of this paper was presented, it may be premature to talk about any kind of failure as yet. As the title of this volume suggests, nation-building in Latvia is still an ongoing process, and this inspires cautious optimism.

---

36 J.E.E. Dalberg-Acton, "Ideas as Historical Forces," in *Selected Writings of Lord Acton, Volume III. Essays in Religion, Politics, and Morality* (Indianapolis: Liberty Fund, 1985), 643.

Why Remember Paul Schiemann?

David J Smith, University of Glasgow

1. Introduction

On 28 and 29 February 2016, events were held at the *Latvijas Saeima* and *Rīgas Dome* to mark the launch of Latvian- and Russian-language editions of John Hiden's book "Defender of Minorities" (2004)—a biography of the interwar German Latvian politician and journalist Paul Schiemann (1876–1944).[1] Initiated by Aivars Sinka, a second generation Latvian from the post-war *émigré* community in the United Kingdom, the not-for-profit project to translate Hiden's work had taken three years to organise and complete. In the process, it attracted support and encouragement from a wide cross section of politics and society in Latvia, including two former Prime Ministers, the Ministry of Culture and the current Mayor of Rīga.[2] Why did the life of Schiemann (a prominent public figure in the 1920s, but—it would be fair to say—still largely unknown to today's general public in Latvia) arouse such interest among forces which in some cases still differ fundamentally in their vision of present-day Latvia and its identity? The current chapter considers this question, using Schiemann's career (and some of the academic debates surrounding it) to reflect upon a century of state- and nation-building.

The support garnered by Aivars Sinka's initiative testifies perhaps first and foremost to Schiemann's obvious courage and the strength of his convictions, as well as to the breadth and richness of his activity as a politician, journalist, theoretician and cultural critic during the interwar period. Having first been drawn to his subject during the 1960s, during archival research on the place of the

---

[1] First published in English as: John Hiden, *Defender of Minorities. Paul Schiemann (1876–1944)* (London: Hurst & Co., 2004); in Latvian as Džons Haidens, *Paul Šīmanis: Minoritāšu Aizstāvis* (Rīga: Laika Grāmata, 2016); and in Russian as Dzhon Khaiden, *Paul' Shiman: Zashchitnik Men'shinstv* (Rīga: Laika Grāmata, 2016). Video footage of the launch event at the Saeima can be found at www.saeima.lv/en/galleries/video/4967 (accessed 1 November 2016). See also: Viesturs Sprūde, "Integrācijas padomi no pagātnes," *Latvijas Avīze*, 29 February 2016; Pauls Raudseps, "Laba vēstures grāmata palīdz meklēt risinājumus arī mūsdienu problēmām," *Ir*, 2 March 2016.

[2] The translated versions contain a full list of the organisations and individuals who financially backed or otherwise supported the project.

Baltic States within Weimar German *Ostpolitik*, John Hiden understood that he had happened upon a figure of international significance who merited further study in his own right. The eventual biography (winner of the 2006 biannual book prize of the US-based Association for the Advancement of Baltic Studies) helped to take Schiemann beyond the narrow realm of Baltic German historiography to which he had hitherto been largely consigned since World War II, and bring him more firmly to the attention of an English-speaking academic audience. The title of the book highlighted Schiemann's significance as an international minority rights activist during the 1920s. Not least, it underlined the importance of his ideas for the work of the European Nationalities Congress, a transnational coalition of minority organisations from 15 states, during the initial period of its existence from 1925–1932. Schiemann's work for the Congress (in which he served as a Vice Chairman), led his contemporaries to dub him the "Thinker of the European Minorities Movement."[3]

There can be little doubt that this epithet was richly deserved. While Schiemann was one of many activists promoting the idea of minority rights in 1920s Europe, "the impression remains that [he] had a clarity of intellect, independence, consistency and commitment to transferring his principles into practical life which was not so evident in those around him."[4] At the same time, the labels "Thinker of the Minorities Movement" and "Defender of Minorities" only partly capture the essence of the man and his contribution to the time in which he lived. As Hiden rightly remarks in the biography, published at the very moment Latvia was acceding to the European Union and NATO, Schiemann can also be regarded as a "Forgotten European", whose work at the international level anticipated the moves towards European integration that would begin to take shape after 1945. His lifelong commitment and intellectual and practical commitment to the cause of European peace and unity have yet to receive the full attention they deserve.[5]

---

3   Hiden, *Defender of Minorities*, 127–148.
4   Martyn Housden and David J. Smith, "A Matter of Uniqueness? Paul Schiemann, Ewald Ammende and Mikhail Kurchinksii Compared," in Martyn Housden and David J. Smith, eds., *Forgotten Pages in Baltic History: Diversity and Inclusion* (Amsterdam and New York: Rodopi, 2011), 178.
5   Hiden, *Defender of Minorities*, 250.

In Latvia itself, a memorial plaque on Rīga's Herder Square, erected in 1994 on the 50th anniversary of Schiemann's death, acknowledges him (in Latvian and German) as an "opponent of totalitarianism of any kind."[6] Also a fitting epitaph, it reflects Schiemann's unflinching opposition to both Nazism and Soviet Communism, and to the events of 1939–1944 that continue to shape identity-building processes in Latvia right up to the present day.[7] But, how familiar is the wider Latvian public with Schiemann's previous work, as a member of the Constituent Assembly of the Republic of Latvia, a Deputy in all four interwar *Saeima* and a member of Rīga City Council. not to mention his role as Editor-in-Chief of Latvia's largest and most influential German-language newspaper, the *Rigascher Rundschau* from 1919–1933? Aivars Sinka, who first learned of Schiemann in the mid-2000s through a lecture that John Hiden gave about his new book at the Latvian Embassy in London, was immediately convinced that the book needed to be read in Latvia, and read both in Latvian and in Russian. This conviction was further strengthened by the appearance (also in Latvian- and Russian-language editions) of Valentīna Freimane's memoir "*Ardievu, Atlantīda!*", in which the author recalled her personal acquaintance with Schiemann and regretted the fact that John Hiden's biography had not yet been made available to a wider readership in Latvia.[8] Sinka's subsequent initiative to do this was driven by a conviction that Schiemann remains one of "Latvia's silent heroes," whose voice is insufficiently acknowledged within his homeland.[9] The initiative can be seen as especially timely as Latvia prepares to mark

---

6   John Hiden, "A Voice from Latvia's Past: Paul Schiemann and the Freedom to Practise One's Culture," *The Slavonic and East European Review*, 77, 4 (1999): 698–699.
7   An international conference on Schiemann was also held in Rīga in 2000, resulting in a published collection of his translated articles from the international press during 1933–1940: Dietrich Loeber, ed., *Pauls Šimanis. Raksti 1933-1940* (Rīga: 2000). A further translated collection of writings appeared in Detlef Henning, *Pauls Šimanis. Eiropas Problēma. Rakstu izlase* (Rīga: 1999). For an overview of some more recent Latvian works, see: Ivars Ījabs, "Strange Baltic Liberalism: Paul Schiemann's Political Thought Revisited," *Journal of Baltic Studies*, 40, 4 (2009).
8   Taken from the text of Aivars Sinka's short speech at the *Saeima* on 28 February 2016, attended by the author.
9   Also from Sinka's speech. "Latvia's Silent Heroes" ("*Latvijas klusie varoņi*") is the name of a broader programme involving organisations such as the Museum of the Occupation of Latvia, the Žanis Lipke Memorial Museum and the Vītolu Fonds and designed to commemorate those (Schiemann included) who, during World War II, risked their own lives to save the lives of others. From author's personal communication with Pēteris Bolšaitis, translator of John Hiden's biography into Latvian, Rīga, February 2016.

the 100th anniversary of the original Declaration of the Republic back in 1918. The centenary year will provide ample opportunities to reflect on the events of that year and on the legacies of the interwar period more broadly. In undertaking this reflection, the contribution of Paul Schiemann to the life of Latvia can hardly be overlooked.

2. Schiemann and the Establishment and Consolidation of the Latvian State

The November 1918 Declaration of Independence came as the Latvian national movement struggled to assert itself against simultaneous challenges from the Bolsheviks and the forces of Imperial Germany. The democratic republic that emerged from this struggle was declared within ethnographic boundaries but established in the name of a civic nation of Latvia ("*Latvijas tauta*"), within which all ethnic groups inhabiting the territory were to have rights to cultural autonomy.[10] These were principles with which Paul Schiemann was immediately able to identify. Born in 1876 in Mitau (present-day Jelgava), to a family of *"Literaten"*, he had come of age in an era that was marked both by rapid processes of socio-economic modernisation and by policies of Russification promoted by Tsar Alexander III. The combined force of these developments was by this time beginning to erode the traditional dominance of the small Baltic German elite within what had hitherto been a rigid, estates-based society. Among other changes, the introduction of Russian in place of German as the language of instruction at the University of Dorpat (present-day Tartu) led Schiemann's father to send him to Germany to complete his university studies in Law. These culminated in the award of a doctorate from the University of Greifswald in 1902. Having imbibed (among other influences) the liberal ideas of Friedrich Naumann during his time abroad, Schiemann returned to his homeland with a world view (and personal lifestyle) that placed him at odds with much of a conservative Baltic German elite still clinging tenaciously to the privileged status it had enjoyed for centuries.

Beginning his career as a journalist, first in Dorpat (Tallinn) and soon in Rīga, Schiemann was alarmed by the violence and radicalism of the 1905 Revolution

---

10 Andrejs Plakans, *The Latvians. A Short History* (Stanford: Hoover Institution Press, 1995), 126–127.

in the Baltic Provinces. Seeing all too well the possible implications for society as a whole and for his own emerging "national" community in particular, he urged his fellow Baltic Germans to embrace Tsar Nicholas II's October Manifesto, acknowledge the growing claims by Latvians and Estonians for greater national self-determination and to join with them in transforming the crumbling estates-based society into a new civil society. In so doing, he sought to emphasise that the Baltic peoples and local Germans had a shared interest in resisting the totalising contours of state-sponsored Russian nationalism.[11] With the outbreak of war in 1914, however, Schiemann joined the tsarist army as a reserve officer in a cavalry regiment—an early indication, perhaps, of his consistently held belief that the political rights and duties of belonging to a *state-based* community must be placed above loyalties defined solely in ethnocultural terms. His position as a Baltic German officer in the Russian armed forces, however, became increasingly untenable following the Bolshevik Revolution. In March 1918, he deserted and returned to Livland, where, in the face of the turmoil wrought by war and revolution and the recent extension of German occupation to the whole of the Baltic Provinces, Latvian national activists were already starting to turn their thoughts towards complete independence.

Schiemann's arrival in Rīga coincided with a Brest-Litovsk Treaty that detached the Baltic Provinces from Russia and placed them (for the time being) under the ambit of Germany. In this situation, his own sympathies lay firmly with the reformist political forces in Berlin who insisted that the principle of national self-determination enshrined in the Treaty had to be applied in full to the former subject peoples of the Russian Empire. This view was not shared by the German military authorities on the ground, who colluded with local conservative elements in an effort to create a united "Baltic State", dominated by the local German elite and in union with the Prussian crown. That Schiemann was soon arrested by the occupying authorities and banished to Germany speaks volumes. As Hiden observes, however, in taking this step his enemies arguably did their own cause more harm than good, for Schiemann had many influential connections in Berlin upon which he could draw in order to advance his own alternative vision for the future of the Baltic Provinces.[12] German-led plans of

---

11 Hiden, "A Voice from Latvia's Past," 685.
12 Hiden, *Defender of Minorities*, 29–31.

any kind would in any case soon start to be overtaken by events, as the subsequent collapse of the Monarchy and the armistice with the Western Powers finally provided Latvian national activists with a window of opportunity (however narrow at first) to assert their own claims for self-determination. In the aftermath of the 18 November 1918 Declaration of an independent Latvia, Schiemann (at that point still in Berlin) rejected calls by the Baltic German National Committee for co-founding rights in the new state, backing instead the vision of the state's founding fathers.[13]

Schiemann's permanent return to Rīga in summer 1919 coincided with a decisive shift in the balance of power towards the Latvian Provisional Government, following the defeat of the *Baltische Landeswehr* at Cēsis and the signature of the Versailles Peace Treaty. Thereafter, as the new leader of the German Balt Democratic Party and head of the wider coalition of Baltic German parties, Schiemann worked tirelessly to mobilise his community behind the new democratic parliamentary politics and the considerable task of building functioning structures of independent statehood. *Inter alia*, as the new Chair of the Nationalities Commission created by the Latvian government at the end of 1918, he oversaw the adoption of a December 1919 "Law on the Schooling of Minorities in Latvia", which would form the basis for what was widely acknowledged as one of the most liberals system of minority governance in Europe during the 1920s. Typically, and as noted by Marina Germane elsewhere in this volume, Schiemann's work in this area was motivated not simply by the particular needs of his own German community, but by the principled commitment to defending the rights of all minorities that would later make him so influential within the European Nationalities Congress. In this regard, the Law on Schooling, however generous in scope, was seen as just the first step towards implementing a more far-reaching system of national-cultural autonomy, based on the precepts first elaborated by the Austrian Social Democrats Karl Renner and Otto Bauer at the turn of the 20th century (on which, more below).

---

13 Hiden, *Defender of Minorities*, 40–44.

Alongside this domestic activity, Schiemann—who could already be credited with an important role in securing the support of the Weimar German government for Baltic independence[14]—also worked hard to consolidate Latvia's position on the international stage. In a *Rigascher Rundschau* editorial published in 1925, he claimed that "the establishment of the Baltic states as a new political factor in east Europe is perhaps the most significant event following the world war, demanding a rethink of European policy as a whole," concluding that "a threat to the security of the Baltic states is a threat to the peace of Europe as a whole."[15] To mitigate this threat, Schiemann worked to encourage the development of a democratic Germany favourable to Baltic independence. He sought to promote mutually beneficial economic and political ties between the Weimar Republic and Latvia, and to integrate both countries into a pan-European security system in which small states could counterbalance any attempt at dominance by Great Powers. As noted later in this chapter, Schiemann's thinking at this time cannot be divorced entirely from the "liberal imperialism" of Naumann's *Mitteleuropa* that had previously shaped his ideas during World War I, nor from the "patrician"—to use Hiden's phrase—views he had expressed towards the Baltic peoples during 1918.[16] Nevertheless, there stands clear blue water between his ideas and those of *völkisch* nationalist Baltic German commentators of the period such as Max Hildebert Boehm (an avowed enemy of Schiemann and all he stood for), whose 1923 book *Europa Irredenta* argued that "the dependence of the small on the large is a fundamental in the lives of individuals and peoples, whose brutality can be modified and its form changed, but which in essence is inescapable."[17]

Schiemann's vision during the 1920s was instead premised on rendering the dichotomy between the "small" and the "large" redundant, through the construction of a United Europe. A strong advocate of the League of Nations from the outset, he also envisaged the future Coal and Steel Community that would lay to rest the enmity between France and Germany and provide the foundation

---

14   In this regard, see John Hiden, *The Baltic States and Weimar Ostpolitik* (Cambridge: Cambridge University Press, 1987).
15   Hiden *Defender of Minorities*, 113.
16   Hiden *Defender of Minorities*, 30.
17   Max Hildebert Boehm, *Europa Irredenta* (Berlin: Hobbing, 1923), 311–312. Cited in David J Smith and John Hiden, *Ethnic Diversity and the Nation State: National Cultural Autonomy Revisited* (London and New York: Routledge, 2012), 20.

for the European Community after World War II. Among other things, he saw a united democratic Europe as offering the best defence against the threat of Bolshevism, whose economic, political and cultural precepts he had attacked already in his 1918 work "The Fiasco of Russian Democracy." Nevertheless, Schiemann argued that Europe should—as far as was realistically possible— engage economically with Soviet Russia, seeing this as the best way to provide a stable framework for the development of the new border states. As a consistently fierce opponent of both Bolshevism and the tsarist imperialism that had preceded it, Schiemann argued that for Russia, "building anew would come not by restoring past borders but only through 'work within'", to use John Hiden's phrase.[18]

3. Schiemann's Conception of Nation and State and its Critics

This broader vision of a stable, united and democratic Europe also formed the cornerstone of Schiemann's work as a minority rights activist, within first the Association of German Minorities in Europe (*Verband der deutschen Minderheiten in Europa*, established 1923) and later, from 1925, the European Nationalities Congress. Both organisations bore the essential imprint of Schiemann's ideas until the start of the 1930s, not least in their insistence that discussion of minority rights must be divorced from that of territorial borders. Expression of irredentist sentiments and attacks on individual governments were thus expressly prohibited at meetings both of the *Verband* and of the Congress; the focus was firmly on general legal principles of interest to all minorities. What these organisations sought instead to challenge was the internal socio-political configuration of the new states that had emerged in Central and Eastern Europe as a result of the peace settlements at the end of World War I. These settlements had, of course, applied themselves to the question of national self-determination that had arisen so powerfully during the conflict. Yet, in so doing, they had applied what Karl Renner termed the "territorial principle", whereby newly created states were seen as "belonging" to particular nations defined in ethnocultural terms. The pronounced ethnic diversity of societies in the region, however, meant that ethnonational and territorial boundaries were in no case wholly congruent, meaning that all the new states were home to minority

---

18 Hiden, *Defender of Minorities*, 61.

groups whose own aspirations for national self-determination had remained unfulfilled. In response to this situation, the Western Powers that drew up the peace settlements had insisted that the new states sign "Minority Treaties," to be overseen by the newly-created League of Nations. Yet, while these treaties prohibited discrimination on ethnic grounds, they did not incorporate provisions for autonomous institutional structures geared to longer-term reproduction of minority cultures within states. Rather, they saw provisions for schooling in minority languages as a short-term measure, designed to encourage the "merger" of minorities into the national communities "to which they belonged."[19]

In an attempt to counter the inadequacies of the League framework for minority "protection" and alleviate the tensions it engendered, Schiemann relied on the ideas of Karl Renner and Otto Bauer to which he had been drawn during 1919. Renner and Bauer's model of national-cultural autonomy had been devised during 1899–1907, in an attempt to "convert the Austro-Hungarian Empire from a decaying conglomerate of squabbling national communities into a democratic confederation of nations."[20] It departed from the assumption that such a confederation could not be established according to the "territorial principle" (i.e. by assigning each group a territory "of its own" within the overall state), since all such units would inevitably contain new minorities subject to cultural domination by the majority. Instead, Renner and Bauer argued that nationality issues should be resolved according to "personality principle", whereby nations were defined as "communities of persons", bound by adherence to a shared cultural identity and with the right to maintain that identity regardless of where they lived within the state. This was to be achieved, in Renner's words, by "[cutting] in two the ... activities of the state, separating national and political matters": power was to be devolved to individual regions within the Habsburg state, but on a strictly territorial, non-ethnic basis; in parallel with these structures, each national group within the state would have the constitutionally-enshrined right to establish its own institutions of cultural self-government, on the

---

19 From a speech by British Foreign Minister Austen Chamberlain to the League of Nations Council in 1925, cited in Bastian Schot, *Nation oder Staat. Deutschland under der Minderheitenschutz* (Marburg: Herder Institut, 1988), 169.
20 Ephraim Nimni, "National-Cultural Autonomy as an Alternative to Minority Territorial Nationalism," in David J. Smith and Karl Cordell, eds., *Cultural Autonomy in Contemporary Europe* (London and New York: Routledge, 2008), 10.

basis of individual citizens freely determining their ethnic affiliation and voluntary enrolling on separate national registers. These would then be used to elect cultural councils, with responsibility for administering education and other cultural matters specific to the relevant group, and with a remit extending to the state territory as whole.[21] With national-cultural autonomy for all ethnic groups guaranteed in this way, it was reasoned, the territorial institutions of the state would be free to attend to "nationally neutral" matters of concern to all citizens, such as defence, economy, health and transport.[22]

Renner and Bauer's model inspired Schiemann's own critique of external efforts to graft the culturally homogenous Western nation-state model onto the plural societies of Central and Eastern Europe, while also shaping his own alternative normative concept of an "anational state", built around autonomous ethnocultural communities inhabiting a shared territorial space.[23] In Schiemann's thinking, preservation of one's particular ethnocultural identity should be seen as a basic human right, which could only be properly guaranteed by accepting cultural diversity as a defining characteristic of any state-based political community and establishing public-legal institutional structures that would ensure possibilities for long-term reproduction of different cultural identities within the population. At the same time, belong to a particular ethnocultural group was not determined by birth, but rather a matter of free affiliation for each individual. Nor should adherence to an ethnocultural identity distinct from that of the majority be seen as in any way inconsistent with loyalty to the state in which a person lived. Indeed, in Schiemann's eyes, minority identities were inseparable from the territorial setting in which they had developed. This thinking is perhaps best summed up in his famous maxim that "politics must be for the good of the place where one resides—any diversion to other ends is suicide."[24]

---

21 Quotation from R. Springer (pseudonym of Karl Renner), *Grundlagen und Entwicklungsziele der österreichisch-ungarischen Monarchie* (Vienna: 1906), 208.
22 Or, as Renner put it: "all nationalities govern and administer themselves ... they deal with their nationally specific affairs alone and their common affairs together." Karl Renner, "State and Nation," 1899 article reproduced in Ephraim Nimni, ed., National-Cultural Autonomy and its Contemporary Critics (London and New York: Routledge, 2005), 24.
23 On this, see Hiden, *Defender of Minorities*, 127–134.
24 Cited in Hiden, *Defender of Minorities*, 144.

With regard to his own community, for instance, Schiemann consistently argued that the key to long-term survival of Baltic German culture and influence lay in embracing minority status and working positively to gain acceptance: in other words, only by first acknowledging minority status would Baltic Germans ultimately be able to transcend it.[25] In appealing to the national majorities within the new states of Central and Eastern Europe, meanwhile, Schiemann argued that granting cultural autonomy was the best way of countering potential threats of irredentism and ensuring the loyalty of minority populations. By way of evidence, he and other activists within the *Verband* and the European Nationalities Congress pointed to the positive experience of Estonia (where Renner and Bauer's model formed the basis for a Law on Minority Self-Government passed in 1925) but also of Latvia, where, although public-legal NCA bodies were never created, the existence of autonomous national sections within the Ministry of Education served as a functional (and some would say superior) equivalent.[26] These examples—unique in the Europe of the day—were used to support the argument that national-cultural autonomy should form the basis for a pan-European system of minority rights to replace the much more limited provisions of the League of Nations.

As Schiemann's continued support for the League makes clear, he fully recognised that moves towards greater accommodation of cultural diversity within states was contingent upon external geopolitical factors as well as internal relationships between different ethnic groups.[27] In order to lay to rest ongoing nationalist tensions and conflicts and ensure their long-term security, he argued, European states would need to devolve sovereignty not only downwards to autonomous institutions amongst their own populations, but also upwards to

---

25 Hiden, *Defender of Minorities*, 140.
26 The "essential task of the minority movement," Schiemann noted in 1925, had taken "by far the most positive forms in Latvia and Estonia." Cited in Hiden, *Defender of Minorities*, 131. Estonia is often singled out as having the most comprehensive system of minority autonomy in interwar Europe, by virtue of its 1925 law on minority self-government. However, a detailed comparison of the two cases and their evaluation by contemporaries suggests that minority control over the structure and content of schooling was actually more comprehensive in Latvia. On this, see: Smith and Hiden, *Ethnic Diversity and the Nation State*, 31 & 58–59.
27 An excellent framework for understanding the relationship between the two sets of factors can be found in Harris Mylonas, *The Politics of Nation-Building: Making Co-Nationals, Refugees and Minorities* (Cambridge: Cambridge University Press, 2013).

supranational institutions of a United Europe. In his mind, the two processes went hand in hand, for he often criticised then existing pan-European projects as driven too much from the top-down by state governments, rather than allowing Europe's peoples to participate in a more organic development of unity from below.[28]

Schiemann's prescription for the state, of course, raises the obvious question of how, within this framework, to construct the overarching common identity and sense of solidarity which are today universally acknowledged as an essential component of any integrated, state-based political community.[29] In his 2009 article "Strange Baltic Liberalism," for instance, Ivars Ījabs claims that Schiemann's thinking reduced the state to nothing more than a functional necessity (*Tatsachengemeinschaft*), with no intrinsic ethical or cultural component of its own, and serving merely as a container for different ethnonational groups having few or any points of contact between them.[30] There seems little doubt that in formulating his conception, Schiemann was informed by long-standing traditions of corporatist rule within the former empires, which led him to reject the classic liberal conception of the state as an indivisible and undifferentiated community of individual citizens.[31] Yet, as a thinker and activist whose career

---

28   Hiden, *Defender of Minorities*, 135.
29   On the importance of this, see: Karl Deutsch, *Nationalism and Social Communication: An Inquiry into the Foundations of Nationality (*Cambridge, MA: M.I.T. Press, 1966); Charles Tilly, ed., *The Formation of National States in Western Europe* (Princeton, Princeton University Press, 1975); Juan J. Linz and Alfred Stepan, *Problems of Democratic Transition and Consolidation: Southern Europe, South America, and Post-Communist Europe* (Baltimore, Md., London: Johns Hopkins University Press,1996), 16.
30   Ījabs, "Strange Baltic Liberalism": 506.
31   The same can be said of Renner and Bauer's original model, which sought to challenge the "atomist-centralist" principle (the state as the sum of its smallest parts—i.e. individual citizens) that had taken hold as part of the progressive centralisation of territorial states from the mid-16th century onwards (see: Nimni, *National-Cultural Autonomy*, 12). Renner and Bauer's model, of course, envisaged corporate minority structures based on free affiliation by individuals. It has, nevertheless, been criticised for essentialising ethnicity, for while it allowed individuals to "choose" their ethnocultural identity, the implication is that each person has only one. This, it is said, runs the risk of limiting the space for individuals who hold multiple cultural affiliations, and thereby hardening ethnic boundaries in contexts where they may in fact be quite fluid (see, for instance: Rainer Bauböck, "Territorial or Cultural Autonomy for National Minorities?" IWE Working Paper No. 22, Austrian Academy of Sciences (2001), at: http://www.eif.oe aw.ac.at/05workingpapers/archive05.html. Interestingly, it is for this reason that the Minorities Secretariat of the League of Nations viewed the interwar Latvian Law on Minority Schooling more favourably than the better-known Estonian cultural autonomy

was in many ways a perpetual journey from one world to another[32], Schiemann was not simply some backward-looking romantic: he was acutely aware of the new modernising realities taking shape around him, and gave them due consideration.

Take, for instance, the founding programme of the Nationalities Congress in which Schiemann was so influential. In his words, the Congress was:

> "striving basically for the inclusion of minorities in normal state life. A minority that is more concerned with its own interests than with the general good acts against public interest and violates the fundamental idea of our Nationalities Congress, *which seeks not to set minorities apart from the state but to engage them in its life* [my italics—DS]. We want to show the world that granting rights to minorities does not threaten the state but strengthens it. We can only win this trust by taking an honourable line in all matters concerning the generality."[33]

To this end, while the Nationalities Congress founding programme of 1925 advocated rights for use of minority languages, it stated plainly that the majority language should be the sole official language of government at the state level.[34] For persons belonging to minorities, learning the majority language was portrayed not only as a duty but also as a *right*, which would enable their effective participation in the wider political community. Dissimilation—or separation—of national communities was therefore not part of the Congress agenda. By the same token, its Chairman Josip Wilfan would declare in 1932 that "the *right* to assimilation, though we oppose this idea, we grant to anyone who wishes to

---

law, for while the latter required individuals to opt for and publicly declare an ethnicity, the Latvian system had no such requirement—rather, pupils could register for minority language schools simply on the basis of declaring that this was the main language spoken in the home. See: L. Krabbe, "L'Autonomie culturelle comme solution du problème des minorités." Note de M. Krabbe au date du 18 nov. 1931. League of Nations Archive, Geneva, R.2175-4-32835.

32 The memoir that Schiemann dictated covered the period 1903–1919 was entitled "Between Two Eras". Paul Schiemann *Zwischen zwei Zeitaltern. Erinnerungen 1903–1919* (Lüneburg: Verlag Nordland-Druck GmbH, 1979).

33 From Schiemann's editorial "Minderheitenziele," *Rigascher Rundschau*, 23 April 1927. Cited in Hiden, *Defender of Minorities*, 139.

34 Although in areas where minorities made up a predominant share of the local population, the relevant minority language should have official status alongside the majority one. See: "Resolutions of the European Nationalities Congress", *Rossiiskii Gosudarstvenii Voennyi Arkhiv*, F.1502, O.1, D.113, pp. 34–35.

assimilate: the *obligation* to assimilation we reject [my italics—DS]."[35] All things considered, the most apt word to describe the Congress' agenda would surely be "integration."

Furthermore, as John Hiden puts it in his book, the state envisaged by Schiemann was far from being simply a "night watchman" for separate national communities.[36] For instance, Schiemann's theory of autonomy argued against devolving any social welfare functions to the jurisdiction of ethnic communities. This, he claimed, "would be to abandon the dictates of love of humanity and replace them merely with love of one's own kin—quite clearly the inspiration of a nationalism injurious to ethics."[37] Schiemann also reflected at length on processes of cultural interaction, remarking that "different nationalities who look back together on a shared past on the same territory ... also have an element of culture in common. Therein lies their strength."[38] He continued that:

> "Where nations live beside each other for decades, a fragment of common culture emerges alongside national cultures; common customs, common history, and the feeling of togetherness take shape ... We can see then, how alongside the nation as a cultural community, a second form of nation can evolve from the state community."[39]

In order to promote this end, Schiemann advocated common schooling for different nationalities after the primary level, seeing this as a vital factor supporting social and national solidarity amongst citizens of the state.[40]

Thus, one can argue that when Schiemann spoke of an "anational state", he did not mean a state with no shared cultural component at all, but rather one that was as ethnoculturally neutral as it could possibly be. Ivars Ījabs is entirely correct when he says that Schiemann's ideas were in many ways particular to the time and context in which they evolved. Nevertheless, Ījabs is also right to point out that these ideas in many ways anticipated the contemporary minority

---

35 Cited by Hildrun Glass, "Die deutsch-judische Kontroverse auf dem europäischen Nationalitätenkongress," unpublished paper presented at the Simon Dubnow Institute, Leipzig, 2005. Cited in Smith and Hiden, *Ethnic Diversity and the Nation State*, 88.
36 Hiden, *Defender of Minorities*, 143.
37 Hiden, *Defender of Minorities*, 143.
38 Hiden, *Defender of Minorities*, 143.
39 Paul, Schiemann, "Volksgemeinschaft und Staatsgemeinschaft, *Nation und Staat*, 1, 1 (1927): 38. Cited by, among others, Ījabs, "Strange Baltic Liberalism": 507.
40 Hiden, "A Voice from Latvia's Past": 693.

rights model which the European Union has advocated as a template for promoting integration in today's Latvia.[41] While this "liberal pluralist" approach is often seen as something to be "exported" to Eastern Europe from the West,[42] Schiemann writings from the interwar period highlight an indigenous tradition of thinking in this area that should not be overlooked today.[43] It also bears repeating that Schiemann was not an "ivory tower" academic, but someone whose ideas were shaped by sustained political work to overcome the legacies bequeathed to Latvia by the tsarist Empire and several hundred years of feudal rule by the Baltic Barons.

These legacies included an absence of any prior common institutional framework uniting different ethnic groups and a lack of experience of democracy. Both were factors that undermined Latvia's parliamentary system of the 1920s and contributed to the onset of authoritarian rule in 1934. As Ījabs reminds us, Paul Schiemann's own views inevitably bore the imprint of his upbringing in a society still dominated by the Baltic German elite. This, coupled with his experience of revolutionary upheaval, left him with a rather elitist understanding of democracy and political participation. Schiemann's suspicion of mass politics meant that he never devoted much effort to putting his ideas across to the wider Latvian public, preferring instead to operate within the narrow confines of the political elite and producing most of his journalism and other published works in German.[44]

In this sense, too, Schiemann long maintained a rather uncritical belief in the superior liberal qualities of Baltic German culture, which he thought would by default place itself at the centre of a new civil society and provide a model for Latvians to follow in their own cultural development.[45] His background also perhaps meant that he could never fully grasp the depth of the inherited social divisions between Latvians and Germans. Common history, he said, was crucial to promoting a feeling of togetherness amongst different nationalities; but,

---

41 Ījabs, "Strange Baltic Liberalism": 508–512.
42 Will Kymlicka and Magda Opalski, eds., *Can Liberal Pluralism be Exported? Western Political Theory and Ethnic Relations in Eastern Europe* (Oxford: Oxford University Press, 2001).
43 Ījabs, "Strange Baltic Liberalism": 511–512.
44 Ījabs, "Strange Baltic Liberalism": 499–503.
45 Ījabs, "Strange Baltic Liberalism": 502–503.

looking back over the previous seven centuries, it was difficult to find very much common ground uniting Latvians and Germans. For reasons discussed elsewhere in this volume, Schiemann's pluralistic conception of political community always envisaged a continued space for German culture and political influence that was larger than most Latvian politicians of the time were willing to allow.[46] The shift to a more "nationalising" state policy from the late 1920s in turn strengthened the hand of conservative and *völkisch* elements within the Baltic German population (and its diaspora) who wished to remain separate from the Latvian majority and who ultimately hankered after restoring their former dominant position within the territory of Latvia.

4. Conclusions

In sum, one can say that the domestic challenges of building a democratic Latvia in the 1920s were formidable. But, they may not have been insurmountable had it not been for the chronically unstable international situation of the day. In this regard, the Great Depression of 1929 further undermined the foundations of Latvia's parliamentary system, but it also destroyed any remaining credibility enjoyed by the League of Nations and heralded Hitler's rise to power in Germany. Schiemann (who had been an outspoken opponent of Nazism from the very start) famously spoke in 1932 of a "new nationalist wave" crashing over Eastern Europe from the West and sweeping in its wake whatever positive work had been achieved during the 1920s.[47] From 1933, Latvia found itself caught directly between the expansionist ambitions of Nazi Germany and a Stalinist USSR determined to reassert control over the territories "lost" by Russia following the 1917 Revolution. The stage was thereby set for the Molotov-Ribbentrop Pact and the 1940 Soviet annexation. Among other things, this development spelled the end of the Baltic German community in Latvia via a Nazi-sponsored resettlement that Paul Schiemann—it need hardly be said—refused

---

46 See especially the contributions by Plakans, Germane and Kott. Anti-Bolshevism was, of course, one shared orientation that bound the Germans to most of the Latvian political elite. However, even this basis for solidarity had been undermined by the actions of the *Baltische Landeswehr* in 1919.

47 This was the title ("*Die neue nationalistische Welle*") of a speech delivered to a meeting of the *Verband der deutschen Minderheiten in Europa* in June 1932, in which Schiemann forcefully reiterated the original founding principles of the Nationalities Congress to a group by now increasingly under the sway of nationalist forces in Germany. See Smith and Hiden, *Ethnic Diversity and the Nation State*, 86.

to join. Schiemann was by this time in very bad health, and had been for several years. Pressures of work had taken their toll, as had Schiemann's incessant smoking. He lived through the Soviet occupation of 1940–41 and died in 1944 while under Nazi house arrest at his home in Rīga. In the course of the Nazi occupation, he and his wife sheltered the young Valentīna Freimane, to whom Schiemann began to dictate his memoirs and who, fittingly, provided the introduction to the new translations of John Hiden's book.

Faced with a set of events that had destroyed everything he had worked for during his career, Schiemann recognised that his belief in the inherent liberalism of the Baltic Germans had been misplaced. He could also see only too well how German nationalist forces had been able to manipulate his ideas on minority rights and subvert for their own ends the international movement that he had helped to found. And yet, for all this, Schiemann never lost his faith in the basic ideals he had developed during the first three decades of the 20th century.

If one fast-forwards to 1997–2004, when John Hiden researched and wrote the biography, there seemed many grounds to suggest that Schiemann's ideals were in the process of being reaffirmed. Having reattained its statehood in 1991, Latvia was by this time already on course to join the EU and NATO and become part of a framework for European integration that appeared in many ways to embody the longer-term vision Schiemann had set out back in the 1920s. At the same time, while accession to and subsequent membership of these two international organisations has undoubtedly offered important "external anchors" (to quote Vanags, in this volume) for state-building, Latvia continues to grapple with challenges that appear no less formidable than those of the interwar period. Integration with European and Euro-Atlantic structures, for instance, has not banished insecurities deriving from the country's geopolitical positioning as an eastern "border state". Indeed, relations between Russia and the West have grown progressively more tense during the Putin era, particularly following Russia's annexation of Crimea and intervention in Eastern Ukraine during 2014. The Kremlin leadership claims that these actions were undertaken to guard against further Western encroachments that threaten Russia's claims to a sphere of influence over its "near abroad", if not the continued existence of Russia itself. However, they could more plausibly be portrayed as an attempt to shore up the domestic legitimacy of the Putin regime in a situation where—to borrow Schiemann's phrase from the 1920s—real "work within" to secure Russia's economic and political renewal has all but ground to a halt. As Li Bennich-Björkman observes elsewhere in this volume, geopolitical and security anxieties were already an important factor in shaping the citizenship policies adopted by Latvia at the start of the 1990s. These gave rise to additional new lines of societal division which, although alleviated, were not entirely resolved by entry to the European Union and NATO. While the state continuity principle underpinning citizenship policy is grounded in principles of international law, one can hardly deny that it also carries ethnopolitical connotations bound up with ensuring the hegemony within the state of an historically-wronged and endangered ethnic Latvian core nation. This in turn has much to do with the demographic changes of the Soviet era, which meant that Latvians acquired a consciousness akin to that of an embattled minority within an increasingly Russified public sphere. On the one hand, the wide support attracted by the initiative to translate Hiden's biography of Schiemann (encompassing both a Ministry of Culture headed by the most nationalist Latvian political party and a Rīga City Council run by a party—Harmony Centre—still often characterised as "pro-Russian") can be seen in its own small way as a testament to the remarkable progress that has been achieved since 1991 in terms of "de-ethnifying" the political sphere. Nevertheless, as Matthew Kott points out in another contribution to this volume, one should not underestimate the scale of the challenges that remain. Aivars Sinka, indeed, made a similar point when publicly introducing the translations in February 2016.

Today, efforts to build a stable, inclusive and prosperous Latvia have to reckon not only with the continued weight of inherited structural obstacles, but also with a growing sense of crisis currently besetting Europe. Latvia may have ridden out the post-2008 economic slump, but it has lost too large a share of its population through out-migration to an EU whose unity and cohesion is being tested as never before by the simultaneous challenges of currency stability, Russian aggression in Ukraine, Syrian refugees and now Brexit. Were Paul Schiemann still with us, he would doubtless offer analyses of all these issues every bit as trenchant as those he produced between the wars. Present-day Latvia (and, indeed, Europe) is very different to that of the 1920s, and it would be too simplistic to claim that the solutions advocated by Schiemann back then could simply be transplanted into a contemporary setting. Nevertheless, his core message of peace, tolerance, mutual acceptance and common work for the general good is one that bears repeating today, and it was this consideration above all others that motivated Aivars Sinka to arrange for the translation of the Hiden biography into Latvian and Russian.[48]

In this regard, the main conclusion to be drawn from Schiemann's work is that rights of minorities are ultimately a means to the end of democratisation and—to use the phrase of a more contemporary theorist—"citizenisation": defined in this way, the present-day concept of "multiculturalism" (which Schiemann so obviously anticipated in his writings) does not entrench, but rather *challenges* cultural identities, both of national majorities *and* minorities.[49] In this respect, one should be wary of those who—like the *völkisch* German nationalists of the interwar period—would simply take arguments for minority autonomy and use them as a basis for promoting separation rather than integration. By the same token, Latvia's current leaders should not simply emphasise Schiemann's own patriotism and his call for minorities to adapt themselves to a Latvian state, without also reflecting on how the majority itself should adapt in order to accommodate them.

Seen in this light, states and the "imagined national communities" that continue to sustain them are perpetual "works in progress", within which ethnocultural diversity remains both a fact of life and (if embraced and properly harnessed) a resource for enriching society. Diversity, moreover, must surely increase in the future, if European states are serious about addressing the decline in the economically active share of their populations. While this may not make for comfortable reading in some circles, the experience of the 1930s shows only too clearly the dangers of succumbing to the "new populist wave" currently sweeping Europe. With this in mind, it is perhaps even more timely to remember Paul Schiemann and his ideas today than it was in 2004.

---

48 From Sinka's speech at Rīga City Council, 29 February 2016.
49 Will Kymlicka, "The Rise and Fall of Multiculturalism? New Debates on Inclusion and Accommodation in Diverse Societies," in S. Vertovec and S. Wessendorf, eds., *The Multiculturalism Backlash* (London and New York: Routledge, 2010), 32–49.

The Return of the Gods? Authoritarian Culture and Neo-Paganism in Interwar Latvia, 1934–1940

Deniss Hanovs, Rīga Stradiņš University
Valdis Tēraudkalns, University of Latvia

1. Introduction

In 1937 Ernests Brastiņš, the leader of the Latvian neo-pagan movement *Dievturi* (The "God-keepers"), congratulated the head of the Republic of Latvia Kārlis Ulmanis on his 60th birthday, stating in his address to the authoritarian president that Ulmanis was a genius and a man sent by God.[1] In sending his congratulations Brastiņš followed the general pattern which dominated the public sphere during the last six years of independent interwar Latvia: glorification of the central figure of the *coup d` état* of May 15, 1934—the Prime Minister, the State President, Father of the Nation, the Leader (*Vadonis* in Latvian) K. Ulmanis. Ulmanis shaped the Latvian version of authoritarian culture until the end of June 1940, when Soviet troops entered the territory of Latvia and he was forced to accept political changes that led to Latvia's transformation into one of the Soviet republics.

The leader of the authoritarian regime was further variously acclaimed as the guardian of Latvian youth, friend of Latvian sailors and the leading expert in many fields, including foreign policy and agriculture (the latter at least had some justification, because Ulmanis had studied agriculture before World War I in Latvia, Germany, Switzerland and the United States). This pattern of ascribing various heroic roles to the leader of the non-democratic regime was more than just a function of a Latvian authoritarian propaganda concentrating on the figure of the leader of the new political formation. For, as Italian researcher Fallasca-Zamponi has stated in her short analysis of the image of Mussolini, propaganda alone cannot explain the success of non-democratic

---

1 Brastiņu Ernests, "Laimīgā diena," in *Kārļa Ulmaņa 60 gadi: 1877. 4. Septembris—1937.: svētku raksti* (Rīga: Zemnieka domas, 1938), 305.

regimes in different countries of Europe.[2] The phenomenon of authoritarianism and totalitarianism should not be analysed as a distortion of an Enlightenment political culture that included the principles of separation of powers and democratic participation as well as various basic freedoms of a civic society, including minority rights. Rather, the present authors would agree with Zamponi's claim that the role of propaganda can only be understood within the context of established political and cultural structures of European societies, structures which assisted non-democratic ideologies and regimes in coming to power either through the attainment of a parliamentary majority and democratically expressed mass support or through non-resistance by the majority of the population after power had been seized by means of a *coup*.

In analysing non-democratic regimes, it is therefore essential to consider the role played by elements of Europe's "pre-democratic" cultures, such as the legacy of monarchism (e.g. the culture of the German Reich, the Italian culture of leadership during the glorified *Risorgimento* movement) or even—in the case of Russia—absolutism, which persisted right up until the breakdown of the regime in the spring of 1917.

Traditionalism in interwar European societies is another complicated issue that will be briefly addressed as part of our discussion of this period of interwar state- and nation-building. Ivan T. Berend argues that the peasantry remained excluded from modernising nation-state projects before World War I and only thereafter attained political articulation via the right and radical right wing of the new and old parliamentary cultures[3]. In this regard, the fragmented political landscape of Latvia provided a favourable environment for the growth of a peasant party (The Agrarian Union, established in 1917) to which the future Leader of the state (Ulmanis) belonged. Agrarian reforms meant that traditionalism became a vital political tool in all three Baltic States, and was used as an instrument of political rhetoric by conservative parties.

---

2   Simonetta Falasca-Zamponi, "Mussolini's Self-Staging," in Hans Jörg Czech, Nikola Goll, Hrsg., *Kunst und Propaganda im Streit der Nationen 1930–1945* (Dresden: Sandstein Verlag, 2007), 89.
3   Ivan T. Berend, *Decades of Crisis: Central and Eastern Europe Before World War II* (Berkeley: University of California Press, 1998), 290–291.

In their earlier publications, the present authors have reflected in detail on the place of traditionalism within Ulmanis' political formula of restoring political stability and rescuing society from the long-lasting chaos and political insecurity "caused" by parliamentary pluralism and a culture of small, short-lived parliamentary coalitions.[4] In this chapter we will reflect upon the traditionalist idea as expressed in the ideological concept of "recovery" of the native Latvian culture. This concept attained preeminence within the political discourse of the authoritarian regime very soon after the *coup* of 15 May 1934. The major message this conveyed was the need to create a "Latvian Latvia" in which Latvians would attain predominant status amongst the various ethnic groups which inhabited Latvia and which had enjoyed freedom and cultural autonomy during the parliamentary phase (1922–1934). The first governmental declaration following the *coup* talked about a "Latvia where Latvianness will triumph and all that is foreign will vanish."[5] In 1937 the Minister of Welfare Vladislavs Rubulis declared in a public speech that "Latvians will remain the basis of this land. The other nations should prove their love of Latvian land and nation."[6] Latvians were defined as a society without social stratification or rather as a mass without social conflicts, but shaped by peasantism in various areas: aesthetically, politically, culturally. Performative aspects of the regime were aimed at propagating this image of a society of liberated subalterns: festivals, mass productions, media content, youth organisations, even agricultural policies were all viewed as instruments for liberating Latvians from a parliamentary past of ethnic, social and political divisions and conflicts. These propaganda activities were presented as a true articulation of people's thoughts, hopes and voices.

After May 1934, the narrative of the traditional peasant culture of the farmstead (*viensēta* in Latvian) became the predominant image of the nation, which, according to various messages from the new regime, was longer no subject to social and regional differences, but instead represented a unified, homogeneous cultural group in a quasi-sacred personal and collective union with the

---

4 See, for example, Deniss Hanovs, Valdis Tēraudkalns, "Happy Birthday, Mr. Ulmanis! Reflections on the Construction of an Authoritarian Regime in Latvia," *Politics, Religion & Ideology* 15:1 (2014), 64–81.
5 "Valdības manifests," *Jaunākās Ziņas,* 16 May 1934, 1.
6 "Norādījumi Latgales zemniekiem," *Jaunākās Ziņas,* 16 March 1937, 6.

guardian of the state Ulmanis. At the time of the *coup* Ulmanis was Prime Minister, but in 1936 when the mandate of his former fellow member of the Agrarian Union (all parties were dismantled after the *coup*) Alberts Kviesis ended, he also became the State President.

One of the visions of traditional society, however, did not fit with the new concept of reviving ethnic culture. Latvian neopaganism was not accepted by the new regime as part of its harmonising ideological construction of recovering true Latvian identity. Why did the government block the development of the *Dievturi*, who pretended to be true bearers of Latvian pre-Christian traditions? Why was the spiritual traditionalism of the movement developed by Brastiņš and others not incorporated into an authoritarian system that supported Latvianness across a wide spectrum of public activities such as folklore studies, arts, sporting activities and even details of everyday life like the design of apartments?

In what follows we will reflect briefly on the *Dievturi* movement within the context of the authoritarian ideology of the Ulmanis regime. The interaction between the new regime and the Latvian neo-pagan movement will be analysed by reference to the political semiotics of authoritarianism. The regime will be examined in terms of its contacts with groups that either did not fit with the image of the authoritarian culture or were opposed to it. The article also will examine how the regime responded to the desire of the *Dievturi* movement to be included into the mainstream narrative of the constructed traditional Latvian culture.

The main focus of the chapter is therefore not on the religious aspects of the *Dievturi* movement. Rather, we seek to contribute to the study of how the authoritarian national ideology was constructed, by illustrating the selective politics of the Ulmanis regime in this area.

2. *Dievturi*—a Concise Dossier on a Neo-Pagan Movement

The *Dievturi* movement emerged during the 1920s, amidst debates among Latvian intellectuals on how to Latvianise religion. The dominant religious confession amongst Latvians—Lutheranism—was perceived as too German and associated with the suppression of Latvian identity during 700 years of serfdom. One outcome of these debates was the Latvianisation of Lutheranism, a project that was more consistently developed under the authoritarian regime when it enjoyed support from the state. One extreme manifestation of this was the "Latvian Christianity" movement spearheaded by Lutheran pastor Jānis Sanders. Following a conflict with the church leadership over his rejection of the Old Testament, Sanders established a separate Latvian Christian Congregation, which acquired legal status in 1937. He Latvianised terms derived from Hebrew such as *amen*, *alleluia* and *hosanna* and repeatedly expressed anti-Semitism. His congregation was similar to that of the German Christian movement.[7]

Another outcome of debates among intellectuals was the establishment of the *Dievturi* movement, which was registered by Latvia's Council of Spiritual Affairs in July 1926. The registration document was not issued to Brastiņš (although he was among those who signed a petition in favour of registration) but to Kārlis Marovskis-Bregžis. From the very beginning the movement lacked unity. Already in 1927 Brastiņš established a rival *Dievturi* organisation. Later, the role of Bregžis diminished and the whole movement became more associated with the name of Brastiņš. But, it is important to note that the two branches of the movement were different not only organisationally but also doctrinally. Bregžis was against *Dievturi* involvement in politics. His version of Latvian neo-paganism was more intimate, practised in the family or small community. Brastiņš, however, developed teaching that was more aimed at attracting people and was more categorical in its statements.[8] Brastiņš is described by writer Anšlavs Eglītis as a gifted speaker and organiser who was able to fill the masses with enthusiasm.[9] Already before the formal establishment of the *Dievturi* Fellowship (*Dievturu sadraudze*), a small brochure was published providing a summary of its beliefs. In it we can see a fascination with the East, characteristic of European Romanticism, including the assertion that "traces of ancient *dievturība* can be found in India."[10] Brastiņš did not hide his sympathies for romanti-

---

7   For more on the Latvian Christian Congregation, see Deniss Hanovs and Valdis Tēraudkalns, *Ultimate Freedom-No Choice: The Culture of Authoritarianism in Latvia, 1934–1940* (Leiden, Boston: Brill, 2013), 238–245.
8   Agita Misāne, "Dievturība Latvijas reliģisko un politisko ideju vēsturē," *Reliģiski-filozofiski Raksti* X (2005), 106–107.
9   Anšlavs Eglītis, *Pansija pilī* (Rīga: Liesma, 1991), 243.
10 Ernests Brastiņš, Kārlis Bregžis, *Latviešu dievturības atjaunojums* (Rīga: 1926), 5.

cism, because according to him "the romanticist is irrational, as is the nationalist. The Nation is a group of people bound strongly by nature itself."[11] The *Dievturi* tried to reconstruct the religion of ancient Latvians based on folk songs (*dainas*), folk beliefs and practices. The movement was never widespread. According to the reports of the Political Police the total number of worshippers attending its ceremonies varied from some dozens up to 600 (in 1937). Starting from 1937 the movement introduced an attendance fee because of financial problems.[12] After the Soviet occupation the movement was banned and continued its existence in emigration. In Latvia, it was reestablished under the leadership of Eduards Detlavs at the beginning of the 1990s after Latvia regained independence.[13]

3. Using the New Language of Authoritarian Discourse: How the *Dievturi* Tried to Follow the Rules

As already mentioned, the leader of the *Dievturi* movement Brastiņš initially participated in the general glorification politics of the Latvian authoritarian regime aimed at defining the leader of the new regime as the saviour of the political order from the chaos of interwar Europe—economic crisis, political instability and threats from the regime of Stalin. "Follow your Leader of the nation because geniuses speed up the progress of their nation many times," wrote Brastiņš.[14] The *Dievturi* quoted Ulmanis in their journal "*Labietis*" as well as in their meetings to show that their ideas were in accordance with the Leader's thoughts. For example, at the opening of the *Dievturi* congregation in Jelgava Jēkabs Bīne repeated Ulmanis' words that "only one culture can and is allowed in Latvia—the Latvian culture."[15]

The political changes that had occurred in Latvia were in accordance with Brastiņš' version of nationalism, which he summarised as follows: "the nation is the highest value, goodness and sacredness. The nation is at the centre of

---

11 Ernests Brastiņš, "Nacionālisms kā romantika," in Romāns Pussars, ed., Ernests Brastiņš. *Tautai, Dievam un Tēvzemei* (Rīga: Zvaigzne, 1993), 70.
12 Misāne, "Dievturība Latvijas reliģisko un politisko ideju vēsturē," 108.
13 "Vēsture," http://www.dievturi.org/vesture.htm (as of 10 April 2014).
14 Ernests Brastiņš, "Nekur citur", in Romāns Pussars, ed., Ernests Brastiņš. *Tautai, Dievam un Tēvzemei* (Rīga: Zvaigzne, 1993), 102.
15 "Vakar Jelgavā nodibināja jaunu draudzi," *Zemgales Balss* 5 February 1940, 4.

the world! The nation is higher than anything else. The nation is in the first place!"[16] For Brastiņš the nation was not a backwards-looking, static reality: "national identity is not something complete (...) it has unfinished and growing potency that hides in itself new, unseen opportunities."[17] Already before the *coup* Brastiņš had been no friend of the democratic system, as can be seen from his publications of the time. However, he developed this position extensively during the authoritarian period. In an article published in 1931 Brastiņš outlined a political concept called *naciokrātija* (Natiocracy)—the rule of the state nation. According to this concept, power lies in the hands of one nation. Ethnic minorities should have cultural freedom but they should not be allowed to participate in elections. Indeed, elections *per se* were not important to Brastiņš because in brackets he adds ("if such were still to be held").[18] Minorities "at best would be looked upon as guests who enjoy hospitality and respect. As guests, they would have freedom but not power."[19] The supreme power in this imagined state belonged to the Leader, the one who "understands the goals of the nation and who is able to turn its dreams into ideals and ideals into concrete patterns."[20] Italy and Germany are mentioned as examples of this system. "Not equality but unity is what natiocracy tries to realise in the nation."[21] It is difficult to reconcile this statement with the more tolerant assertion that "Latvianness means loving what is ours and respecting the other."[22]

In "*Labietis*", Brastiņš did not limit his glorification of Ulmanis to statements about the heroic role of the Leader in creating the Latvian Latvia and bringing peace and prosperity. In September 1935, he published the script of a play called "Fruitful Master" (*raženais saimnieks* in Latvian).[23] Its plot resembled other examples of authoritarian theatrical discourse during the six years of the

---

16 Ernests Brastiņš, "Latvietība kā jauna tikumība", in Romāns Pussars, ed., *Ernests Brastiņš. Tautai, Dievam un Tēvzemei* (Rīga: Zvaigzne, 1993), 54.
17 Ernests Brastiņš, *Tautības mācība* (Rīga: Zemnieka domas, 1936), 52.
18 Ernests Brastiņš, "Demokrātija un naciokrātija," in *Latviskas Latvijas labad: mājieni un aicinājumi 1925–1935* (Valmiera: Valmieras skolu valde, 1994), 59.
19 Brastiņš, *Tautības mācība*, 264.
20 Brastiņš, *Tautības mācība*, 246.
21 Brastiņš, *Tautības mācība*, 246.
22 Ernests Brastiņš, "Diezgan zaimots un glaimots!" in *Latviskas Latvijas labad: mājieni un aicinājumi 1925–1935* (Valmiera: Valmieras skolu valde, 1994), 29.
23 Ernests Brastiņš, "Raženais saimnieks," *Labietis* 5 (1935), 89–106.

regime, starting with an open-air performance called "The Song of Revival" staged on 20–22 July 1934, soon after the *coup*. The Latvian variant of non-democratic regime displays various similarities with different types of sport and theatrical performances which combined mass actions with theatrical experiments developed by Italian and Russian futurists before and after World War I, with Dadaist works and what can be called flash mobs of classical European modernism, as Roselee Goldberg has illustrated in her updated research on post-World War political performance.[24]

The non-democratic regimes across Europe used and reinterpreted the experience of artistic pluralism and opposition to elite cultural production accumulated during the pre- and post-war period and put mass culture patterns and scenarios of aesthetic influence on the mass spectator into a new frame. For dictatorships, mass involvement entailed a passive audience accepting the new interpretation of recent political events (*coups*) and a remote past in which nations were shaped in terms of the culture of a homogeneous society without political pluralism.

Instead of using Ulmanis' image directly, Brastiņš in his play created the image of the Master and Mistress of the rural estate who act alongside allegoric figures of the rural extended family, such as: old man (grandfather), old farm labourer, female tutor, mother. The example of the "Song of Revival" demonstrates that the direct use of the dictator's name or that of other political figures was not welcomed. The "Song" ignored this by staging the apotheosis scene with Ulmanis played by a professional actor. However, the prohibition was adhered to in the text written by Brastiņš, for here Ulmanis was not directly present, but rather depicted as the "Peasant of all Peasants", and identified with agrarian society and its virtues. Further characters represented the modernised administrative presence of the state authorities, such as a schoolteacher and a head of the local community administration, while another set of *dramatis personae* were spiritual forces, such as Jumis (God of the Harvest) and his female counterpart Jume.

---

24 Rouzly Goldberg, *Iskusstvo performansa. Ot futurizma do nashih dnei* (Moskva: Ad Marginem Press, 2014), 52.

Typically for an authoritarian drama, there were also two personages of the physical world, who represented dichotomous political powers—one, called the Confuser (*Jaucējs*), depicts himself as the one who is always present where Latvians come together (scene II).[25] The antipode of the Confuser is the Caller (*Saucējs*), who argues with the Confuser and stresses the necessity for joint work. He then sends the Confuser away, arguing that the people have no need of him. In scene III the choir, consisting of members of the youth organisation *mazpulki* (similar to boy scouts, and used by the Ulmanis' regime as a means of involving youth in collective activities organised by the authorities) and peasants, asks who should be acclaimed and why; in turn, they receive proof of the benevolence of the Master. The peasant landowner, the master of the land, should be acclaimed as the custodian of traditional ancient rites and virtues, including fertility of the land.[26]

The Master himself appears shortly after these acclamations and in a long monologue asks God and the ghosts of the ancestors to safeguard Latvia, where order, law and prosperity now rule. The first reference to Ulmanis comes from the replica of the Master, who asks the ghosts to give support to the Master of all Masters, who established Latvianness and whom all other heads of farmsteads serve: following the example of various peasants, who deal with seeds and harvest, putting together all the fruits of the season, Ulmanis, called "The Great Master" (*Dižais Saimnieks*) is acclaimed as the saviour of the nation from political Others.[27] The end of the play follows the usual pattern of apotheosis directed at the Leader of the state: the Master states that all his successes and his dominant role would not have been possible had the Leader of the state not provided the peasants with peace and security:

> "I would not be the Master of my home,
> without my chief Master`s clever action,
> to him should the glory and honour be!"[28]

The play ends with scene XIV, in which the choir of all present (both rural and urban Latvians who overcame social and economic differences) ask the Master

---

25 Brastiņš, "Raženais saimnieks," 90.
26 Brastiņš, "Raženais saimnieks," 92.
27 Brastiņš, "Raženais saimnieks," 93.
28 Brastiņš, "Raženais saimnieks," 106.

who is this Great Master. The Master of Latvia is described as the person who is superior to all others in all "places and all actions".[29] Ulmanis is called "The Fruitful Master of Latvia", the term *Vadonis* is used repeatedly and Ulmanis is depicted as the one who returned Latvia to the Latvians.

The play used a pattern similar to other patriotic performances staged during the authoritarian regime in the capital Rīga and in regional centres (such as Rēzekne, etc.). It depicted the teleological destination of Latvian history, proclaiming the *coup* as a quasi-religious form of liberation, heralding eternal peace after the final struggle. This and other examples from the legacy of the movement illustrate how *Dievturi* activists attempted to participate in the discourse of authoritarianism using tools defined and propagated by the politics of the state. Following the tradition of authoritarian festive culture, the play was intended as the *Dievturi*'s contribution to the developing cult of the personality of the state leader, grounded in the movement's polytheistic vision of an agrarian traditionalism inhabited by spirits and pre-Christian gods.

Why did the head of the state not respond favourably to the offer to create a new, ethnic, "authentic" religion and thereby refuse to grant the *Dievturi* movement official status? To answer this question, one must analyse how the state ideology responded to the proactive politics of the movement.

4. Regime Responses: The Interplay of Religion and Political Radicalism

Brastiņš grew disappointed with the regime and during an interrogation by the Political Police in 1936 openly admitted that he did not trust Ulmanis' politics and that his enthusiasm for the Leader was a mistake.[30] Police reports suggest that those who gathered around Brastiņš were mainly right-wingers who did not feel accepted by the regime and were excluded from the political elite.[31] Ulmanis had no intention of granting neo-pagans a privileged role within the state. The *Dievturi* had to reregister as a nongovernmental organisation and were no longer officially recognised as bearers of a separate religion.

---

29 Brastiņš, "Raženais saimnieks," 105.
30 Misāne, "Dievturība Latvijas reliģisko un politisko ideju vēsturē," 113.
31 Misāne, "Dievturība Latvijas reliģisko," 115.

Ulmanis was pragmatic when it came to church-state relationships. His principal objective was to secure the support of the main religious organisations. He had to respect the fact that the dominant Churches (Lutheran, Catholic and Orthodox) were much more influential than a small neo-pagan group. On the one hand, the Churches (as well as Jewish religious communities) received money from the state; at the same time, the state increased control over them and involved them in propaganda campaigns, using them as tools for raising patriotic feeling. For example, the newly built Lutheran church in the town of Viesīte was named the Church of Freedom after the Latvian independence battles.[32] Religious newspapers had to publish editorials praising the regime. Ulmanis followed models developed by other dictatorships of the time. His policy towards small religious groups was similar to the one in Germany, his educational policy—to relationships between school and church in Italy.[33]

There was also a difference in strategy. Brastiņš saw the *coup* as just one of the steps towards a total Latvianisation of the country, which, according to his scenario, meant a dominant role for the *Dievturi*:

> "The Latvian nation has twice been liberated from everything foreign and unnecessary. The first time soldiers liberated the country from foreign forces. The second time the guards (*Aizsargi* in Latvian) saved the country from the disaster of political parties. The *Dievturi* are bidding to liberate Latvians for the third time—to free their spirit from non-Latvian religions. The total liberation will be work of the *Dievturi*."[34]

Brastiņš' words clearly convey a sense of dissatisfaction with the present. In the same article published in December 1934, he further opined that "the *Dievturi* are the best part of the Latvian nation. But for the time being they are only exemplary Latvians who are trying to like Latvians and to create Latvian cultural values".[35] Similar sentiments were expressed by other contributors to "*Labietis*" such as Žanis Ventaskrasts, whose claim that "those people start showing interest in our culture who previously did not demonstrate any interest

---

32 Z. Cīrulis, "Viesītes Brīvības baznīca," *Jaunatnes Ceļš* 1 (1940), 2.
33 Inese Runce, *Mainīgās divspēles. Valsts un baznīcas attiecības Latvijā: 1906–1940* (Rīga: Filozofijas un socioloģijas institūts, 2013), 321.
34 Brastiņu Ernests, "Vai mēs esam tauta?," *Labietis* 12 (1934), 91.
35 Brastiņu, "Vai mēs esam tauta?," 90.

in our national particularity"[36] hints at the hypocrisy of many who were now striving to be part of the political elite.

Ulmanis' ethnic policy did not go so far as to embrace fully Brastiņš' ideas. The government introduced discriminatory practices towards ethnic minorities. For example, in 1935 restrictions were launched in the timber trade aimed at decreasing the significant ratio of Jews in this sphere.[37] Restrictions were also placed upon Latvians who spoke Latgalian, the regional language spoken in the eastern part of Latvia bordering the USSR. The Latgalian language and culture were considered peculiar and did not fit the concept of a unified nation. Negative rhetoric was also used when speaking about Germans, who were considered the main ethnic Other. The Latvian media responded positively to the mass exodus of Germans under an agreement with Nazi Germany in 1939. However, Ulmanis' ethnic policies were moderate and there was no ethnic cleansing. This was proved by symbolic public actions. In 1934, for example, Ulmanis sent congratulations to the synagogue in Jelgava on the occasion of its 150th anniversary.[38] During his trips around Latvia Ulmanis also visited synagogues. If some Jewish organisations were closed, these were mainly the structures of secular, leftist Jews.

Another reason for the rejection of the *Dievturi* was political—Brastiņš was a member of the radical right-wing political group *Pērkonkrusts* ("The Thunder Cross"), which was illegal during the authoritarian period. He shared with it hostility to ethnic minorities and opposition to leftist political ideas. In 1939 the Political Police concluded that most of the people that attended the *Dievturi* meetings conducted by Brastiņš were from *Pērkonkrusts*. The small printing house located in Brastiņš' apartment also printed materials for *Pērkonkrusts*. Part of the money collected by Dievturi was used to support political radicals.[39] This cooperation was vital for *Pērkonkrusts* as an underground movement, be-

---

36 Žanis Ventaskrasts, "Cienīsim savējo!", *Labietis* 4 (1935), 87.
37 Aivars Stranga, *Ebreji un diktatūras Baltijā (1926–1940)* (Rīga: Latvijas Universitātes Jūdaikas studiju centrs, 2002), 183.
38 "Ministru prezidenta Dr. K. Ulmaņa apsveikums Fridliba sinagogai," *Jaunais Zemgalietis* 20 November 1934 (no pagination).
39 Anita Stašulāne, "The Dievturi Movement in the Reports of the Latvian Political Police (1939–1940)," *The Pomegranate* 14 (1) (2012), 37.

cause it used *Dievturi*-operated venues for its activities. Ulmanis saw *Pērkonkrusts* and similar radical political groups as rivals because they also disliked parliamentary democracy and used nationalist rhetoric. Ulmanis and his collaborators justified the *coup* by reference to the threat posed by these radicals. This is a weak argument, because the radicals were small in number and were under constant surveillance by the Political Police. One radical group, *Leģions* (The Legion), did plan a *coup* shortly before events of 15 May, but its leadership was arrested. According to the information of the Political Police, radical groups negotiated about a possible merger but were not able to agree on who the main leader should be. Despite having similar ideologies, they saw each other as competitors and were suspicious of each other.[40] After the *coup* Pērkonkrusts published a manifesto in which the new government was described as "masonic" and not nationalistic enough. At the same time, it suggested that members of *Pērkonkrusts* should use new opportunities to fight Marxists, Germans and Jews.[41]

5. Conclusion

In the state-supported political discourse on the revival of ethnic dominance of the Latvians after the *coup* of 15 May, the *Dievturi* movement proclaimed aims which did not correspond to the leading version of traditionalism. The ruling regime rejected the movement's ideas because of the radicalism of the religious upheaval that they advocated. The new religion did not find space within the narrative of regaining freedom, security and stability. Christianity was shared at least on a formal level by most of Latvia's inhabitants, including the rural population, and its rejection would have created various tensions. Implementation of *Dievturi* traditionalism would have been too revolutionary because it would have meant breaking with continuity and tradition within Latvian society. Nor did the new regime cherish the *Dievturi* ideal of revival, as this would

---

40 No Politiskās pārvaldes aģenta X-2 ziņojuma par Latviešu tirgotāju un rūpnieku arodorganizāciju savienību "Saimnieciskais centrs" un biedrību "Latviešu saimnieciskais centrs" in Valters Ščerbinskis, Ēriks Jēkabsons, eds., *Apvērsums. 1934. gada 15. maija notikumi avotos un pētījumos* (Rīga: Latvijas Nacionālais arhīvs, Latvijas Arhīvistu biedrība, 2012), 147–148.

41 "Latviešu tautas apvienības "Pērkonkrusts" uzsaukums "Pērkonkrusts ir nomodā," in ibid., 282–285.

have implied new centres of spiritual dominance. Instead, Ulmanis' person-centered authoritarianism was more interested in staging itself as an order that embodied the ideal of a return to stability, avoiding political radicalism even if this meant rejecting new offers of ethnic ideology.

Following the classification of European interwar dictatorships offered by Besier and Stokłosa in their latest comparative analysis, the Latvian authoritarian regime could be defined as a traditionalist regime with elements of monarchist symbolism, which staged the leader as the educator of the nation.[42] Opposition by Latvia's Christian churches to a new religion that categorically rejected Christianity would in turn have meant massive opposition to the authoritarian regime. While the leadership of the churches formally supported the regime, the latter could not ignore the fact that some church leaders had belonged to the now abolished parliament (Catholic Bishop Jāzeps Rancāns was deputy Chair of the *Saeima* while Orthodox Archbishop Jānis Pommers and Jewish Rabbi Mordehajs Dubins were also members).[43] The churches were handled with care even by fascism in Italy and by Nazism in Germany. In Latvia, the discourse of the *Dievturi* on the return of authentic gods was viewed as another form of radicalism and thus as an unacceptable political rival to the authoritarian regime. The link to *Pērkonkrusts* was just another pretext for the negative attitude towards an intellectual movement that aspired to a role in shaping a new vision of authentic Latvianness.

The relationship between the contemporary *Dievturi* movement and right-wing radical groups remains ambivalent. Some members of the movement have close links with *Pērkonkrusts*, others not. When the *Dievturi* Fellowship of Latvia decided to replace its logotype with a symbol that resembles the swastika, one congregation ("Rāmava") published an open letter of protest complaining that this gives the wrong impression (even though this visual similarity should not be taken to mean that the *Dievturi* are flirting with neo-Nazism).[44] Nowadays *Dievturi* serves as an umbrella term for a fragmented movement that consists of various small groups. Some of them see themselves as guardians of

---

42 Gerhard Besier, Katarzyna Stokłosa. *European Dictatorships: A Comparative History of the Twentieth Century* (Cambridge: Cambridge Scholars Publishing, 2013), 16.
43 Runce, *Mainīgās divspēles. Valsts un baznīcas attiecības Latvijā: 1906–1940*, 266.
44 "Atklāta vēstule," http://www.marasloks.lv/public/?id=176&ln=lv (as of 13.04.2014.)

beliefs developed by Brastiņš, while others take a position that is more flexible. Based on fieldwork carried out among the *Dievturi*, researcher Gatis Ozoliņš concludes that the perspectives of contemporary *Dievturi* are diverse and are drawn from various sources (Latvian folklore, Eastern religions, Christianity etc.).[45] As is the case with many other contemporary pagan groups around the world, the *Dievturi* are innovators in rituals. Canadian Latvian Maruta Voitkus-Lūkina describes the rite of "washing away foreign ideology" developed together with "Beverīna", the *Dievturi* congregation in Valmiera, Latvia. Participants must swim over to the other side of a lake to bring back a bulrush and then burn it as an offering to the Mother of Fire.[46] One part of the *Dievturi* is rather pessimistic about the future. Marģers Grīns, the leader of the movement declared in 2001 that "today the prospects of existence for Latvians in the world are not favorable because majority of the nation has moved away from a Latvian lifestyle".[47] The movement thus remains nationalistic and its vision of the nation is generally primordial.

---

45 Gatis Ozoliņš, "Mūsdienu latviešu dievturu grupu *habitus*," *Letonica* 18 (2008), 196.
46 Maruta Voitkus-Lūkina, *Ar balto dvēselīti* (Rīga: Lauku avīze, 2013), 130–133.
47 Marģers Grīns, *Mēs esam* (Rīga; Māra, 2001), 118.

"Come on Latvians, Join the Party—We'll Forgive You Everything": Ideological Struggle during the National Communist Affair, Summer 1959

Geoffrey Swain, University of Glasgow

At the end of the closed plenum of the central committee of the Latvian Communist Party (LCP), held on 7–8 July 1959 to decide the fate of Latvia's National Communists, the smooth-running of proceedings was disrupted by Indrikis Pinksis, a candidate member of the Latvian Central Committee Bureau and the President of the Latvian Trade Union Council. Given that his political career was about to be brought to an abrupt end, he insisted on making an impassioned personal statement. For two days, he said, the plenum had been talking about anti-Russian discrimination in cadre policy and the registration of migrants in Rīga, "questions in which I did not take an interest and took no part". Yet he was on the list of those to be disciplined. Ignoring the "noise from the hall" Pinksis continued: "maybe it is wrong to express myself like this, but my whole life I have struggled in the underground, in prison, at the front—and so I think this is unjust". This protest did no good, Pinksis was removed from the LCP Bureau on 8 July and sacked as President of the Trade Union Council at the end of the month.[1] Pinksis had indeed fought for the cause of communism all his life, but he had fought for an understanding of communism that was no longer acceptable to the conservative core at the heart of the Soviet Communist Party.

Pinksis was right. Throughout the long discussions around the National Communist Affair in summer 1959—the May investigation by a "brigade" from the CPSU Central Committee's Department of Party Administration, its subsequent report to Moscow, Khrushchev's visit to Rīga on 9–13 June, the meeting of the LCP Bureau on 20–21 June in the presence of Presidium member Nuridin Mukhitdinov, the discussion between the LCP leadership and Khrushchev on 1 July, the resumed LCP Bureau meeting on 4 July, and the closed plenum

---

1 Latvian State Archives (*Latvijas Valsts arhīvs*), fonds 101, apraksts 22, lieta 15, lapa 170—hereafter 101.22.15.170. For the removal from the trade union post, see 101.22.28.151.

of the LCP Central Committee on 7–8 July—discussion kept reverting to what critics of the National Communists saw as the linked issues of cadre policy, language policy and registration in Rīga which were all, allegedly, being conducted by the National Communists in an anti-Russian spirit. The brigade's report, delivered to the CPSU Central Committee in Moscow on 8 June, argued that at least 14 cases had been uncovered where cadre policy had been violated and the best qualified candidate, a Russian, had been passed over and replaced by a less qualified Latvian. That report then went on to list a series of accusations, which would be repeated again and again over the course of the summer, amongst them the key charge that the policy of registration in Rīga had been used to prevent Russians settling there.[2] These were the issues on which the two most prominent leaders of the National Communists, Vilis Krūmiņš and Eduards Berklavs, chose to mount their defence.

However, by the closed plenum of 7–8 July, the agenda had subtly changed. Pinksis and others were also subject to attack, and this attack was mounted on ideological rather than organisational grounds. Of central importance here was the charge of "Beriaism", something not mentioned on 20 June but a key charge by 7–8 July. This chapter explores how that agenda changed, the quixotic non-intervention of Khrushchev in the row, and the key role played in this process by Arvids Pelše, Ideological Secretary of the LCP, on the one hand, and the CPSU's Department of Party Administration on the other. The way ideological and organisational matters operated hand in glove over the summer of 1959 paved the way for the party apparatus to assert a clearly ideological role in the later years of Khrushchev's rule.

1. Cadres Policy

Although at the LCP Bureau meeting of 20 June Krūmiņš stated that he did not want to make an issue of the inaccuracy of the brigade's report, he nonetheless did precisely that. He made clear that "not all those letters which were sent to the Central Committee in Moscow are completely accurate, and it is difficult to

---

[2] *Regional'naia politika N S Khrushcheva: TsK KPSS i mestnye partiinye komitety, 1956–64 gg* (Moscow: ROSSPEN, 2009), 227.

decide issues properly when things are interpreted inaccurately".[3] The accusation that incompetent Latvian cadres had been appointed to replace competent Russian cadres simply did not stand up to scrutiny. The Rēzekne Party Secretary had been sacked, but not because he was a Russian but because he had been a speculator in pig feed. Former Deputy Premier Nikolai Ponomarev had a long record of confrontations with party activists and during a visit to Czechoslovakia had blatantly engaged in "contraband"; he might feel "insulted as a Russian", but that was not why he had been sacked. On Ponomarev, Krūmiņš won a small concession from the authors of the report: the brigade representative at the meeting accepted that the Party Control Commission had reviewed Ponomarev's dismissal and concluded that he had been "correctly sent to work in the ranks".[4]

Berklavs was more outspoken than Krūmiņš. Although later accused of "juggling with statistics", he was determined to give chapter and verse in his rejection of the allegation that cadre policy had been in any way anti-Russian.[5] One specific allegation that he had personally decided the fate of the Russian who headed the Pharmacy Directorate by getting up a press campaign in the newspaper *Rīgas Balss*, was simply "untrue"; his dismissal on 5 May had been because he had failed to take measures to counter widespread financial irregularities concerning the supply of medicines to hospitals and clinics.[6] "There was," Berklavs said, "no basis to the suggestion that some sort of replacement of non-Latvian cadres by Latvian cadres had begun", and he then proceeded to reel off figures which he would repeat at the closed plenum on 7–8 July: in the republic's Council of the National Economy only 202 of the 552 departmental directors were Latvian; in the Rīga office of the Ministry of Internal Affairs only 361 of the 1,334 employees were Latvian; and only 18 of the 44 doctors in the country's leading medical facilities were Russian. Equally there was no truth to the allegation that the registration policy in Rīga had deliberately targeted Russians. The truth was, he insisted, that of the 28,000 registrations for residency in Rīga which took place in 1959 only 10,500 went to Latvians,

---

3   101.22.54a.39.
4   101.22.54a. 39 &107–8.
5   101.22.15.91–2.
6   101.22.26.18.

while for the first half of 1959 the equivalent figures were 8,500 and 3,000. The allocation of flats in Rīga showed a similar pattern: over the previous 18 months 3,355 flats had been allocated in Rīga, but only 1,089 to Latvian families. "I cannot believe that comrades travelled down from Moscow with malicious intentions," Berklavs suggested, "but it is clear that someone has brought them into a state of confusion."[7]

The brigade's report made clear that it had been "anti-Leninist" of the LCP in December 1956 to set a two-year deadline for all its cadres in day-to-day contact with the population to have fluency in both Latvian and Russian. It was the gradual introduction of this policy in spring 1959 which had prompted first letters of complaint to Moscow, then more organised lobbying and finally the decision to send the brigade to investigate. On the language issue Krūmiņš and Berklavs were willing to make concessions. Krūmiņš mused that it might have been better not to pass a resolution on the matter but to arrange language classes over the radio and television, and to provide more in the way of textbooks—it emerged during the debates on 20 June that the relevant text books had only been printed early in 1958. Berklavs also accepted that "the question of the time-scale [of language preparation] was not entirely correct".[8]

It was Pinksis, rather than Krūmiņš and Berklavs, who based his defence on principle rather than practice. He told the LCP Bureau meeting of 20–21 June just why the language decision had been taken in 1956: it was because Latvian workers stood aside from the party on the grounds that they considered it "Russian". It was because the word on the street was already that after Khrushchev's visit to Rīga earlier that month "there'll be another commission and the Latvians will be driven out".[9] Pinksis already had a bit of a reputation as a trouble-maker with the Department of Party Administration—in 1956 he had been criticised by it for the speed with which he had pulled down portraits of Stalin in Liepāja where he was party secretary[10]—and at the closed plenum on 7–8 July he challenged the ideological assumptions of the brigade's report. The

---

7   101.22.54a.58,63;101.22.15.34.
8   101.22.54a.65, 138&168–9.
9   101.22.54a.101–4.
10 *Doklad N S Khrushcheva o Kul'te Lichnosti Stalina na XX S"ezde KPSS: Dokumenty* (Moscow, ROSSPEN, 2002), 502.

report had made clear that while it was "good practice" for cadres to know both Russian and Latvian, it was "un-Leninist" to put administrative pressure on cadres to learn a language.[11] Pinksis pointed out that in 1919, when Soviet power was restored in Ukraine, Lenin had stated that "all workers in Soviet institutions should know the Ukrainian language"[12].

2. Reviving Working Class Support

Pinksis told the LCP Bureau on 20 June that in many factories where the majority of workers were Latvian, all the leading positions in the factory—the party, Komsomol and trade union organisations—were held by people who did not speak Latvian. "How," he asked, "was that meant to strengthen friendship among peoples?" After Pinksis had given a list of examples where such Russian predominance was absolute, the Presidium representative Mukhitdinov agreed that such things were "completely incorrect". "Well," responded Pinksis, "that is how it is with us, and so it is impossible to ignore language when serving the republic."[13] Later, at the closed plenum on 7–8 July, Pinksis explained how the presence of only Russian-language slogans and posters at the giant VEF industrial plant had alarmed him, since this was somewhere regularly visited by official foreign delegations.[14] Pinksis was supported by Kārlis Ozoliņš, President of the Latvian Supreme Soviet, a veteran communist who pointed to the practical consequences of such incidents for the LCP; its links with the working class were weak. When the party had emerged from underground in 1940, he said, it had over 60 members in the factory now called the Red Textile Worker, in 1959 it had only 10 members; in the Red Metallurgist Works a party conference had been held in 1940, but now there were also just 10 party members. The fact was that the word on the street was this: "there were the Latvian years, then came the German occupation and now we have the Russian years".[15]

How best to address the lack of Latvian workers in the party was the theme of a controversial article written by Berklavs and published in February 1959 in the evening newspaper *Rīgas Balss*. The article "Conversation from the Heart"

---

11 101.22.54a.9.
12 101.22.15.114.
13 101.22.54a.99.
14 101.22.15.115.
15 101.22.54a.85.

(*Sarune no sirds*) proved extremely controversial, indeed the editor of the official LCP newspaper *Cīņa* Pavels Pizāns, in every other way one of the most outspoken of the National Communists, refused to publish it.[16] In the article Berklavs pondered on why it was that, in his recent discussions with activists in industry, culture and health care, many were not party members, "especially among the Latvians". Most of those he had talked to readily agreed "in the justice and superiority of Soviet power", so "why did many of these best, most energetic, most educated people not join the vanguard?" He asked himself, "for how much longer, would they look on from the side". It had to be, he suggested, "only a misunderstanding" which prevented such people joining the party, they had not "properly thought it through". So, he wrote, "hold out your hand, we are waiting for you", because in assessing a person for membership perfection was not necessary, just the ability to be a model for others, other considerations could be put on one side.[17]

In later years Berklavs felt he had delayed too long in writing "Conversation from the Heart"; good honest Latvians could have changed the "relative balance" in the party sooner.[18] The article was discussed by the LCP Bureau on two occasions, the second time after a phone call was received from Moscow, but the criticism it received was "gentle": on 14 April the LCP Bureau decided that "it was incorrect to give open recognition in the article to the fact that many of the best people in the republic, especially those of Latvian nationality, were not joining the party". Berklavs had gone on to call on workers to be more active in joining the party, but framing the issue as he had done had "stirred up a variety of comments amongst certain communists"; the LCP Bureau therefore resolved to "bring to the attention" of Berklavs that the article had not helped "the correct understanding within party organisations of the question of expanding party ranks".[19]

At the reconvened LCP Bureau meeting on 4 July, Nikolai Saleev, the editor of the Russian language daily *Sovetskaia Latviia*, put his finger on the nub of the

---

16 101.22.54a.116.
17 *Rīgas Balss*, 25 February 1959. I am grateful to Mike Loader for helping me obtain a copy of "Conversations from the Heart".
18 E Berklavs, *Zīnat un Neaizminst* (Rīga: Eraksti, 2011), 19–20.
19 101.22.54a.126,139,177&181;101.22.25.125.

issue. He argued that no person reading the article could fail to notice that an overly nationalist position was being adopted. According to him, one paragraph of the article formulated this absolutely clearly: "Berklavs stated that Latvians needed to be moved forward to various posts, that there were few Latvians in the party, so come on, Latvians, join the party, we'll forgive you everything."[20] The phrase "we'll forgive you everything" did not appear in Berklavs's article, it was Saleev's embellishment, his suggestion of what the hidden agenda of the National Communists actually was. The orthodox Marxist-Leninist ideology, as it has evolved from the Great Patriotic War, was that there was only one narrative, the heroic struggle of the Soviet people against German fascism. In a country like Latvia, where this narrative simply did not match the reality of wartime experiences, what the National Communists saw as opening up to the population at large, their opponents saw as forgetting the past and letting potential "enemies" into the party. Saleev's stance was that all Latvians were potentially suspect—no wonder Krūmiņš accused him of being "afraid of his shadow".[21]

In the two years since the National Communists had gained control of the party in spring 1958 they had done much to try to win over public opinion. *Rīgas Balss*, founded by Berklavs, was a newspaper of a new type, written and printed in a western style and consciously adopting both an engaging and a campaigning tone; it quickly became very popular.[22] National Communists gave much stress to developing Latvia's own revolutionary heritage, and recruitment had been good with 8,000 new members and 8,500 new candidate members, over a third of them young people.[23] There is some evidence that at this time there was a relaxation of some of the more stringent rules surrounding recruitment. A teacher was let into the party despite having a brother who was a former legionary; investigations had revealed that the brother was mobilised into the Latvian Legion rather than having volunteered, a crucial distinction but

---

20 101.22.54a.177.
21 101.22.54a.178.
22 William D. Prigge "Power, Popular Opinion and the Latvian National Communists," *Journal of Baltic Studies* 45,3 (2014), 311–3.
23 101.22.26.4-5. On revolutionary heritage, one example was the *Komsomol*, which had a campaign "to know the revolutionary past of your motherland" and encouraged survivors to gather treasured possessions from the years of underground struggle and save them for posterity. See 201.1.1072, 150.

one which was not always taken into consideration.[24] Recruitment within the *Komsomol* was equally good at this time: membership rose from 117,950 in March 1958 to 125,030 in March 1960, and part of this growth was achieved by relaxing rules on admission; thus in 1959 a teenager joined the *Komsomol* even though in 1949 her family had been on the list of those to be deported since her father had served in the Latvian Legion and one of her uncles had fought as a national partisan.[25]

Where relaxing party recruitment policy might lead was highlighted by the First Deputy in the CPSU Central Committee's Department of Party Administration Petr Pigalev, who had headed the brigade which visited Latvia that May. At the closed plenum, he reminded those present that the former Latvian Social Democrat leader Fricis Menders, recently released from prison but able nonetheless to obtain a flat in Rīga, had praised "Conversation from the Heart", since essentially what it said was "let's put on one side the usual considerations" for party recruitment. The attitude of Pelše was the same, essentially what Berklavs had asked was "why not join the party?"[26] Neither man had been placated when the Rīga Secretary tried to explain on 20 June that recruitment to the party was often complicated by a specifically Latvian issue, the fact that those of Latvian ethnicity were often unwilling to sponsor party members since this meant that their own past would be investigated and unpleasant circumstances like a family association with the Latvian Legion uncovered.[27]

At the closed plenum on 7–8 July Pigalev also raised the ideological implications of what Pinksis had supposedly said at the 20 June meeting of the LCP Bureau. As he recalled it—although these were in fact the words of Ozoliņš who spoke after Pinksis[28]—Pinksis had stated that people on the streets said "Latvia once belonged to the Latvians, then the Germans and now belongs to the Russians", adding that Pinksis had also referred to comments like "the Russians liberated Latvians socially but enslaved them nationally". For Pigalev simply to report such a comment, whether or not it was true, was to act like "a

---

24 Daugavpils University Oral History Centre, Interview 548.
25 *Ocherki istorii Leninskogo kommunisticheskogo soyuza molodezhi Latvii, 1919–85* (Rīga, 1985), 462. Daugavpils University Oral History Centre, Interview 884.
26 101.22.15.54,153.
27 101.22.54a.135.
28 101.22.54a.85.

bourgeois nationalist". Pigalev's fantasy world extended back into history, as he also expressed alarm at the film *The Story of the Latvian Rifleman*, suggesting that the film "tore away" the Latvian Rifleman from their "truest allies" the Russian Riflemen.[29] Pigalev's ignorance of the role played by the Latvian Riflemen in Russia's Revolution and Civil War was breath-taking, but it reflected the orthodoxy established by Stalin which was still dominant in the party apparatus: that there could be no revolutionary tradition other than one led by Russians, was a conviction that the apparatus was determined to uphold.

3. Pelše and Pigalev

It was the turn of the debate towards ideological issues which led to the decision to include Pinksis amongst those to be disciplined, a decision pushed through by both Pelše and Pigalev acting together. What enabled this to happen was Khrushchev's decision, in apparent contradiction of his intemperate outburst at Rīga airport on 13 June, not to make a big issue of the behaviour of the National Communists. As William Prigge has shown, and Mukhitdinov confirmed in an interview given in 1990, Khrushchev's own position on the policies of the National Communists was much more ambiguous than the version given in the brigade's report.[30] After the LCP Bureau meeting on 20 June Berklavs was summonsed to be present while a phone call was put through to Khrushchev. To the surprise of those present, Khrushchev flatly rejected any notion that Berklavs should be put on trial and insisted that the affair be handled in as low key a way as possible; he even told Krūmiņš that he considered Berklavs to be "straightforward, honest but obstinate".[31] It is true that at the meeting held between the Latvian leadership and Khrushchev on 1 July, Khrushchev initially ranted and raved about Ulmanis being able to sleep peacefully in his grave since his work was continuing, but once he had calmed down, he was much more emollient. Krūmiņš proposed putting on one side the accusations made by the brigade and concentrating on the essentials: if cadres did not

---

29 101.22.15.150-2.
30 William D. Prigge "The Latvian Purges of 1959: A Revision Study," *Journal of Baltic Studies* 35, 3 (2004), 220; "1959 god v Latvii: vzgliad izvne—inter'viu s Mukhitdinovym," *Kommunist Sovetskoi Latvii* 5 (1990), 90–91. I am grateful to Mike Loader for providing me with a copy of this interview.
31 V Krumin'sh, "Dolgaia doroga k demokratii" *Kommunist Sovetskoi Latvii* 4 (1990), 88.

know Latvian, would it ever be possible to construct Soviet power in Latvia? After a break in the proceedings, Khrushchev appeared to agree. He recalled his own time in Ukraine when he had always insisted that those communists who knew Ukrainian should use it, and he even criticised Latvian First Secretary Jānis Kalnbērziņš for speaking Russian that June in Rīga when Khrushchev had introduced him to his visiting guest, GDR President Walter Ulbricht. "I consider that for you Latvian is the state language", Khrushchev stated.[32]

And so, Khrushchev decided that the National Communist affair should be left to the Latvians to resolve by themselves. He had been "in a scathing mood", he said, when flying back from Rīga on 13 June, but now he saw no need to "maim" people. He was sure "an absolute majority" of both the party and people in Latvia supported Soviet power, so there was no point making a gift to enemies by talking of a crisis in nationality policy, that would create a crisis where none existed at present. "We have emerged from the sauna with our pores cleared", he declared in typically idiomatic style.[33] Mukhitdinov confirmed that after the Presidium discussion there was no formal decision and all the documentation was "returned to Latvia to let them decide".[34] However, what Khrushchev had failed to understand was that "letting the Latvians decide" meant handing things back to Pelše and Pigalev, who had been working together since at least May and who had very clear ideas about what sort of shower was needed to wash away the dirt exposed by the sauna.

When the brigade arrived in Rīga in May, a close relationship was established with Pelše at once. The brigade refused to make contact with the Latvian leadership and worked only with the local Department of Party Administration, then headed by the Russian Latvian and future LCP leader Augusts Voss. Helped by Ponomarev, it interviewed all those with concerns about the current leadership.[35] According to Saleev, ironically one of the leading critics of the National Communists, the behaviour of the brigade had been appalling: it had behaved like "Lady Muck", refusing to have any contact with any member of the Latvian Central Committee nor any of its secretaries—for all his hostility to the National

---

32 *Arkhivy Kremlia: Prezidium TsK KPSS 1954–64* (Moscow: ROSSPEN, 2003), 376.
33 *Arkhivy Kremlia*, 381–2.
34 "1959 god v Latvii," 90–1.
35 Krumin'sh, "Dolgaia doroga k demokratii," 87.

Communists, Saleev did accept that "many Russian comrades do not respect the culture of the Latvian people".[36] However, the brigade worked extremely closely with Pelše. Mukhitdinov recalled: "it was agreed with Kalnbērziņš that Pelše would head the work of this brigade and act as its co-author and that it would report only to Kalnbērziņš.[37] Pigalev had occupied the post of First Deputy in the CPSU Central Committee's Department of Party Administration for most of the 1950s; prior to that he had spent the years 1943–1947 working in the Secretariat, followed until 1950 with a brief spell as Second Secretary in Perm. He was an apparatus man if ever there was one.

The brigade's report might have lain on a shelf unread if Ponomarev had not been a friend of General N S Demin, who was in turn an old wartime companion of Khrushchev. On 12 June, when Ulbricht had already returned to Berlin and Khrushchev had an evening to himself, Demin contacted him to outline how Russians were being persecuted by the "bourgeois nationalists" running the LCP. It was this that led to a clash between Khrushchev and Berklavs at Rīga airport on 13 June and ensured that the brigade's report was considered in Moscow on 18 June. It was this meeting which decided to send a Presidium member down to Rīga to investigate, along with Pigalev and the other authors of the report.[38] In his 1990 interview, Mukhitdinov made clear that he had not been the original choice to represent the Presidium in Rīga. Since ideological issues clearly stood at the heart of the matter, it was Mikhail Suslov, Pelše's brother-in-law, who was originally delegated to go to Rīga, but he fell ill and so Mukhitdinov was chosen to take his place. Before the LCP Bureau meeting started on 20 June, Mukhitdinov held separate meetings with Kalnbērziņš, Krūmiņš, Lācis and Ozoliņš, but Pelše was present at all of these; at the meeting with Kalnbērziņš, Pelše was chosen to head the commission which would prepare a draft resolution on the way forward.[39]

When, after the meeting with Khrushchev, the LCP Bureau reconvened on 4 July there was some confusion over precisely what had happened in Moscow.

---

36 101.22.54a.127–8.
37 "1959 god v Latvii," 87.
38 Prigge "The Latvian Purges of 1959," 218; Regional'naia politika, 232.
39 "1959 god v Latvii," 88.

Saleev accused Krūmiņš of trying to "soften" the resolution passed by the Presidium in Moscow; Krūmiņš insisted all he had done was to telephone Pelše and argue that any draft resolution should only reflect what had been agreed in Moscow.[40] The point was, however, that nothing had been decided by the Presidium in Moscow, Khrushchev had left it to the Latvians, and, as things unfolded, that in practice meant that the decisions which emerged reflected the wishes of Pelše and Pigalev. Pelše had been clear from the start that the brigade's report was not the result of some sort of misunderstanding, as Berklavs had implied, but the result of policies being pursued which were reminiscent of those of the interwar leader Ulmanis, those of "Latvia for the Latvians". Pelše said as much at the LCP Bureau meeting on 20 June and this phrase was echoed by Pigalev at the closed plenum on 7–8 July; only these two speakers went as far as making this incendiary comparison.[41]

4. Beria's Boys

The absence of a clear decision by Khrushchev enabled Pelše and Pigalev to draw up additional demands, extending the charges beyond language and into the realm of ideology, and extending the list of those to be disciplined to Pinksis and others. This caused some controversy, but Saleev believed that Berklavs and Pinksis had long formed a common front within the LCP Bureau and those who on 4 July tried to resist extending the attack to Pinksis "could not have been in the same hall as the rest of us", so clear was his guilt.[42] Pelše and Pigalev were keen to cement their ideological victory by branding the views of their opponents as a Beria-inspired heresy: to this end they demanded that the decisions of the 1953 June Plenum of the LCP Central Committee needed to be repealed, something given great prominence in Kalnbērziņš's speech to the closed plenum on 7–8 July, but which had not been mentioned during the discussions of the LCP Bureau on 20 June.[43]

Not long before Beria's arrest on 26 June 1953, Khrushchev had drafted a report on the extent of Russification within the Latvian Communist Party, as a

---

40 101.22.54a.176.
41 101.22.15.146 &101.22.54a.78-9.
42 101.22.15.104] & 101.22.54a.177.
43 101.22.15.22.

result of which the Latvian Communist Party held a plenum on 22–23 June which, among other momentous decisions, ended the tradition of the Second Secretary being a Russian and appointed Krūmiņš to that post instead. Later Krūmiņš had been replaced by the Russian Fedor Kashnikov, but at the 15th LCP Congress in January 1958 Kashnikov received what amounted to a vote of no-confidence and by May it had been agreed he would stand down and Krūmiņš take over the post again.[44] When the Baltic Sector of the Soviet Communist Party Central Committee learned of Kashnikov's removal it looked to Khrushchev for guidance, but he was relaxed about the change. To be on the safe side, Krūmiņš raised the matter with Khrushchev personally and was assured that "Beria had nothing to do with it", the decisions of the June 1953 Plenum were still in force.[45] After the closed plenum of 7–8 July, that was no longer the case. Point 16 of the resolution adopted then was "to rescind the decision of the 23 June 1953 Plenum entitled 'Shortcomings in directing the political work and cultural development of the republic' as politically incorrect and as imposed by the enemy of the people and state, L Beria".[46]

The attitude of the party apparatus towards those accused of "Beriaism" was made clear in the so-called Čerkovskis Affair. Pāvils Čerkovskis, the Deputy Minister of Culture, was sent to Daugavpils in October 1958 to try to enforce the ruling on language knowledge. Čerkovskis met with a hostile reception, there was an almighty row, later Čerkovskis' behaviour was criticised, but as part of the settlement of the dispute the head of agitation and propaganda in Daugavpils was expelled from the party on the grounds that he had made "anti-party" comments. On appeal to the Party Control Commission however, the head of agitation and propaganda was reinstated, and reinstated on the grounds that his language could not be considered "anti-party"—what he had done was to call the LCP Bureau "Beria's boys". Clearly bad-mouthing a declared enemy of the people like Beria could not be considered "anti-party", but the Party Control Commission ignored the fact that behaviour of this sort undermined the centralised hierarchy of the party, weakened the authority of Rīga

---

44 D Bleiere (et al) *Istoriia Latvii XX vek* (Rīga: Jumava, 2005), 371.
45 Krumin'sh, "Dolgaia doroga k demokratii," 86.
46 *Latvija padomju režīma varā: 1945–1986: Dokumentu krājums* (Latvijas Vēstures Institūta Apgāds, 2010), 221.

and turned the head of agitation and propaganda into a local Daugavpils hero.[47] Beria was also at the forefront of Mukhitdinov's thoughts. At a private meeting on 20 June he said to Berklavs: "Comrade Berklavs, Beria was shot for similar views—what do you suggest we do with you?"[48] Mukhitdinov had been sacked by Beria as the Uzbek Prime Minister in May 1953 and so had little sympathy with his attempted reform.[49]

The degree to which Pelše and Pigalev had pushed beyond what Khrushchev had envisaged for the LCP became clear in November. The early autumn of 1959 was a busy time for Khrushchev. In the second half of September he went on his dramatically successful visit to the United States, followed by a hasty visit to Beijing to explain the reasoning behind making friendly overtures to "imperialists". It was not until later in the autumn that he returned to the need to replace Kalnbērziņš as First Secretary of the Latvian Communist Party with someone more forceful. He summoned Kalnbērziņš, Krūmiņš and Pelše to Moscow and asked what Pelše would do if he became First Secretary; Pelše responded that he would "request a Second Secretary from your apparatus", thus signalling a return to the procedure favoured by Stalin and overthrown by Beria. Khrushchev went red with fury, calling the idea "garbage" and defending Krūmiņš who, by implication, was clearly about to be sacked.[50] Later, when the Presidium discussed a replacement for Kalnbērziņš, Mukhitdinov seemed belatedly to recall what it had told the 21st Party Congress in January 1959—that "Lenin condemned the smallest appearance of nihilism and scornful or lordly attitudes to national peculiarities and feelings".[51] Mukhitdinov recommended that Krūmiņš replace Kalnbērziņš but Suslov recommended Pelše; it was Pelše who was appointed.[52]

---

47 101.22.54a.106–7, 111 & 101.22.15.156–7.
48 Prigge "The Latvian Purges of 1959," 223.
49 N Mukhitdinov *Gody provedennye v Kremle* (Tashkent: izdatel'stvo narodnogo naslediya imeni Abdully Kadyri, 1994), 109–115.
50 Prigge "The Latvian Purges of 1959," 225.
51 *Vneocherednoi XXI S'ezd Kommunisticheskoi Partii Sovetskogo Soyuza: Stenograficheskii Otchet* (Moskva 1959), 394.
52 "1959 god v Latvii," 91.

5. A Fear of Shadows

What began in spring 1959 as a whinge from those Russian cadres in Latvia who felt it was beneath their dignity to learn Latvian, became by autumn a struggle to stamp out as "Beriaism" any notion that there could be another revolutionary tradition to that led by Russians. The obsessive fear of enemies among the Latvians was not something shared by Khrushchev, but in this affair it was the apparatus, in the form of the Department of Party Administration, which emerged as the arbiter of "revolutionary correctness", not the party leader. Khrushchev intervened only occasionally to stop excesses, like the idea of putting Krūmiņš and the other National Communists on trial in 1961.[53]

Back in June 1953, at the time when Beria's proposals were being discussed, the Latvian Prime Minister Vilis Lācis met with Khrushchev and told him:

> "We have a fear of the shadow of the past... we have cadre workers who continue to live by, to be governed by *curricula vitae* which are fifteen or twenty years old and completely ignore what citizens did in the Soviet years. *Aizsargs, Mazpulka*, Boy Scout, member of a student corporation, served in the Legion, such words act like a scarecrow, hanging over their whole life."[54]

At the LCP Bureau meeting on 4 July 1959 Krūmiņš said something similar when he had accused Saleev of being "afraid of his shadow".[55] The context was the same: whether or not opening up to the Latvian people would simply let "enemies" take over or allow Latvians to celebrate their own revolutionary heritage. When Krūmiņš and the other National Communists had been in charge of the *Komsomol* in the last Stalin years they had tried to make membership dependent on what young people had done under Soviet rule, not what had happened in the past.[56] In 1959 they were adopting the same approach in the party, but adapting to Latvian realities was no more acceptable to conservative ideologues in the apparatus than it had been a decade earlier.

---

53 Krumin'sh, "Dolgaia doroga k demokratii," 90.
54 *Dokumentu krājums*, 193.
55 101.22.54a.178.
56 The *Komsomol* in the late Stalin years is discussed in this author's "Before National Communism: Joining the Latvian Komsomol under Stalin," *Europe-Asia Studies* 64,7 (2012), 1239–70.

"At First We Missed our Latvia...":
Attitudes towards the Latvian State during the Soviet Period

Irēna Saleniece, University of Daugavpils

1. The People and the State

The Latvian state has a history dating back just 100 years. Moreover, during only half of this time has the country been free and independent. The 20th-century political history of Latvia encompasses: a period of independent statehood (parliamentary republic and authoritarian regime) from 1918–1940; successive periods of Soviet, Nazi and Soviet occupation, each with a corresponding socio-political order, from 1940–1991; and—since 1991—reconstruction of the independent state. In each period, there existed a respective organisation of power (state) and a legitimating ideology that greatly affected the population's understanding of the state's origin, objectives and functions.[1] However, the impact of the state and its institutions always runs up against the standpoint of the people—the way they perceive the state and behave towards it.[2]

During the half century between the so-called First Republic of Latvia and its lawful successor—the present-day state—the territory of Latvia and its people were under the rule of foreign powers. What, then, was the attitude of the Latvian population towards the state of Latvia during the Soviet period, when the ruling power and its ideology not only openly negated the concept of independ-

---

1 The impact of ideology becomes obvious even in relation to defining seemingly neutral concepts such as "state". Here, a wide range of different interpretations come into play, from liberal and democratic—'political community organized under a government, nation, civil government' (*The Penguin Concise English Dictionary* (London: Bloomsbury Books, 1991), 707); 'a politically unified people occupying a definite territory; nation' (*Random House Webster's* (New York: Random House, 1997), 1260)— to communist: 'a political organization founded by the ruling class in a country with the task of maintaining the ruling order in it and suppressing the opposition of other classes' (*Latviešu valodas vārdnīca* (Rīga: Avots, 1987), 840.).
2 Joels Veinbergs, *Piramīdu un zikurātu ēnā: cilvēks seno Tuvo Austrumu kultūrā* (Rīga: Zinātne, 1988), 133.

ence but also sought to erase all memory of it? This was a period of considerable demographic change, as thousands perished or emigrated from Latvia[3] while Soviet immigrants settled in large numbers on the territory of Latvia[4]. The major part of the Latvian population who stayed in their homeland learned to live alongside the Soviet regime and its supporters while secretly keeping memories of *their own* lost country.

2. The Interwar Generation and Latvia

Taking into consideration the diversity and complexity of Latvia's political history, one cannot expect the entire population to have been united in their attitude towards the Latvian state. However, continued diversity of outlook was not only determined by individual differences—account must also be taken of differences arising from a person's belonging to a particular generation. According to Paul Thompson, the family remains the main channel for the transmission of many of the fundamental aspects of culture and identity, including "habits of the heart"—attitudes to emotions and relationships.[5]

In this chapter, I argue that—broadly speaking—four generations may be singled out in contemporary Latvia whose life experience differs greatly, especially if regarded from the aspect of political life. These are:

- 1st generation (born in 1910–1935)—older representatives of this group witnessed as children World War I, the foundation of the Republic of Latvia and its parliamentary period, as well as the *coup* by Kārlis Ulmanis, the authoritarian regime and the shift of powers in 1940–1941.
- 2nd generation (1935–1960)—the childhood memories of its older representatives are related first and foremost with World War II; representatives of this group also witnessed the period of Stalinism and destalinisation.

---

3 Pārsla Eglīte, "Padomju okupācijas ilglaika demogrāfiskās sekas", in *The Soviet Occupation Regime in the Baltic States 1944–1959: Policies and Their Consequences. Materials of the International Conference. 13–14 June 2002, Rīga* (Rīga: Latvijas vēstures institūta apgāds, 2003), 256–66.
4 Jānis Riekstiņš, *Migranti Latvijā* (Rīga: Latvijas Valsts arhīvs, 2004), 244.
5 Daniel Bertaux and Paul Thomson, *Between Generations: Family Models, Myths & Memories* (New Brunswick (USA) and London (UK): Transaction Publishers, 2005), 5.

- 3rd generation (1960–1985)—they spent the early period of their lives under the conditions of "developed socialism and construction of communism", i.e. during the period of stagnation—and they lived up to the regaining of independent statehood.
- 4th generation (1985–2010)—unlike the preceding generations, they have not experienced any rapid political changes during their conscious lives, living continuously in an independent Latvia becoming more and more integrated with the European community.

People of each older generation share much of the same experience as younger generations. Yet their attitude towards commonly shared experience may differ, because older people have their own judgement and they treat events according to their own values developed while they were growing up. Unlike the 2nd and 3rd generations who were brought up as the "Soviet people" and educated in conditions of a dominant communist ideology and total censorship, representatives of the 1st generation grew up in the independent state of Latvia. At school[6], in their family, in the surrounding environment they not only acquired their first social experience but also notions of the system of values of their society, with their own state occupying a certain place within this.

The legitimacy of the independent state of Latvia was self-evident for members of this generation. Though the propaganda of the Ulmanis regime had managed to discredit much of the political practice of the parliamentary period, all in all they recognised the rights of the Republic of Latvia to exist in the form of a civic state based on representation, rule of law, division of powers and participation. The communist idea of "world-wide revolution" and dictatorship of the international proletariat as offering the only possible path to a bright future was largely alien to them. It is this fact that makes the attitude of the 1st generation towards the Latvian state especially interesting. Various historical sources could be used in order to discern this attitude, including archival documents, letters, diaries and oral history interviews.

---

6   Gaston Lacombe, "Nationalism and Education in Latvia, 1918–1940," *Journal of Baltic Studies* 38, 4 (1997); Aldis Purs, "'Unsatisfactory National Identity': School Inspectors, Education and National Identity in Interwar Latvia," *Journal of Baltic Studies* 35, 2 (2004).

Only occasionally do archival documents reveal information about the attitude of the first generation towards power and the state during the Soviet period. For instance, in the correspondence of the Central Committee of the Communist Party of Latvia in 1945 one can read:

> "In Rīga Secondary School No.6 at a meeting after Stalin's order of 1 May and the occupancy of Berlin by the Red Army all school teachers refused to speak... the headmaster did not even mention the Red Army and Soviet power. He talked about duties and the duty of the sons of Latvia for their Motherland, he said that everybody would understand one's duty and would do what the Motherland asked him to. The speech was followed by stormy applause of learners. <..> In Secondary School No. 3 school girls wear national colours on their clothes and flowers in vases are arranged so that they resemble the flag of the bourgeois republic."[7]

However, such evidence from archival documents is episodic and incidental and can, therefore, be seen as indirect. Information about the Soviet time is presented differently in the life-stories of so-called "ordinary people." Here, narrators relate their own vision of the past that very often reveals patterns of behaviour and mood characteristic of diverse social groups. The present article is based on oral history sources from the collection of the Oral History Centre of Daugavpils University (hereafter—DU OHC).[8] These are life-stories of people residing mostly in eastern Latvia during the Soviet period. The impressions and emotions experienced then return also now in their recollections, making it possible to recreate the socio-psychological atmosphere as it was perceived by the "common people" of that time. These oral history sources thus give us the possibility to reconstruct from a present-day perspective the attitudes that ordinary people held towards the Latvian state.

---

7   The Latvian National Archives—the State Archives of Latvia (LNA LVA-PA). F. 201, apr. 4, l. 48, lp. 8
8   The Oral History Centre of Daugavpils University (DU OHC) was founded on 2 December 2003. The aim of the OHC is to promote the theoretical research and practical use of oral history. Its main activities are recording of the life-stories of the inhabitants in Eastern Latvia and putting them into archives as well as using oral history sources in the research of 20th-century Latvian history. By 2014 the number of oral history sources of the DU OHC collection had reached 1040 records. This article is based on analysis of around 400 life histories of narrators born in 1910–1935.

In attempting to do this, the present chapter employs the method described by Paul Thompson as "reconstructive cross-analysis". In this approach, the historian's argumentation is constructed on the basis of information provided by oral history sources. However, the overall shape of the system of arguments and, hence, reconstruction of the past is not predetermined by the life stories, but emerges from the inner logic of reconstruction designed by the historian.[9] At the same time, a comprehensive reconstruction should embrace evidence extracted from different interviews and compared with evidence from historical sources of other types. In the article, only those life-stories that are relevant to the aspects highlighted in the research have been quoted.[10]

3. Capturing Narrators' Life Stories through Oral History

The "starting position" for narrators' reflections on the state of Latvia is usually 1940, and the first encounters with Soviet soldiers as representatives of another state. Later, narrators were able to compare according to their own experience the treatment of the population by Latvian state power and Soviet power. It may be stated with considerable assurance that for the majority of Latvian children and youth in 1940 the entrance of the Red Army and the establishment of the Soviet order were neither understandable nor acceptable. Neither Latvians nor Latvian citizens of other ethnicities knew how to behave according to the new situation. Some narrators testify that local Russian people were most confused:

> "'Soviets'—what kind of a state is it? In childhood, we didn't know such a thing ... there was Russia, I knew after my mother's stories, but Russia ceased to exist, "Soviets" came to exist, Bolsheviks... they went along a highway, Soviet troops... they speak like us— Russian. I was surprised: 'Soviets' and speaking the same language, Russian."[11]

---

9   Paul Thompson, *The Voice of the Past: Oral History* (Oxford: Oxford University Press, 2000), 269–271.
10 References to quotations from life stories in the chapter indicate the DU OHC collection name and interview number (DU MV: no).
11 Ivans Kudrjašovs' life-story, interview undertaken by Diāna Stalidzāne in Preiļi, 8 July 2010 (145 minutes, in Russian), DU MV: 782.

Contemporaries testify that part of the Latvian population was panic stricken and had a premonition of bad things to come. A narrator who was 17 years old in 1940 reveals the emotions of local people:

"[..] at first we missed our Latvia. Oh, we did suffer, we thought—that's all, the world has come to an end. [..] At first, we cried bitterly for the time of Latvia. Oh, how we agonised, my Goodness, my Goodness, we thought—that's the end, the world has fallen to pieces."[12]

A narrator who was only nine years old in 1940—too young to assess the situation—recalls her mother's reaction and expresses the dominant feeling of that time—the sense of loss. At the same time her story refers to local people (though unnamed) who participated in the dismantling of the "old order":

"[..] By the school [in Indra] there was a [sculptural] portrait of Kārlis Ulmanis and they (mum, when they returned after that meeting having seen that, mum was crying bitterly) smashed Ulmanis, they took it publicly out at the station where people had gathered... atheists started acting at once...
– But that Ulmanis, the bust of Ulmanis was smashed by the local people or the newly arrived?
– I think that the local people did it, if there was a political leader (*politruk*), he would not do it but there were no others..."[13]

Among the narrators there are some who tell about their activities in line with the demands of the Soviet power already in 1940–1941 (e.g. becoming pioneers,[14] joining the *Komsomol*[15]). They account for this in terms of a thirst for romantic deeds and a desire (typical of youth) to try something novel, as well as a hope for the victory of social justice declared by the Soviet regime.[16] Nowadays, however, even those who at first welcomed the establishment of Soviet

---

12 Staņislava Maļinovska's life-story, interview undertaken by Iveta Bogdanoviča & Inese Ruļuka, in Demene parish of Daugavpils district, 28 June, 2006 (80 minutes, in Latvian), DU MV: 356
13 Janīna Gekiša's life-story, interview undertaken by Irēna Saleniece, in Krāslava, 13 July 2009 (340 minutes, in Latvian), DU MV: 656.
14 Vladimirs Rustamovs' life-story, interview undertaken by Irēna Saleniece & Geoffrey Swain, in Krāslava, 11 July 2009 (197 minutes, in Russian), DU MV: 623.
15 Ivans Bogdanovs' life-story, interview undertaken by Irēna Saleniece, Geoff Swain & Zane Stapķeviča, in Daugavpils, 27 January 2011 (112 minutes, in Russian), DU MV: 831 (1).
16 Mikhail Afremovich, *Bolshaya molekula: Povest' o shkole* (Rīga, 2004), 68–70.

power express far greater appreciation for Ulmanis-era Latvia than they do for Latvia within the USSR.

The absolute majority of narrators, looking back to events of the past, the consequences of which are well known today, do not hide their indignation about the harm and injustice done to Latvia and its people (themselves included). As one Russian respondent (born 1926) recalled during an interview:

> "– You mentioned: 'When the Red Army entered in [19]40, we were so uncertain.' Yet your family is Russian, so one might think logically that they could be 'your own people' who came...
> – What logic?! We were absolutely sure... in our family we talked that we were annexed or occupied (I don't know how they called it at that time), that it is unfathomable, that the only president [Kārlis Ulmanis] in the whole world suffered such treatment being arrested and deported. There has been no other fact like that, it was nonsense! Nowhere in the world there has been something like that [*indignation in the narrator's voice*] ..."[17]

Though extended reflections by the narrators about the Latvian state and their bond with it are scarce, they still refer to this topic in their life-stories. Hence, it is possible to reconstruct the common picture and see the historically and socially determined common and individual attitude to the state and its elements. In all their reflections, narrators mention—as the basic elements of the state— territory, residents/citizens, power (principles, character and role of the ruler, etc.). A stance of critical evaluation can certainly also be discerned—i.e. agreement on the part of the majority about "good" or "hard" times, just or unjust power and "good" or "bad" rulers.

In order to fit into the hitherto unfamiliar socio-political order introduced after World War II, respondents born during the 1920s and 1930s had to replace their "love for the state of Latvia" cultivated in the time of Ulmanis[18] ("bourgeois nationalism" in communist parlance) with the amorphous "love of the socialist Motherland and the socialist countries"[19]. They had to forget loyalty to the state of Latvia and instead accept the Soviet Union as "their own". Rīga as a capital

---

17 Zoya Gulayeva's life-story, interview undertaken by Irēna Saleniece, in Rīga, 30 June 2013 (75 minutes, in Latvian), DU MV: 1028 (1).
18 "Likums par tautas izglītību" *Valdības Vēstnesis*, 17 July 1934.
19 "Moral Code of the Builder of Communism" in https://en.wikipedia.org/wiki/Moral_Code_of_the_Builder_of_Communism (20.10.2014.)

city had to be replaced by Moscow with the Mausoleum on the central square (previously in the Latvian press it had been described as an oddity); instead of Latvian police and army officers and soldiers people had to address Soviet militia and military personnel whose appearance and conduct seemed dubious to them;[20] the symbols of the Latvian state had to be replaced by the red flag, "Internationale", five-pointed star, and so on.

Some young people in Latvia found this sudden transformation unacceptable. Though no national level resistance was organised against the Soviet invasion, the more patriotically minded school pupils of the Ulmanis years often spontaneously expressed indignation about the occupation of their country. Latvian historians have carefully studied archival documents testifying to the resistance by youth against the Stalinist regime both in 1940–1941[21] and again from 1944 right up until the 1950s[22]. From the perspective of the security bodies of the USSR/LSSR, those were "evil malefactors" (despite their young age) who intentionally denied the "sanctity" of communism and therefore deserved the severest punishment, including death. Memories of contemporaries reveal the scene of the past and enable us to make more trustworthy judgements about people's actions. Latvian society was confused; people were aware only of the fact that they were not satisfied with the novelties of the Soviet regime. In this context, youth—who are always especially active—tried to organise them-

---

20 Irēna Saleniece, "Die sowjetishen Soldaten in den Augen der Einwohner Lettlands: Die 1940er Jahre (nach mündlichen Quellen)", in *Narva und die Ostseeregion = Narva and the Baltic Sea Region: Beiträge der II. Internationalen Konferenz über die politischen und kulturellen Beziehungen zwischen Russland und der Ostseeregion (Narva, 1.–3. Mai 2003) = Papers Presented at the II International Conference on Political and Cultural Relations between Russia and the Baltic Sea Region States (Narva, 1–3 May 2003)* / herausgegeben von / edited by Karsten Brüggemann (Narva: TÜ Narva Kolledž & Autoren, 2004), 311–324.
21 Tālivaldis Vilciņš, *Skolu jaunatne nacionālajā cīņā (1940–1941)* (Rīga: Latvijas Valsts arhīvs, 1997), 80.
22 Heinrihs Strods, "Latvijas skolu jaunatnes nacionālā pretošanās kustība (1944. gads— 50. gadu vidus)", in *Totalitārie režīmi un to represijas Latvijā 1940.–1956. gadā: Latvijas Vēsturnieku komisijas 2000. gada pētījumi = Totalitarian regimes and their repressions carried out in Latvia in 1940–1956: Research of the Commission of the Historians of Latvia (2000)* (Rīga: Latvijas vēstures institūta apgāds, 2001), 666–674.

selves in order to express their dissatisfaction. One of the former "state criminals" (born in 1929) who was convicted and sent to the GULAG for having participated in an "anti-Soviet organisation" of school pupils recalls that:

> "[...] in Russian times we started talking at school and sometimes at home and started organising something and we had something like an anti-state organisation..."[23]

Memories[24] testify how vague and spontaneous the youth's resistance in many cases was. Unlike the punishment that followed—definitely, brutally, inevitably—as soon as the slightest suspicion was aroused on the part of supporters of the regime. Historical sources indicate, that Soviet security institutions not only punished actually existing resistance groups and strictly limited efforts to provide help and support for the repressed, but also "created" resistance networking. It is about both "imagined" resistance groups in the territory of Latvia[25] and "imagined" help networks that supposedly linked the Latvian people to the *Gulag* and places of special settlement of those deported from Latvia.[26] It must be taken into consideration that both adults and youths were poorly informed about the situation in the USSR—the reality of the communist regime—and often could not imagine what consequences their actions may have. Any oppositional posture aroused the displeasure of Soviet functionaries and automatically led to repressions:

> "...in secondary school there was a small group, they spread some kind of slogans. And that girl was just among the classmates and for them [security service] it was enough. [..] The girl was convicted for twenty-five years."[27]

---

23 Voldemārs Vētriņš' life-story, interview undertaken by Marija Andrejeva, in Daugavpils, 12 August 2006 (64 minutes, in Latvian), DU MV: 393.
24 Voldemārs Vētriņš' life-story; Olegs Jegorovs' life-story, interview undertaken by Diāna Stalidzāne, in Krāslava, 12–13 June 2009 (122 minutes, in Russian), DU MV: 634.
25 See: Vilciņš, *Skolu jaunatne,* 30–31.
26 It is possible that though this kind of falsification, members of the security apparatus sought to raise their profile in the eyes of management and further intimidate the local population. More generally, though, this provides us with a more detailed understanding of the nature of the Soviet communist society and shows that Latvians (as well as residents of the other Baltic states) who grew up and had been educated in "bourgeois" countries were always suspected of having a disloyal attitude towards the Soviet order.
27 Ilga Bakarte's life-story, interview undertaken by Irēna Saleniece, in Aknīste, Jēkabpils district, 3 July 2008 (179 minutes, in Latvian), DU MV: 548.

As the communist regime became more consolidated, people acquired greater awareness of the new state of affairs and the number of underground resistance organisations started falling. Yet, individual acts of resistance[28] continued throughout the Soviet period, with Latvian patriots becoming especially active around the anniversaries of the proclamation of the Republic of Latvia (18 November) and the Ulmanis *coup* (15 May):

> "Guys there had good brains and they decided to hoist the Latvian flag on the water tower of the secondary school [on 18 November]. And so they did. My cousin and other guys [..] climbed the water tower, hoisted the flag and got on their bikes. The rode their bikes to the lake, others took their bikes but they crossed the lake in a boat. Dogs took the track until the road [..] by the lake the track was lost. That's it! Until the present day: only memories and the waving Latvian flag."[29]

However, as the Soviet regime stabilised and Sovietisation began to intensify during the late 1940s and 1950s, young people in Latvia ceased to insist on their own state and with greater or lesser enthusiasm began to adapt themselves to the Soviet system. Judging by the narrators' memories, the main motive for doing so derived from the expanded opportunities for social mobility— through education and career development—that Soviet power offered to more needy sections of the population:

> "With all the shortage of money I went to study at Daugavpils Teacher Training Institute. We got a grant and could cope somehow if we took some bread from home. [...] The six years spent in the institute were the most carefree time in my life: we were learning, went to clear away the post-war debris, built the tram rails, worked in the support farm of the institute and those six years passed unnoticed. In 1952 I graduated from Daugavpils six-year teacher training institute. Then I started working as a teacher."[30]

Whatever the individual experience of the narrators of the first generation, one cannot help noticing that today they have no absolute unanimity concerning the existence of the independent state of Latvia. The overwhelming majority is

---

28 Heinrihs Strods, "Nevardarbīgā pretošanās Latvijā (1944–1985)" in *Nevardarbīgā pretošanās: Latvijas neatkarības atgūšanas ceļš 1945–1991* (Rīga: Latvijas Zinātņu akadēmija, 2008), 63–159.
29 Raisa Žilinska's life-story, interview undertaken by Zane Stapķeviča, in Vabole parish of Daugavpils district, 30 June 2003 (95 minutes, in Latvian), DU MV: 54.
30 Valentīna Valērija Guḑlevska's life-story, interview undertaken by Evēlija Želve, in Aglona parish of Preiļi district, 11 April 2006 (40 minutes, in Latvian), DU MV 321(1).

favourably disposed, though rather often with some reserve caused by the unsatisfactory social provision in present-day Latvia; very seldom, though, does one encounter a negative attitude or indifference towards the very concept of Latvian statehood:

> "Well, as I had reconciled with the Soviet power, I did not think that we needed free Latvia by all means. We had to work anyway. Now we also have to work. Labour determines the person's worth. No matter with what government he lives and no matter what country..."[31]

A very critically minded historian could state that the narrators had switched sides *en masse* with the beginning of the so-called Third Awakening in the late 1980s. However, in listening to them it must be assumed that long before that they had been hiding their true attitude. They chose outer obedience but inner resistance:

> "... [when it became known that Soviet power arrived] we all started crying and guardian angels probably said; we were watching and drying eyes with handkerchiefs, feeling that something evil was approaching but we endured, did not surrender, did not surrender, we endured. That language was Russian but we didn't speak it among ourselves, we spoke Latvian, Polish [*in a whisper*]. Now they [defenders of the Soviet order] also impose all kinds of things, now they need a state [Russian] language, imagine, in another country and they dictate what we need."[32]

The choice of such a "hypocritical" strategy of conduct was determined not only by rational justification based on criticism of the negative sides of the Soviet regime and recognition of the advantages (mostly the lost ones) of the independent Latvia. It seems that greater significance was attributed to the bond of the narrators with Latvia and awareness of their belonging to the brutally destroyed Latvian state.

The negative features of the Soviet period most commonly alluded to by narrators were as follows:

---

31 Emīlija Mežaraupa's life-story, interview undertaken by Jānis Liniņš, in Bebrene parish of Ilūkste district, August 2010 (44 minutes, in Latvian), DU MV: 833.
32 Helēna Zarakovska's life-story, interview undertaken by Renāte Vilmane, in Daugavpils, 27 March, 2010 (37 minutes, in Latvian), DU MV: 692.

- Repressions and oppression in many spheres (ethnic; religious; private business; aesthetic and artistic etc.);
- Living in fear, especially during the Stalinist period;
- Expropriation of the people through nationalisation of private property and collectivisation in the countryside;
- Russification;
- Denigration towards the independent Republic of Latvia;
- Disparity between words and deeds on the part of the authorities;
- The need to hide one's true opinions.

Even leaving aside terror, repression of "enemies of the people" and intimidation of the rest, the communist authorities evoked dislike due to the constant discrepancy between the ideals they declared and the everyday practice of their rule:

> "[..] all kinds of slogans, all kinds. I don't even want to remember those times. But we were working. And working well. So, the life passed. [...] Praise everything! Well, it wasn't all bad. We were working and it seemed all right. The time was like that, we grew up like that and worked our time span. [...] In childhood, in the times of Ulmanis, it had been completely different. We are, see, such Soviet time people. Driven away from the church. Only secretly [...]"[33]

The other narrator who had managed to finish 6-year basic school during the period of independent Latvia tells about the great discrepancy between the officially expressed experience and her own. In the press, in the process of learning, even in fiction, there were statements, especially concerning the pre-war Latvia, that the narrator could not agree with. However, she was not allowed to express her opinion:

> "[..] I came to realise as I grew older. It became clear that it was one way, [but] you had to speak this way. Say something completely different. [..] When I analysed those works, the novel 'Up the Hill' ['*Pret kalnu*'] by Anna Sakse, I wrote the way I was supposed to. But I never had that certainty. There were also people who with their low culture level wrote and they condemned everything [concerning the period of the independent state of Latvia]—'bourgeois.' [..] And I could not understand either, I thought: how can you say

---

33 Anna Bernāne's life-story, interview undertaken by Zane Stapķeviča, in Preiļi, 9 July, 2010 (85 minutes, in Latvian), DU MV: 800.

that, did you live here, how can you call them names like that?! ... And, first, that language, very illiterate. Very illiterate. Everywhere: 'kulaks', 'bourgeois.' Never mind what the article will be—those words will be there."[34]

Other people express the same thought about the "specific" understanding of a word during the Soviet period in the form of sarcastic aphorisms and anecdotes. For instance, "In the Soviet Union 'nationalists' are those who can speak at least two languages (Latvian and Russian) but 'internationalists' speak only Russian"[35]; "A [Soviet] migrant writes to his family in his homeland: 'Life in Latvia is good, only there are too many Latvians'."[36]

In 1961 "The Moral Code of the Builder of Communism" was adopted at the 22nd Congress of the Communist Party of the Soviet Union, as part of the new Party programme. One witness recalls how this became the occasion for a vast propaganda campaign:

> "All communists cited the moral code [of the builders of communism]; there was a fashionable magazine 'Огонёк' [...] Everyone was crazy about communism then, it was so fashionable."[37]

But declarations, promises and propaganda did not entail real progress in society and in people's everyday life:

> "Khrushchev condemned Stalin very much. But he wasn't there for long, that Khrushchev, so there was no great break away. From Khrushchev's times I remember dark grey bread in the store for which I queued up in a terribly long line. [..] Me and my husband, we were both going to town [..] early in the morning queuing up by the butcher's, there was a line since the night and we were both standing, standing, to get a bigger piece. When our turn comes, only ears, heads, cow's hooves are left. [..] You know, we heard that things had become [better] but was that true?"[38]

---

34 Ilga Bakarte's life-story.
35 Voiceks Juhņevičs' life-story, interview undertaken by Rihards Kokins, in Višķi parish of Daugavpils district, 23 June 2004 (81 minutes, in Latvian), DU MV: 157 (1).
36 Antons Guģis' life-story, interview undertaken by Irēna Saleniece, in Dunava parish of Jēkabpils district, 1 July 2005 (90 minutes, in Latvian), DU MV: 296.
37 Renāte Pudāne's life-story, interview undertaken by Zane Stapkeviča, in Vabole parish of Daugavpils district, 4 July 2003 (106 minutes, in Latvian), DU MV: 110.
38 Ērika Kampāne' life-story, interview undertaken by Andris Dunskis, in Daugavpils, 29 December 2003 (40 minutes, in Latvian), DU MV: 140.

Oral history sources make it possible to trace the parallel lives lived by the first Latvian generation in their public and private spheres during the Soviet period. Using communist phrases in public by no means bore witness to their real convictions. This was all the more so given that communist ideology was totalitarian in essence and demanded that its supporters accepted fully and unquestioningly all its dogmas: the rejection of private property and industry, Soviet patriotism, communist internationalism, atheism. The local residents who had grown up in pre-war Latvia often could not accept the whole diet of beliefs.

Summarising the content of the life stories brings out the major advantages of the "time of Latvia" in the eyes of narrators: harmonious inter-ethnic relations; freedom of religious belief; acceptable, rational action by the authorities in economic and other practical issues; the opportunity to participate in decision making on socially important questions; a subjective sense of freedom.

In the 1920s and 1930s the majority of the population was engaged in agricultural work. In the course of the agrarian reform of 1920s many families, especially in Latgale, became legal landowners for the first time. Though the size of the landed properties was small (around 10 hectares), they gave peasants a new sense of social stability and the opportunity to become engaged in trade of agricultural produce (also in state organised export) and to enhance the material and social status of their families. For instance, a narrator who is descended from an Old-Believer family and who later became the director of a collective farm relates the notion that he formed in childhood about private property (especially land) and owner status as essential values. As his family had benefitted from these values only once—in the "times of Ulmanis"—he held this period in especially high regard:

> "-Well, my father was hardly literate, he never went into politics, you see... the power for us always, well...
> **-You must accept the power as it is...**
> -Accept is one thing, another is that it seemed all right. Imagine, having 4 cows and 20 hectares [of land] he lived decently—a landowner!"[39]

---

39 Grigorijs Lavreckis' life-story, interview undertaken by Irēna Saleniece, in Saliena parish of Daugavpils district, 2 July 2004 (120 minutes, in Russian), DU MV: 214.

The narrators' accounts also suggest that youth living in early Soviet Latvia had since childhood developed the notion that independent employment is the best lifestyle, often inheriting values of initiative, industriousness and responsibility—from parents or other adults.[40] In this respect it is only natural that the majority of people of this generation never accepted the fact that their family property was nationalised/collectivised in the course of Sovietisation and that, during the Soviet period, they worked hard to make money and placed a high value on material wellbeing.

During the interwar period people in Latvia started to become accustomed to assuming responsibility for their own society. They could independently decide upon important questions such as building schools for local community children:

> "[..] I started going to the old school on the premises of Pilcene estate in [19]38. Mum had said in a parents' meeting: 'Can't we build a good school for our children that they need to learn in this narrow space.' Others supported her and so they started raising money, breeding and selling cattle, and the head of the civil parish Ezeriņš had supported the parents' idea, he had also got married to one of the young teachers, Eleonora. Later they were deported in [19]41 because they had been active in building the school, Ezeriņš died as a martyr. [..] Parents brought logs, gravel, went on *corvée*. I remember going to form two in the autumn, like rivers, like streams they came from all sides, brought to the school yard, drew logs with horses and gravel and stones, the school was growing, growing bigger and bigger. In a year's time the school was built."[41]

However, the major factor determining the positive attitude towards the Latvian state was the sense of belonging—national identity[42]—the features of which are obvious from those narrators of the first generation raised in independent Latvia. For instance, a narrator (born 1926, Russian, Old-Believer) cites a letter (in Latvian) that she received during the 1940s, in which the author, a young Russian man to whom she was romantically attached, states that he considers Latvia to be his *native* land and Latvian—his *native* language:

---

40 See, for instance, Vladislavs Purpišs' life-story, interview undertaken by Irēna Saleniece & Geoff Swain, in Krāslava, 11 July 2009 (109 minutes, in Russian), DU MV: 622; Vladimirs Rustamovs' life-story.
41 Anna Babre's life-story, interview undertaken by Ligita Strode, in Malta, Rēzekne district, 16 August 2003 (75 minutes, in Latvian), DU MV: 131.
42 Entonijs D. Smits, *Nacionālā identitāte* (Rīga, 1997), 19.

"He[43] was searching for me through Swiss Red Cross [*reading a letter*]: 'Dear Zoya, I wrote to you several times but did not receive any reply and I would like to get a letter from you. I am fine, on vacations now, on 15 October the new semester will start. I have to study much because very little is left till the end. When we receive "*Cīņa*", I am glad that at least that little is possible to be read in my native language from my native land."[44]

Adherence to the pre-war Latvia and faith in the Latvian state manifest themselves in various ways in the life stories of the first generation. Sometimes they are declared in the first person:

"I was born in 1918, I spent my childhood and all life here, in Latvia, this is my native land. I am a patriot of Latvia, though Polish by nationality but my parents had been living here all the time and they were very well-disposed to this country. And the country gave me education [..] we are the true patriots, we always knew that our nation is with us and we ate Latvian bread and walked Latvian ground, therefore we have to be very, very thankful to our country."[45]

There are also stories about national identity manifestations of other contemporaries:

"...When there was the first Popular Front meeting in a culture centre in Kraslava, it was in [19]89 [...] The house was full to the utmost... and people were singing for the first time the national anthem 'God, Save Latvia' ... and as they started [singing] behind me I knew that there were Old-Believers, those local Russians... I heard their voices, I turned, tears filled my eyes, they knew..., all these long years..., they knew this song.[46]

4. Conclusion

Based on the information obtained from the oral history sources, the most characteristic attitudes of the generation born in the 1920s and 1930s towards the statehood of Latvia can be summarised as follows. First, these respondents felt a sense of belonging to an independent Latvian state mostly on an emotional level: they recognised the independent Latvian state as "one's own" due to mostly happy memories of childhood and youth, and they opposed the So-

---

43 N. B., born in 1926, Russian, Old-Believer; after serving in the Latvian legion he emigrated to the West, where he became a well-known economist.
44 Zoya Gulayeva's life-story.
45 Helēna Zarakovska's life-story.
46 Janīna Gekiša's life-story.

viet state. Witness, for instance, one narrator—a deeply religious Russian Orthodox woman of 82 years—who, when looking through 70-year-old photographs, exclaimed: "Here's our Ulmanis for whom I pray. And this is the bishop [Pommers] killed by the Soviets... Good Grief, Good Grief! How we lived in the times of Latvia!"[47]

Another characteristic feature is poor information about the political system of the interwar Republic of Latvia and the changes made to it in the 1930s. Not all respondents differentiate between the years of the parliamentary republic and the years of Ulmanis' authoritarian rule. For the majority, this whole period is reduced to the "times of Ulmanis". However, all respondents identify the "times of Latvia"—the time of the independent Latvian state before war—and relate to it positively. The attitude towards the LSSR is mostly negative, though the Soviet social policy of the 1960s–1980s is compared positively to that which exists in the "reconstructed Latvia" of today. Yet, while narrators from this generation are far from unanimous in their attitude towards the Latvian state, their patriotism and civic identification cannot be denied:

> "...as long as God grants me I will live. But I will die with the Latvian flag on my chest, I told my children to put a small tiny Latvian flag across the pillow [in the coffin] because *I have lived only for my Latvia, my Latgale*. And the folk costume of ancient Latgalians will be on me when I pass away, this is my most honourable apparel, of all I have had and won't have any more..."[48]

Overall, the representatives of this generation had a decisive role in the reestablishment of Latvia's statehood. They formed a bridge between two periods of independent Latvia—the *interbellum* and the contemporary. Their concrete knowledge about the state order, traditions and symbols was passed down to the generations that followed. Their enthusiastic and positive attitude towards "their own" state ensured that their children and grandchildren stood up for restoration of independence during the 1980 and 1990s.

---

47 Vera Hrebtova's life-story, interview undertaken by Ināra Jefimova, in Daugavpils, December 2002 (60 minutes, in Russian), DU MV: 5.
48 Anna Babre's life-story.

Latvians in Exile and the Idea of the Latvian State

Ieva Zake, The College of New Jersey

1. Introduction and Theoretical Considerations

This chapter offers a brief review of a conception or idea of Latvian statehood that formed and was propagated by Latvians in North America—arguably the largest Latvian diaspora in the period between the early 20th century and the 1990s. It is not my intention to analyse the conceptions of Latvian statehood among the current diaspora, as I believe these to be different from the one held by earlier Latvian exiles. Nor do I claim that the exile idea of Latvian statehood that emerges from my analysis reflects the full spectrum of political views among Latvians in the United States and Canada and beyond. Rather, my chapter points toward a few discernible trends that emerged from the discussions and controversies among the *émigrés* around the issue of the past and future of the Latvian state. This is a generally descriptive study that analyses historical accounts of the exile community, political documents and various published materials circulated among exiles. I treat the public voices of intellectuals, journalists and political activists as speaking not only for themselves, but for the exile community as a whole. The Latvian press in exile was highly engaged and it strived not to just inform, but also to influence and shape its readers' minds and attitudes. My sources come mainly from the archival documents and periodicals of exile Latvians stored at the Latvian National Archives in Rīga and the Immigration History Research Center at University of Minnesota. The periodicals discussed here include such diverse sources as *Svešos Krastos* (published in Philadelphia), *Oregonietis* (published in Oregon), *Saulainā Krasta Vēstis* (published in Florida), *Laiks*, *Jaunā Gaita*, *Dauvagavas Vanagu Mēnešraksts* and others.

From a theoretical point of view, this chapter explores what has been identified by Ladis Kristoff as the "state idea", that is, "a philosophical and moral conception of a state's destiny and mission in terms of universal human teleology" in relation to the "national idea"—a "semiconscious tendency rooted in the collective psychology of national tradition and inhibitions."[1] According to Kristoff, the state idea is usually articulated by political and intellectual elites and is goal-oriented, while the national idea relates to the masses and is focused on traditional beliefs and cultural features of the group. In the context of new and small nations, such as those of Eastern and Central Europe, this distinction works differently. For them, the predominant idea is that of a nation-state as a political structure serving the interests of an ethnically defined nationhood. The cultural and ethnic identity of the nation is actively defined and shaped by the elite, which advocates for a state that is ethnically and culturally-rooted. Consequently, the state is not just a civic institution for small nations, but an entity with primarily cultural and social obligations.

The search for the nation-state idea leads one to explore varied discourses of the state circulating within and among groups. Discourses are thought and conversation processes, reflected in, for example, public debates and the press. Political discourses shift over time and are contextual. They are also conflicting and ambivalent and depend on the social and cultural, even physical (as in the case of diaspora) positions of the groups that produce them. Ethnic and national discourses tend to be preoccupied with issues of legitimacy, that is, the grounds on which a state or a nation proclaims itself as a political actor.[2] It is in these kinds of discourses that the nation-state idea is born.

What is the relevance of looking at the idea of a Latvian nation-state through discourses taking place among exile groups? First, some of the most politically astute and articulate groups of Latvians found themselves in exile in different periods of history, so their conversations are a meaningful element of political conversations among Latvians and about Latvia; second, the influence of the exile nation-state idea was felt in various forms in the homeland itself if not during the period of Soviet occupation, then certainly during the independence movement and after. In general, exile is a unique study site for the construction of the nation-state idea. As suggested by some researchers, diaspora or exile

---

[1] Quoted in David Knight, "Statehood: A Politico-Geographic and Legal Perspective," *GeoJournal* 28, 3 (1992): 311–318.

[2] Kristine Barseghyan, "Rethinking Nationhood: Post-Independence Discourse on National Identity in Armenia," *Polish Sociological Review* 144 (2003): 399–416.

communities already distinguish themselves from the concept of a state, namely, their host country, because they perceive it as a short-term place of residence to which they have little connection. The state as such appears as something external to them. Moreover, diaspora is all about crossing and questioning national borders and living in a trans-state position where politically and territorially defined states are not important. Thinking about the nation-state requires an ability to operate in terms of integrity and unity, something of which diaspora or exile community are not always capable: "any political project of diaspora, dealing with nation and national identity, will have a tendency to reflect the moment of its borderlessness and to rearticulate the ethnic concept of nation of ethnic-civic dichotomy."[3] In other words, the experience of being an exile and living in a perceived no-man's land has a direct impact on the fluidity of the conception of statehood among émigrés. I inquire whether these notions of border-questioning and statelessness characterised the nation-state idea among Latvians.

It has to be made clear that I will not discuss the national idea (what it means to be Latvian), even though, as stated above, this forms the foundation of the nation-state idea for small nations such as the Latvians. I am focusing primarily on what exile Latvians meant when they referred to Latvian statehood. To summarise, the goals of the chapter are to describe the conceptions of a Latvian nation-state among Latvian exiles in the US and Canada before 1940 and after World War II; and to analyse the discursive features of their idea of Latvian statehood.

2. The Latvian Nation-State Idea among the "Old Latvians"

Latvian exiles of the early 20th century—or the so-called "Old Latvians" —began to formulate their initial conceptions of Latvian statehood during World War I, more specifically around 1918. Since the Latvian state did not exist at the time, some of the Old Latvians even came to believe that the idea of national statehood had actually originated with them.[4] At a meeting on 30 June 1918 in Boston, Latvian émigrés developed a public statement in which they not only con-

---

3 Barseghyan, "Rethinking Nationhood," 405.
4 Līdumnieks, "Latvijas Brīvvalsts," *Amerikas Vēstnesis*, 1 August 1918, 1.

firmed their loyalty as US citizens, but also expressed support for Latvia's independence efforts. They expressed gratitude to Woodrow Wilson for his contribution to the statehood aspirations of small nations and loudly voiced their concern about Germany and Russia's attempts to restrict the freedoms of Latvians.[5] Meanwhile, American Latvian newspaper *Amerikas Vēstnesis* passionately discussed the future of Latvian statehood. Overall, it came out in support of independence and democracy because it celebrated national identity and argued that Latvians who had fought against the German forces during World War I were entitled to national autonomy.[6] Old Latvians also perceived themselves as valuable agents in the struggle for independence because they could effectively communicate with the US government and President and convince both to support Latvia's state. In fact, some of them did so very effectively.[7]

For Old Latvians, the nation-state was the Latvian nation's opportunity to have sovereign governance. They acknowledged that Latvians might be able to exercise this opportunity due to the revolution in Russia, but only if the Tsar's rule was replaced with a moderate and democratic government. The Old Latvians were astute in their understanding of political potentialities when they warned against investing too much hope in either pro-monarchist counter-revolution or Bolshevik radicals. Nationalist oriented Old Latvians saw that neither of these groups would ensure a stable future for Latvia's national independence.[8] They loudly advocated for democracy above all and praised the United States as an example of the best political system because of its respect for the individual's rights.[9] Thus nationalist exiles took care in expressing their full loyalty to the USA, while they also came out as supporters of Latvia's national independence.

When independence was actually declared, nationalistically-oriented Latvian Americans were somewhat surprised, mainly because most of them had expected to see a Bolshevik and pro-Russian government in Latvia. Nevertheless, they welcomed the new state as a positive development. In January 1919,

---

5 "Bostonas Latviešu Rezolūcija," *Amerikas Vēstnesis*, 15 July 1918.
6 Anonymous, "Latviešu tautas karogs," *Amerikas Vēstnesis* 15 April 1918, 4.
7 Anonymous, "Vēl reiz Latviešu lietā," *Amerikas Vēstnesis*, 15 April 1918, 4.
8 Anonymous, "Baltijas stāvoklis pirms viņas krišanas. Krīt kauliņi," *Amerikas Vēstnesis*, 15 April 1918, 1–2.
9 Līdumnieks, "Demokrātijas uzvara," *Amerikas Vēstnesis*, 1 August 1918, 4–5.

about 30 participants of the Latvian National Congress officially recognised the new Latvian government, although a few members of the gathering expressed doubts as to whether Latvia should in fact be independent. Officially, American Latvians encouraged President Wilson to apply the principle of self-determination to the Baltic nations and to acknowledge their state-building efforts. American Latvians also engaged in a few debates with Lithuanian *émigrés* who propagated territorial claims on parts of the fledgling Latvian state. The Old Latvians who supported independence believed that the Latvian state had to be designed to protect the interests of ethnic Latvians against the German landed aristocracy. Due to this, exile Latvians' conception of Latvian statehood at times clashed with the *Realpolitik* of Latvian democracy, especially as far as compromises with the German minority were concerned.

In sum, the idea of the Latvian state as propagated by the Old Latvians was democratic, loyal to the US and based on America's democratic principles such as respect for individual rights and liberties, while at the same time highly protective of interests of the Latvian nation especially against Germans. In other words, while this conception was democratic, it was non-compromising on the ethnic issues.

It should be noted that this understanding of the Latvian state was formed in conversation or rather—conflict—with pro-communist and pro-Bolshevik ideas among other Latvian *émigrés*.[10] Nationalist oriented *émigrés* such as Ravins, Ozols, Roze, Podins and others therefore collaborated eagerly with Latvian provisional government, providing them with information and financial support and promoting national independence. But it was important to the nationalistically-oriented Old Latvians to ensure that the American political establishment did not perceive all Latvians as dangerous communists, especially as the Red Scare was underway. Consequently, their underlying goal in their pro-independence thinking and activism was to oppose the Latvian Bolsheviks in the US.

Bolshevik *émigrés*' conception of the future of Latvia was not fully a notion of statehood, since it was supposed to usher in a dictatorship of the proletariat under which the state would eventually "wither away." The radical socialist and

---

10 Anonymous, "No Filadelfijas," *Amerikas Vēstnesis*, 15 April 1918, 3.

communist *émigrés* of the post-1905 period maintained strong beliefs about the working-class revolution and many of them went to Russia to join the Bolsheviks during the Civil War or continued their extremist activities in the US, even during the Red Scare.[11] Bolshevik Latvians were convinced that "independence" meant liberation from all of the "masters"—Latvian as well as German—who enslaved the Latvian working class. These *émigrés* could not understand opposition to communist ideas and Russia, because in their minds the Russian Bolsheviks were the Latvians' best allies against the German landowners. For this reason, any political compromises that the Latvian government made with the German minority were entirely unacceptable to the proponents of the working-class Latvia. Their conception of the Latvian non-state was deeply opposed to the way that Latvian independent statehood went on to develop during the 1920s and 1930s. They saw this statehood as a product of the petit bourgeoisie and as antagonistic to the needs and interests of the working class.

The idea of the Latvian state was therefore caught in between radically opposed notions—independence vs. inclusion in the larger proletarian state-like structure (Bolshevik Russia), working class dictatorship vs. liberal democracy, opposition toward the bourgeois class both Latvian and German vs. opposition to Germans and Russians on ethnic grounds. This fundamental inconsistency of the Latvian idea of the state was due to the differences in the political beliefs of Latvian *émigrés* themselves. The conflict was rooted in the fundamentally opposed self-conceptions of the *émigré* groups. While some were deeply invested in loyalty to the US and therefore pronounced democracy as the perfect political system (while still believing that Germans should not get any rights), others were fundamentally alienated from American society and perceived themselves as international agents of working class revolution. Consequently, the nationalist notion of Latvian statehood was basically an affirmation of the American state idea in a Latvian context. Since this was questioned by the radical leftist anti-statists, it made those in favour of Latvian statehood invest political and symbolic capital in protecting it. Thus, the Latvian state that was then coming into being already had to be protected and defended in exile.

---

11 Osvalds Akmentiņš, *Vēstules no Maskavas: Amerikas latviešu repatriantu likteņi Padomju Krievijā 1917–1940* (Lincoln, Nebraska: Gauja, 1987).

3. The Latvian Nation-State Idea among Post-World War II Exiles

For post-World War II Latvian *émigrés*, the issue of the past, present and future of Latvian statehood was of highest priority. If the Old Latvian community dealt with a notion of the Latvian state-to-be, the post-World War II group was focused on the Latvian state-as-it-used-to-be. In other words, its conceptions of the Latvian state were more backward-looking, in the sense that they sought ideas from what the Latvian state had or had not been.

The politically engaged parts of Latvian *émigré* society were firmly convinced that liberation of the Latvian state was its mission. Latvian *émigrés* perceived the idea of an independent Latvia as a message that needed to be conveyed to the world, as a claim that had to be reasserted and repeated to make sure that no one would forget about it: "activities of the exile will be noticed only when both friends and enemies will see that regardless of external circumstances, Latvians' goal always remains free Latvia."[12] American Latvians of the post-World War II period believed that the message of returning Latvia to independence had to be brought to heads of state; it had to be publicised in the media and promoted in any political way possible.[13] For example, in a manifesto issued by the Baltic States Freedom Council on June of 1968, *émigrés* declared that it was their duty to accuse the Soviets of aggression, appeal to the free world to understand the injustice done to the Baltics and reaffirm the determination of the Baltic people to be free.[14] They saw the independent state as a political notion that needed to be continuously advocated for and kept alive in the political memory of the West. In addition, Latvian *émigré* society itself was both to embody and to exhibit in its activities the idea of Latvian state. Its actions had to display the longing of the Latvian nation to have its state again. In this context, the idea of the state took on a cyclical or retroactive nature where the future was essentially an attempt to reassert the past. Remembering

---

12 Alberts Eglītis, "Tumsa un gaisma skan novembrī," *Daugavas Vanagu Mēnešraksts* 5 (1975): 2; Laimonis Streips, "Domas par Latvijas valsti," *Jaunā Gaita* 62 (1967): 41.
13 Jāzeps Grodnis, "Domas par Latvijas valsti," *Jaunā Gaita* 64 (1967): 45–47; Alfreds Puķīte "Daugavas Vanagi un trimdas sabiedrība," *Daugavas Vanagu Mēnešraksts* 1 (1987): 4–6.
14 Manifesto, Baltic States Freedom Council, June 1968, Raimunds Čaks files, Box 5, Folder 12, Immigration History Research Center, University of Minnesota.

and reaffirming national independence both defined and guided Latvians in exile, because they symbolised the historic injustice done to the Latvian state. Due to this, the older generation of émigrés who had actually experienced the period of national independence held leadership roles in the exile community for a considerable time. It took a while before the second generation could assert itself as a political agent and achieve a significant role in the exile community organisations.

Furthermore, émigrés viewed the Latvian state as an historical and political entity to be returned to its normal condition of independence and preserved in its historical borders. Statehood was an ideal to believe in, thus turning political goals and tasks into a type of secular religion that presented politics in messianic terms:

> "We know that our time will come, too. Therefore, we should never succumb to hopelessness. In full trust we have to hope and wait until free Latvia will have again its place in the free world."[15]

Regaining national sovereignty was portrayed in terms of salvation:

> "the policies of Free Estonia, Latvia and Lithuania will be oriented toward human progress, social justice and international cooperation based on mutual respect for national sovereignty and territorial integrity."[16]

By interpreting the struggle for national independence in quasi-religious terms, émigrés presented the state itself as helpless, subjugated and in need of protection and defense.[17] It was to be delivered by historical circumstances, as it was not really perceived as a political agent in its own right. It had to be, in the words of émigré activist Jānis Peniķis, "returned to its legal owners"[18]—like a possession that had been taken away.

Due to this messianic and almost sacral attitude towards Latvian statehood, the exile society throughout its undeniably active and politically saturated years

---

15 Vaira Vīķe-Freiberga, "Par brīvību un humānisma vērtībām," *Jaunā Gaita* 122 (1979): 3–9, 61.
16 Manifesto, Baltic States Freedom Council.
17 See, for example, Voldemars Korsts, "Skatisimies patiesibai seja," *Saulainā Krasta Vēstis* 6 (1980): 9–11.
18 Jānis Peniķis, "Darbs brīvībai un mūsu uzskati," *Jaunā Gaita* 32 (1959): 205.

had little by way of a substantive conversation about the actual political system in the liberated Latvia of future.[19] Attempts to generate a debate about the political content of this messianic statehood were often perceived as deliberate fragmentation and weakening of the *émigré* society that would undermine its dedication to the ultimate goal.[20] The idea of the Latvian state was not filled with concrete political recommendations. Instead, it remained a noble and utopian mission.[21] For example, prolific publicist Ernests Blanks argued that national independence alone was the goal of the exile political struggle and Latvia's political system could be decided later, when it might turn out to be democracy or communism or another system. [22] National independence first, everything else later—this was often the motto of the Latvian exile community.[23]

This should not be a surprise, given that Latvian *émigrés*, like any other community of political exiles, was explicitly self-centred and isolated. As presented in a well-written, slightly tongue-in-cheek "letter to a friend Peter in Soviet Latvia" by an *émigré* political activist, Jānis Peniķis, *émigrés* had little to no knowledge about the political ideas, desires and leanings of Latvians under the Soviet regime. Due to this, passionate conversations about the future of the Latvian state were essentially internal to the *émigré* community. Or, as stated by Peniķis:

"I understand, my friend, that I do not understand much about what Your ideal Latvian state will look like when You finally will have a chance to draw it. It is much easier for me to write this letter as a monologue because then You will not confuse my smooth arguments with Your objections. (...) Now you understand why we here, in the West, have such serious debates about You and what You are thinking."[24]

---

19 Historian Andrievs Ezergailis lamented this fact in his political writings throughout the 1970s (see, for example, "Vai ir vajadzīga jauna trimdas nacionālpolitika?" *Jaunā Gaita* 122 (1979): 12–13.
20 See, for example, Pēteris Aigars, "Nacionālie centieni nemirst," *Daugavas Vanagu Mēnešraksts* 5 (1968): 9; Jānis Frišvalds, "Tēvzemei un brīvībai," *Daugavas Vanagu Mēnešraksts* 1 (1976): 4.
21 On this, see for example, Peniķis, "Darbs brīvībai un mūsu uzskati," 208.
22 Ernests Blanks, "Latviešu komunistiem dzimtenē," *Daugavas Vanagu Mēnešraksts* 5 (1970): 6–7.
23 A. Karps, "Latvijas nākotnei darāmie darbi," *Daugavas Vanagu Mēnešraksts* 2 (1969): 1–2.
24 Jānis Peniķis, "Domas par Latvijas valsti," *Jaunā Gaita* 65 (1967): 48–49.

Peniķis' writing suggests an awareness that conversations about Latvian statehood inside the *émigré* community were limited and vague, with only a general understanding of (or willingness to understand) the current situation in the homeland. This attitude towards Soviet Latvia was driven mainly by a fear that by acknowledging the present reality, *émigrés* would tacitly give it legitimacy. Consequently, their isolation on the issue of future Latvia's state was politically motivated and self-imposed, for the purpose of preserving the perfect ideal of Latvia's past as well as future.

Thus, the *émigré* community's internal conversations about Latvia's future statehood revolved around issues that were crucial to the community itself, and not so much around Soviet Latvia and Latvians. Among them were, for example, strong generational differences and disagreements on the question of Ulmanis' authoritarian regime from 1934–1940. The younger generation wanted its ideas about the future Latvian state to be less dependent on the visions of older *émigrés*, but more aware of the present-day Latvia. Therefore, some of them speculated that Latvians inside Soviet Latvia might, in fact, want to build a state based on socialist ideals and that *émigré* society needed to be prepared for that.[25] Some even argued that only those Latvians who currently resided in Latvia had to the right to make decisions regarding its political system and that they might choose to preserve the social and economic ties that had developed between the Latvian SSR and its neighbouring countries. Thus, they might not even necessarily want an independent state, but rather choose to join some sort of European confederation. Most importantly, the younger generation stressed that "the year 1939 is not going to return and even less so the year of 1934,"[26] meaning that fear of past calamities was a bad guide for the future.

As noted, these ideas evolved largely as opposition to those influential and older members of the *émigré* community who propagated Kārlis Ulmanis' authoritarian regime as the best model of the future state well into the 1980s, especially on the pages of the publication *Daugavas Vanagu Mēnešraksts*.[27]

---

25 Ingvars Kalniņš, "Domas par valsti," *Jaunā Gaita* 11 (1957): 188–189. Similar ideas were expressed 10 years later by Jāzeps Lelis, "Latviešu trimdas sabiedrības izvērtējums," *Jaunā Gaita* 63 (1967): 40–48.
26 Streips, "Domas par Latvijas valsti," 44.
27 Jānis Daģis, "Kārli Ulmani pieminot," *Daugavas Vanagu Mēnešraksts* 4 (1977): 1–9; Jānis Radziņš, "Manas atmiņas par K. Ulmani," *Daugavas Vanagu Mēnešraksts* (1977):

They glorified Ulmanis as an economic genius and admirable political leader with high ideals and moral standards. Even if it was admitted that his politics had been non-democratic and authoritarian, this was explained away as an historical necessity. Moreover, it was argued that had World War II been avoided, Ulmanis would have restored democracy anyway.[28] Parts of the older *émigré* generation insisted that Ulmanis' political system was not a dictatorship. Rather, he was the "master of the land"—like a farmer who took care of everyone's needs and left his subjects satisfied.[29] Or, alternatively, it was argued that the so-called people's democracies of the interwar period were so inefficient that there was no other choice but to institute authoritarianism. In fact, it was the minority parties that kept politics in Latvia hostage and actually predetermined the arrival of Ulmanis' *coup*. Authoritarianism had a positive effect on Latvia and everyone else in Europe was doing it at the time, so it seemed like a logical decision of which Latvians did not need to be ashamed.[30]

Meanwhile, opponents of pro-authoritarianism asked the *émigré* society to look soberly at the threats to individual freedom that were built into the ideology of authoritarianism, even if it did not turn into a full-fledged dictatorship.[31] They positioned parliamentarism and multi-party democracy as the only viable option for the future of the Latvian state.[32] They also suggested that Latvians both under communism and in exile had gone through a great "school" of history preparing them to build a democratic political system.[33] Thus, by the early 1960s it seemed that the fascination with Ulmanis and the *coup* of 15 May was already disappearing among most of the *émigrés*, mainly because they were

---

10–11; Valdis Zants, "'Var punduri tev ešafotu taisīt...'," *Svešos Krastos* 24 (1977): 8–12; Alberts Eglītis, "Tauta saulē un važās," *Daugavas Vanagu Mēnešraksts* 5 (1980): 8–10; Aleksandrs Zaube, "15. maiju atceroties," *Čikāgas Ziņas* 125 (1988): 3.

28 A. Liepiņa, "Kārlis Ulmanis," *Daugavas Vanagu Mēnešraksts* 5 (1978): 15; Kārlis Lezdkalns, "Par kardinālām aplamībām kādā kompilācijā par Kārli Ulmani," *Svešos Krastos* 38 (1981): 17–19; rs, "Pirms 50 gadiem," *Svešos Krastos* 49 (1984): 1.

29 Alberts Raidonis, "Kārlis Ulmanis un viņa laiks," *Čikāgas Ziņas* 85 (1984): 1–2.

30 Arturs Neparts, "Autoritārās Latvijas ideoloģija: Komentāri par komentāriem," *Jaunā Gaita* 37 (1962): 146–147.

31 Gunārs Irbe, "Autoritārās Latvijas ideoloģija," *Jaunā Gaita* 33 (1961): 216–219; Jānis Rudzītis, "Režīms un literatūra," *Jaunā Gaita* 38 (1962):187–196.

32 Jānis Peniķis, "Latvijas parlamentārais posms: sasniegums vai neizdevies eksperiments?," *Akadēmiskā Dzīve* 26 (1984): 3–15.

33 Jāzeps Grodnis, "Domas par Latvijas valsti," *Jaunā Gaita* 64 (1967): 45–47.

exposed to a well-functioning democracy. In addition, the younger generation who had grown up under American democracy began to play an increasingly important role in this community's affairs. Some suggested that émigré Latvians were gradually being "cured of authoritarianism."[34] Still, as late as 1989 certain voices continued to discuss the respective merits of a parliamentary versus a presidential political system, recommending that the failures of parliamentary democracy and the benefits of authoritarianism had to be taken into consideration when shaping the potential new state.[35]

Another point of discussion within the émigré society was the purpose of Latvian statehood as such. For many émigrés, the state's mission was to protect ethnic Latvians and to assert their place and role in the international political arena. The destruction of the Latvian state was seen as an injustice done to ethnic Latvians, because having no state threatened their survival and thus violated their human rights. No other legal and political mechanism except statehood could ensure the full exercise of Latvians' ethnic rights. These discourses showed explicit distrust towards and concern regarding non-Latvians who had entered the territory of Latvian SSR during the Soviet occupation. These groups were perceived as colonist-oppressors and as a barrier on the way to full implementation of human rights for Latvians.[36]

But, while some demanded that the state served to defend Latvians' human rights, others questioned the model of the nation-state *per se*, since it clearly had not helped to solve the ethnic problems of the 20th century. Drawing states along ethnic lines had not only failed to ensure peace amongst groups within them, but had also led states to engage in disastrous warfare with each other. In sum, the nation-state as a shell that was supposed to protect its ethnically

---

34 Kārlis Dzelzitis, "Lielā plaisa sāk aizvērties," *Jaunā Gaita* 44 (1963): 233–234.
35 Alberts Raidonis," Kādu demokrātiju nākotnes Latvijai?," *Daugavas Vanagu Mēnešraksts* 1 (1989): 13–14.
36 See, for example, Visvaldis Klīve, "Pārdomas un meklējumi," *Jaunā Gaita* (1955): 28–29; Ernests Blanks, "De Jure," *Daugavas Vanagu Mēnešraksts* 1 (1971): 6–8; Rita Liepkalne, "Mērķi un ceļi," *Daugavas Vanagu Mēnešraksts* 5 (1977): 3–5; Vija un Visvaldis Klīve, "Mums vēl daudz jādara," *Laiks* April 9, 1980, p. 2; Ernests Blanks, "Lielkrievu šovinisma purvā," *Daugavas Vanagu Mēnešraksts* 2 (1973): 7–8.

defined "content" had proved to be highly problematic. Reflecting on this history, some *émigrés* proposed that it might not be in the best interests of the Latvian nation to pursue this type of statehood at all.[37]

In addition, as more and more states began to unite into wider federations or unions, their cultural uniqueness found itself under threat of extinction. Some *émigrés* warned that this could happen to Latvians as well and therefore the goal of the state, if it was ever to exist for Latvians, had to be protection and maintenance of Latvian ethnic and linguistic heritage.[38] These *émigrés* argued that the essence of Latvian future was in its cultural distinction, not political sovereignty. The Latvian state therefore had to be envisioned as serving cultural, not political purposes: "The future of Latvia is possible only as the future of a cultural state. The materialistic position needs to be largely replaced with a focus on ideas."[39] In other words, it was argued that drawing political borders around Latvians could hardly ensure the future of Latvians as an ethnic group. Instead, the true purpose of the state was to realise Latvian ethnocultural difference. Independence, they argued, had to be a cultural conception and, at the same time, national culture had to be the motivator for the struggle for independence.[40] Moreover, national culture fueled political resistance behind the Iron Curtain and it was the only real bridge that connected Latvians inside and outside of Latvia.[41] Therefore, the future Latvian state had to be a cultural, not a political entity.

4. Conclusion

The foregoing brief analysis of the North American Latvian exile community's internal discourse allows one to identify the ideas and realities that had the strongest influence on how this group defined Latvian statehood. In a post-World War II context, these were: 1) dominance of memory and remembrance in how exiles thought of themselves, which granted more social and political

---

37 Fricis Dravnieks, "Nacionālisms un tā perspektīvas," *Akadēmiskā Dzīve* 18 (1976): 38–40.
38 See, for example, Arnolds Ruņģis, "Akūta nacionālā problēma," *Akadēmiskā Dzīve* 4 (1961): 15–17.
39 V. Dulmanis, "Nacionālisms—mūsu pastāvēšanas pamats," *Archivs II* (1961): 195.
40 Ezergailis, "Vai ir vajadzīga jauna trimdas nacionālpolitika?", 11–12.
41 On these ideas, see, for example, Jānis Andrups, "Šīs trimdas vēsturiskais uzdevums," *Ceļa Zīmes* 51 (1973): 117–118.

authority to those who held first-hand knowledge of life before exile; 2) exiles' urge or sometimes necessity to use the political goal of freeing their homeland as a tool for mobilising and unifying their community, which occasionally led to creating thought control and internal group censorship; 3) exiles' self-imposed isolation from the present realities of the homeland, which tended to produce a patronising and even infantilising attitude towards those who had stayed behind and, ironically, towards the concept of Latvian statehood itself. In both the pre- and post-World War II community, one can point to: 1) exiles' unclear sense of their own future, which they projected onto the future of Latvian statehood; 2) exiles' fear of assimilation that led them to passionately, but also narrowly concentrate on ensuring the cultural survival of their group. Most notably, in both time periods, North American Latvians constructed their notions of Latvian statehood through passionate and engaged discussions amongst themselves. Exile Latvians never fully agreed on anything and their notion of Latvian statehood reflected that. This leads me to conclude that the experience of exile as such played the most significant role in how this group chose to envision the political future of its homeland. The conception of the Latvian state among exiles was not tied to the actual, present-day realities of Latvia and Latvians "over there", but rather reflected internal moods, ideas and conflicts of the exile community itself. Consequently, the way that exiles thought and talked about the Latvian state should be perceived as more of a self-portrait than a vision of Latvia in its own terms.

This suggests that the idea of Latvian state among exiles Latvians was not borderless, as suggested by the theories discussed earlier. Although loyalty to the US was a big part of the *émigré* identity, this did not necessarily have an impact in terms of bringing to bear a transnational perspective. Instead, the idea was closely tied to notions of the historical borders of Latvia (see, for example, the passionate discussions with *émigré* Lithuanians and emphasis on territorial integrity of the interwar Latvia among post-WWII *émigrés*) and, even more so, the social and cultural borders around and within the exile community itself. The idea of Latvian statehood in exile was focused on protection and preservation as opposed to openness and inclusivity.

International Reactions to the Independence of the Baltic States: The French Example, 1989–1991

Una Bergmane, Cornell University

1. Introduction

On 11 March 1990 Lithuania became the first Soviet republic to declare its independence. Soon after, on 30 March and 4 May, Estonia and Latvia declared the beginning of a transitional period toward independence. Commenting on these events on 19 April of that year, French President François Mitterrand told his American counterpart George Bush: "We are in a terrible contradiction. Our interests are in keeping Gorbachev where he is, and in supporting Lithuanian Independence."[1] The French President advised Bush not to rush into recognising the restoration of Baltic independence and made it clear that France would recognise the three countries only when a negotiated agreement between Tallinn, Rīga, Vilnius and Moscow had been arrived at.[2]

Paradoxically, one year and three months later, on 25 August 1991, France recognised the restoration of the Baltic countries' independence 11 days before the Soviet Union and one week before the United States. No agreement had been reached at this point between the Soviet Union and the Baltic States. It can therefore be asked why there was such a gap between the intentions of the French President in April 1990 and the actions of his government in August 1991? In order to understand the factors that influenced the French decision regarding the independence of the Baltic States in August 1991, this chapter will analyse the French policy regarding the Baltic claims for independence between August 1989 and the summer of 1991 and then describe how this policy was brought to an end by the failed *putsch* in Moscow.

In this way, the chapter contributes to an emerging literature on the external factors that played a role in the reestablishment of Baltic independence and

---

1 The White House, Memorandum of Conversation, subject: meeting with President Mitterrand of France, April 19, 1990, 10:30 am–1:05 pm, Key Largo, Florida, George Bush Presidential Library (http://bushlibrary.tamu.edu/research/pdfs/memcons_telcons/1990---04---19------ Mitterrand%20[1].pdf), 4.
2 The White House, Memorandum of Conversation, 4.

the fall of the Soviet Union. Since 1991, many scholars have analysed the Baltic and Soviet internal dynamics that made Baltic independence possible,[3] while decision-makers from different countries have written about the Baltic problem in their memoirs.[4] Those by Roland Dumas, Hubert Védrine and Anatoly Chernayev have been particularly useful for the elaboration of this chapter. Scholars working on the end of the Cold War have briefly mentioned the Baltic Question in the context of tensions between Lithuania and the USSR in spring 1990. This chapter has especially benefitted from the works of Frédéric Bozo and Mary E. Sarotte, which have helped the author to see the events described

---

3   Amongst them: Richard J. Krikus, *Showdown: The Lithuanian Rebellion and the Breakup of the Soviet Empire* (Washington, DC: Brasseys, 1997); Rasma Karklins, *Ethnopolitics and the Transition to Democracy: The Collapse of the USSR and Latvia* (Washington, DC: Woodrow Wilson Center Press, 1994); Ainius Lasas, "Bloody Sunday: What Did Gorbachev Know About the January 1991 Events in Vilnius and Riga?," *Journal of Baltic Studies* 38, 2 (2007): 179–194: V. Stanley Vardys and Judith Sedaitis, *Lithuania: The Rebel Nation* (Boulder: Westview Press, 1997); David Pryce-Jones, *The War That Never Was: Fall of the Soviet Empire, 1985–91* (London: Weidenfeld & Nicolson, 1995); Astrid S. Tuminez, "Nationalism, Ethnic Pressures, and the Breakup of the Soviet Union," *Journal of Cold War Studies*, 5, 4 (2003): 81–136; Daina Stukuls Eglitis, *Imagining the Nation: History, Modernity, and Revolution in Latvia* (University Park: Pennylvania State University Press, 2002); R. Kh. Simonyan, "Strany Baltii v gody Gorbachevskoi perestroiki," *Novaia i noveishaia istoriia*, 2 (2003): 44–65; William E. Watson, *The Collapse of Communism in the Soviet Union* (Westport, Conn: Greenwood, 1998).
4   From the US: Addison Baker and Thomas M. DeFrank, *The Politics of Diplomacy: Revolution, War, and Peace, 1989–1992* (New York: Putnam, 1995); Michael R. Beschloss and Strobe Talbott, *At the Highest Levels: The Inside Story of the End of the Cold War* (Boston: Little, Brown, 1994); George Bush and Brent Scowcroft, *A World Transformed* (New York: Knopf, 1998); George H. W. Bush, *All the Best, George Bush: My Life in Letters and Other Writings* (New York: Scribner, 1999); Robert L. Hutchings, *American Diplomacy and the End of the Cold War: An Insider's Account of US Diplomacy in Europe, 1989–1992* (Baltimore: The Johns Hopkins University Press, 1997); Jack Matlock, *Autopsy on an Empire: The American Ambassador's Account of the Collapse of the Soviet Union* (New York: Random House, 1995). From France: Jacques Attali, *Verbatim*, vol. III (Paris: Fayard, 1995); Roland Dumas, *Le Fil et La Pelote: Memoires* (Paris: Plon, 1996); Hubert Védrine, *Les Mondes de Francois Mitterand: a l'Elysée, 1981–1995* (Paris: Fayard, 1996). From Germany: Helmut Kohl, *Je Voulais l'Unité de l'Allemagne* (Paris: Éd. de Fallois, 1997); From Sweden: Lars Peter Fredén, *Baltijas brīvības ceļš un Zviedrijas diplomātija 1989–1991* (Rīga: Atēna, 2007); Sten Anderson, *I de lugnaste vattnen...* (Stockholm: Tiden, 1993); From Finland: Mauno Koivisto, *Witness to History: The Memoirs of Mauno Koivisto, President of Finland 1982-1994* (Carbondale: Southern Illinois University Press, 1997); From the UK: Margaret Thatcher, *The Downing Street Years* (New York: Harper Audio, 1993).

in the context of German Reunification and European construction. For instance, Bozo's analysis of the Franco-German joint letter to the Lithuanian president as an attempt to improve Franco-German relations has inspired the present author to focus more fully on the German factor when analysing French attitudes toward the Baltic Question.[5] Kristina Spohr has worked on German policy regarding the Baltic Question and published a very interesting article on Western reactions in the face of the struggle for Baltic independence.[6] Meanwhile, Mark Kramer has analysed the impact that the fall of socialist regimes in Eastern Europe had on the Soviet republics, especially Lithuania, Latvia and Estonia.[7] The present chapter focuses on French reactions to the Baltic claims for independence, which are not discussed by Kramer and mentioned only very briefly, without using primary sources, by Spohr.

In 2011, German scholar Tilo Schabert published an essay on Franco-Baltic relations during the presidency of François Mitterrand.[8] As such, the present chapter does not focus exclusively on the attitudes of the French President (already covered by Schabert), but relates them to the reactions of the press, French diplomats, Foreign Ministry officials and members of the National Assembly. The Baltic example shows that even though the President of the Republic determines the foreign policy of France, he is obviously unable to control

---

5   Mary Elise Sarotte, *1989: The Struggle to Create Post-Cold War Europe* (Princeton: Princeton University Press, 2011); Frédéric Bozo, *Mitterrand, La Fin de la guerre froide et L'unification Allemande: de Yalta à Maastricht* (Paris: Odile Jacob, 2005), 250–251.
6   Kristina Spohr-Readman, *Germany and the Baltic Problem After the Cold War: The Development of a New Ostpolitik, 1989-2000* (London and New York: Routledge, 2004); Kristina Spohr-Readman, "The Baltic Question in West German Politics, 1949–90," *Journal of Baltic Studies* 38, 2 (2007): 153–178; Kristina Spohr-Readman, "Between Political Rhetoric and Realpolitik Calculations: Western Diplomacy and the Baltic Independence Struggle in the Cold War Endgame," *Cold War History* 6, 1 (2006): 1–42. See also her contribution in John Hiden, Vahur Made, and David J. Smith, *The Baltic Question during the Cold War* (London and New York: Routledge, 2008), 100–133.
7   Mark Kramer, "The Collapse of East European Communism and the Repercussions Within the Soviet Union (Part 1)," *Journal of Cold War Studies* 5, 4 (2003): 178–256; Mark Kramer, "The Collapse of East European Communism and the Repercussions Within the Soviet Union (Part 2)," *Journal of Cold War Studies* 6, 4 (2004): 3–64; Mark Kramer, "The Collapse of East European Communism and the Repercussions Within the Soviet Union (Part 3)," *Journal of Cold War Studies* 7, 1 (2005): 3–96.
8   Tilo Schabert, "France and the Baltic States during the Presidency of François Mitterrand," *Baltic Worlds* 2 (2011): 8–14.

everything, and thus decisions on smaller questions are influenced and sometimes even determined by other actors.

While the present author agrees entirely with Schabert's thesis that Mitterrand supported the idea of finding a balance between the interests of the Soviet Union and the Baltic States, she cannot agree with the contention that Mitterrand was continuously willing to be involved in Baltic-Soviet relations. On the contrary, this chapter argues that the Baltic issue *per se* was not important for France at the presidential level and that France was cautiously adjusting its policy to the very prudent German position in order either to support Gorbachev or to work on Franco-German cooperation. In the same way, this chapter will demonstrate that France's recognition of Baltic independence in August 1991 was not (as Schabert argues) the logical culmination of a consistent policy toward the Baltic States. Rather, it represented a drastic change of sides in the conflict between Gorbachev and the Balts that can be explained only by putting this decision into an international as well as a French domestic context.

This chapter is based on still classified French Presidential and Diplomatic Archives that the author has been able to consult with special permission. Documents from the Archives of the Bank of France, George Bush Library as well as Latvian and Estonian archives are also used. All in all, these documents reveal the variety of ways in which the Baltic Question was perceived by those who had a voice in French foreign policy.

2. French Policy towards the Baltic Claims for Independence, August 1989–August 1991

François Mitterrand's claim that "we are in a terrible contradiction. Our interests are in keeping Gorbachev where he is, and in supporting Lithuanian independence" describes well the French position in 1990. In general France was favourably disposed towards Baltic aspirations for independence, but at the same time it was a strong supporter of Mikhail Gorbachev. The terrible contradiction that Mitterrand spoke about arose from the fast escalating conflict between Gorbachev and the Lithuanian, Latvian and Estonian leadership.

The Velvet Revolutions and the fall of the socialist bloc had a considerable impact on the psyche of Lithuanians, Latvians and Estonians and raised hopes that their drive for independence would not be crushed by force.[9] This optimism was largely based on how the Balts perceived their relations with the Soviet Union. Lithuanians, Latvians and Estonians emphasised that their states had been illegally annexed in 1940 and were therefore not formally part of the USSR. As was stated later by Vytautas Landsbergis, the leader of the Lithuanian independence movement *Sąjūdis*: "We were occupied and wanted to become free. (...) The USSR was not made up of fifteen republics but at most twelve. The other three were independent countries that has been invaded."[10] Thus, from the point of view of the Balts, Gorbachev could and should "let them go" in the same way that he had other Eastern European States which did not form part of the USSR.

The Soviet leadership obviously did not share this understanding of the situation. For Mikhail Gorbachev, the Baltic States were an integral part of the Soviet state. Thus, after Lithuania had proclaimed its independence on 11 March 1990, the Kremlin promptly established an oil and gas embargo against it. On 30 March, Estonia's Supreme Council ruled that the USSR had no legal authority and declared the start of a gradual transition toward independence. Although the Estonian approach was far less radical than the proclamation of Lithuanian independence, Gorbachev similarly threatened Estonia with an embargo. On 4 May, the Supreme Council of Latvia also declared the annexation of Latvia by the USSR illegal and decided to start a transition toward full independence. In an attempt to obtain Gorbachev's support, Anatolijs Gorbunovs, President of the Latvian Supreme Council, sent the Soviet leader an emotional letter arguing that Baltic independence was a logical result of Gorbachev's reforms:

> "Five years ago you were brave enough to take the historic step that began a new era. [...] we believed in you, we followed you [...] The statement of 4 May opens the door for

---

9   Archie Brown, *The Gorbachev Factor* (New York: Oxford University Press, 1996), 194.
10 Vytautas Landsbergis, *Un Peuple sort de prison* (Vilnius: Baltijos Kopija, 2007), 302–303.

a transitional period, a period of honest dialogue. We believe that our neighboring States are facing a new phase of close economic, political and personal cooperation."[11]

Gorbachev perceived the Baltic drive for independence not as the consequence of the democratisation process he had started, but as a betrayal, and responded with two executive orders declaring the Estonian and Latvian statements invalid.

The problem that the West had to face in this situation is effectively summarised in a note that Spain, then president of the European Economic Community (hereafter EEC), sent to its partners already in December 1989:

> "The Western world is faced with an obvious contradiction: either lose this opportunity to support the Baltic states, with the consequent breakdown of the principles held until today (non-recognition of the annexation), or rather support openly the Baltic claims for independence, reducing Gorbachev's maneuverability and creating new difficulties for *perestroika*."[12]

In the French case, as seen in Mitterrand's "contradiction" remark, the name of Gorbachev came before that of Lithuania. For France, supporting Mikhail Gorbachev was a more important task than supporting the Baltic States. The caution of French decision makers in the face of the Baltic claims for independence was not a French specificity, but part of a broader Western attitude toward the problem of Soviet nationalities.

In 1990, the main goal of Western policy toward the USSR was to preserve the relationships developed since the arrival of Mikhail Gorbachev in the Kremlin, and to ensure that he remained at the head of the USSR. This attitude can be explained by a series of objectives Western countries hoped to achieve in the short term, but also by expectations and fears about the long-term fate of the USSR and Europe. During spring 1990, these short-term objectives were to achieve the "grand bargain" on the Reunification of Germany between the West and the Soviet Union, which necessarily involved maintaining good relations

---

11 Letter from Anatolijs Gorbunovs, Chairman of the Supreme Council of the Republic of Latvia to the President of the USSR Mikhail S. Gorbachev, Rīga, 4 May 1990, State Archives of Latvia (LVA), f.270, a.8, I.8, 158.
12 COREAU (Correspondance Européenne), origine: Madrid, destinataire: Ministère des Affaires Etrangères de la France, Madrid, le 16 janvier 1990, French Diplomatic Archives, URSS (1986–1990), 6592.

with the USSR.[13] American President George Bush was concerned not only with achieving the accession of a united Germany to NATO, but also about arms limitation talks with the Soviet Union. For German Chancellor Helmut Kohl, the reunification of Germany was of course the most important issue, and he did everything to avoid any possible links between the German and the Baltic Questions.[14] In May 1990 Kohl went as far as to ask Lithuanian Prime Minister Kazimiera Prunskiene to put on hold Lithuanian national aspirations so that they would not jeopardise the realisation of German ones.[15] Obviously, the Balts had no wish to do this. Just as the whole of Eastern Europe did not want to continue to live under undemocratic regimes for the sake of general stability,[16] or the Japanese did not care about the success or failures of *Perestroika* but about the Kuril Islands,[17] the main concern of the Balts was their independence.

As for France, the Baltic Question was never crucial. Historically it never had strong links with the Baltic nations and the Lithuanian, Latvian and Estonian communities in France were very small. As observed by Yves Plasseraud, after 1945 "(...) the public lost the memory of the Baltic states and one only spoke about the peoples living on the periphery of USSR as national minorities that seemed to always have belonged to the Soviet Union."[18] Meanwhile, good relations with Germany were extremely important for France in the context of ongoing negotiations on German Reunification and European integration. As a result, Mitterrand seized the opportunity to boost Franco-German relations by elaborating a common *Ostpolitik* on an issue that was far from being crucial for France.

In the long term, Western leaders were concerned about the uncertain future of the USSR. Bush, Mitterrand and Kohl agreed that Gorbachev must resist the

---

13 Bozo, *Mitterrand*, 211.
14 Spohr-Readman, "Between Political Rhetoric and Realpolitik Calculations," 17 & 24.
15 Sarotte, *1989*, 158.
16 Pierre Grosser, *1989, L'Année où le monde a basculé* (Librairie Académique Perrin, 2009).
17 Sarotte, *1989*, 158.
18 Yves Plasseraud, "La Connaissance de l'Estonie en France," in: Antoine Chalvin (ed), *France-Estonie, regards mutuels: Actes du colloque franco-estonien, Tallinn-Tartu, 16–20 juin 1991* (Association France-Estonie, 1997), 115.

intense pressure he faced from Soviet conservatives.[19] The spectre of a *coup d'état* in Moscow pushed Western leaders to avoid as far as possible the destabilisation of Gorbachev's position. Yet, the independence of the Baltic States endangered not only Gorbachev's power, but also the integrity of the USSR, and the fall of the USSR was considered dangerous for security and stability in Europe. The fear of seeing the Soviet empire riven by civil wars, as well as concern about the future of the Soviet nuclear arsenal led Western leaders to be extremely cautious regarding the possible disintegration of the Soviet Union.[20] François Mitterrand's feelings on the question can be well illustrated by the reflection he made to Anatolijs Gorbunovs, the acting President of Latvia, in May 1991:

> "Are we going to witness a general break—up of Europe? Even if it's for a just cause, we wonder what will emerge from this disorder? A destabilisation of the whole continent."[21]

One would think that in such a situation, Baltic claims for independence could find no support in France. However, this was not the case. Several factors played in favour of the Baltic States. First, François Mitterrand had inherited a diplomatic tradition that he could not change and which required the French president to speak in favour of the independence of the Baltic countries. This tradition was the non-recognition of the annexation of the Baltic countries. The annexation of Lithuania, Latvia and Estonia by the Soviet Union in 1940 was considered illegal not only by the Balts themselves, but by most Western countries. On 23 July 1940, the United States protested for the first time against the occupation of Latvia, Estonia and Lithuania that took place on 16–17 June 1940. Basing its position on the Stimson doctrine, enacted in 1931 during the

---

19 Bush and Scowcroft, *A World Transformed*, 215; "Deutsch-französische Konsultationen, Paris, 26. April 1990," in: *Dokumente zur Deutschlandpolitik. Deutsche Einheit Sonderedition aus den Akten des Bundeskanzleramtes 1988/90*, (München: R. Oldenbourg Verlag, 1998), 1056.

20 Védrine, *Les Mondes*, 483; John T. Wooley, Gerhard Peters, Remarks and a Question-and-Answer Session at a White House Briefing for the Board of Directors of the National Newspaper Association, http://www.presidency.ucsb.edu/ws/?pid=18258 (accessed 23 December 2011).

21 Présidence de la République, Entretien du Président de la République avec M. Gorbunovs, Président de la République de Lettonie, le 16 mai 1991 à 18H, Archives Nationales, 5 AG 4/ CD 314, dossier 13.

occupation of Manchuria, the American government stated that according to the principle *ex injuria jus non oritur*, no territorial changes effected by force could be recognised as legitimate.[22]

In general, France (like all Western European states except Spain, the Netherlands and Sweden) followed the American example, but its positions were less firm and clear. Its stand on the Baltic Question was taken only when the governments were faced with practical problems related to the legal status of the Baltic States, such as Baltic assets in its banks and Baltic property on French soil. In 1932, Latvia and Lithuania deposited in the Bank of France 999 kg and 2,246 kg of gold respectively. After 1944, the Soviet Union, considering itself the owner of the Baltic property, demanded that the gold be transferred to Moscow. France refused to do so and maintained this position throughout the Cold War. However, the fact that the buildings of the Baltic embassies had already been given to the USSR in 1940 and then again in 1945 shows that this firm stand on the gold owed more to the institutional culture of the Bank of France than it did to the official position of the French Republic itself.[23]

In 1954, when the Bank of France questioned the Ministry of Foreign Affairs about the official French position regarding the Baltic States, the latter declared that it would give an official response only at the request of a court.[24] Internal correspondence of French institutions from the 1970s shows that for French

---

22 Ineta Ziemele, *State Continuity and Nationality: The Baltic States and Russia. Past, Present and Future as Defined by International Law*, (Leiden, Boston: Martinus Nijhoff Publishers, 2005), 22.
23 On 11 August 1940, Molotov informed the Ambassador of France in Moscow that the diplomatic and consular buildings of the Baltic States must be handed over to the USSR before 25 August 1940. Meanwhile, representatives of the Baltic States in Paris received an order from the new ministries of foreign affairs of their countries, now Soviet republics, to leave the Legations. Baltic diplomats refused to hand over the keys of their Legations to the Ambassador of the USSR, but declared they were ready to give them to the French authorities. On 14 August 1940, representatives of the Baltic Legations gave the keys to the Prefect of Police of Paris. Following the instructions of the Nazi authorities, the Prefect in turn gave the keys to the Soviet Union on 25 August 1940. After the war between Nazi Germany and the Soviet Union began, the Germans occupied the Baltic delegations. After the Liberation, the French government gave the buildings to the Soviet Embassy.
24 Le Gouverneur de la Banque de France à Monsieur le Ministre des Finances, le 11 octobre 1954, Archives de la Banque de France, Direction des études, N° bordereau: 1397199403, N° boîte: 7, 2.

diplomats and other civil servants, it was obvious that France did not recognise the annexation; however, no official declarations were made.[25] Only in 1975, when France had to sign the Final Act of Helsinki, did the President of the French Republic state in vague terms that "the text signed does not imply the recognition of situations which it would not have recognised otherwise".[26] Nevertheless, this statement did not make the headlines in the French press.

It was only in 1987, when the activities of the Baltic independence movements attracted the interest of French journalists, that they slowly started to reintroduce the Baltic Question to public debates. In the period from 1987 to 1989 news from Estonia, Latvia and Lithuania was mainly framed in terms of a discussion about nationalist movements at the Soviet periphery. The historical origins of the Baltic problem were evoked, but they were not discussed any more than other aspects of the Baltic drive for independence such as the situation of Lithuanian Catholics, protests by the Russian speaking part of the population in Estonia, Russification in Rīga, or Baltic economic performance.

The turning point came on 23 August 1989, when the Baltic Way[27] efficiently communicated to the World the main argument for independence. In the following days, French newspapers retransmitted the Estonian, Latvian and Lithuanian message to the French society. *Le Monde* and *Libération* explained why the existence of the Molotov– Ribbentrop pact allowed the Balts to question the legality of the annexation of their countries.[28] In *Le Figaro,* Pierre Bocev highlighted the dilemma presented to the Kremlin by the relevance of Baltic arguments.[29] Olivier Weber (*Le Point*) concluded that "the desire for independence has a legal basis in the Baltics."[30] Finally, *La Croix* stated that "the Soviet occupation in the Baltic States has come to an end." Only the newspaper *l'Humanité*, the organ of French Communist Party, claimed that there was no link

---

25 See: Archives de la Banque de France, Direction des relations internationales, Direction générale des études et relations internationales 1940-1992, N° bordereau 1489200403.
26 Note a/s: des pays Baltes, French Presidential Archives; 5 AG 4/CD 242, Dossier 4.
27 A human chain from Tallinn to Vilnius via Rīga, organised to commemorate the 50th anniversary of the Molotov –Ribbentrop Pact.
28 "Les Pays baltes contestent la légalité de leur rattachement à l'URSS," *Le Monde,* 24 August 1989; "600,000 baltes marchent contre L'annexion," *Libération,* 24 August 1989.
29 Pierre Bocev, "Le Kremlin face à L'histoire," *Le Figaro,* 28 August 1989.
30 Olivier Weber, "Le Défi des pays baltes," *Le Point,* 3 September 1989.

between the annexation of the Baltic countries and the Molotov—Ribbentrop Pact.[31]

As the situation in the Baltics became increasingly tense towards the end of 1989, French journalists and the opposition started to question the policy of the French Republic regarding the Baltic Question. In response, President Mitterrand and the Minister of Foreign Affairs emphasised more and more often that France had never recognised Baltic annexation, as well as the fact that Lithuanian and Latvian gold was still in the Bank of France.[32] Ironically, by force of repetition, this narrative (which was largely intended to cover for French caution and inaction in the face of the Baltic drive for independence) popularised the idea of the illegality of Soviet power in the Baltic.

Consequently, French leaders became trapped in their own discourse.[33] The non-recognition policy and all the historical aspects of the Baltic problem, which for 50 years were minor issues concerning only particular diplomats and civil servants, suddenly became part of public debates. Moreover, Mitterrand's perception of the Baltic Question was far from being the only way this issue was regarded among those who aspired to a voice in French policy. The strongest critics came from the opposition in the National Assembly and French Senate. The right-wing parties, *l'Union pour la Démocratie Française* and *Rassemblment pour la République,* demanded stronger government support for Baltic

---

31 Bernard Frederic, "Les Tensions nationalistes," *l'Humanité*, 25 August 1989.
32 See French Presidential Archives 5AG 4/CD 242, dossier 4: Communiqué de R. Dumas le 12 mars 1990, François Mitterrand "7 sur7", le 23 mars, 1990; Conférence de presse conjointe de François Mitterrand et de Vaclav Havel, le 20 mars 1990; Conférence de presse conjointe de Monsieur François Mitterrand, Président de la République Française et de Monsieur Georges Bush, Président des Etats Unis, Key Largo, le 19 avril 1990; Conférence de presse conjointe de Monsieur François Mitterrand, Président de la République et de Monsieur Helmut Kohl, Chancelier de la République Fédérale d'Allemagne à l'issue des 55ème consultations franco-allemandes, Palais de l'Elysée, le 26 avril; Présidence de la République, Service de Presse, Conférence de Presse conjointe de Monsieur François Mitterrand Président de la République et de Michail Gorbatchev, Président de l'Union des Républiques Socialistes Soviétiques, Moscou— Vendredi le 25 mai 1990.
33 Spohr-Readman ("Between Political Rhetoric and Realpolitik Calculations," 29) notes that "In the Baltic context, most Western governments appeared locked into a Cold War rhetoric and thus into Cold War policy, when their new *Realpolitik* priorities clearly lay elsewhere." This idea is certainly true in the American case, but the Baltic Question was not a part of French Cold War discourse.

independence and often recalled the illegality of Soviet actions in 1940 and the French non-recognition policy.[34] In the summer of 1990, a parliamentary group of deputies (opposition parties and the ruling Socialist Party) supporting Baltic independence was established in the French Senate and National Assembly.[35] During the period 1990–1991, members of these two groups helped to organise visits by Baltic officials to Paris and became advocates for the Baltic cause in France.[36] One of their lines of approach carried deep historical and symbolical meaning: authorised by the governments of the three Baltic States, Michel Pelchat, the president of the group at the National Assembly, took to court the case of the Baltic embassies previously handed over to the USSR.[37]

At the same time, members of different branches of the French Foreign Service seemed more inclined than President Mitterrand to consider Baltic arguments. Moreover, French diplomats in Moscow who were circumspect regarding the rapid Baltic push for independence seemed more understated when it came to the historical explanation behind the Baltic campaign.[38] By the end of 1989, the chief of the Soviet Affairs Subdivision of the French Ministry of Foreign Affairs stated that Baltic claims had strong moral legitimacy precisely because of the

---

34 Assemblée Nationale, Constitution du 4 octobre 1958, 9e Législature, Seconde session ordinaire de 1989-1990, (4e séance), 1e séance du mercredi 4 avril 1990, Politique de la France à l'égard des Pays de l'Est, 72.
35 Communiqué Association Parlementaire France–Pays baltes, Paris, le 28 juin 1990, Estonian Diplomatic Archives, Taustamaterjal Prantsusmaa, 1990-1991, Box 4.1.3; Groupe d'études sur l'Estonie, La Lettonie et Lithuanie, Estonian Diplomatic Archives, Taustamaterjal Prantsusmaa, 1990-1991, Box 4.1.3.; Michel Pelchat, Député de l'Essone à V. Landsbergis, Président du Conseil Suprême de Lituanie, Paris, le 25 juillet, 1990, Latvian Diplomatic Archives, Box 1990_39_216.
36 Michel Pelchat, Député de l'Essone à François Mitterrand, Président de la République, ND, Latvian Diplomatic Archives, Box 1990_39_216.
37 Lettre du Ministre des Affaires Etrangères de l'Estonie Lennart Meri à Michel Pelchat, Président de la Groupe d'Études sur les Pays Baltes à l'Assemblée Nationale, Tallinn, le 22 avril 1991.
38 L'Ambassadeur de France en URSS à S.E. Monsieur le Ministre d'Etat, Ministre des Affaires Etrangères, a/s: mission en Lituanie (10---12 mars1991), French Diplomatic Archives, Europe (1991---1995), URSS 7667; République Française, Ambassade de France en URSS, note a/s: Lituanie et question balte, Moscou le 10 mai 1990, French Diplomatic Archives, Europe (1991–1995), URSS 6686.

INTERNATIONAL REACTIONS   167

way the Baltic States were attached to the USSR in 1940.[39] The analyst of the Ministry's Analysis and Prevention Centre also explained that the Yalta system could not be considered to have been destroyed as long as the Baltic States had not recovered their independence.[40] The most favourable point was made by the Department of Legal Affairs at the *Quai d'Orsay*, namely that:

> "(...) in our opinion the Baltic States still exist. (...) The recognition that we granted to these States after the 1914 War is still valid. In our view, the legal personality of these States has survived the annexation, even though these States have not exercised their sovereignty."[41]

All in all, as claimed by Aina Nagobads-Ābols, the Representative of Latvia in Paris in 1990–1991 and later Ambassador, the Balts found in the Ministry of Foreign Affairs people who were a "gift of fortune" for their cause.[42] Working day-to-day with Soviet affairs, they were more favourable to Baltic independence, and sometimes even personally attached to it.[43]

Ideas that circulated at the Ministry level reached the President via a report written by Jacques Blot, Director of the European Affairs Department. This document, entitled "The conflict of two legitimacies", criticised the French approach to the Baltic problem, judging it too Soviet-oriented. Firstly, Jacques Blot described the two existing points of view—the Baltic and the Soviet—about what implications history carried for the actual legal status of the Baltic States. His second observation was that these conflicting points of view were leading to

---

39 Ministère des Affaires Étrangères. Direction d'Europe. Le Sous Directeur d'URSS. République Française. Paris, le 22 septembre 1989, French Presidential Archives, 5AG4 / CD 242 dossier 4.
40 Ministère des Affaires Étrangères, Centre d'analyse et de prévention, note a/s: de "L'Etat de droit au droit de l'Etat" ou la Lituanie martyre, Paris le 16 janvier 1991, Europe (1991–1995), URSS 7667.
41 Ministère des Affaires Étrangères, Direction des affaires juridiques, rédacteur Mr. D'Haussy, note pour la Direction des affaires politiques, objet: la position française à l'égard des Républiques Baltes, le 9 mars 1990, Archives Nationales, 5 AG 4/CD 242, dossier 4, p. 1.
42 Aina Nagobads–Ābols, *Parīze, Madride, Lisabona Un Atpakaļ Rīgā*, (Rīga: Zinātne, 2000), 36.
43 Lettre de René Roudaut, sous---directeur de la sous---direction URSS à Lennart Meri, Ministre des Affaires Étrangères de l'Estonie, sans date, Estonian Diplomatic Archives, Taustamaterjal Prantsusmaa, 1990---1991, Box 4.1.3.

Soviet repression in the Baltics and that France had to have a plan of action in case force was used. As Blot explained:

> "If the current escalation continues, soft in its progression, implacable in its fatality, we would be forced to imperceptibly accept the unacceptable: the crushing of the desire for freedom of nations whose annexation by the Soviet Union we have never recognised."[44]

The President commented that the report expressed "an interesting point of view."[45] Still, he did not decide to follow Blot's guidelines for a stronger stand on the Baltic Question. Instead, when publicly speaking about it, he tried to embrace both the Soviet and the Baltic points of view about history and the present. For example, during a press conference in Moscow he stated that "France did not recognise the annexation. This is the history, as is the right legal point of view from the perspective of my country".[46] At the same time, he acknowledged that "today Lithuania is enclosed in the constitutional reality of the Soviet Union. Here we have two views that are hard to reconcile. I do not want to be the judge". Mitterrand repeated similar points of view on several occasions and even told Lithuania's Prime Minister Kazimiere Prunskiene: "This is a clear case; Lithuania has the right to its own sovereignty. But the reality is that Lithuania has been dissolved into the USSR".[47]

The French position regarding the Baltic claims to independence was, therefore, the result of interactions between different actors—the President, the Ministry of Foreign Affairs and members of the National Assembly and Senate. The policy resulting from these interactions can be described as small steps in favour of the Baltic States followed by immediate retractions provoked by fear of destabilising Gorbachev, or by German attempts to downplay the Baltic Question. In April 1990, France and Germany sent a letter to Lithuanian president Landsbergis inviting him to suspend the Lithuanian Declaration of Independence, in order to facilitate negotiations between Lithuania and the USSR. How-

---

44 Direction d'Europe, le Directeur, note a/s.: Pays baltes: le conflit des deux légitimités, le 3 avril 1990, AN, AG 4/CD 242, dossier 4.
45 Direction d'Europe, le Directeur, note a/s.: Pays baltes: le conflit des deux légitimités.
46 Présidence de la République, Conférence de Presse conjointe de François Mitterrand et de Mikhaïl Gorbatchev, Moscou, Vendredi le 25 mai 1990.
47 Présidence de la République, compte-rendu, entretien du Président de la République avec Madame Prunskiene, Premier Ministre de Lituanie, Jeudi le 10 mai 1990 18 h 45; French Diplomatic Archives, AN, 5AG4/DM 48, dossier 11.

ever, Mitterrand refused to act as a mediator in these negotiations when it became clear that the Germans were unwilling to be more involved in the Lithuanian crisis, and that the Soviets were in fact upset by the Franco—German move.[48] In November 1990, France invited the Baltic States to participate in the CSCE meeting in Paris, but when Gorbachev expressed outrage at their presence, the Baltic Ministers had to leave the Conference.[49] In January 1991, Roland Dumas and Hans-Dietrich Genscher sent a letter to Eduard Shevardnadze condemning Soviet use of force against civilians in Vilnius and Rīga and calling it a "blow against democracy and international law."[50] Privately, however, both François Mitterand and Helmut Kohl made sure Mikhail Gorbachev knew that they understood the complexity of the situation in the Baltic and supported him.[51] This policy of small steps and caution only came to an end in August 1991, when the French position radically changed due to the *putsch* in the Soviet Union.[52]

3. Recognition of the Independence of the Baltic States—Consequences of the *Coup* in Moscow

The decision to restore relations between France and the Baltic States after the failed *putsch* in Moscow was influenced by three factors: (1) severe criticism from the French press and parliamentary opposition regarding the way

---

48 République Française, Ministère des Affaires Etrangères, Direction d'Europe, Paris, le 9 mai 1990, note a/s: l'occident face aux évènements en Lituanie, 4; Lettre de V. Landsbergis à F. Mitterrand et la correspondance du côté français concernant cette lettre. Le 2 mai 1990. Publié dans: Landsbergis, *Un peuple sort de prison*, 427–428.

49 Interview with Roland Dumas, Minister of Foreign Affairs, 1988–1993 (Paris, March 2010); interview with Ambassador Philippe de Suremain, Deputy Director of European Affairs Division, 1989-1991 (Paris, 11 March 2010); interview with Ambassador René Roudaut, Director of the USSR Subdivision, 1990-1992 (Budapest, 15 April 2010).

50 Déclaration commune des ministres des affaires étrangères de France et d'Allemagne, le 13 janvier 1991, AN 5AG 4/CD 242, dossier 4.

51 Yuri Doubinine, *Moscou–Paris dans un tourbillon diplomatique: témoignage d'ambassadeur* (S.l.: Imaginaria, 2002), 368; Christian Neef, "The Gorbachev Files: Did Gorbachev Know About Violent Crackdowns?" *Spiegel Online*, 8, 2011, http://www.spiegel.de/international/europe/the---gorbachev---files---secret---papers---reveal---truth---behind---soviet---collapse---a---779277---2.html.

52 The text of the preceding two paragraphs is substantially reproduced from Una Bergmane and Louis Clerc, "Beyond 'Caution, Pragmatism and Cynicism'? France's Relations with the Eastern Baltic in Times of Crisis (1918-1922; 1988-1992)," *Ajalooline Ajakiri*, 3/4 (2016): 316-317. Permissions to use this material have been obtained.

Mitterrand responded to the *coup d'état* in Moscow, (2) cooperation and competition between France and its European partners including Germany, and finally (3) the redistribution of power in the USSR.

In August 1991 François Mitterrand faced harsh criticism after quoting on national television the letter sent by the organisers of the *putsch* and calling them "the new leaders of the Soviet Union". In his memoirs, Hubert Védrine, diplomatic adviser to François Mitterrand, claimed that by quoting the letter, the President only wanted to "lock the *putschists* into their own promises."[53] Meanwhile, in 1991, the attitude of the French President was perceived as anti-Gorbachev by Russian democratic forces[54] and criticised in France as overly cautious and inappropriate by the press and the opposition led by former President Valéry Giscard d'Estaing.[55] Furthermore, during the hours that corresponded to the day of 19 August in the USA and the night of 19–20 August in Europe, the USA toughened its stand on the issue. Thus, the Elysée Palace had to quickly change the course of its policy. Within the context of this "correction du tir",[56] the Baltic issue reappeared on the international scene: on 20 and 21 August respectively, the Estonian and Latvian Parliaments voted for the end of the transition period and declared the renewal of their independence.

The second factor that influenced the French decision to recognise Baltic independence was the international context and the position of French partners. On 22 August, Iceland became the first country to recognise the independence of the three Baltic States and expressed its willingness to restore diplomatic relations. In the coming days, it was followed by all other Scandinavian countries including Denmark, a member of the European Economic Community. A day later, Belgium announced its intention to renew diplomatic relations with the Baltic States and requested a common EEC Declaration. Most importantly of all, news from Bonn showed that Germany was leaning towards the recognition of the Baltic States. In this situation, France did not want to again be seen

---

53 Védrine, *Les Mondes*, 510–511.
54 Doubinine, *Moscou-Paris*, 401; *Diary of Anatoly Chernyaev 1991*, National Security Archive, p.101 (http://www.gwu.edu/~nsarchiv/NSAEBB/NSAEBB345/The%20Diary%20of%20Anatoly%20 Chernyaev,%201991.pdf).
55 Pierre Favier and Michel Martin-Roland, *La Décennie Mitterrand, tome 4: Les déchirements* (Paris: Le Seuil, 1999), 38.
56 Bozo, *Mitterrand*, 367.

as being slower than its partners and late in its responses to the developments in the East.[57]

Finally, the third factor that influenced the French decision was the attitude of Boris Yeltsin. Following the failure of the *putsch*, the distribution of power in the Soviet Union changed dramatically—Gorbachev's authority radically diminished, and Yeltsin emerged as the *de facto* new leader of the USSR. Previous relations between France and the Russian president were not the warmest, for the same reasons that had pushed France to be cautious when dealing with the Baltic independence question: Yeltsin's activities destabilised the power of Mikhail Gorbachev.[58] However, after the *putsch*, when Yeltsin's political power and influence in the USSR rose considerably, France tried to show its alignment with Yeltsin as well as with Russian democratic forces in general. 24 August was the decisive moment, for on this day Yeltsin, in his capacity as the President of the Federal Republic of Russia, recognised the independence of the three Baltic States and called upon Mikhail Gorbachev to follow his example.[59]

Already on 22 August, the Quai d'Orsay and more specifically the Soviet Affairs Subdivision had insisted that France must recognise the renewal of independence.[60] The Elysée Palace, however, resisted this idea for a further three days. After Yeltsin's move on the evening of 24 August, Roland Dumas, Minister of Foreign Affairs, asked François Mitterrand what position France should now adopt. That same day, René Roudaut, director of the Soviet Affairs Subdivision, conveyed to his superiors information received from intelligence services: the Soviet Army was evacuating its missiles from the territory of the three Baltic States.[61] At that point, the President left the decision to the Minister, answering: "Do as you feel."[62] Thus, the same night, Roland Dumas announced on national

---

57 Interview with Roland Dumas.
58 Bernard Lecomte, Le Bunker. Vingt ans de relations franco-soviétiques (JC Lattès, 1994), 220-222; Doubinine, *Moscou et Paris*, 378.
59 Dokumenti par Latvijas valsts starptautisko atzīšanu, neatkarības atjaunošanu un diplomātiskajiem sakariem 1918–1998 (Rīga: Nordik, 1999), 222-232.
60 Védrine, *Les Mondes*; In his book, the former spokesperson for the Elysée gets confused and describes the events of August 1991 as having taken place in March 1990.
61 Interview with Ambassador René Roudaut.
62 Védrine, *Les Mondes*; Lecomte, *Le Bunker*, 236.

television that France recognised the reestablishment of the independence of the Baltic States and that a formal Declaration would be adopted at an extraordinary meeting of the European Community.

Philippe de Suremain, Deputy Director of the European Affairs Division, was sent to the Baltics to communicate Dumas' message in person to the three acting Baltic presidents. On 29 August, Dumas' plane landed in Vilnius and the French Minister proceeded to visit all three countries. At the time, the French press noted with some irony that Roland Dumas was the first "in the race to Vilnius."[63] French historian Suzanne Champonnois would later describe Dumas' trip as an attempt to "come to the rescue of victory."[64] At the same time, it must be emphasised that when the EEC and France recognised the independence of the Baltic States and the French Minister visited the three capitals, neither the Soviet Union nor the United States had yet recognised their independence and the situation on the ground was still very unclear. When, on the evening of 26 August, Philippe de Suremain arrived in Lithuania from Warsaw, it was not obvious whether the border he crossed separated Poland and the USSR or Poland and the Republic of Lithuania. When the French diplomat asked the person who checked his passport if he represents the Soviet Union, the border guard answered "Yes, for the time being." When Roland Dumas arrived in Vilnius three days later, two border guards, one Lithuanian, the other Soviet, argued for a considerable time over which of them had the right to verify the French Minister's passport.[65] These incidents showed that the debate about who possessed the sovereign power in Lithuania was not yet over.

4. Conclusion

In conclusion, we can say that during 1989–1991, France saw the Baltic Question as closely linked to the question of the future of the Soviet Union. In the perception of the French President, Baltic independence risked destabilising the Soviet Union and its President. For François Mitterrand, it was in the best interests of France and Europe to preserve the Soviet Union as such, and to

---

63 Pierre Haski, "Dumas premier dans la course vers Vilnius," *Libération*, 30 August 1991.
64 Suzanne Champonnois, "French Policy towards the Baltic States 1939–1990: from Abandonment to Reunion" in: John Hiden, Vahur Made and David J. Smith, eds., *The Baltic Question during the Cold War* (London, New York: Routledge, 2008), 98.
65 Interview with Roland Dumas.

maintain Gorbachev as its president. In this situation, international norms, pressure from the opposition and the differences between the Quai d'Orsay and the Elysée played in favour of the Baltic States.

At the time of the recognition of independence, internal struggles between Mitterrand and the opposition and competition between France and its European partners all played in the favour of the Baltics. Yet the most important factor remained the redistribution of power in the USSR. The victory of the Russian Democrats, who had been even more neglected by the French Presidency than the Balts, diminished the French desire and need to help Gorbachev. Thus, the victory of the Russian Democrats was at the same time the victory of the Balts. It is frequently overlooked that history would have been very different if Yeltsin had not supported the independence of Estonia, Latvia and Lithuania.

"You Are Not the People": Revisiting Citizenship and Geopolitics

Li Bennich-Björkman, Uppsala University

1. Introduction

In the great transformation from Soviet republics to independent states, Latvia, along with neighbouring Estonia, did not opt for what at the time was called the "zero option" approach to granting citizenship. This distinguished them from other former Soviet republics, which, in line with the *jus soli* principle, basically offered citizenship to all residents then living on their territories. Instead, the political majority in Latvia decided to restrict entitlement to citizenship to those who either had been citizens before 1940 or who had close relatives who had been. This *jus sanguinis* principle was justified by the legal argument that what was being effected was in fact the restoration rather than the creation of an independent state. The constitutional choices made resulted in an electorate dominated, and still so, by the 'titular' Latvian nationality (living both in Latvia and abroad), since most Russian-speaking residents—constituting the major minority—were immigrants or descendants of immigrants who had arrived during the 1940s and 1950s. Post-war immigrants and their descendants were required to apply for citizenship through a naturalisation process requiring language tests and declarations of loyalty. As such, they did not automatically become members of the political community of the new Latvia, but rather non-citizens or, in certain cases, citizens of Russia. Despite international pressure, Latvia has clung to its chosen citizenship policies, even if these were appreciably softened over the course of some years.

The third Baltic state of Lithuania, which had frequently adopted the most nationalistic attitudes during the struggle for independence in the late 1980s, did not choose this path. All who resided in Lithuania at the time of independence were given the opportunity to apply for citizenship according to *jus solis*. Lithuania's demographic situation was, however, quite different. The Soviet period had not changed the ethnic composition as radically as it had in Latvia and Estonia. Over 80% of the population were ethnic Lithuanians, and the minorities included not only Russians (who constituted about 10%), but also among others Poles. For Latvia and Estonia, the Russian-speaking minorities were large, between 30 and 40%. The Central Asian republic of Kazakhstan constituted one of the few parallels in this respect, in that Kazakhs were reduced to slightly less than 50% of the population during the Soviet period, which lasted over 70 years.[1] But, Kazakhstan did not adopt the principle of *jus sanguinis* as the basis for citizenship.

The choice made by Latvia's political leaders was clearly controversial at the time, and was questioned if not from a strictly legal then from a democratic point of view. Because of its willful actions in a situation that was unstable in terms of security policy, Latvia's relations with its powerful neighbour Russia immediately became very tense.[2] The country also ran the risk of having its reputation as a democratic state called into question by the international community—something that would soon become apparent.[3] Latvia has over the years been called an "ethnic" democracy, and is constantly accused by Russia of discriminating against Russian-speakers. In assessing this situation, many authors have claimed that emotions, revenge and justice were the major reasons behind the constitutional choices taken.[4] The famous political scientists

---

[1] The comparison between Latvia and Kazakhstan is not as far-fetched as it might seem, insofar as the theoretical literature points to these two republics as the ones most likely to experience ethnic conflict and violence. Ethnic conflicts have instead become the most profound in Moldova (with the break-away republic of Transnistria). Cf. Pål Kolstoe, *Nasjonsbygging. Russland og de nye statene i öst* (Oslo: Universitetsförlaget, 1999); Pål Kolstoe, "Conclusions," in Pål Kolstoe, (ed.), *National Integration and Violent Conflict in Post-Soviet Societies. The Cases of Estonia and Moldova* (New York: Rowman and Littlefield Publishers, 2002).

[2] See, for example, Rein Ruutsoo, "Hard and Soft Security in the Baltic Sea Region," A Report from a Seminar Held in the Ålands Islands August 29–21, 1997 (Stockholm: The Olof Palme International Center, 1998), 63 & 65; Pami Aalto, *Constructing Post-Soviet Geopolitics in Estonia. A Study in Security, Identity and Subjectivity* (Helsinki University: Department of Political Science, 2001), 40 ff. Lee Kendall Metcalf describes how Yeltsin used strikingly harsh formulations and referred to what took place in Latvia and Estonia as "ethnic cleansing" and a form of "apartheid". The Russian leadership consequently undertook countermeasures and threatened economic sanctions and the suspension of troop withdrawals. Lee Kendall Metcalf, "Outbidding to Radical Nationalists: Minority Policy in Estonia, 1988–1993," *Nations and Nationalism*, 2, 2 (1996), 213–234.

[3] Metcalf, "Outbidding to radical nationalists"; Kjetil Duvold & Sten Berglund, "Democracy, Citizens and Elites," in Sten Berglund & Kjetil Duvold (ed.), *Baltic Democracy at the Crossroads. An Elite Perspective* (Kristiansand: Høgskoleforlaget, 2003), 257.

[4] Snyder, "Nationalism and the Crisis of the Post-Soviet State," *Survival*, spring 1993, 5.

Juan Linz and Alfred Stepan, for instance, have concluded that "In order to understand Estonia's and Latvia's policy in respect to the Russian minority, we must never forget the legacy of totalitarianism and history prior to independence."[5] In a similar vein, Anton Steen has stated that:

> "in Estonia and Latvia the nationalists' fear of the large Russian-speaking minority groups who had settled there mainly during the Soviet period soon challenged the idea of inclusive democracy."[6]

While an outright ethnic dimension in party politics has been downplayed in Estonia, in Latvia it continues to evoke harsh rhetoric and mutual accusations between Latvian and Russian parties.

In this chapter, my purpose is to reconsider the choices on citizenship made during those turbulent and formative years. Whereas the motives of the nationalists have been dominating the picture, the choice of the pragmatists—those politically active in *Tautas Fronte* and elected to the Supreme Councils who initially wanted the zero-option but finally decided otherwise—has yet to be fully explained. Were the pragmatists forced into a process of nationalist outbidding, as has been suggested? Because of the nationalists' accusations of "Soviet friendliness,"[7] did it become politically impossible in the heated and complex historical situation that prevailed to adopt positions that were more open with regard to citizenship?[8] Here, I put forward the argument that geopolitical motives contributed to the provocative position that was ultimately adopted. To say this should not be taken to imply—as is often the case—that local Russian-speakers did not want Latvia to be independent, for many of them supported the demands for sovereignty.[9] Nevertheless, more pragmatic Latvian politicians viewed Russian-speakers as a population group that had strong historical

---

5 Juan Linz and Alfred Stepan, *Problems of Democratic Transition and Consolidation. Southern Europe, South America, and Post-Communist Europe* (Baltimore and London: Johns Hopkins University Press, 1996), 409 & 415.
6 Anton Steen, "Accessing Liberal Compliance? Baltic Elites and Ethnic Positions under New International Conditions," *International Journal on Minority and Group Rights,* 13 (2006), 187.
7 Paul Kolstoe, *Russians in the Former Soviet Republics* (London: Hurst and Company, 1995); Metcalf, "Outbidding to radical nationalists".
8 Linz and Stepan, *Problems of Democratic Transition and Consolidation,* 409.
9 Research by Latvian sociologist Brigita Zepa suggests that 85% of ethnic Latvians and 26% of non-ethnic Latvians opted for independence in 1990. By the time of the March

and cultural ties to the Russian and Slavic cultural sphere, and which consequently regarded a continued close connection to this sphere as a given in the situation that had arisen. Much has been written over the years about the origins, underlying motives and effects of the citizenship policies of the Baltic States and their effects on relations between the ethnic groups in these countries.[10] While the geopolitical explanation has been touched upon by a few researchers before, among them Vello Pettai and Klara Hallik,[11] Rein Ruutsoo[12] and Kjetil Duvold,[13] it has not gained enough attention. The recent developments in Ukraine, where geopolitical division is one of the major hurdles to political integration, shows the importance of geopolitical belonging in the borderlands of Russia and Europe, a space to which the Baltic States also used to belong.

1991 referendum on independence, the figures had grown to 94% and 38% respectively. Brigita Zepa, "Sabiedriskā doma pārejas periodā Latvijā: Latviešu un citlatviešu uzkatu dinamika," *Latvijas Zinātņu Akadēmijas Vēstis*, 10 (1992). Cited in Artis Pabriks and Aldis Purs, eds., *Latvia: The Challenges of Change* (London and New York: Routledge, 2001), 61, 64.

10 There is an extensive literature on citizenship and language policies in Latvia and Estonia, which have attracted great international interest. See, for example, Anatol Lieven, *The Baltic Revolution. Estonia, Latvia, Lithuania and the Path to Indepedence* (New Haven: Yale University Press, 1993); Romuald Misiunas and Rein Taagepera, *The Baltic States. Years of Dependence 1940–1990* (London: Hurst and Company, 1993); Kolstoe, *Russians in the Former Soviet Republics*; Linz and Stepan, *Problems of Democratic Transition and Consolidation*; Metcalf, "Outbidding to radical nationalists"; Mikko, Lagerspetz, *Constructing Post-Communism. A Study in the Estonian Social Problems Discourse,* Turku: Department of Sociology (dissertation), 1996); Aalto, *Constructing Post-Soviet Geopolitics in Estonia*; Vello Pettai and Klara Hallik, "Understanding processes of ethnic control: segmentation, dependency and co-optation in post-communist Europe," *Nations and Nationalism*, 8, 4 (2002), 505-529; and Kjetil Duvold, *Making Sense of Baltic Democracy. Public Support and Political Representation in Nationalising States* (Örebro: Örebro Studies in Political Science 14, 2006).

11 2002, 524. Kolstoe (ed.) 2002 also compares Estonia and Moldova in regard to ethnic integration, with Estonia avoiding ethnic violence while civil war broke out in Moldova in 1992. It is interesting to note that in Moldova, where ethnic violence became a reality, citizenship was based on the constitutional principle of *jus solis*.

12 Ruutsoo, "Hard and Soft Security", 77.

13 Duvold, *Making Sense of Baltic Democracy*, 134, 160 & 166-167. Duvold touches upon the question of why Latvia and Estonia chose *jus sanguinis* and suggests voter-strategic motives. He writes that "If Estonia and Latvia had chosen the so-called zero-option— granting all residents citizenship at the moment of independence—the transition from communism, the introduction of a market economy, and their international political orientation would have been much different" (134).

2. Latvia in the Midst of Geopolitical Uncertainty

In order to better understand and explain what took place, it is thus time to return to the years that are so central to the story—the period between 1990 and 1994, when Latvia and the other Baltic republics shed their skins as controlled units of a centralised empire and once again became independent democracies.

Two elections of great and decisive significance were held during this important period. The first was in March 1990, when Latvia was still part of the Soviet Union; the second was in June 1993 after it had regained its independence. This was also the period in which the new constitution was prepared, with the definition of citizenship being one of the most important questions. Prior to independence, there was a quite broad consensus within the pragmatic leading political strata of both Latvia and Estonia that citizenship should be made inclusive, so that all those who came to the country after World War II would have had the possibility of opting for citizenship without any further conditions, as was the case in the other former Soviet republics.[14] However, a decisive change of opinion took place as preparations were being made for the first post-independence elections.

The 1990 "Supreme Council" Elections

The Popular Front of Latvia (*Latvijas Tautas Fronte*) was formed in October 1988. This was a broad umbrella organisation that gathered together reform-

---

14 As discussed later in this chapter, an updated constitution and full citizenship law for today's Latvia were adopted only after parliamentary elections had taken place. In the interim, the original 1922 constitution was deemed still to be in force following the official declared end of Soviet occupation in May 1990, while a resolution adopted by the Supreme Council in October 1991 conferred renewed rights of citizenship upon all who had held them prior to the Soviet takeover of 1940 (thus excluding Soviet-era settlers and their descendants from participation in the June 1993 elections). On political questions of state continuity and citizenship, see Jouni Reinikainen, *Right Against Right. Membership and Justice in Post-Soviet Estonia* (University of Stockholm: Department of Political Science (dissertation), 1999), 10–11. Some have explained the earlier readiness to follow the line of inclusive citizenship as playing to the gallery in order to garner the support of Russian-speakers (and Western opinion) for the demands for independence. See, for instance, Alexei Semjonov, "Estonia: Nation-Building and Integration: Political and Legal Aspects," in Kolstoe, (ed.), *National Integration and Violent Conflict in Post-Soviet Societies*.

minded communists, intellectuals, cultural workers and various types of activists. Under overwhelming pressure from public opinion, its initially moderate demands for autonomy within the framework of the Soviet Union were quickly radicalised into calls for complete independence. Popular Fronts of this type emerged in a number of Soviet republics, inspired by their Baltic counterparts. In Latvia and Estonia, where communist participation led nationalist forces to consider the popular fronts as illegitimate, parallel and in part competing organisations for popular mobilisation were soon established.[15] Taking Gandhi's Indian independence movement as a model, these were named Citizens' Committees, and the most outspoken nationalists were to be found there. Their aim was to register all who had been citizens before the 1940 occupation and their descendants in order to thereby establish an electorate that was legitimate according to the principle of legal continuity. The Popular Fronts, in contrast, promoted an inclusive line, and gathered together different ethnic groups as well as different ideological perspectives. The Latvian politician and former member of parliament Ruta Marjaša, who was a member of the Popular Front, participated in the constitutional convention, and was a member of the *Latvijas Ceļš* (Latvia's Way) party, recalls that:

> "*Tautas Fronte* was not homogeneous; it consisted of both the rightist, middle, and left. But we had a problem with what the Latvia of the future would look like. The question was whether we should give citizenship to all Latvians (that is, to everyone who lived in Latvia). I had serious doubts about that."[16]

The Communist Party first permitted electoral competition in the local Supreme Soviet elections of February and March 1990. Candidates were put forward by the Communist Party, the Popular Front, and the strongly pro-Moscow *International Front* (*Interfront*). In the process, the Supreme Soviet was re-christened the Supreme Council. These spring 1990 elections came to be decisive for the eventual balance of power between, on the one hand, the opposition that was formed around the popular front and, on the other, the old communist elites (those elements which did not line up on the side of the reform forces). The

---

15 No such parallel organisation emerged in Lithuania, where the local Communist Party had a greater legitimacy and also cooperated more closely with forces working for national independence.
16 Interview with Ruta Marjaša, Member of Latvian Parliament, Rīga, 13 November 2006.

existence of *Interfront* as a third actor in Latvia related to the fact that the local Communist Party lost legitimacy among parts of the Russian-speaking electorate, was greatly weakened, and was considered to be non-competitive.

While many Russian-speakers in Latvia clearly cast their votes for pro-independence forces, those candidates that were strongly loyal to the Soviet Union and Moscow garnered nearly all their support from amongst the Russophone population. Latvian politicians explained this in terms of the Baltic Russians having a different political and cultural allegiance that they did not hesitate to express whenever the possibility to do so arose. The period when elections to the Supreme Council took place was consequently highly tense and polarized; relations between the Baltic States and Moscow were strained, and the survival of the Soviet Union was uncertain. Had the elections been held in calmer and less threatening circumstances, voting patterns amongst Baltic Russians might possibly have been different.

The Citizens' Committees organised elections to a parallel "parliament," the Citizens' Congress, at the same time as the Supreme Council elections were held. Only those who registered as citizens in accordance with the procedure indicated above had the right to vote. After the elections, at least in Estonia, two parallel political structures were formed: The Citizens' Congress, led by Tunne Kelam, and the Estonian Supreme Council, headed by Arnold Rüütel. An agreement between the two in April 1990 resulted in a division of labour: whereas the Supreme Council had a stronger say in matters of economy and social matters (reform policies), the Citizens' Congress got the upper hand in matters of citizenship and border agreements (constitutional policies).[17] Relations between the two bodies were marked by mutual respect, as can be seen from the following assessment by a prominent member of the Congress:

> "I can say that both people by and large, the PF people and the other people were real Estonians: they were looking for the best possible solution for Estonia. But they just had different assessment of the situation."[18]

---

17 Interview with Tunne Kelam, founding Member of the Citizens' Committees, later MEP for *Isamaaliit* (Pro Patria), 21 August 2008.
18 Interview with Trivimi Velliste, Member of Citizens Congress and Estonian Heritage Society, Ambassador, 20 February 2004.

In Latvia, however, the Citizens' Congress did not become an equivalent parallel structure, and the Popular Front-led Supreme Council was more dominant up until 1992.

The 1993 Elections to the Saeima

Latvia declared independence in August 1991. Its first democratic elections as a free state were the June 1993 elections to the *Saeima* (parliament). In contrast to the elections held in 1990, only citizens of the interwar Republic of Latvia and their descendants were now able to vote.[19] Consequently, Baltic Russians on the whole stood outside the political community and had no possibility to exercise political influence. Within the course of two years the atmosphere had thus changed from the more inclusive line of the Popular Front, which had prevailed over the 1990 elections, to a restrictive citizenship policy. The new state had taken a very large and decisive step that had many far-reaching consequences.

Are those researchers correct who maintain that emotional motives, namely, an understandable but as it may seem politically irrational desire for revenge, had gained the upper hand? Were the pragmatic politicians who had dominated the earlier period steamrollered by nationalists in a process that basically no one wanted? Or did this reversal originate in a strategic and rational judgment based on the information *then available* concerning the voting preferences of the Russian-speaking population?

The nationalistic forces—chiefly *Tēvzemei un Brīvībai* (*For Fatherland and Freedom*) and *Latvia's National Independence Party*—gained wind in their sails as the Popular Front weakened during its years in power and split apart. The Citizens' Congress provided a basis for their positions, and there is no doubt that their argumentation—that citizenship for all who lived in the two countries involved an indirect recognition of the legitimacy of the 1940 Soviet annexation along with a series of other consequences concerning, for example, ownership rights to property that had been confiscated—met with sympathy. But there

---

19 See fn. 14 above. The constitutional process in Latvia was somewhat drawn out. It was judged that the new constitution should be approved by the newly elected independent parliament since it was of such central importance. The constitutional legislation was approved by the parliament that was formed after the June 1993 elections.

were also many other significantly less ideological and more pragmatically oriented politicians and parties in the picture.

> "If we would have taken easier way (zero-option), we would not have been in EU and NATO. Why? Because 40% of the population would then be strongly in favour of Moscow and with little or no support for western organisations like EU and NATO. We would have been like Moldova (where a region also is controlled by Russia and where there was civil war and ethnic violence)."[20]

The above quote is from Tunne Kelam, one of the most influential actors on the nationalist side in Estonia during these formative years. Kelam's view conveys the understanding of the Estonian but also the Latvian Citizens' Congress regarding the geopolitical consequences of the "zero option" approach to granting citizenship. Loyalty to the state was interpreted as being loyal to the goal of joining Western institutions. Such loyalty did not exist among the Russian-speaking population, which preferred a geopolitical orientation towards the Commonwealth of Independent States (CIS).[21] Hence, it is highly likely that representatives of the Citizens' Congress could have used these kinds of geopolitical arguments, rather than those based on revenge or "primordial" rights, to convince pragmatists within the Councils about the citizenship legislation.

The pragmatists drew conclusions regarding the question of citizenship also from how voters and parties on the "Russian" side conducted themselves during the period after 1990. Three issues in particular stand out. First, the way Baltic Russians voted in the 1990 Supreme Council elections constituted an important basis for their concerns. It indicated that these voter groups preferred "Moscow-friendly" alternatives to a not insignificant degree. Secondly, it seemed ever more clear that a future association with the West, which was both ardently desired and in principle unquestioned among the Latvian and

---

20 Interview with Tunne Kelam. The diplomat Lars Peter Fredén has written two well-informed books about the liberation of the Baltic countries based upon his own experiences and participation. In his comments on the citizenship question, he calls attention to the fact that the aim of legislation was to avoid giving political influence "to inhabitants whose loyalty was assumed to lie not with the homeland, but with the neighbouring great power" (Lars Peter Fredén, *Återkomster. Svensk säkerhetspolitik and de baltiska ländernas första år i självständighet 1991–1994* (Stockholm: Atlantis, 2006), 95.
21 Interview with Tunne Kelam, 21 August 2008.

Estonian political elites, was not at all viewed with the same degree of enthusiasm by their Baltic Russian counterparts, either amongst elites or the public. Continued cooperation within the framework of what had been the old Soviet Union under Russian dominance was their given alternative. For example, a survey taken in July and August 1990 indicated that the preferred future option for 62% of non-Latvians was that Latvia either remain autonomous within the framework of the Soviet Union, or form a confederation with other (former) Soviet republics. Only 12% of Latvians and Estonians shared these same views— an enormous difference.[22] Among the Russian-speaking groups, people quickly began to categorise the new Baltic States as "nearby foreign countries," with the unstated but understood implications of continued integration which that involved.[23] Hence, the connection to the West that has today become a reality by virtue of EU and NATO membership was far from self-evident.[24]

Third, the way in which the representatives of the Baltic Russians in the Supreme Council conducted themselves, the arguments they used, and the positions they adopted on the questions of vital importance at the time provided additional essential information to the "pragmatists" among Latvian politicians. The rhetoric and bellicose tone of Interfront's representatives in the Supreme Council surprised many: "The Interfront fraction was indeed aggressive and focused on defending the Soviet system and the existing state of affairs", Ruta Marjaša recalls.[25] Anna Seile, a key figure in Latvian politics at that time, shares the same thinking.[26]

In general, the Baltic Russians' preferences at both voter and party levels concerning the geopolitical future of Latvia were that the orientation towards Russia and the other republics of the former Union be continued. This was a deeply

---

22 This survey material collected by Klingeman and Gibowski is reproduced in Linz and Stepan, *Problems of Democratic Transition and Consolidation*, 413.
23 Fredén, *Återkomster*, 108.
24 Compare Duvold (*Making Sense of Baltic Democracy*, 160), who states that while it might appear quite obvious with hindsight that Estonia, Latvia, and Lithuania would be allied with the West, "such scenarios seemed quite far-fetched at the beginning of the 1990s. Given the comprehensive integration with other Soviet republics and Moscow's use of brute force, a more plausible alternative was closer ties to Russia and the newly established Commonwealth of Independent States."
25 Interview with Ruta Marjaša.
26 Interview with Anna Seile, Rīga, 12 November 2006.

disturbing situation for Latvian representatives, who had diametrically opposed geopolitical preferences for swift and unconditional Western integration. Latvian politicians might well have expected—at least considering the information they then had—that the Baltic Russian political representatives would evidently pursue continued integration with Russia and the other new states on the far-flung territory that had been the Soviet Union. Were people now headed towards a situation in which liberation would be combined with continued integration under Russian dominance, albeit in freer forms than previously?

From the perspective of Latvian politicians at that time, a divided electorate and consequently a divided political elite concerning the "geopolitical question"— which most likely could be a consequence of inclusive citizenship—could be devastating for any possibility of gaining future membership in attractive Western organisations. There was initially no strong interest on the part of the EU or NATO that the former "Eastern states," not even the Central European Visegrad countries, should become members. This was instead a process driven by the countries in question. With citizenship laws that excluded the Russian-speaking population groups who had other geopolitical preferences, such possibilities appeared much brighter. It would then be the ethnic Latvian voters who would leave their mark on the governing institutions during the essential years of the 1990s and thereby guarantee a broad consensus on a "return to Europe" policy.

"Pragmatists" within the Popular Front, who still dominated the political scene in 1991 and 1992, thus began to consider the possibility of excluding Baltic Russian voters from further influence, not least against the background of geopolitical questions. The Moscow *putsch* in August 1991 further strengthened the perception that the Soviet Union was weakening.[27] Ruta Marjaša, however, describes the Latvian *Tautas Fronte*, which dominated the Supreme Council, as remarkably divided on whether citizenship should be granted to everyone who lived in Latvia. Several possible alternatives were discussed. She states that:

---

27 Interview with Vello Pettai, journalist with the Estonian Independent/Baltic Independent (1989–90) and Professor of Political Science, University of Tartu, 20 August 2009.

"I was very careful: if we gave everyone the right to vote, would we not soon return to the situation that we wanted to get away from?" She adds that "After long, intense discussion, we decided that by law all former citizens, their children, and their grandchildren would have the right to become citizens. We thus decided who could vote for the next parliament."[28]

3. "You Are Not the People"

Was it a struggle for historical justice and an "immature" desire for retribution that drove forward Latvia's provocative citizenship policies? Many researchers have maintained, and with a certain justification, that this was in fact the case. But why then did Lithuania, which shared the communist fate of its neighbours, not long for this type of revenge? Others have pointed to a fear that the "nation," its language, and its culture would succumb if the Russian-speakers were allowed to be seriously involved in the formation of the new states. But why did not for example the Kazakhs—who like the Latvians were almost a minority in their own country—take a similar decision on the basis of *jus sanguinis*?

Even if the analysis could be taken further, there is enough to suggest that the constitutional process in Latvia involved more than ethnic survival and coming to terms with the "colonial" past. Nationalists and pragmatists came to be united around the decision to apply the principle of legal continuity. Pragmatists made their choice of constitutional alternatives in respect to citizenship for the purpose of ensuring a political consensus for Latvia's future as a Western-oriented country. This also meant a departure, however, from the democratic principles that were regarded as being of symbolically central importance in the repudiation of the former authoritarian regime. Nevertheless, *Realpolitik* carried more weight. Consensus was chosen over democratic inclusion.

The design of the citizenship law and its outcome likely served to indirectly ensure Latvia's remarkably fast and smooth association with the West and its membership in NATO and the EU, as well as rapid and liberal reform policies. From our perspective in time, we regard developments "after the fact" and thus tend to write the history of the winners. Western integration is today firmly established and seems almost self-evident where the Baltic States are concerned. But, as we have seen, things could have been completely different.

---

28 Interview with Ruta Marjaša.

Not only geopolitical aspects should be emphasised. Vello Pettai, who was then a young Estonian-American working for the "Estonian Independent" (later "Baltic Independent"), and is now Professor of Political Science in Tartu, also refers to consequences for reform policies:

> "Mart Laar would never have been elected, and that would have meant much less radical economic reforms. The indirect effects of this choice are quite obvious. The same is true for Latvia, maybe even to a higher extent".[29]

The story of emotional and immature "Baltic nationalists" who could not restrain themselves has long dominated the West's understanding of the political line concerning citizenship that was pursued in Latvia. Why, one may ask? One obvious answer is that the pragmatists have not been particularly eager to defend these choices, while the nationalists proudly wrote "their own" story. Another is that normatively complicated questions are raised when we consider the pragmatists' actions, making the "black and white" condemnation of the choices made in Latvia less straight-forward. Was it wise—in order, for example, to reach a goal that made Western integration and collective security possible—to deviate from what many viewed as fundamental democratic principles? Furthermore, did the exclusion of the Russian-speaking population from the electorate work to prevent ethnic mobilisation, such as that which shook, for example, Moldova with the civil war over Transnistria's secession as a result, or the Ukrainian situation of a geopolitically torn country that clearly is seen today? The answers are far from self-evident. Moreover, EU-membership has had clearly positive effects, including the creation of new opportunities to work in Europe not least of all for young Baltic Russians.

At the same time, however, democracy is inescapably rule not for, but *by* the people who are affected by decisions. Perhaps Latvian and Estonian politicians drew hasty conclusions about how Baltic Russians were going to act. Previous history has indeed shown that people are wiser than the holders of power believe. Nevertheless, what the holders of power believe—regardless of whether it is well-founded—is always essential for the outcome of politics.

---

29 Interview with Vello Pettai.

Post-Soviet Latvia: A Consolidated Democracy in the Third Decade of Independence?

Geoffrey Pridham, University of Bristol

1. What is Democratic Consolidation?

On 21 March 2013 Latvia recorded the 7,884th day since the restoration of its independence in 1991. This was one day more than the length of the first independent republic which lasted from 18 November 1918 to 17 June 1940[1]. Time is obviously one vital factor in a new democracy's achievement of consolidation, although by no means the only one. By and large, this process takes a couple of decades, ranging between two or three depending on the country in question and the extent of its legacy and transition problems. When the Southern European countries were establishing their new democracies nearly four decades ago, there was some debate among transitologists (political scientists analysing transitions to democracy) about the length of consolidation between minimalists and maximalists. The former pointed for example to the brevity of the Colonels' regime of only seven years in Greece, arguing with some justification that this required only a brief transition before becoming established. It does, however, depend on what is exactly understood by the tasks of democratic consolidation.

Whereas democratic transition usually involves mainly elite level decisions, such as constructing the institutions of a new democracy—though popular protests may form part of this early regime change—with democratic consolidation deeper changes are necessary, leading notably to a remaking of the country's political culture that may help to root that new democracy. With the democracies that emerged in Central & Eastern Europe in the early 1990s, the tasks facing their consolidation were considerable and far greater than those in the case of the Southern European new democracies in the later 1970s and the 1980s which involved only replacing one type of political system with another. The previous regime legacies from a near half century of communist rule were more profound than those from the long-lasting Iberian dictatorships by virtue

---
1 Latvian News Agency (LETA), 21 March 2013.

of the nature of the system with its thorough and penetrative mechanisms of one-party control in the cause of socio-economic transformation. In turn, that meant a formidable task in post-communist regime change embracing concurrent political system and economic system replacement, the latter with market economies being introduced following the dismantling of command economies. In some post-communist countries, a third systemic change occurred with the construction of new nation-states following national independence on the collapse of the Soviet Union and of Yugoslavia. Added to these multiple fundamental changes there was the "rebirth of history", as it was called at the time, a phenomenon whereby old historical patterns suppressed under communist rule—notably nationalism and ethnic divisions—reappeared to have a determining effect on the politics of these post-communist countries.

It is hardly surprising, therefore, that post-communist democracies have taken a long time to consolidate and, moreover, that some of them may not yet have achieved this. If Latvia is included among the latter, then this country would not be exceptional. It is essential when assessing the progress of democratic consolidation to focus on broad over-time patterns and not too much on particular problems except when these have a real systemic importance. No liberal democracy, let alone a new one, can be a perfect model and is therefore marked by some defects, as sometimes highlighted in the media.

In late 2008, *The Economist* recorded that Latvia's political system was "notable for fragmented parties, squabbling mediocrities, dodgy business lobbies and abuse of power."[2] This comment contained observable truths even if marked by exaggeration, but ignored positive aspects of the system, especially democratic changes since the end of communism. More authoritative was the democracy audit carried out by the University of Latvia which concluded that "a significant portion of Latvia's population is not satisfied with the democratic development in the country" and warned: "Democracy is not just democratic institutions and procedures; democracy cannot function effectively if it is not rooted in public confidence." At the same time, there was overwhelming support for the view that democracy has some shortcomings yet it is better than

---

2   *The Economist*, 20 December 2008.

any other form of government.³ It should be pointed out that this report was first issued barely a decade and a half after independence, well before full democratic consolidation could be expected. More recently, a global democracy index published in late 2011 described Latvia as having a "democracy with flaws", being rated high for the electoral process and pluralism as well as civil liberties but low for the functioning of government, political participation and political culture.⁴

Democratic consolidation may be defined as the stabilisation, institutionalisation and legitimation of patterns of democratic behaviour leading to the dissemination of democratic values through the internalisation of the new rules and procedures. For the purpose of analysing its progress, it is useful to disaggregate democratic consolidation into its essential component parts by adopting the "partial regimes" approach focussing on linkages between governing authorities and political actors and between institutions and civil society and based on the realistic assumption that some aspects of a new democracy consolidate more easily or quickly than others.⁵ This approach is now applied to post-Soviet Latvia in two ways by focussing in turn on key levels of consolidation and then three dimensions—the structural, the attitudinal and the behavioural. The latter, which provide a thematic summary of consolidation's progress, reflect on the degree to which that has acquired any depth.

---

3   Commission of Strategic Analysis and Advanced Social and Political Research Institute, *How Democratic is Latvia: Audit of Democracy* (Rīga: LU Akademiskais Apgads, 2005), 14–15. This report was updated by a much briefer version in 2007. Editor's note: a new version of the report, published in 2014 after this chapter had been submitted and approved, substantially confirms the findings herein—noting significant progress in areas such as anti-corruption and NGO development during 2005–2014, the report nevertheless highlights continued challenges in the areas of socio-economic inequality, alienation between power holders and the general public, and settling relations between Latvia's major ethnolinguistic groups. For a useful summary, see: Juris Rozenvalds, "Introduction," in Juris Rozenvalds, ed., *How Democratic is Latvia? Audit of Democracy 2005–2014* (Rīga: University of Latvia, 2014), 16–19.
4   LETA, 20 December 2011.
5   See Philippe C. Schmitter, "The Consolidation of Political Democracies" in G. Pridham, ed., *Transitions to Democracy: Comparative Perspectives from Southern Europe, Latin America and Eastern Europe* (Aldershot: Dartmouth, 1995), 556–58.

2. A Comparative Framework: Levels of Democratic Consolidation

The State and its Institutions

The political institutions in Latvia are fixed and stable, there having been no real debate about constitutional revision as has occurred in several other post-communist countries (apart from occasional discussion of the possible direct election of the President and the recent initiative for a preamble to the Constitution). The 1992 Constitution adopted that of 1922 of the interwar republic with some minor changes and so there was a clear choice of a parliamentary system. Despite this stability, institutional development has revealed several serious defects.

Although some governments have lasted longer (e.g. the Bērziņš government from May 2000 to November 2002; the second Dombrovskis government from October 2011 to January 2014), most governments—invariably multi-party coalitions—are short-lived, making an average of somewhat over a year. By 2014, when this chapter was written, Latvia had had 17 governments since independence in 1991.[6] This instability of governments may be qualified by the continuity of centre-right parties represented in them and to some extent by the effective role of the Presidency within its strict constitutional limitations. Moreover, there has remained low public confidence in the political institutions as recorded by successive Eurobarometer surveys (e.g. only 21% trusting the Parliament and 25% the government in spring 2006).[7] This is despite the effective performance of some governments, notably those of Dombrovskis during 2009–2014, in handling the financial crisis—efforts which were, however, much more praised abroad than they were at home, where the effects of budgetary cuts were severe. Other institutions like the judiciary also lack public confidence despite more success than in other post-communist countries with establishing its independence. Efforts were made to counter this problem by introducing in 2004 new administrative courts to adjudicate disputes and conflicts between the public and national or local public servants including policemen. The Constitutional Court has also become an important recourse for those dis-

---

6 Editor's note: by mid-2016 the country was already on its 20th government.
7 Commission of Strategic Analysis, *How Democratic is Latvia: Monitoring of Democracy 2005–2007* (Rīga: Zinatne, 2007), 54–55.

satisfied with public policy, which, through a name for fair decisions, has fostered public trust.[8] In general, administrative reform was promoted by EU accession somewhat in the face of political reluctance and it has had real but limited effects.

The political system has been known for its lack of transparency, but gradually the law on access to information has had some positive effects qualified only by political passivity. Websites are available for all ministries and the directives and planned agendas of Cabinet meetings are also available online.[9] As a whole, trust tends to be higher in local government than it is in the national institutions. Democratic procedures are well in place there, such as open council and committee meetings and freely available minutes with recognised access to council members and executive officials and complaints procedures [10].

It must be remembered that legacies from the communist period, such as a basic mistrust towards the state and towards politics, take some time to work through. One other legacy from this past is that governments have been formed by Latvian parties while those representing the large Russian minority have been excluded. Now the latter have been united in the electorate of the Harmony Centre party and because of its relative popularity its possible role in a national coalition has been publicly discussed beginning with the 2011 election (its leader, Nils Ušakovs has been mayor of Rīga since 2009). In principle, the participation of this party in national government should enhance the legitimacy of the state cross-ethnically, for ultimately democratic governance depends for its survival on the ability of the main political elites to work together consistently. But now the crisis over Ukraine and Russian ambitions to restore the Soviet Union have driven a wedge between the ethnic political communities in Latvia, raising in a more painful way than before the question of loyalty towards the Latvian state.

Intermediary Actors: Political Parties, NGOs and the Media

Structurally, the party system is problematic: it is multi-party with no real leading parties; there is no viable political Left, with the traditional Social Democrats having failed to make the grade, although the Harmony Centre has in effect

---

8   Juris Dreifelds, "Latvia" in Freedom House, *Nations in Transit 2010: Democratization from Central Europe to Eurasia*. (Lanham: Rowman & Littlefield, 2011), 315.
9   Dreifelds, "Latvia", 309.
10 Dreifelds, `Latvia", 314.

filled that gap, meaning the Left/Right divide has become ethnicised; and, most of the Latvian parties are grouped in the centre-Right, thus dividing that side of the ideological spectrum. There has continued to be a certain instability in the life of some parties allowing new ones to emerge (dramatically in 2002 when a brand-new party, New Era, won the election that year and became the leading party of government after only a few months of existence). Parties tend to have small memberships and sometimes are little more than personal vehicles for their leaders or are aligned with particular economic interests, with politicians using their political leverage to benefit materially. Most notoriously, there are some big-time oligarchs (sometimes known as "grey cardinals") who have special links with certain parties, such as Ventspils mayor Aivars Lembergs with the Greens and Farmers' Party. It is not totally surprising that parties have a consistently very low trust rating in the Eurobarometer reports (e.g. only 5% in the survey published in January 2009), one even worse than those for the political institutions.

In the last few years efforts have been made to overcome some of the party system's defects. In the 2010 election, various party alliances were formed especially among centre-Right Latvian parties to counter party fragmentation and some like the Unity alliance have persisted. At the same time, new parties have continued to be formed like Zatlers' Reform Party for the 2011 election, despite pressures for its leaders to join with Unity. Then, in May 2011, Zatlers when still President made a brave speech denouncing the oligarchs and their influence on the country's politics (effectively undermining his re-election chances just afterwards) and calling for a referendum on having new elections.

Latvia's democracy lacks a serious internal enemy. There are no overt antisystem parties whose existence taking historical examples from other countries may point to a crisis of democracy. All Latvian parties are firmly democracy-supportive. The Russophile Harmony Centre works clearly within the political system at different levels but there are some grey areas, notably over the nature of its cooperation agreement of 2009 with Putin's party in Russia, United Russia, such as whether financial support is forthcoming from Moscow. Harmony Centre took an ambiguous position during the 2012 referendum on making Russian the second official language, which proved very divisive. During the Ukraine crisis Harmony Centre has taken a different line from the Latvian parties for instance in abstaining in the *Saeima* vote in March 2014 condemning Russia's annexation of Crimea. Given the implied threat to Latvia's own national security from Russia's expansionist ambitions, this crisis has therefore pushed Harmony Centre somewhat out on a limb at a time of enhanced interethnic tension, thus putting at risk its ability till now to mobilise significant support from Latvian voters as well as Russian ones.

NGO development has been slow, remaining largely urban based, i.e. concentrated in Rīga, for some time and hampered by a low level of participation due to former regime mentalities inhibiting a culture of engagement. Gradually, EU accession had some beneficial effects through various assistance programmes and especially support from the Soros Foundation, engagement with experienced European NGOs and involvement in projects under the Structural Funds. Furthermore, the demands of EU affairs on Latvia as a member state prompted efforts to regulate relations between the state and NGOs such as through cooperation agreements between individual ministries and relevant NGOs, a change assisted by the recognition of the rights of NGOs as cooperation partners by EU institutions. In 2004 the Civic Alliance was formed as an umbrella organisation to promote cooperation among Latvian NGOs, to improve their working environment and to strengthen their combined influence in lobbying EU institutions.[11] There are now many NGOs but they usually have small memberships with a low organisational capacity and shortage of finance. But there are some more active NGOs such as in the environmental and women's rights field and one of the largest is the European Movement (EKL). There tend to be separate Russian NGOs which look to the interests of their ethnic community. It is clear overall that European integration has had a far more beneficial effect on NGOs than on political parties. While the EU transnational parties have provided a useful career outlet for some national politicians as MEPs, they had no profound effect on party development inside Latvia, failing for instance to help overcome party fragmentation as had occurred in a few other post-communist democracies.

---

11 Geoffrey Pridham, "Post-Soviet Latvia—a Consolidated or Defective Democracy? The Interaction between Domestic and European Trajectories", *Journal of Baltic Studies* 40,4 (2009): 484.

The media present a mixed picture. They perform a valid role in a democratic society, but they have their limitations. There is a good legislative framework for independent journalism (editorial independence and freedom to disseminate information and views subject only to libel considerations) and evidence of public understanding of the need for diverse media outlets to reflect different political opinions and to criticise those in government (with the media becoming more effective in this role). However, there has been a certain lack of transparency about media ownership, limited development of investigative journalism and a division between the Latvian and Russian language media (plus the tendency of Latvian Russians to listen to the media from Russia) thus reinforcing the ethnic divide[12]. Despite their limitations, the media are generally trusted in Latvia—radio and television rather more than the press—certainly more so than the political institutions; and there has been a gradual increase in internet use.

Civil Society and the Economy

Dissatisfaction with the functioning of Latvia's post-Soviet democracy has focussed mainly on the political institutions and parties. Since this persistent attitude has combined with overwhelming support for liberal democracy as a type of political system, it is pertinent to ask about the evolving political culture and about civil society, which is usually crucial in underpinning a new democracy. Political culture has been slow to develop in this post-Soviet society with its heavy legacy problems from the post-war past, as reflected in the difficulties of NGO development; but there has generally an upwards trend. At a formal level, fair and free elections have been well established from soon after independence, with political competition as witnessed by the wide choice before the voters, reasonably effective voting procedures and the readiness of political forces to accept the electorate's preferences. Voter turnout is reasonably high (with recent signs of some decline), but participation in political life between elections has remained low and there has been very limited involvement in the political

---

12 Sergejs Kruks and Ilze Šulmane, "The Media in a Democratic Society" in *How Democratic is Latvia* (2005), 143–147.

parties.[13] Political passivity has been marked, perhaps related in a complex way with public scepticism about the performance of Latvia's democracy, although there have been occasional flashes of public discontent notably in the "umbrella revolution" of protests outside the *Saeima* in December 2007 leading directly to the resignation of the Kalvītis government and then the riots of January 2009 over economic distress and dissatisfaction with politicians demanding the dissolution of the *Saeima* which influenced the formation of the Dombrovskis government a few weeks later.

There are of course different areas of civil society to investigate in any new democracy; but two rather basic problems have great importance in the Latvian case: corruption and the Russian ethnic minority. The first reflects strongly on respect for the rule of law which is fundamental to a democracy's impact and capacity for survival; the second, an exceptionally large Russian minority (the largest in percentage terms of all ex-Soviet republics apart from Russia itself) has had implications not only for political pluralism but also for democratic legitimacy.

Fighting corruption was one of the major political conditions imposed by the EU as a precondition for membership. This was all the more necessary in a country like Latvia which had at the time one of the worst ratings across Europe. But corruption was widespread and deeply rooted, deriving much from practices developed in the communist period to circumvent authority and its frustrating bureaucratic rules. EU pressure meant the problem became a political issue and this enhanced public awareness, although that did not in itself automatically translate into action. The accession period was too short for any resolution of the problem; but one crucial item of good news deriving from outside pressure was the creation of the Corruption Prevention and Combatting Bureau (*Korupcijas novēršanas un apkarošanas birojs*—KNAB) shortly before EU entry. This has been assiduous and persistent in its actions, sometimes brave ones in the face of vested political interests, as a result of which it has over time emerged as one of the most trusted institutions in the country. There have

---

13 Jānis Ikstens and Andris Runcis, "Free and Fair Elections" in *How Democratic is Latvia* (2007), 43–4; Zinta Miezaine and Mara Simane, "Political Participation" in *How Democratic is Latvia* (2005), 151–52.

been several high-profile cases involving action against certain local governments and most notably against national political elites such as over the sensitive area of party financing. KNAB has in effect responded to the public desire for a counter force to what are regularly seen as corrupt politicians; but the latter have attempted unsuccessfully to undermine this agency.

One should distinguish between small or petty corruption at the public level, ever present for instance in the health system, and high-level corruption which is more relevant to the theme of democratic consolidation. One of the most long-standing obstacles to fighting corruption has been the considerable amount of money of unknown origin available to public officials and economic interests. Public surveys have pointed to government as the sector where bribery is perceived as the most widespread, but more recently there have been signs of a decline in state capture.[14] KNAB has developed ever more sophisticated anti-corruption efforts such as over lobbying activities and protecting whistle-blowers (the latter being significant in view of the public's reluctance to come forward with evidence, the so-called "mentality of silence"). The 2014 European Commission anti-corruption report on Latvia concluded:

> "Latvia has made progress in preventing and addressing corruption, with a searchable online database of political donations and a track record of KNAB investigations. Moreover, anti-corruption laws are gradually being developed and refined, although implementation in practice remains uneven. Further efforts can help address corruption risks in public procurement and improve the accountability of elected officials as well as the transparency of state-owned companies."[15]

In principle, a country's treatment of ethnic and other minorities reflects on the quality of democracy, namely the degree of political pluralism and toleration. Severe and persistent problems might well inhibit its consolidation in the case of a new democracy. With Latvia, there is a serious ethnic minority problem because of its size of over one-third of the population (29% Russians plus nearly 9% other Slavs in 2005) making Latvians hardly dominant in their own country (only 52% in 1989 rising to 59% in 2005). Two other linked problems have made this more difficult; the past, namely the Soviet period with strong

---

14   Valts Kalniņš, "Minimizing Corruption" in *How Democratic is Latvia* (2007), 73–74.
15   European Commission, *EU Anti-Corruption Report: Latvia*, 3 February 2014, 11.

and painful memories of it among Latvians; and the present where neighbouring Russia has made a major issue claiming mistreatment of Latvian Russians. The problem has remained essentially unresolved consensually, this being the only way for the sake of strengthening Latvia's post-Soviet democracy. It is a deeply emotional and divisive issue (as shown by the experience of the referendum on Russian as an official language in February 2012) that has at times gained high international visibility, touching on such matters as citizenship (the proportion of non-citizens, at 13%, was still high in 2014), education and of course role in the political system.

Some progress was achieved during accession because of pressure from the EU and other international organisations like the OSCE and the Council of Europe, such as over the citizenship laws. In 2002 a new Ministry of Social Integration was established only to be disbanded some years later due to a lack of sustained commitment among the political elite. In 2005 the Council of Europe's Framework Convention on the Protection of National Minorities was ratified after a decade's delay although its implementation has been unsubstantial. Since EU entry, there has been a tightening of regulations over the language question. This reverse pattern has been evident in other areas of minority rights as shown by expressions of homophobia which would have been undiplomatic during EU accession when political conditionality was still applicable. The problem of ethnic minority rights represents perhaps the weakest point in Latvia's democracy, particularly if acerbated by action from Russia with threats to the country's security.

The state of the economy is obviously one vital underlying factor in a country's progress towards democratic consolidation. Early difficulties are likely to delay that process and indeed in Latvia's case economic adjustment in the first part of the 1990s proved very difficult. After a period of more than a decade's growth in which Latvia joined the EU there followed the financial crisis which hit the country badly. The government adopted a policy of sharp austerity and reform within a fixed currency (the Lat was pegged to the Euro), with assistance from the IMF, the World Bank and the EU. This involved deep cuts in sectors like health and education, thus weakening the country's social infrastructure. Opinion surveys showed increasing pessimism about the economic future but at the same time a public understanding of the need for austerity (as confirmed in the re-election of the government in 2010 and 2011). There were no overt threats to democracy as a result of this crisis, which could have proved dangerous; and Latvia has emerged from its major slump into a new trend of fast growth.

External Actors

Basically, there has been a contrast with Latvia's interwar democracy which ultimately suffered from the dual challenge to its existence from aggressive totalitarian states in Nazi Germany and Stalin's Russia, the two countries which successively occupied Latvia in World War II and one of which incorporated that country into its own system for half a century. Memories of this period and particularly the Molotov-Ribbentrop Pact of August 1939 are still painful. Nevertheless, since independence in 1991 Latvia's restored democracy has benefitted from a much more benign international environment with a fully democratic Germany to the West, one which is an EU and NATO partner since Latvia joined both organisations in 2004. This situation has undoubtedly enhanced the prospects of Latvia's democracy, the EU accession process having itself acted as a spur to the country's post-Soviet democratic development through the pressures of political conditionality, the aim of which was to strengthen democratic institutions and procedures as well as promote good governance and political pluralism and human rights. In general, EU institutions enjoy distinctly more public trust than national institutions as evidenced by regular Eurobarometer reports. Within the EU framework there is also close cooperation between Latvia and the other Baltic States as well as Scandinavian countries.

The relationship with post-Soviet Russia has been more complicated. For most of the independence period so far that country has not presented an aggressive totalitarian state as before. However, it has hardly been a friendly neighbour country either, given disputes over the status of Russians, and especially the many non-citizens, in Latvia. There has been growing concern about Russian penetration of Latvia by means of business and criminal activity as well as covert mechanisms of "soft power" such as funding Russian cultural programmes—half of all money now invested in Latvia comes from non-resident depositors most of whom live in Russia and former Soviet republics. EU diplomatic sources have confirmed that Russian intelligence agencies are highly active in Latvia ("they have successfully penetrated Russian elites in this country" according to one such source). It is assumed that Latvia's geographical position bridging Russia and the West made it an ideal entry point for such activity and that Russia's ultimate intention is to reverse Latvia's strategic direction from pro-West to pro-Moscow through greater dependence.[16] In addition, Russia has staged major military exercises just across the border with Latvia in recent years. This kind of evidence provides an uneasy background to growing concerns about Latvia's national security during the Ukraine crisis, despite efforts by NATO to strengthen its military presence in the Baltic area in reaffirmation of article 5 of the NATO Treaty to come to the defence of any NATO member state if attacked.

3. A Thematic Framework: Dimensions of Democratic Consolidation

The Structural

The picture presented by Latvia's post-Soviet democracy is one of established structures which are also legitimate but whose credibility, if one includes the whole range of institutions as well as the political ones, is rather variable. Public lack of trust or confidence in some of them is worryingly low. In part this is historical, deriving from the Soviet period (lack of trust in the state as represented by Moscow), but it is also due to difficulties of democratic performance since then, this not being helped by the generally unimpressive quality of the political elites. The party system structure remains weak and this has not promoted democratic consolidation. A basic problem is that of participation in the political system and in particular the limited role of the large Russian minority in the state institutions apart from the *Saeima*. There has been no real alternation in power at the national level. But no serious systemic alternative has been presented, nor is it likely to gain significant popular support.

The Attitudinal

The political elite has remained essentially democracy supportive but evidence of democratic learning—as shown by transparency problems –could be

---

16 See detailed report in *The Guardian*, 24 January 2013. In answer to the author's question whether Russia showed signs of coming to terms with Latvia's new membership of the EU and NATO, a prominent politician involved in the country's foreign affairs replied in an interview in 2004 that, on the contrary, Russian intelligence activity had increased since entry to both organisations.

stronger. Pressures from EU accession did produce adaptation on a number of conditionality matters, but this was significantly driven by opportunism over accession as suggested by some backtracking since EU entry. The weight of historical legacies, heavy from the Soviet experience, is still evident after more than two decades of independence, as shown by the impact of historical memory which is stronger than in most other post-communist democracies. Some politicians have recently advocated resolving issues of the past and constructing common historical memories to underpin national unity; but that is not easy to achieve except over a long period of time and in any case such ideas have not been free from political interest. Altogether, it may be said that this problem has limited the full achievement of democratic consolidation.

The Behavioural

It may be concluded that deeper and wider changes deriving from Latvia's post-Soviet democratisation have been slow in coming. A vibrant democratic political culture underpinning the political system and including basic trust in its institutions and tolerance towards political opponents that strengthens political pluralism is rather lacking. There is the need for a stronger modern political elite, as highlighted by President Zatlers' attack on the role of the oligarchs in the country's politics in summer 2011, although some individual top politicians may be said to represent that category. Some aspects of democratic life nevertheless look more positive bottom-up than top-down, such as inter-ethnic relations which are far more intense in national and Rīga city politics than they are at the local level. Overall, changes in political behaviour have nevertheless been evident compared with two decades ago.

4. Conclusion: An Ongoing Process

Latvia's post-Soviet democracy is defective in some important ways. However, it has survived and endured and, taken in the round, has far stronger prospects of survival than the interwar republic not least because of the EU's beneficial effects both during accession and during membership since. Only drastic international circumstances like fundamental economic collapse or military aggression are likely to shake its foundations. It shows no signs of transmuting into a more authoritarian mould as happened in Latvia from the mid-1930s. In fact, Latvia's record of democracy emerges as quite positive when compared with some other post-communist systems, whether the violent inter-ethnic strife in the Western Balkans or recent signs of democratic inversion in other EU states like Romania and more seriously Hungary under Orban's rule.

In summary, referring to the introductory definition of democratic consolidation, there are both positive and negative aspects: the routinisation and institutionalisation of democracy has occurred but its legitimation has been limited and slow while the dissemination of democratic values and the internalisation of the new rules and procedures still suffer from serious weaknesses. Until remaining problems like that of inter-ethnic relations are eventually solved, Latvia's democracy cannot be considered as fully consolidated. It could be that at least three decades are really needed to achieve this.

The Europeanisation of Latvia's Public Policy: The Case of Foreign Aid Policy, 2004–2010

Pēteris Timofejevs Henriksson, Södertörn University

1. Introduction

In Latvia, as in other Central and East European countries (CEECs), state-building processes coincided with three other mutually-intertwined processes of change during the 1990s and early 2000s: transition to democracy, transition to a market economy, and integration into European and Transatlantic organisations[1]. Integration into the European Union (EU) is a particularly noteworthy process, because it overlapped with and reinforced the processes of democratisation, economic transition and state-building. Accordingly, a large portion of the literature studying these processes focuses on one aspect only, namely that of how the EU influenced the public policy of the CEECs[2]. Known as the "Europeanisation East" literature, this body of scholarly literature examines how and through which causal mechanisms the EU succeeded in effecting domestic change, both during the run-up to accession and in the post-accession period[3]. An ongoing dialogue between two theoretical schools—Rationalists and Constructivists—has focused on the question of how to explain the EU-induced change in the CEECs—as a strategic adaptation to external incentives provided by the EU or as a process of norm-based socialisation? Taking this

---

1 Mitchel A. Orenstein, Stephen Bloom, and Nicole Lindstrom, "A Fourth Dimension of Transition," in Mitchel A. Orenstein, Stephen Bloom, and Nicole Lindstrom, eds., *Transnational Actors in Central and East European Transitions* (Pittsburgh: Pittsburgh University Press, 2008), 5.
2 See, for instance: Frank Schimmelfennig and Ulrich Sedelmeier, eds., *The Europeanization of Central and Eastern Europe* (Ithaca: Cornell University Press, 2005); Bengt Jacobsson, ed., *The European Union and the Baltic States: Changing Forms of Governance* (London: Routledge, 2010); Wade Jacoby, *The Enlargement of the European Union and NATO: Ordering from the Menu in Central Europe* (Cambridge: Cambridge University Press, 2004).
3 For an overview of the literature, see Ulrich Sedelmeier, "Europeanisation in New Member and Candidate States," *Living Reviews in European Governance* 1 (2006). http://europeangovernance.livingreviews.org/Articles/lreg-2006-3/ (Accessed 10 July 2014).

theoretical discussion within the Europeanisation literature as the point of departure, this chapter revisits and further interrogates the nature of the relationship between EU membership and public policy. In so doing, it focuses on the evolution of foreign aid policy in Latvia (one of the smallest and poorest EU member states) during the post-accession period. This policy area—being part of a wider policy area of external relations—is close to the core of state sovereignty that, usually, is seen as being "safeguarded" from EU intervention. This area can be used as a metaphoric "litmus test" indicating the depth of EU influence on the new member states—in this particular case, Latvia.

In examining the evolution of foreign aid policy in Latvia, the chapter seeks to explain the following puzzle: as I have argued elsewhere[4], Latvia, at least partly, adopted its foreign aid policy as part of the EU-imposed conditions in order to be admitted to the EU (known as "EU conditionality") in the pre-accession period. According to the Rationalist theories, the CEECs, after their accession to the EU, were expected to stall or even reverse the policies and reforms introduced due to the pre-accession pressure which was no longer present after 2004[5]. Latvia, upon its accession to the EU, was the poorest new member state, and even in 2010 it was among the three poorest countries in the EU[6]. Following the Rationalist theoretical predictions, one could expect that

---

4 Peteris Timofejevs Henriksson, "'You Cannot Sell It': Initiation and Implementation of Latvian Development Co-operation Policy (2000–2010)," in Henrik Lindberg, ed., *Knowledge and Policy Change*, (Newcastle upon Tyne: Cambridge Scholars Publishing, 2013), 201–219; Peteris Timofejevs Henriksson, "The Europeanisation of Foreign Aid Policy: Slovenia and Latvia 1998–2010" (PhD dissertation, Umeå University, 2013).

5 See, for instance: Klaus H. Goetz, "The New Member States and the EU: Responding to Europe," in Simon Bulmer and Christian Lequesne, eds., *The Member States of the European Union* (Oxford: Oxford University Press, 2005), 262; Frank Schimmelfennig and Ulrich Sedelmeier, "Conclusions: The Impact of the EU on the Accession Countries," in Schimmelfennig and Sedelmeier, eds, *The Europeanization of Central and Eastern Europe*, 226–227.

6 Officially, the OECD Development Assistance Committee listed Latvia, even upon its accession to the EU, as an aid recipient country under the category "Countries and Territories in Transition." See OECD DAC, "DAC List of Aid Recipients—As at 1 January 2003." http://www.oecd.org/investment/stats/2488552.pdf (Accessed 7 July 2014). That Latvia was the poorest new member state in 2004 is confirmed by the Eurostat index of GDP per capita in purchasing power standards (PPS), according to which Latvia had the value of 47 (if EU-28=100) in 2004. In 2010, Latvia's GDP per capita in PPS amounted to 55, and only Romania and Bulgaria had lower indicators—51 and 44

it would be among the first new members that would have stalled or reversed its decision to provide aid to developing countries. Nevertheless, as will be demonstrated in what follows, the case of Latvia did not comply with the Rationalist expectations. Even throughout the economic depression in 2008–2010 the country continued providing both bilateral foreign aid, even at a significantly smaller scale than before the crisis, and multilateral foreign aid. The ambition of the chapter is therefore to explain why this relatively small, poor country decided to continue developing its own foreign aid policy even after 2004 and to examine the role of the EU in the policy evolution processes. I will be arguing that Rationalism explains only certain aspects of foreign aid policy evolution, but it fails to answer to the more significant question—why policy reversal did not occur in Latvia after accession. I will therefore argue that the policy evolution can be explained by socialisation processes that shaped Latvia's identity as a modern European country. Interpreting the socialisation processes in retrospect, it is also suggested here that, like all states, Latvia was most probably seeking not only physical, but also ontological security[7], and it continued providing aid after the accession, because Latvia strove to appear consistent with its evolving identity of being a modern European (donor) country that can transfer its transition experiences to other, lesser developed countries.

The chapter is structured as follows. First, I examine the theoretical discussion between Rationalists and Constructivists on how to explain the policy changes in the CEECs during and after the pre-accession period. This is followed by a short discussion about the methodological aspects of the study. The section that follows then presents my empirical findings, which focus on the evolution of foreign aid policy in Latvia and the main causal factors explaining the process. The chapter concludes with a discussion of the main findings and their theoretical implications.

---

respectively. See Eurostat, "GDP per capita in PPS." http://epp.eurostat.ec.europa.eu/tgm/table.do?tab=table&init=1&plugin=1&language=en&pcode=tec00114 (Accessed 7 July 2014).

7 Jennifer Mitzen, "Ontological Security in World Politics: State Identity and the Security Dilemma," *European Journal of International Relations* 12 (2006): 341–370; Brent J. Steele, *Ontological Security in International Relations: Self-Identity and IR State* (London: Routledge, 2008); Brent J. Steele, "Ontological Security and the Power of Self-Identity: British Neutrality and the American Civil War," *Review of International Studies* 31 (2005): 519–540.

2. Two Theoretical Approaches—Rationalism and Constructivism

There is an abundance of different definitions of Europeanisation.[8] For the purposes of this study, Europeanisation will be understood as "processes involving both 1) the EU adaptational pressures to adopt a certain policy or follow certain policy goals and 2) a domestic response from states at which the EU adaptational pressures are targeted"[9]. Europeanisation is not a theory in itself, but rather a concept that can be used to ask "interesting" questions.[10] The two main theoretical schools within the Europeanisation research that focuses on explaining the EU-induced changes in the CEECs are Rationalism and Constructivism. Here I will focus on three slightly contrasting explanations provided by the two schools—legacy of EU conditionality, veto players, and socialisation through identification.

Mainstream Explanation

The mainstream explanation of the policy changes in the CEECs is provided by Rationalism, which has its roots within the Rational Choice Institutionalist stream of political-science research. Rationalism posits that agents (either individual or collective) are rational and tend to strategically maximise their utility. The changes introduced in the CEECs are explained as strategic adjustments which were carried out as a response to the external incentives provided by the EU before the CEECs were admitted to the EU.[11] To explicate this incentive structure, Rationalists introduce the concept of "EU conditionality" that refers to the conditions that the CEECs had to fulfil in order to be admitted to the EU. Thus, EU membership is the ultimate reward that is granted to those candidate countries which have fulfilled all the conditions (such as introduction of all the EU rules, known as the *acquis communautaire*). In contrast, if the candidate countries do not comply with the EU conditions or do not fully implement the

---

8   Johan P. Olsen, "The Many Faces of Europeanization," *Journal of Common Market Studies* 40 (2002): 921–52.
9   Timofejevs Henriksson, "The Europeanisation of Foreign Aid Policy," 13–14.
10 Kyriakos Moumoutzis, "Still Fashionable Yet Useless? Addressing Problems with Research on the Europeanization of Foreign Policy," *Journal of Common Market Studies* 49 (2011): 607–629.
11 Frank Schimmelfennig and Ulrich Sedelmeier, "Introduction: Conceptualizing the Europeanization of Central and Eastern Europe," in Schimmelfennig and Sedelmeier *The Europeanization of Central and Eastern Europe*, 10.

requested norms, the EU may choose to punish them by withholding the desired benefits.[12]

Regarding the outcomes of compliance, Rationalists expect strategic compliance from the CEECs in the form of either discursive or formal adjustments in the pre-accession phase; a behavioural change implies too high adjustment costs for the domestic actors which are assumed to be interested in minimising the adjustment costs.[13] If the adjustment costs increase beyond a level that powerful domestic actors perceive as tolerable, they may choose to veto the policy introduction or implementation; such powerful domestic actors are therefore described as "veto players".[14] After the accession, the CEECs were expected to stall the reforms, or reverse them (the reversal thesis) because the EU could no longer punish non-compliance once the candidate states had become member states.[15] It was feared that such policy reversals in the CEECs would constitute an "Eastern problem" for the functioning of the EU after the accession.[16] Moreover, it was proposed that veto players, which were constrained by the EU conditionality before the accession, would become more salient and would be more willing to play an active role and block the disagreeable policies after the accession.[17]

Rationalists argue that EU conditionality produced "pervasive" effects and I, too, have argued that EU conditionality, at least partly, can explain the foreign aid adoption in Latvia in the pre-accession period[18]. What is not equally clear is whether Rationalism can explain developments in the post-accession period, which, according to the "reversal thesis", should be characterised by stalling or reversing the policies adopted under the EU pressure before accession. In fact, there are reasons to doubt the "reversal thesis" because the CEECs have shown an exemplary transposition record,[19] even if the actual implementation

---

12 Schimmelfennig and Sedelmeier, "Introduction," 11–12.
13 Schimmelfennig and Sedelmeier, "Introduction," 17.
14 Schimmelfennig and Sedelmeier, "Introduction," 16–17.
15 Goetz, "The New Member States and the EU," 262; Schimmelfennig and Sedelmeier, "Conclusions," 226–227.
16 Ulrich Sedelmeier, "After conditionality: post-accession compliance with EU law in East Central Europe," *Journal of European Public Policy* 15 (2008): 807.
17 Schimmelfennig and Sedelmeier, "Conclusions," 226–227.
18 Timofejevs Henriksson, "The Europeanisation of Foreign Aid Policy," 250.
19 Sedelmeier, "After Conditionality," 807.

of EU rules is assessed as lagging behind.[20] Therefore, it has been suggested that a specific legacy of pre-accession conditionality influences the public policy processes in the CEECs. The argument is based on the fact that, in the run-up to accession, many CEECs had introduced special legislative procedures that promptly transposed the EU rules into domestic legislation. These "fast-track" legislative procedures, it is suggested, could account for the positive transposition record in the countries where the procedures are still present.[21]

Alternative Explanation

The main alternative explanation to the dominant Rationalist explanation is provided by Constructivists. Constructivism is based on the ontological assumption that the policy changes in the CEECs were driven by EU normative influence (i.e. EU norms were seen as "appropriate") and that the domestic decision-makers were socialised into believing that that, for instance, foreign aid policy adoption was the right thing to do.[22]

Constructivists point out a specific causal mechanism that accounts for the policy changes and that I call here "socialisation through identification" or simply socialisation. According to this theory, the domestic decision-makers strove for their country's EU membership, because they identified with the EU as their "reference group" to which they wanted to belong and which they emulated in order to ensure that their country appears as a "proper" European country.[23] Due to their high level of identification with the EU, or, once the CEECs have become member states, the domestic decision-makers should be particularly susceptible to what can be called "social influence" or "peer pressure" from the

---

20 Frank Schimmelfennig, and Florian Trauner, "Introduction: Post-Accession Compliance in the EU's New Member States," *European Integration Online Papers* 13 (2009). http://www.eiop.or.at/eiop/pdf/2009-SpecIssue-2_Introduction.pdf. (Accessed 19 January, 2010).
21 Sedelmeier, "After conditionality," 807.
22 Schimmelfennig and Sedelmeier, "Introduction," 18.
23 Schimmelfennig and Sedelmeier, "Introduction," 19; Jeffrey T. Checkel, "Why Comply? Social Learning and European Identity Change," *International Organization* 55 (2001): 563; Alastair I. Johnston, "Treating International Institutions as Social Environments," *International Studies Quarterly* 45 (2001): 499; Bengt Jacobsson and Anders Nordström, "Soft Powers (In a Community of the Willing)," in Bengt Jacobsson, ed., *The European Union and the Baltic States: Changing Forms of Governance,* (London: Routledge, 2010), 168.

members of their reference group. According to Constructivism, it is the fear of opprobrium from peers rather than material punishment that motivates the compliance from the member states (or aspiring member states).[24]

A slightly modified version of this argument is found also in the discussion on the legacies of EU conditionality. It has been suggested that the CEECs internalised the European Commission's monitoring and ranking of CEECs according to their performance in transposing the acquis. Therefore, the CEECs, still in the post-accession phase, are more "susceptible" than the Western EU members to the "shaming strategy of the EU compliance system" and the CEECs are therefore more prone to "conceive of good compliance as appropriate behaviour".[25]

Despite the slight differences in these two accounts, they seem to converge on the expectation that, in the post-accession phase, the new members will not reverse or stall the adopted policies, but rather continue implementing them because "everyone else does that", or, alternatively, because that is the "right" (or "appropriate") thing to do.

Some even imply that agents need not believe in appropriateness of the policy, but rather simply be interested in avoiding opprobrium from their peers.[26] This line of reasoning resonates with the Constructivist theories on states seeking ontological security (understood as "a sense of continuity and order in events"[27]). These posit that states tend to follow the course of action which complies with their "sense of self-identity" and which eventually has a positive impact on their self-esteem[28]; when states act in ways that are incongruent with

---

24 Johnston, "Treating International Institutions as Social Environments," 499.
25 Sedelmeier, "After conditionality," 808.
26 Johnston, "Treating International Institutions as Social Environments," 502. See also Jeffrey T. Checkel, "International Institutions and Socialization in Europe: Introduction and Framework," *International Organization* 59 (2005): 810–812.
27 Anthony Giddens, *Modernity and Self-identity: Self and Society in the Late Modern Age* (Cambridge: Polity Press, 1991), 234.
28 Steele, "Ontological security and the power of self-identity," 526. Also, Alexander Wendt has argued that states tend to seek "collective self-esteem," which he defines as a "group's need to feel good about itself, for respect or status." See Alexander Wendt, *Social Theory of International Politics* (Cambridge: Cambridge University Press, 1999), 236. On the role of self-esteem in pursuing a foreign policy that aims at ontological security, see Richard Ned Lebow, *A Cultural Theory of International Relations* (Cambridge: Cambridge University Press, 2008), especially, 25–26.

their self-identity, they experience shame.[29] This argument also provides an answer to the Rationalist confusion as to why the CEECs continued to exhibit exemplary transposition behaviour, even if there was no conditionality or even implicit threats that the EU could retaliate against non-compliers.

3. Methodological Aspects: Operationalisation and Research Design

In this section, two methodological aspects are reviewed: first, the operationalisation of Rationalist and Constructivist theories in the specific context of foreign aid policy evolution, and, second, the research design of the study. When operationalising the Rationalist theory of legacies of conditionality, we should expect to find a specific legislative procedure that has been inherited from the pre-accession period and that has significantly contributed to a faster adoption of the EU rules regarding foreign aid. Operationalising the second factor—the existence of powerful veto players—involves conducting in-depth interviews with the relevant politicians and civil servants that can uncover the dynamics behind the policy decisions taken. Veto players can be expected to be present if the interviewed decision-makers can point out which individual or collective actors have tried or succeeded in delaying the policy decisions and how they did it.

Constructivism, on the other hand, is more challenging to operationalise, as it presumes that the policy decisions were taken against the background of the socio-psychological processes of socialisation. As it is naturally impossible to directly observe such processes, socialisation is operationalised here through proxy measures.[30] First, the in-depth interviews with the domestic decision-makers will be examined as to whether they perceived EU peer pressure, understood here as experience of explicit or implicit opprobrium from the European Commission or other member states. Also, when examining the policy documents, one should expect to find statements that contain arguments concerned with, for instance, the country's reputation in the international community.

---

29 Steele, "Ontological Security and the Power of Self-Identity," 527.
30 For a similar approach, see, for instance, Jeffrey T. Checkel, "Tracing Causal Mechanisms," *International Studies Review* 8 (2006): 367.

As this chapter revolves around Latvia's foreign aid policy, the research design is that of single case study. It aims at generating a causal explanation by employing the process-tracing methods which are particularly useful when analysing causal mechanisms.[31] As I aim to understand the dynamics behind the taken policy decisions, I have conducted 28 in-depth interviews with domestic decision-makers (both relevant politicians and civil servants), representatives from relevant non-governmental organisations (NGOs) and academics in 2009 and 2010.[32] Moreover, I have also collected and analysed relevant policy documents to triangulate the interview data.

4. Findings: Foreign Aid Policy Evolution, 2004–2010

Although, upon Latvia's accession to the EU in May 2004, the EU conditionality was no longer effective, the country still faced a new kind of adaptational pressure from the EU. Already in 2002, the EU agreed to significantly increase the official development assistance (ODA) to contribute to the achievement of the globally agreed Millennium Development Goals that among others aimed at halving poverty.[33] Specifically, the member states agreed 1) to individually reach the target of allocating at least 0.33% ODA/ GNI by 2006 and 2) to collectively reach the target of 0.39% ODA/ GNI by 2006.[34] These agreed targets and also other policy goals outlined in the Council Conclusions came later to be known as the "Barcelona commitments". Nevertheless, the member states tasked the European Commission with conducting a specific monitoring exercise of member states' progress towards reaching the agreed goals.[35] Later, in 2005, the EU agreed to new financial targets for increasing aid: the new member states (such as Latvia) were expected to reach the targets of allocating

---

31 On process-tracing methods, see Derek Beach and Rasmus Brun Pedersen, *Process-Tracing Methods: Foundations and Guidelines* (Ann Arbor: The University of Michigan Press, 2013).
32 Not all interviews are referenced here; a full interview list is available upon request.
33 Council of the European Union, "Agreement reached by Foreign Ministers with a view to the International Conference on Financing for Development (Monterrey, Mexico, 18–22 March 2002). 7274/02 Presse 76. Brussels, 14 March 2002." http://register.consili um.europa.eu/pdf/en/02/st07/st07274.en02.pdf. (Accessed 11 July, 2014).
34 Council of the European Union, "Agreement".
35 Council of the European Union, "2464th Council meeting, General Affairs, 14184/02 Press 351, Brussels, 19 November 2002." http://europa.eu/rapid/press-release_PRES-02-351_en.htm?locale=FR. (Accessed on 11 July 2014).

0.17% ODA/ GNI by 2010 and 0.33% ODA/ GNI by 2015, while the old member states were expected to reach significantly higher targets.[36] In sum, the EU had far-reaching foreign policy ambitions of playing an important role in the developing world, and the member states were expected to contribute to this overarching goal by mobilising resources to increase their ODA to developing countries.

Latvia's response to these developments at the EU level is measured along two main dimensions: formal (institutional developments, such as building new aid-providing institutions, adopting policy planning documents, etc.), and behavioural (measured here as increasing the foreign aid in order to reach the EU commitments). Although Latvia's response, all in all, can be assessed as mixed, there was at least some progress to be reported.

Latvia selected Georgia, Moldova and Ukraine as its primary partners for development cooperation. In 2006, a special policy planning document, "Programme for Latvian Development Cooperation 2006–2010", was adopted, thus granting a state budget line that to some extent institutionalised foreign aid policy as an independent state policy, albeit still being under the umbrella of the wider category of external relations.[37] Following the praxis of Western donors, co-operation with Latvian NGOs was established and the ambition was both to develop a close co-operation with civil society that could implement at least a certain part of Latvia's development cooperation projects and to boost local knowledge and expertise in development issues[38]. Still, throughout the period, most of the development projects were implemented by various state institutions (such as line ministries or specialised state agencies whose primary *raison d' être* was not development cooperation) that transferred their expertise to the partner countries[39]. In 2008, the Law on International Assistance was

---

36 Council of the European Union, "Conclusions of the Council and Representatives of the Governments of the Member States Meeting within the Council, Brussels, 24 May 2005, 9266/05." http://register.consilium.europa.eu/pdf/en/05/st09/st09266.en05.pdf. (Accessed 11 July 2014).
37 Cabinet of Ministers, "Program for Latvian development co-operation, 2006–2010." http://polsis.mk.gov.lv/view.do?id=1898. (Accessed on 12 July, 2014).
38 Interview with a middle-level civil servant at Latvia's Ministry of Foreign Affairs, Rīga, 12 October, 2010.
39 Timofejevs Henriksson, "The Europeanisation of Foreign Aid Policy," 208.

adopted specifying the legal framework for policy conduct and the main institutions. The Law provided that the Ministry of Foreign Affairs (MFA) would retain responsibility for policy planning, but that a special implementing agency would also be set up.[40] However, in 2008, Latvia was hit by the financial crisis, which reduced its GDP almost by 20% during the period 2008–2010.[41] The crisis forced the postponement of the plans to establish a special implementing agency.[42]

Regarding the behavioural dimension, mixed results emerge too. As Table 1 indicates, Latvia's foreign aid expressed in absolute terms increased by 600% in 2004, jumping from EUR 1 million to EUR 7 million. While further increases were not equally impressive, the foreign aid volumes peaked in 2008, when EUR 15 million was allocated to ODA. As was the case with the development of the policy's institutional aspects, the financial crisis had a direct and negative impact on foreign aid volumes, as the planned bilateral aid was severely cut in both 2009 and 2010.[43] All in all, foreign aid increased by approximately EUR 5 million (or 71%) during the period from 2004 to 2010.

---

40 "Starptautiskās palīdzības likums." [Law on International Assistance.] http://likumi.lv/doc.php?id=175254. (Accessed 12 July, 2014).
41 Eurostat. "Real GDP growth rate—volume." http://epp.eurostat.ec.europa.eu/tgm/table.do?tab=table&init=1&plugin=1&language=en&pcode=tec00115. (Accessed 12 July, 2014).
42 Interview (a group interview) with a middle-level civil servant and three desk officers at Latvia's Ministry of Foreign Affairs, Rīga, 20 October 2009.
43 Timofejevs Henriksson, "The Europeanisation of Foreign Aid Policy," 205–206.

Table 1: Latvia's foreign aid 2003–2010

Aid type	2003	2004	2005	2006	2007	2008	2009	2010
Foreign aid, in total, EUR, million	1	7	8	9	12	15	15	12
Multilateral aid, as % of the total aid	No data	No data	91.3	92.2	90.4	80.5	90.5	89.6
Bilateral aid, as % of the total aid	No data	No data	8.7	7.8	9.6	19.5	9.5	10.4
Foreign aid/ GNI (%)	0.01	0.06	0.07	0.06	0.06	0.07	0.07	0.06

Sources: European Commission, "Memo: Publication of preliminary data on 2013 Official Development Assistance." Accessed 10 July, 2014, http://europa.eu/rapid/press-release_MEMO-14-263_en.htm; European Commission, "Communication from the Commission to the Council and the European Parliament: Accelerating progress towards attaining the Millennium Development Goals—Financing for Development and Aid Effectiveness, COM (2005) 133", Accessed 10 July, 2014, http://register.consilium.europa.eu/doc/srv?l=EN&t=PDF&gc=true&sc=false&f=ST%208139%202005%20INIT

Nevertheless, the share of bilateral aid within total aid was not equally impressive. With the exception of 2008 and 2010, the share of bilateral foreign aid was under 10%, which suggests that Latvia was not actively developing its bilateral foreign aid policy. The lion's share of Latvia's foreign aid was allocated to multilateral development institutions (such as the World Bank, the United Nations Program for Development, etc.) and to the EU budget.

Also, the indicator of ODA/ GNI proportion, which was used by the European Commission to follow up Latvia's progress in reaching the EU targets, fluctuated. Throughout the period, Latvia's proportion of ODA/GNI never even came close to reaching the EU's 2010 target for the new member states. It increased from 0.06% in 2004 to 0.07% in 2005, but fell back to the 2004 level in 2006 and stayed there until 2008, when it increased once again to 0.07%. In 2010, Latvia missed the EU target of 0.17% ODA/GNI, as it allocated only 0.06% of its GNI to foreign aid.

In sum, Latvia's response to EU adaptational pressures was mixed. First, the institutional dimension of Latvia's foreign aid policy evolved gradually, but was halted by the financial crisis in 2008–2010. Second, the financial dimension of the policy was developing gradually and, if measured in absolute terms, the increase in the aid budget was significant. Nevertheless, Latvia's ODA/ GNI proportion was lagging behind other CEECs, which on average allocated approximately 0.1% ODA/ GNI throughout the period. All in all, this slow and gradual evolution does not amount to stalling or reversing the policy, as predicted by the Rationalist theories.

5. Analysis of Causal Factors

The main ambition of this section is to explain the evolution of Latvia's foreign aid policy after the accession, in particular why Latvia continued implementing and developing the policy even though the EU had no legal power to enforce compliance after the EU conditionality lost its effect after accession. First, I will examine and evaluate the evidence concerning the Rationalist explanatory factors: legacy of conditionality,[44] and presence of veto players. Second, I will turn to examining the explanatory power of socialisation.

Rationalist Explanation

Considering the first of the two factors suggested by Rationalists—legacy of EU conditionality—I have examined whether any kind of "fast-track" legislative procedure, inherited from the pre-accession period, facilitated an effective transposition of EU rules even in the post-accession period. My conclusion is that the EU foreign aid policy is not a policy area characterised by a high density of binding EU rules that the member states have to transpose in their national legislation. In fact, foreign aid policy is seen as part of the member states' foreign policy, which implies that the most usual outcome of negotiations at the Council of the EU is adoption of so-called "soft law" (Council Conclusions, recommendations, etc.). Even the Barcelona commitments and the succeeding EU commitments on increasing foreign aid mentioned in the preceding section were adopted as "Council Conclusions" (i.e. conclusions of the negotiations held by the member state representatives in the Council of the EU) which, strictly speaking, are not legally binding. In fact, the Law on International Assistance was the only law on foreign aid that was passed by *Saeima* (Latvia's

---

44 As I have indicated above, I treat the second kind of legacy of EU conditionality (continued susceptibility to the EU's shaming strategy) as belonging to the Constructivist school, as it is based on the theoretical premises of Constructivism.

Parliament) in 2008, four years after the accession.[45] Therefore, it can be concluded that this factor cannot explain the continued evolution of Latvia's foreign aid policy in the post-accession period.

Nor can the second factor suggested by Rationalists—veto players—explain why Latvia continued building its aid institutions and increasing its ODA in absolute terms. If there were powerful political players that wished to abolish the foreign aid policy, the post-accession period was the right time to do it, but the policy was not stalled or reversed.

What the veto player theory can explain, however, is the fluctuating dynamics of Latvia's ODA/GNI proportion, which is one important aspect of the evolution of foreign aid policy. Throughout my interviews I found that increasing the foreign aid budget was an issue that was contested in the annual inter-departmental negotiations on drawing up the state budget.[46] The Ministry of Finance in particular argued for a fiscally conservative stance regarding increase of public spending.[47] Some respondents expressed the view that both relevant politicians and also higher civil servants feared a negative public reaction if the public spending was ambitiously increased for a policy area that is not concerned with ensuring and improving domestic welfare.[48] Probably based on that motivation, in 2006 the government adopted a policy document entitled "Concept on Increasing the Financing for Implementation of Latvian Development Cooperation, 2006–2010", which set the goal of increasing ODA only to

---

45 Although the Law is based on the "principles and best practice" of several international organisations (*inter alia*, also the EU), it cannot be deemed as a case of binding EU rules being transposed into national legislation.
46 Interview with Latvia's former Minister of Foreign Affairs, Rīga, 23 October, 2009; Interview with Latvia's former Minister of Foreign Affairs, Rīga, 22 October, 2010.
47 Interview with Latvia's former Minister of Foreign Affairs, Rīga, 23 October, 2009; Interview with a former senior civil servant at the Latvian Ministry of Finance, Rīga, 12 October, 2010; Interview with chairman of the Committee for Foreign Affairs, *Saeima* (Latvia's Parliament), Rīga, 13 October, 2010; Interview with Latvia's former Minister of Foreign Affairs, Rīga, 22 October, 2010.
48 Interview with a former senior civil servant at Latvia's Ministry of Finance, Rīga, 12 October, 2010; Interview with a former senior civil servant at Latvia's Ministry of Finance, Rīga, 20 October, 2010.

the level of 0.1% ODA/ GNI by 2010. This implied that Latvia would miss the EU's 2010 target for the new member states of 0.17% ODA/GNI.[49]

However, during the early stages of the financial crisis, as some interviewees recalled, the decision to cut the funding for bilateral aid was taken internally within the Ministry of Foreign Affairs.[50] As the former foreign minister related in an interview, he had two choices—either cut the bilateral aid, or cut funding for the diplomatic network—and he decided to cut the bilateral aid[51]. In this case, the foreign minister functioned as a political actor that was able to influence the further evolution of foreign aid policy. By severely cutting aid, he constrained Latvia's already limited ambition to increase its ODA.

Based on the analysis of these historic episodes, the veto player theory can explain why Latvia did not reach the EU target of 0.17 ODA/ GNI by 2010. Still, this theory does not provide an explanation for why Latvia continued its foreign aid policy in the first place. Therefore, I turn now to the Constructivist explanation.

Constructivist Explanation

As noted above, the Constructivist explanation revolves around the socio-psychological processes of socialisation and, in particular, socialisation through identification with the EU as the reference group. Despite the fact that the "Barcelona commitments" were domestically seen as the "soft" *acquis* (implying no material sanctions against non-compliers)[52], the domestic decision-makers I interviewed recalled having discussed the topic of increased ODA with their colleagues at various meetings at the EU level.[53] A high-level civil servant even

---

49 Cabinet of Ministers, "Koncepcija finansējuma palielināšanai no valsts budžeta 2006.—2010. gadā Latvijas Republikas attīstības sadarbības politikas īstenošanai." [Concept on increasing the financing for implementation of Latvian development cooperation, 2006–2010.] http://polsis.mk.gov.lv/view.do?id=1899. (Accessed 12 July, 2014).
50 Interview (a group interview) with a middle-level civil servant and three desk officers at Latvia's Ministry of Foreign Affairs, Rīga, 20 October, 2009; Interview with Latvia's former Minister of Foreign Affairs, Rīga, 22 October, 2010.
51 Interview with Latvia's former Minister of Foreign Affairs, Rīga, 22 October, 2010.
52 Interview with a senior civil servant at Latvia's Ministry of Foreign Affairs, Stockholm, 26 October, 2010.
53 Interview with a senior civil servant at Latvia's Ministry of Foreign Affairs, Stockholm, 26 October, 2010; Interview with a former senior civil servant at Latvia's Ministry of Finance, Rīga, 20 October, 2010.

noted that she had received "reproaches from some member states" when discussing Latvia's performance in reaching the EU financial targets.[54] It was also explained that, for Latvia, the commitment to increase the ODA was about demonstrating solidarity with the old EU member states.[55] A lower-rank civil servant also acknowledged the existence of such peer pressure from the European Commission and other member states, noting that the European Commission's annual reports on member states' performance in meeting the EU targets constituted an important part of such pressure.[56]

When examining the policy documents, there was, naturally, no explicit mention of "peer pressure". Subtle references to it could nevertheless be read between the lines. For instance, the policy document "Concept on Increasing the Financing for Implementation of Latvian Development Cooperation, 2006–2010", despite recommending a break with the EU targets for the new member states, contained references that can be read as evidence that Latvia was concerned about its image in the EU and in the international community. For instance: "For Latvia, it is essential to demonstrate the resolution to gradually increase the financing for development cooperation taking into account the international commitments."[57] Moreover, the document did not even consider the option that Latvia could stall or reverse its decision to provide aid to developing countries. The document argued for increased financing for foreign aid, albeit to a lower level than foreseen by the EU commitments. It seems that the government's decision to adopt the document can be interpreted as a balancing act: the government, probably, was constrained domestically not to increase ODA too ambitiously; but, at the same time, it was aware that increasing the ODA was the right thing to do. The dilemma was rather to what extent Latvia should increase its ODA in order to avoid opprobrium from other member states.

---

54 Interview with a senior civil servant at Latvia's Ministry of Foreign Affairs, Stockholm, 26 October, 2010.
55 Interview with a senior civil servant at Latvia's Ministry of Foreign Affairs, Stockholm, 26 October, 2010; Interview with a former senior civil servant at Latvia's Ministry of Finance, Rīga, 20 October, 2010.
56 Interview (a group interview) with a middle-level civil servant and three desk officers at Latvia's Ministry of Foreign Affairs, Rīga, 20 October, 2009.
57 Cabinet of Ministers, "Koncepcija finansējuma palielināšanai."

All in all, the perceived peer pressure and fears of opprobrium (or reputational costs stemming from non-complying with the expected behaviour) from the EU (both the European Commission and other member states) provides a plausible explanation for why Latvia did continue its foreign aid policy even after accession. Even if Latvia was not prepared to wholeheartedly implement the EU targets on ODA, it seems that a complete policy discontinuation was not an option that was seriously considered by domestic decision-makers.

6. Conclusions

At the outset of this chapter, I outlined the research puzzle concerning the continued evolution of foreign aid policy in Latvia after its accession to the EU. According to the Rationalist predictions, we should expect that, after accession, Latvia would have stalled or reversed the policies and reforms introduced under the pressure of EU conditionality. As this chapter has demonstrated, Latvia, despite being one of the poorest new member states, did continue gradually building its foreign aid policy structures and providing aid to developing countries. This is an outcome which does not comply with the Rationalist expectations. Consequently, the observed outcome prompted the question regarding what factors can explain the continued policy evolution in the post-accession era.

Rationalists have suggested that new member states might have inherited special legislative procedures facilitating quick transposition of the EU rules. This chapter, however, demonstrates that such legacies do not explain the case of foreign aid policy, as there were few binding rules that had to be transposed. Nor does the veto player theory, also proposed by Rationalists, explain the fact that Latvia continued providing aid and increasing it in absolute terms throughout the post-accession period. The veto player theory can explain those aspects of the policy that concern reaching the EU's targets for the new member states. Indeed, it seems that powerful domestic decision-makers did constrain Latvia fulfilling its international commitment of reaching the 0.17 % ODA/ GNI target by 2010.

The findings here seem to support the Constructivist explanation that point to the role of socialisation as the main factor behind why Latvia continued providing aid to its development partners, developed its policy structures and strove to increase the foreign aid budget even in the post-accession period. It can be inferred from the findings that the domestic decision-makers perceived peer pressure and feared opprobrium from their peers in the EU. It is difficult to say whether Latvian decision-makers had internalised their susceptibility to the peer pressure already in the pre-accession phase when the country was subjected to EU conditionality and the European Commission conducted a thorough monitoring and ranking of aspiring member countries according to their performance.

I propose that this sensitivity to the EU's strategy of shaming need not be linked with EU conditionality. The susceptibility to shaming, at least partly, could stem also from the new member states' quest to appear as "proper" European countries that has been noted by other authors.[58] I further propose the following interpretation: the quest to affirm Latvia's "Europeanness" was linked to its need for ontological security.[59] The concept of ontological security is still novel and controversial in the discipline of international relations.[60] I, for one, find it useful, because the concept suggests that states may "feel" a need to present and act according to a coherent narrative of state identity that would not only appeal to both a domestic and an external audience, but would, in doing so, also sustain a sense of coherent Self and ensure the credibility and predictability of their respective countries within the wider international community[61]. As noted above, ontological security is pursued in order to avoid feeling shame at doing something that is incongruent with one's self-identity and to increase the feeling of self-esteem. Appearing as a "proper", and thus predictable, Western-oriented and credible European country might be a very essential strategy for a small country like Latvia, especially after the Crimean annexation when the domestic elites must assure themselves and the population of Latvia that the country will be protected in a hypothetical crisis situation.

---

58 Jacobsson and Nordström, "Soft powers (in a community of the willing)," 168.
59 Mitzen, "Ontological Security in World Politics," 341–370; Steele, *Ontological Security in International Relations*.
60 For a critique of the concept, see, for instance, Alanna Krolikowski, "State Personhood in Ontological Security Theories of International Relations and Chinese Nationalism: A Sceptical View," *Chinese Journal of International Politics* 2 (2008): 109–133.
61 Mitzen, "Ontological Security in World Politics," 344; Steele, *Ontological Security in International Relations*, 2–3.

If the evolution of Latvia's foreign aid is interpreted through the lens of ontological security, asserting oneself as a "proper" European country implies following certain behavioural models that stem from the conceived idea of how "proper" European countries behave in the international community;[62] for instance, that they provide aid to developing countries. In such a case, it is probably not important how large (or small) aid volumes are provided (as there is also a wide difference in the aid volumes allocated by the old member states[63]), but rather the fact that the new member states share the European practice of providing aid. Finally, such an interpretation considering Latvia's aid-giving activities as part of its quest for ontological security implies that Latvia, most likely, had gained a certain sense of agency as a small state. It probably meant that even the small sums that were allocated to foreign aid allowed the country and its elites to feel that they were not only reacting to the developments in their neighbourhood, but also to some extent actively shaping that environment (i.e. the situation in the recipient countries) by providing aid. After all, one of the main reasons that countries provide foreign aid is to seek to influence the development (or at least the behaviour) of the aid recipient countries.

---

62 On the importance of following practices that sustain self-identity, see Mitzen, "Ontological Security in World Politics," 344, 347. On the importance of following material practices that pertain to sustain an aspired identity, see Michelle Murray, "Identity, Insecurity, and Great Power Politics: The Tragedy of German Naval Ambition Before the First World War," *Security Studies* 19 (2010): 663–665.

63 For instance, according to the data compiled by the European Commission, the old member states that provided the highest aid volumes (measured as percentage ODA/GNI) in 2013 were Sweden (1.02%), Luxembourg (1.0%) and Denmark (0.85%), while the old member states that provided the lowest aid volumes (measured as percentage ODA/GNI) in 2013 were Greece (0.13%), Italy and Spain (both provided 0.16%). See European Commission, "Memo: Publication of preliminary data on 2013 Official Development Assistance." http://europa.eu/rapid/press-release_MEMO-14-263_en.htm (Accessed 10 July 2014).

Paradoxes of Power: Gender, Work and Family in the New Europe

Daina S. Eglitis, George Washington University

1. Introduction

The goal of this chapter is to illuminate some of the key paradoxes of power in the New Europe, with a particular focus on Latvia and the 25 years following the reestablishment of independence in 1991. The work is set in a context that I argue is characterised by enduring and doxic patriarchal structures and practices that exist together with a substantial population of weak male actors whose educational attainment, labour force participation, earning power, health status and longevity, and assumption of family roles and responsibilities have declined markedly in the period since independence was reestablished. My argument is that the past decades have seen the evolution of an acute social crisis among a significant segment of men in the "new Europe," that is, in the post-communist space that has been integrated in the past two decades into European structures like the European Union. While much has been written on post-communist societies, patriarchy, and the discriminatory effects of transition processes on women in the region, less attention has been paid to the paradox of a population of marginal men in a societal context that privileges male actors and masculinity. Arguably, the roots and depth of the crisis may be masked by the persisting economic and political domination of male elites in key institutions and the cultural domination of masculinity.

This chapter highlights the dimensions and sociological roots of the crisis, including declining educational attainment among men, substantial labour market changes and persistently high rates of alcohol and even drug use. It also considers the implications of this crisis for society at both the micro and macro levels, focusing in particular on the institutions of the family and the economy.

2. The Phenomenon of "Male Crisis"

The notion in Western societies that there is "trouble with men" is not entirely new. In sociology, it dates back to the Chicago School of urban sociology, which was active in the 1920s and 1930s. In the 1980s, the research of sociologist William Julius Wilson on the crisis in black urban America introduced the concept of "male marriageability" and the "unmarriageable man" as conceptual links between post-industrial labour market shifts, middle class migration from cities, and the dramatic decline of marriage and rise of non-marital births among poor and working-class African-Americans.[1] Today, the British press— and to a lesser extent, British social science—laments the troublesome lads who are neither in school nor in the labour market, occupying marginal social spaces and locked into unproductive, poor, and sometimes criminal lives.[2]

In the post-Soviet and ex-Communist Bloc countries, one has also historically encountered a paradoxical mix of deeply embedded patriarchal attitudes and structures that exist together with a shared sentiment acknowledging women's autonomy, strength, and resilience in crisis.[3] In Russian culture, for instance, one encounters the folk wisdom that, "Women can do everything and men can do the rest." At the same time, male dominance has been and continues to be normative and structural, with men occupying key positions of power in economic and political fields and masculinity occupying a privileged cultural position in society.

This chapter highlights the manifestations, roots, and implications of what I argue is a *new crisis of men in the post-Soviet space*. The crisis is made visible in social indicators that show changes in areas like educational attainment, labour market participation, health status and longevity, and, arguably, even in demographic data on family formation and fertility. At the same time, the crisis may be made virtually invisible by the continued dominance of males in politics and the economy and the domination of masculinity in culture and society. It may also be difficult to discern because social scientific studies to this point have largely highlighted the post-communist structural and social processes

---

1   William J. Wilson, *The Truly Disadvantaged* (Chicago: University of Chicago Press, 1990); William J. Wilson, *When Work Disappears: The World of the New Urban Poor* (Chicago: University of Chicago Press, 1997).
2   Rebecca Kay, *Men in Russia: Fallen Heroes of Post-Soviet Change?* (Burlington: Ashgate, 2006).
3   Kay, *Men in Russia*.

contributing to women's marginalisation, including discrimination in employment, low levels of political power in the absence of quotas, and cuts to important social supports for mothers and children.[4]

What, then, does the crisis of men look like and how do social indicators show its evolution and direction? Below I examine data on educational attainment, labour market participation and health and mortality, in order to highlight the argument that the dominance of *some* men in structures of power and the preeminent place of cultural norms of masculinity may be obscuring a more broadly experienced and significant crisis of men in post-communism.

Educational Attainment

While in the much of the Western world, women have only recently caught up or surpassed men in advanced educational attainment, in post-communist Europe, for several generations women have had higher average rates of educational attainment than men. In Latvia, an educational gap favouring women opens up in the advanced middle-ages. Notably, this gap, with some fluctuations, has persisted and grown in recent decades.

The gap in higher education is not unrelated to a gap in completion of high school in Latvia, where early school-leaving rates are higher among male students than among their female peers. In 2012,[5] for example, while girls made up about 52% of primary school completers and boys constituted the remaining 48%, high school completers were 56% female and male completers were about 44%. Some of the non-completers may also have moved into vocational education schools, which have a higher proportion of male graduates, but

---

4 Daina S. Eglitis, *Imagining the Nation: History, Modernity, and Revolution in Latvia* (University Park, PA: Penn State University Press, 2002); Barbara Einhorn, *Cinderella Goes to Market: Gender and Women's Movements in East Central Europe* (New York: Verson, 1993); Susan Gal and Gail Kligman, *The Politics of Gender after Socialism* (Princeton: Princeton University Press, 2000); Joanna Regulska and Bonnie G. Smith, eds., *Women and Gender in Postwar Europe: From Cold War to European Union* (New York: Routledge, 2012); Daina Stukuls, "Body of the Nation: Mothering, Prostitution, and the Place of Women in Postcommunist Latvia," *Slavic Review* 58 (2002); Peggy Watson, "Eastern Europe's Silent Revolution: Gender," *Sociology* 27, 3 (1993).
5 Statistical indictors used in this chapter, unless otherwise indicated, are from the database available in Latvian and English at the Central Statistical Bureau of Latvia website: http://www.csb.lv.

higher rates of early school leaving among male students in high school, particularly in rural areas, were noted in Latvia already in the first decade of postcommunism after more stringent Soviet rules on educational attainment were lifted.[6]

The most substantial gap is to be found in higher education, where data show significant differences by sex in enrollment and graduation. First, data on total enrollments in higher education suggest that the disparity between men and women is high, though proportions shift. In the 2000–2001 school year, just over 62,000 women were studying in institutions of higher education; in the same year, about 39,000 men were enrolled. Over a decade later, in 2012–2013, about 55,000 women were enrolled and nearly 39,000 men were enrolled. Men continue to make up the greater share of students in science, maths, computing, engineering, and fields related to manufacturing and construction. All other fields, including health, education, the humanities and the social sciences, are dominated by women: for example, of about 6000 education students in 2012–2013, more than 5300 were women.

Notably, enrollment in higher education is only part of the important story in the male and female education gap. As has been the case in other Western countries,[7] a significant number of male students in higher education leave without completing a degree. This is reflected in graduation figures, which have been relatively consistent across the last decade.[8] In 2012, over 67% of Bachelor's degree recipients were female, as were over 70% of Master's degree recipients, over 64% of higher professional education graduates, and 60% of doctoral recipients.

As noted above, this disparity continues a trend that extends back to the communist era. Christy Glass has written that "Many women compensated for their relative lack of political capital and occupational prestige [in communism] by

---

6 Daina S. Eglitis, "Cultures of Gender and the Changing Latvian Family in Early Post-Communism," *Journal of Baltic Studies* 41, 2 (2010): 151–176; Ritma Rungule, *Izglitiba un dzives apstakli Latvija 1999. gada* (Rīga: Central Statistical Bureau of Latvia).
7 Claudia DiPrete and Thomas Buchmann, *The Rise of Women: The Growing Gender Gap in Education and What It Means for American Schools* (New York: Russell Sage Foundation, 2013).
8 Eglitis, "Cultures of Gender".

seeking high levels of educational credentials."[9] This trend has continued, arguably for similar reasons, in the last two decades as well: the existence and persistence of a gender wage gap in spite of women's relative wealth of educational capital and credentials suggests that higher education is a key path of personal and professional advancement that is fully open to women.

The gender gap in educational attainment points both to women's relative educational and economic progress and, at the same time, a potential social problem, as lack of educational attainment, as I note below, is dysfunctional for active male participation in the formal labour market, particularly as that labour market shifts from Soviet-era reliance on industrial and agricultural production to services, technology, and occupations that demand higher education or specialised skills.

Labour Market Participation

Men have historically had higher labour market participation rates than women, a trend that continues to this day in Latvia, though women's participation rate (72%) approaches that of their economically active male peers (77%).[10] There are myriad reasons for this. In the context of modern waged labour, women have traditionally been expected to leave the labour market, at least temporarily, when children are born. Women have also been paid less than men, even in comparable positions, making their labour force participation less economically valuable and more likely to be sacrificed when an adult is needed at home to care for a child or elderly parent.

In the post-communist period, much has been written about women's disadvantages in the shift from centrally planned economies to the free and largely unregulated capitalist labour market. Indeed, few apparent advantages accrued to women, particularly during the early years of post-communism. Consider for instance the question posed in 1993 by then-Russian Labour Minister Gennady Melikyan: "Why should we employ women when men are out of work?"

---

9 Christy M. Glass, "Gender and Work in Transition: Job Loss in Bulgaria, Poland, and Russia," *East European Politics & Societies* 22, 4 (2008): 759.
10 See: http://data.worldbank.org/indicator/SL.TLF.CACT.ZS

At the same time, in Latvia, women have, judging by statistical data, been more "employable" than their male peers, whose unemployment rate has often been higher in the post-communist period. We might explain women's apparent advantage in the labour market by pointing to the fact that in periods of economic restructuring (including the shift from an industrial to a post-industrial economy), women have been protected by their concentration in fields less vulnerable to change, including the service industry and the public sector. Notably as well, as lower-cost workers, they may benefit from employers' desire to maintain productivity while cutting costs.[11] Paradoxically, then, women's advantage in the labour market may, in part, be built on a foundation of their disadvantage—that is, their concentration in lower-wage sectors of the economy.

Twenty-five years of independence have brought many political advantages and advances to Latvia. Economically as well, many inhabitants have gained new opportunities both professionally and in terms of consumption and lifestyle. At the same time, economic gains have not been shared across the spectrum and one of the persistent maladies of post-communism has been high rates of unemployment and accompanying problems of low-income and poverty. Women's rates of unemployment[12] have tended to be lower than men's for much of the post-communist period. Notably, some of the most substantial gaps in the rate were in the years immediately following the onset of the economic crisis in 2008. In 2008, men's unemployment rate was 8.7% and women's was 7.3%. The following year, men's rate had risen to 21.4% and women's to 14.6%. In 2010, men's unemployment rose to 23% and women's to 16.6%. Both rates took a downward turn the following year, though in 2011, men's rate at nearly 19% was still about five points higher than women's at

---

11 For a similar argument, see, for instance: Eva Fodor, "Gender in Transition: Unemployment in Hungary, Poland and Slovakia," *East European Politics and Societies*, 11, 3 (1997): 470–500.

12 Unemployment was defined by Central Statistical Bureau of Latvia in 2014 as follows: "Unemployed persons are persons aged 15–74 years, whether registered at the State Employment Agency (SEA) or not, and who meet the following three conditions simultaneously: 1) during the reference week neither worked nor were temporary absent from work; 2) had actively sought employment during the past 4 weeks; 3) in case of finding a job, were available to start work immediately (within the next 2 weeks). Persons who already had found a job and will start up within a period of three months are also classified as unemployed."

14% Subsequent years have seen a continuing decline for both sexes, though a gap has remained.[13]

While women have lower levels of unemployment, they are also subject to a persistent gender wage gap. Even in sectors of the labour market dominated by women, such as the hospitality industry (79% female), education (87% female), health and social services (86% female) and public sector bureaucracy (67% female), women have lower average wages: for example, in 2012, women in education earned 85% of what their male colleagues working full-time and year-round earned; in health and social services, the figure was 84%. Notably, in male-dominated and highly remunerative sectors like finance and insurance services, women's average pay is just 61% of the male wage. In 2012, the average monthly earning for women was 426 Lats; for men, it was 511 Lats.

In terms of the labour market, men enjoy some perception of favourable treatment: in a 2004 *Latvijas fakti* (Latvia's Facts) survey, nearly 65% of respondents agreed that, "a man is often hired for a job just because he is a man." Employed men are also more likely to earn a higher wage. At the same time, men are less likely to be employed and, importantly, sectors that historically have been the source of livelihood for less educated men, industrial production in particular, have been largely wiped out by the collapse of the Soviet chain of production and the competition of post-Soviet capitalism.

Health and Mortality

Much has been written in the past decades on the expansive health and mortality crisis that data suggest has characterised much of the post-communist region. Recently, for instance, journalist Masha Gessen (2014) lamented the "Dying Russians," citing data on the overall decline of life expectancy and other

---

13 Unemployment data is not, of course, comprehensive, as it fails to include those who, for instance, have given up looking for work (long-term unemployment is another persistent problem in the region), who work part-time but would like to work full-time hours, and those who work in the informal economy, a sector of the economy that provides opportunities for those whose options in the formal labour force may be limited, but which does not accrue retirement benefits or offer other key benefits of the formal labour force.

health and population indicators.[14] While the precision of some her figures has been disputed,[15] the overall trend of declining health and mortality that appears to take root in the 1990s is in little dispute. In Latvia, social indicators suggest that while overall trend lines have shown both decline and some recovery (though not in the population growth overall), a persisting trend is the dramatic gap between male and female health and mortality indicators.

Life expectancy at birth is a commonly cited indicator in demographic literature, and the historical trend in the modern era has been the steady upward climb of life expectancy as medical advances like antibiotics and public health improvements like modern sanitation have spread. In Latvia, life expectancy at birth for both sexes dropped in the 1990s, particularly in the early years of the decade, which were characterised by destabilising economic crises. By the turn of the millennium, however, stabilisation and then apparent recovery took place. If, for instance, the overall life expectancy at birth was just 66.7 years overall in 1995, then by 2005 it had risen to 70.89 and in 2012 it reached 74. The gradual upward climb, however, masks substantial sex differences in life expectancy at birth: in 1995, when the overall life expectancy was just 66.7 years, it was still 73.1 for women. By 2005, the female life expectancy at birth had reached 76.5, but male life expectancy was just 65.1. In 2012, the male figure improved, but remained below 70 years (69.7 years), while the female figure was nearly 79 years.

Lower male life expectancy reflects substantial health threats and risks that accrue across the life course. Males are more likely than their female peers to succumb to disease, external causes of death, and suicide. For example, while men and women have similar risks of coronary disease or cancer (though men's risk is higher), men's risk of dying from respiratory illnesses is far greater. They comprise nearly 70% of victims, which may be attributable to men's much higher rate of tobacco use: according to the World Health Organisation, about 46% of men over the age of 15 use tobacco, while just 20% of women do. Men

---

14 Masha Gessen, "The Dying Russians," *New York Review of Books Blog*. http://www.nybooks.com/blogs/nyrblog/2014/sep/02/dying-russians/ (Accessed September 2014).

15 Mark Adomanis, "Eight Things Masha Gessen Got Wrong about Russian Demography," *Forbes*, 3 September, 2014. http://www.forbes.com/sites/markadomanis/2014/09/03/8-things-masha-gessen-got-wrong-about-russian-demography/ (Accessed September 2014).

account for about three-quarters of all deaths from "external causes," which includes accidents, violence, and suicide. Taking suicide alone as a cause of death, the difference is even more dramatic: in 2009, for example, the male rate of suicide was 40 per 100,000 population, while the female rate was just 8.2 per 100,000 population. The male rate of suicide has risen in periods of economic crisis (for example, 1993 and 2008–2009) while women's rates have been less sensitive to economic distress.[16] Interestingly, a journalistic account of Latvia's "man shortage" published by the British Broadcasting Corporation in 2010 noted the opinion of a psychoanalyst who treats men that, "Latvia's transition to capitalism…put massive pressure on men to succeed financially." The article continued that, "[the] economic crisis [that began in 2008] has made those ambitions even more unattainable."[17]

While data on problems like alcohol and drug use and abuse are not as rigorous and are more dependent on self-reports, available indicators suggest that these are also contributors to male morbidity and mortality to a degree that women do not share. For example, data on registered cases of addiction indicates that far more men than women (over 16,000 men compared to under 5000 women) were registered in 2011 as alcoholics; while the figures were low for both, more men than women were also registered as psychoactive drug addicts. Alcohol use and abuse have also been linked to regional cultures.[18] As Eglitis writes:

> "The problem of alcohol abuse has become acute, especially in economically depressed areas. Some people who cannot afford commercial alcoholic beverages make their own local version of moonshine. For men who cannot meet the 'masculine' breadwinning norm embraced by both men and women, alcohol may be the chosen salve…"[19]

The persistence of heavy drinking among men is not, however, only linked to economic distress. Rather, anecdotal evidence suggests the rootedness of this practice in masculine culture more generally: the BBC article noted above

---

16 Data is from the World Health Organization (WHO): www.who.int/mental_health/media/latv.pdf
17 British Broadcasting Corporation (BBC), "Latvian Man Shortage Leaves Women Lost for Love," BBC News Europe, 13 October 2010. http://www.bbc.co.uk/news/world-europe-11493157 (accessed September 2014).
18 On Latvia, see Eglitis, "Cultures of Gender"; on Russia, see Kay, *Men in Russia*.
19 Eglitis "Cultures of Gender," 169.

quotes a 28-year-old male engineer suggesting that, "It is kind of perceived that it is manly, that the more alcohol you can handle, the more of a man you are."[20] Heavy use of alcohol can be linked to external causes of death, including accidents and poisonings, as well as suicides. Economic and social consequences can also be significant, as heavy users of alcohol may have trouble getting and keeping paid employment, as well as establishing or maintaining family relationships.

3. Masculinity, Power and Society

The "crisis of men" is rendered visible in social indicators that show lagging relative educational attainment, weak labour market prospects for many less-educated men, and poor health and mortality indicators. At the same time, arguably, the existence and persistence of post-communist crisis is obscured by a dominant culture of masculinity and the dominance of male actors in key societal sectors like politics and the economy.

The assertion of a "dominant culture of masculinity" does not, of course, preclude the recognition of women's power in society or of a phenomenon of denigration of men that can also be found in the region.[21] Alas, it suggests that particular characteristics associated with (stereotypical) masculinity are socially valued, particularly relative to characteristics associated with (stereotypically) feminine traits. Further, it posits that there is a discernible societal perception that men and masculinity are more highly valued in society.

A variety of societal surveys suggest women and men perceive advantages to both male status and associated masculine traits. For example, a 2004 survey published by *Latvijas fakti* (Latvia's Facts) found that nearly three-quarters of respondents agreed with the statement that, "A man is the head of the family"—

---

20 BBC, "Latvian Man Shortage".
21 Kay, *Men in Russia*.

strikingly, however, a 2013 GfK survey found that 50% agreed with this statement.[22] A smaller proportion (just over 50%) agreed that, "Men are better politicians," a proportion that was smaller still in 2013.[23] Significantly for this discussion, over 86% of respondents affirmed the statement that, "A man must be the provider of the family"—while this figure was smaller in 2013 (61%), it still represented a majority opinion and over 73% agreed that "a man must assume the greater responsibility for financial care of the family." In light of the persisting phenomenon of male unemployment and underemployment, particularly among less educated males, this strongly affirmed norm is significant, a point that will be discussed more fully further along.

Survey data also suggest that many respondents hold stereotypical views of women and their social roles. For instance, about two-thirds of 2004 respondents agreed that "A woman must assume responsibility for the household" and, in an echo of Soviet-era concerns about spinsterism that existed in an era of early and widespread entry into marriage,[24] over 43% affirmed the statement that "an unmarried woman who is over 30 is a spinster (*vecmeita*)[25]."

Latvia was the first post-Soviet and post-communist state to have a female head of state: President Vaira Vīķe-Freiberga served in that position from 1999 to 2007. She is still a popular figure in Latvia's society and her opinions continue to command global attention. At the same time, the upper echelons of Latvian politics have been persistently male-dominated. In early 2014, the proportion of female deputies in the Parliament of Latvia was just under a quarter,[26] 78% of Rīga City Council deputies were males, and out of 5 political parties represented in the Parliament in the 11th parliamentary session, only two had female board members. Local politics is also male-dominated: in 2009,

---

22 See survey results in Slide Share at http://politika.lv/article/iespeja-diskusija-sievietes-un-viriesa-loma-politika-latvija.
23 A weakness of this question battery is that it did not offer an alternative: "Women make better politicians." Rather, one is left to guess whether respondents who said "no" would believe that men and women were equally good or that women were better politicians.
24 Eglitis, "Cultures of Gender".
25 As in English, *vecmeita* is a disparaging term rather than a female equivalent of a bachelor. There is no obvious male equivalent for an unmarried man in Latvian.
26 Although 23 is the record number of female deputies, surpassing by 2 women the number in the 8th and 10th sessions.

1138 locally elected deputies (to the equivalent of city or regional councils) were men, while 627 were women.

Women in politics have been more likely to be critiqued in the media about their professional demeanour and their appearance. Recent work conducted by PROVIDUS, a Latvian think tank, points to the persisting stereotype of men as confident, strong and rational politicians and women as emotional and untrustworthy politicians.[27] In the 2013 GfK study, just 1% of inhabitants of Latvia agreed that being a politician is the most appropriate profession for a woman. About three-quarters of respondents indicated that the most appropriate profession for a woman was a kindergarten teacher, a secretary, or a housewife. Paradoxically (considering women's active participation in the labour market), the work also found a continuing stereotype that family and career are mutually exclusive spheres of life for women. Moreover, nearly a third of respondents suggested that a woman who has a high work position is no longer "womanly" (sievišķīga).[28]

Attitudes about gender show discernible progress over the course of the last decades. At the same time, both attitudes and practices continue to privilege male dominance in politics and society and, paradoxically, to reinforce the stereotype of the male breadwinner imperative that both elevates male societal position and marginalises men who fail to reach this goal.

4. Hypothesising the Effects of the Crisis

The growing gender gap in educational attainment and the economic (as well as other) struggles of some groups of men correlate with other dramatic changes in Latvian society in the post-communist period. Among those changes are significant shifts in marital and fertility behaviour.

Demographic data from the Central Statistical Bureau of Latvia show that the crude marriage rate in Latvia fell sharply in the 1990s. In 1970, Latvia (or the Latvian SSR) had a crude marriage rate of 10.1 per 1000 population. A very

---

27 PROVIDUS, *Diskusija „Sievietes un vīrieša loma politikā Latvijā"*. http://politika.lv/article/iespeja-diskusija-sievietes-un-viriesa-loma-politika-latvija.
28 Guntars Laganovskis, "Sieviete—politike vai darbiniece un majsaimniece?" *Latvijas vestnesa portals*, 21 February 2014. http://www.lvportals.lv/print.php?id=261079 (Accessed September 2014).

slow downward trend followed, though change was relatively insubstantial: in 1980, the rate was 9.8 and in 1985, the rate was 9.3. In 1990, the crude marriage rate was 8.9; the years following marked a turning point in the trend, as the rate dropped precipitously. In 1995, it was 4.5 per 1000 and in 2000, 3.9 per 1000. In the decade that followed, the rate fluctuated, creeping upwards to 5.6 in 2005 and back down to 4.4 in 2010. Changing attitudes about marriage, as well as a rise in cohabitation, offer some explanation for the decline of marriage: attitudes expressing comfort with later marriage and with cohabitation before or in place of marriage have been present particularly among young adults.[29] At the same time, marriage has remained among most people an expected event in the life course.[30]

Second, the decline in marriage and rise in cohabitation has been accompanied by a rise in the proportion of non-marital births. This increase is a function both of a real rise in births outside of marriage and a fall of births within legal marriage, as Latvia's total fertility rate has slipped and remained one of the lowest in the world. When marriage rates were high, most births, predictably, were within marriage: in 1980, only 12.5% of births were outside marriage and in 1990, 16.9% of births were outside marriage. A substantial acceleration of the rise of non-marital births took hold in the post-communist period. By 1995, 30% of births were outside of marriage; in 2000, the proportion rose to 40%. By 2005, the proportion was at about 45%, the point where it has, roughly speaking, stayed to the present time.

What is the relationship between these trends and the crisis of men discussed in this chapter? While correlation should not be confused with causation, a relationship between males' educational and economic status and their "marriageability"—that is, their desirability as a partner in the broader marriage pool—has been the subject of sociological study in, among other places, post-industrial America.[31] The desirability of a male partner who is poorly educated

---

29 Pēteris Zvidriņš, Ligita Ezera and Aigars Greitans, *Fertility and Family Surveys in Countries of the ECE Region: Standard Country Report, Latvia* (New York, Geneva United Nations, 1998).
30 Eglitis, "Cultures of Gender".
31 Wilson, *The Truly Disadvantaged*; Wilson, *When Work Disappears;* Katherine Edin and Maria Kefalas, *Promises I Can Keep: Why Poor Women Put Motherhood before Marriage* (Berkeley: University of California Press, 2011).

or significantly less educated than his prospective female partner, or who is unemployed or underemployed, is clearly low. While there is a spectrum of possible reasons for the pattern of non-marriage in communities characterised by high levels of male undereducation or underemployment, the male marriageability hypothesis has received sociological attention and support, both in the U.S. and in the post-communist region, as I discuss in greater detail below.

My work on family and fertility shifts in Latvia suggests that male marriageability has been one factor in the decline of marriage and rise of non-marital births.[32] First, comparatively low levels of educational attainment among men are, notably, among the reasons that some women have characterised (some) men in Latvia as being "unmarriageable." For example, women in my study explained the decline of marriage in Latvia in post-communism with comments including the following:

- "...a woman is more educated and does not need any 'spare furniture' [a male partner] with outdated views." (unmarried Latvian doctor, 25–29, in Rīga)
- "[Many men have] a low level of education and are uncultured." (unmarried Latvian, 25–29, in Rēzekne)
- "There are few educated, intelligent, strong men (I don't mean physically strong)." (unmarried Latvian florist, 19–24, in Rīga).

Second, as the data cited earlier in this chapter suggests, male employment and unemployment in the post-industrial context of independent Latvia are important aspects of the male crisis. Less educated and rural men in particular—though not exclusively—have experienced acute economic dislocation in post-communism. The consequences of this are manifold. It is one factor in the rise of poverty in post-communism.[33] It has also been linked to the growth of alcohol abuse: a respondent in one sociological study pointed out that:

"It has constantly been imbued that a man is one who provides for a family. It turned out that the situation has changed because a man no longer provides for the family. Instead,

---

32 Eglitis "Cultures of Gender".
33 Daina S. Eglitis and Tana Lace, "Stratification and the Poverty of Progress in Postcommunist Latvia," *Acta Sociologica* 52, 4 (2009): 329–349.

the wife does. I think that for the majority of men…it was a heavy blow. And many, who couldn't get over it, because inveterate drunkards. I could list many specific examples."[34]

Indeed, the notion that "the man is the breadwinner in the family" has, despite many social changes in Latvia, remained a strong cornerstone of the gender narrative.

The failure of many men to assume this socially normative role in a post-industrial and newly competitive capitalist context that wiped out many jobs and diminished the earning power of others, can be implicated in the decline of marriageability as well. As noted in an earlier study:

"Data show that unemployment rates have consistently been higher for women than for men. However, men's labor force attachment and success in the workplace are elevated in gender culture in a way that women's are not. That is, a woman who is not working is an acceptable (sometimes even desirable) marriage partner, while a man who is not working is virtually never an acceptable or desirable marriage partner."[35]

The decline of marriage has taken place at the same time as fertility rates overall have fallen, but the rate of non-marital births has risen. Arguably, while some women may forgo marriage, motherhood is still an embraced value in Latvian society and the normative acceptability of single motherhood means that this role is not foreclosed to women who cannot find a partner or choose not to enter legal marriage. In fact, in my study, many women firmly articulated the point that motherhood was strongly desirable, regardless of marital status:[36]

- "It is better to have a child outside marriage [than not to have one at all]. Without children life is worth nothing." (divorced Latvian farmer, 43, in a rural area);
- "A woman must definitely become a mother, if that's possible." (cohabiting Latvian homemaker, 27, in Rīga);
- "Regardless of the circumstances, it is better to become a mother [than not to have a child]." (married Latvian, unemployed, 35, in Rīga).

---

34 Aivita Putniņa, "Men in Latvia: A Situation Sketch," in Pēteris Zvidriņš, ed., *Demographic Situation: Present and Future*, Commission of Strategic Analysis Research Papers 2, 8, 68.
35 Eglitis, "Cultures of Gender, "167.
36 Eglitis, "Cultures of Gender".

Normative shifts and structural obstacles to marriage, as well as a normative stasis in attitudes toward motherhood, suggest that the non-marital birth proportion, which now stands at just below half of all births, is unlikely to change in the near future.

Are low rates of marriage and a high non-marital birth rate social problems? On the one hand, family and fertility decisions are highly personal and what is functional for one family may not be functional for another. On the other hand, historically it has been the case that single women with children are among the groups in any society most vulnerable to poverty. Latvia is no exception to this: in 2012, the group with the highest poverty risk[37] in Latvia was a "single parent (with dependent child/children)", who had a 38.8% risk. By contrast, a family with two adults and a single dependent child had a risk of just over 14%. Interestingly, both single men and women *without* dependent children also show high levels of poverty risk: in fact, the rate for single males (over 34%) is slightly higher than that of females (just below 30%), a phenomenon that is unusual in modern economies and states, where men retain many key economic privileges. The low rate of poverty risk (just over 16%) for a two-adult household without children suggests that marriage or cohabitation may offer some protection from economic deprivation for both men and women.

The data noted above point to some of the economic consequences of the crisis of men that are visited upon society—and on both men and women. The lower levels of educational attainment may be one factor in understanding the somewhat higher rate of poverty risk to be found among single men, which, as noted, is unusual, particularly considering the existing and persisting gender

---

37 The Central Statistical Bureau of Latvia uses the following definition of "at-risk-of-poverty": "Persons with income less than at-risk-of-poverty threshold; or explicitly materially deprived; or employed at work with low intensity are subjected to **at risk of poverty or social exclusion**. It is considered that a person is facing **severe material deprivation** if he/she cannot afford at least four items among the 9 following: i) to pay for arrears (mortgage or rent, utility bills or hire purchase instalments), ii) to keep home adequately warm, iii) to face unexpected expenses, iv) a meal with meat, chicken or fish every second day, v) one-week annual holiday away from home, vi) a personal car, vii) a washing machine, viii) a colour TV, xi) a telephone. The work intensity of the household refers to the number of months that all working age household members have been working during the income reference year as a proportion of the total number of months that could theoretically be worked within the household..."

wage gap. Educational attainment is a good predictor of poverty risk in Latvia, as elsewhere: in 2012, among those ages 18–64, those with a "basic or lower" education had a poverty risk of 33%, while those with a "secondary" (high school or equivalent) education had a risk of 20%. By contrast, for those with higher education, the risk was just over 6%.

The theorisation of effects of a significant number of less educated and/or unemployed or underemployed men on the macroeconomy and indicators like productivity is beyond the scope of this chapter; but, arguably, one linked phenomenon in Latvia has been a decade of high levels of labour migration. As is well-known, Latvia has lost a substantial proportion of its population in the postcommunist period. From an estimated population of 2.3 million at the dawn of restored independence to a diminished population of about 1.9 million at the time of the 2010 Census, the decline of numbers is not trivial. While Latvia's death rate exceeds its birthrate, most population loss is the result of migration. Substantial numbers of men and women have been part of this phenomenon, but it is striking that male emigration figures are higher in periods of economic crisis, suggesting that the lack of economic opportunities is a key driver of male migration: for example, data from the Central Statistical Bureau of Latvia (which is incomplete, as individuals and families leaving Latvia are not required to register their departure and intentions) show that in 2009, more than 20,400 males left and about 17,700 females undertook long-term migration. In 2010, the male figure reached nearly 21,000 and the female figure grew to 18,600. In the years following, the two figures have declined and again become more similar. It is striking that data from 2010–2012 show that three times as many emigrants are single or divorced than are married. Not incidentally, labour migration has been most dramatic from economically struggling regions.

5. Conclusion

This chapter has offered the outlines of an argument that posits the existence of a social crisis of men in contemporary Latvia. Indicators of crisis, however, are submerged beneath culture and practices that privilege masculinity and obscured by the dominance of men in visible positions of power across society. While appropriate attention has been paid in the academic literature on postcommunism to costs of transition borne disproportionately by women, far less recognition has been granted to the marginalisation of men who occupy society's less visible positions. Men who lack education, experience unemployment or underemployment, and inhabit the geographic spaces (particularly rural areas) stripped bare of opportunity in the last quarter century comprise a population that is simultaneously visible and invisible. The effects of this crisis are, however, apparent and reach beyond individual lives to affect society, economy, and family in Latvia.

Reflections on the Political Economy of the Latvian State since 1991: The Role of External Goals. What to Do Now that Externally Defined Goals have been Realised?

Alfs Vanags, Stockholm School of Economics in Riga

1. Introduction

When Latvia regained independence in 1991 it faced (at least) two political economy challenges: one was to disentangle the economy from the Soviet system in which it had been deeply integrated; the second, perhaps more difficult challenge, was to create an independent nation-state. At a formal level, the solution to the latter challenge appeared straightforward—assume continuity of the Latvian state. Effectively this meant reinstating the pre-war constitution, which was indeed done for the most part. Symbolically, this continuity was signalled by, for example, calling the first post-Soviet parliamentary elections held in June 1993 the elections for the 5th *Saeima* (parliament). The elections for the 4th *Saeima* had taken place more than 60 years earlier, in October 1931. At a practical level the challenges were more complex—Latvia had had no practical experience of statehood for nearly 50 years and mistakes were made. For example, Latvia initially diplomatically recognised Taiwan rather than the Peoples Republic of China. This was quickly corrected, but it illustrates the knowledge gap of Latvia's policy makers at the time.

In the economic sphere, there was a presumption that newly independent Latvia should become a market economy, but no consensus on how this should be achieved. This contrasts with Estonia, where a group of "market economy young Turks" was able to implement a kind of "zero option" marked by abolition of tariffs, rapid privatisation and other measures geared to making a decisive break with the Soviet past. In Latvia, there were strong protectionist sentiments and initial privatisation was a muddled process. The creation of the Latvian Privatisation Agency in 1994 regularised the privatisation process, though before that there were significant elements of so-called "spontaneous" privatisation which contributed to the emergence of some of Latvia's so-called oligarchs—for instance, Andris Šķēle who acquired many agribusiness-enterprises and Aivars Lembergs who acquired control of oil and transit interests.

The Agency is still functioning and is not expected to be liquidated until 2018, whereas the Estonian Privatisation Agency started earlier and was wound up already at the end of 2001.

2. The Role of External Anchors

Advice and advisers were abundant in post-independence Latvia. In the early 1990s Latvia was awash with international advisers: the IMF and the World Bank were both present; the Germans were advising on a constitution for Latvia's central bank—the Bank of Latvia; the British were active in public administration reform; Denmark advised on research and higher education and so on. Advice was often conflicting, with different advisers promoting their own visions of structures as models that Latvia should adopt, for instance regarding the legal and education systems.

What the new state needed, however, was not only advice and assistance but explicit policy goals, clear commitments or external anchors to fix a development path. There was a general sense of the desirability of a "return to Europe", but this needed to be made concrete by adopting explicit policy goals. The key external goals which met these requirements and the dates when they were realised included the following:

- World Trade Organisation 1998
- NATO 29 March 2004
- European Union 1 May 2004
- Eurozone 1 January 2014

A final external goal was joining the Organisation for Economic Cooperation and Development (OECD)—a club of developed countries. The bid to join the OECD was launched in 2013 and its membership was confirmed on 1 July 2016, when Latvia deposited its instrument of accession to the OECD Convention. Joining the OECD does not provide a policy agenda as such, but rather represents an acknowledgement of Latvia's progress in social and economic development.

Each of these goals took several years to realise. The effect and significance of the external anchors thereby provided has been that they "depoliticised" many potentially contentious areas of Latvian life. This has been particularly important given the fragmentation that has historically dominated Latvian politics. Thus, in the interwar period no less than 32 different political parties were represented in the *Saeima*. In the early post-Soviet parliaments similar tendencies were observed, with newly created parties emerging as the winners in terms of number of seats in each of the first four elections[1]. The election of 2006 was the first in which the previously largest party was returned as the largest party[2]. The threshold for gaining representation in the *Saeima* was raised from 4% to 5% in 1995 and this has contributed to more stability in the medium term. Nevertheless, between the 1993 election and the 2014 election there have been no less than 17 governments, most of which have been uneasy coalitions of three or four partners with divergent views and interests. In this context, the benefit of external anchors is self-evident.

World Trade Organisation (WTO)

The Latvian WTO accession process started in 1993 when Latvia communicated its intention to seek WTO membership and the working party on Latvia's accession to the GATT was established. In 1995 this was converted to a WTO working party and in September 1998, the working party adopted by consensus the draft report, protocol of accession and the schedules of concessions on goods and services. Latvia also agreed to bring its economic and trade regime into conformity with WTO rules and obligations in all areas.

Thus, WTO accession was a 5-year process, the significance of which was that it contributed to modifying the protectionist sentiments that were rife during the early years of independence. Rather curiously, Estonia, which adopted a radical free trade policy right from the first days of independence, had more difficulties in achieving WTO membership than "protectionist" Latvia. Estonia was obliged to implement additional economic regulations in order to conform to the rules of the WTO and the EU (to which it was committed to join as its WTO application proceeded) and consequently Estonian WTO accession was delayed until 1999.

---

1 This was by default in the 1993 elections when all parties were new.
2 This was the *Tautas partija* (People's Party), but this party had vanished by the 2010 election.

NATO

Latvia became a NATO partner country right from 1991 and was one of seven countries that were invited to begin accession talks to join the Alliance at the 2002 Prague Summit. Full membership was achieved in 2004. The prime goal of NATO membership was the security guarantee provided by the provisions of article five of the North Atlantic Treaty—Latvia was (and still is) regarded by Russia as part of its "near abroad", and has therefore felt particularly vulnerable. Apart from military criteria such as 2% of GDP to be spent on defence (a condition that has never been met) other membership conditions included the creation of the Latvian Anti-Corruption Bureau (KNAB) in 2002 and the liberalisation of citizenship legislation, the latter because NATO was concerned about the prospect of a member state with a large number of non-citizen residents Arguably, neither the creation of the anti-corruption Bureau nor the liberalisation of naturalisation rules would have occurred, or would have occurred when they did, in the absence of the NATO position on these issues.

EU Accession

Overall, the commitment to EU accession was more important and more comprehensive in terms of external constraints than any of the others. The requirement of candidate countries to accept the EU *acquis communautaire* took huge areas of economic and social legislation out of the political arena. The *acquis* defined a comprehensive economic and social template for Latvia. Of course there were negotiations, but these were often about timing rather than substance. For a country like Latvia with its fragmented politics, this was important in securing the modernisation of its social and economic infrastructure. The Copenhagen criteria, laid down at the June 1993 European Council, as well as containing the requirement that candidate countries should become functioning market economies and should have capacity to cope with competitive pressure and market forces within the Union, also included the requirement that, in order to be invited to join the Union, the candidate country should have achieved stability of institutions guaranteeing democracy, the rule of law, human rights, respect for and protection of minorities.

While the economic criteria presented few difficulties of principle for Latvia—most people were in favour of a market economy—the respect for and protection of minorities presented problems for many Latvian politicians. Liberalisation of the citizenship law was therefore resisted until after December 1997, when the rejection of Latvia from fast-track EU accession talks prompted a rethink of the hitherto intransigent position on the quota or "windows" system of phased naturalisation introduced in 1995. The Law was amended and the quotas removed following a referendum held in October 1998. As already noted, NATO was also in favour of liberalisation, being concerned for security reasons about the large numbers of non-citizens living in Latvia. The combined impact of EU and NATO positions therefore resulted in a major turning point in Latvian naturalisation legislation. The same can be said regarding the creation of the anti-corruption bureau KNAB, where EU pressure was also instrumental.

It is hard to over-estimate the impact of EU accession on Latvia. It contributed significantly to creating at least the infrastructure of a modern democratic state—if not always the substance. More importantly, one should ask: what would Latvia be like today if it were not in the EU? Of course, such a counterfactual is rather difficult to be precise about. However, there are sufficient tendencies even now in Latvia to suggest we would observe something like a tax-haven, off-shore economy, probably with weak democratic institutions. EU accession has saved Latvia, and most importantly ordinary people in Latvia, from a fate of this kind.

The Eurozone, Austerity and the International Lending Programme

Latvia's path to the Eurozone provides a salutary case study of what can happen in Latvian policy making when external constraints are either not present or do not bite and of how the establishment of effective external constraints can bring policy back into line. It was originally Latvia's intention to join the EU single currency in 2008, but as the boom of 2006–2007 proceeded it became clear that the inflation target and budget deficit targets of the Maastricht criteria for Eurozone accession could not be achieved and the application was put on hold.

Latvia's boom, which started before EU accession but then strongly accelerated after accession in 2004, was largely home grown and consisted of two driving elements: the credit boom, especially housing loans but also in financing the purchase of consumption goods such as luxury cars;[3] and the explosion of public expenditures, especially public sector wages which grew by 133% between 2004 and 2008 with the annual rate of growth reaching nearly 36% in 2007 alone. Figure 1 illustrates the mechanism of how this happened over time.

What is revealed in Figure 1 is a consistent pattern of higher spending in the fourth quarter of each year,[4] whereby buoyant tax receipts were used to pay higher wages to public sector officials often within the framework of an opaque structure of bonuses, premiums and other "motivation payments", or distributed among the line ministries of the partners of the various coalition governments to finance favoured projects. This phenomenon of supplementary budgets aimed at spending growing revenues is represented in Figure 1 by the last quarter spikes in expenditure. Thus, what could have been a budget surplus was simply spent and spent largely on consumption rather than on productive investment. Arguably, the property boom itself resulted in a huge distortion of resources, with both human and physical resources sucked into unproductive property speculation.

---

3   Visitors to Rīga in 2006–2008 often commented on the density of expensive cars observed on the streets of the capital, exceeding even what might be observed in the most exclusive neighbourhoods of London.
4   This was implemented through a succession of supplementary autumn budgets.

Figure 1: Fiscal irresponsibility in the run up to the crisis: The quarterly dynamics of government expenditure (in millions LVL)

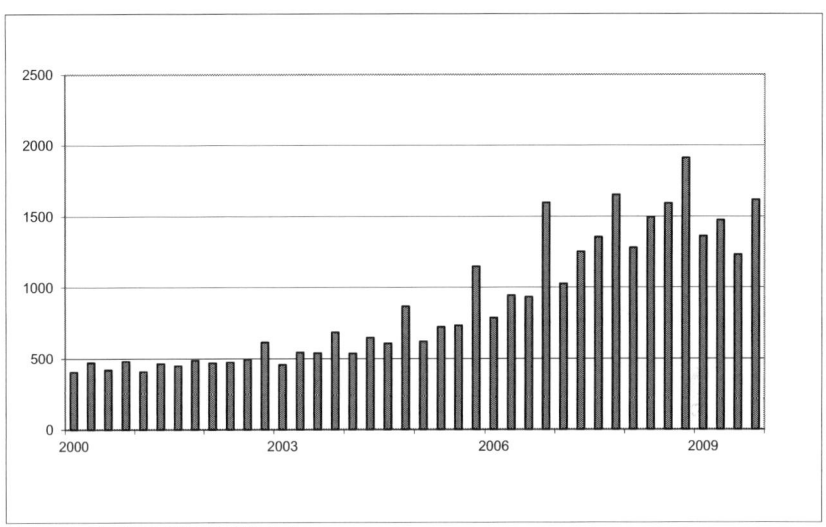

Source: Latvia Competitiveness Report
(http://www.sseriga.edu/download.php?file=/files/news/lcr2013.pdf.)

Thus, the Latvian crisis that emerged in the autumn of 2008 was largely home grown. Despite the problems of Parex Bank, Latvia and Latvia's banking system were not in the first instance victims of the banking crises in the US, UK and other European countries. Rather, as economic activity slowed in 2008 it became clear that the problem was the growing budget deficit. According to the IMF, "The fiscal deficit risked to balloon threatening financing and confidence. Under unchanged policies, the 2009 deficit would have been around 16–18% of GDP."[5] This was apparent to all the players involved, including the Swedish commercial banks who privately indicated to the Latvian authorities in the autumn of 2008 that they were no longer willing to purchase Latvian government debt. Hence, financing the deficit through the market effectively be-

---

5 C. Purfield and C. Rosenberg, "Adjustment under a Currency Peg: Estonia, Latvia and Lithuania during the Global Financial Crisis 2008–09" *IMF Working Paper* WP/10/213 (2010), 17. https://www.imf.org/external/pubs/ft/wp/2010/wp10213.pdf (Accessed December 2014).

came impossible. Faced with the prospect of a disorderly government payments crisis, the Latvian authorities were obliged in November 2008 to seek financial support from the IMF, the EU and Nordic countries, despite earlier having denied even that they were contemplating such support.

The international lenders collectively provided a facility of EUR 7.5 billion, but with it came strict and regular monitoring and supervision by both the IMF and the European Commission. Effectively, fiscal policy was taken out of the hands of the Latvian authorities and in 2009 a net fiscal adjustment of just over 11% of GDP was implemented so that the 2009 fiscal deficit ended up at a relatively reasonable 7%. In fact, much less than the full EUR 7.5 billion was actually used,[6] and over the whole three-year programme nearly 50% of the financing employed went to cover the budget deficit during the adjustment, while 38% was used to pay off government debt. Only 12% was used for "financial stability". This supports the proposition that the crisis was about the public finances rather than the banking system. Against the preferred position of the IMF, Latvia rejected the option of changing the exchange rate as an adjustment instrument, but chose instead to implement a so-called "internal devaluation"[7] as the mechanism for restoring the international competitiveness lost in the excesses of the boom.[8] The result was a cumulative GDP decline of 25% and unemployment soaring to more than 20% in early 2010.

A key part of this episode was the establishment of a new external anchor, namely, the goal of achieving accession to the Eurozone by 2014. This was the exit strategy that was proposed as justifying several years of pain. And, indeed Latvia did successfully join the single currency on 1 January 2014, although in the run up to that date the problems of the Eurozone meant the single

---

6 According to the Finance Ministry, only EUR 4.4 billion had been used as of 20 June 2011.
7 Internal devaluation is in no way a novel policy—it is an adjustment mechanism that was an integral part of the classical gold standard and has nearly always been the initial recourse of any country facing adjustment in a fixed exchange rate regime.
8 Whether the "internal devaluation" actually worked as it was supposed to in theory has been questioned by Blanchard et al (2013) who point out that the observed reduction in private sector wages (the theoretical mechanism for restoring competitiveness) was relatively small. Olivier J. Blanchard, Mark Griffiths and Bertrand Gruss, "Boom, Bust, Recovery Forensics of the Latvia Crisis," Fall 2013 Brookings Panel on Economic Activity, 19-20 September 2013.

currency no longer looked as attractive as it had in 2008–2009, when the Latvian authorities unsuccessfully attempted to negotiate a fast-track Eurozone accession as a "quick fix" solution to their problems.

3. The Political Economy of Latvia Today

In a conference address in 1992, the then prime minister Ivars Godmanis claimed that his ambition was to "develop Latvia as a Swedish style social democracy."[9] Today Latvia is very far from this goal, and arguably an agenda to achieve it has never been implemented or even seriously contemplated. Latvia today is the fourth poorest country in the EU, with GDP per capita in 2013 at 67% of the EU average. Only Croatia, Romania and Bulgaria are poorer. Sweden by contrast has a GDP per capita at 127% of the EU average. It is also a noticeably unequal society, with some of the worst poverty and inequality indicators in the EU, and also a noticeably low tax country. Overall tax revenues in Latvia amounted to 27.9 % of GDP in 2012, which is markedly below the EU-28 average (39.4%). Together with Bulgaria (27.9%), this tax-to-GDP ratio is the second lowest in the European Union after Lithuania (27.2%). This contrasts with Sweden, where the 2012 tax to GDP ratio was 44.2%. These are figures and positions that have remained rather stable over time

These and other problematic aspects of Latvian life and society are home grown and can only be addressed by a home-grown policy agenda. It is hard to imagine external anchors that can address poverty or inequality, that reduce the size of the shadow economy, or can improve the quality of the Latvian higher education system. The discussion below analyses these three internal policy or political economy challenges.

Inequality and Poverty

This is perhaps the biggest political economy challenge facing post-crisis Latvia. In terms of the Gini coefficient[10] of after tax income, Latvia is the most unequal society in the EU. Moreover, this is policy induced: in other words, the

---

9   Personal recollection of the author.
10 The Gini coefficient is a measure of the statistical dispersion of income in a country. A Gini coefficient of zero indicates perfect equality i.e. everyone has the same income while a Gini coefficient of one (or 100%) represents theoretical maximal inequality e.g. where one person has all the income and all others have none.

Latvian tax-benefit system is one of the least redistributive in the EU. This is illustrated in Figures 2 and 3.

Figure 2: Gini coefficients after taxes and transfers (2012)

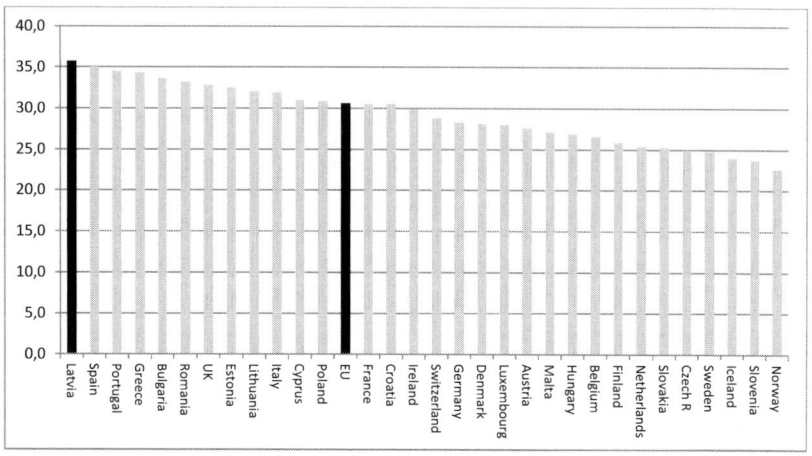

Source: Eurostat
(http://epp.eurostat.ec.europa.eu/cache/ITY_PUBLIC/3-04112014-BP/EN/3-04112014-BP-EN.PDF.)

Figure 3: Gini coefficients before taxes and transfers (2012)

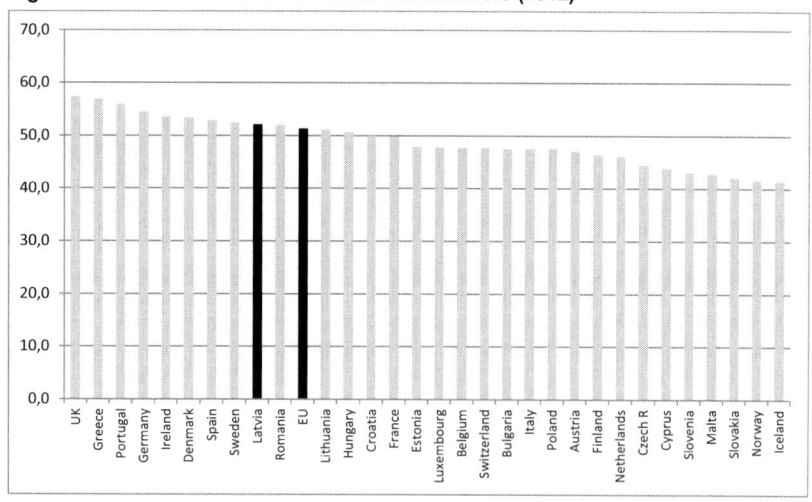

Source: Eurostat
(http://epp.eurostat.ec.europa.eu/cache/ITY_PUBLIC/3-04112014-BP/EN/3-04112014-BP-EN.PDF.)

It can be seen that, while the before tax /transfer Gini for Latvia is close to the EU average, the one after tax is the highest in the EU. In other words, the high degree of inequality in Latvia is the direct result of the very modest redistribution generated by the Latvian tax-benefit system. Although inequality and poverty has emerged as a political issue over the last couple of years, current proposals are unlikely to make a significant impact on either the indicators or on reality.

While the Gini coefficient is a rather abstract concept, Eurostat has in recent years published a more intuitively understandable set of indicators of poverty, namely indicators of material deprivation. Eurostat has defined nine indicators of material deprivation. These are:

- arrears on mortgage or rent payments, utility bills, hire purchase;
- not being able to afford one week's annual holiday away from home;
- not being able to afford a meal with meat, chicken, fish (or vegetarian equivalent) every second day;
- not being able to face unexpected financial expenses;
- not being able to buy a telephone (including mobile phone);
- not being able to buy a colour television;
- not being able to buy a washing machine;
- not being able to buy a car;
- not being able to afford heating to keep the house warm

A person who satisfies three of these is said to experience *material deprivation*, while satisfying four out of the nine defines *serious material deprivation*.

According to Eurostat,[11] in 2013 24% of the Latvian population were severely materially deprived. Only Bulgaria (43%), Romania (28.5%) and Hungary (26.8%) have worse indicators. This compares with 16% in Lithuania and 7.6% in Estonia, while serious material deprivation is as low as 1.4% in Sweden.

Given that overall GDP per capita levels are similar in the three Baltic States, the serious material deprivation gap between Latvia and Estonia and Lithuania cannot be explained in the level of overall wealth. One possible explanation

---

11 Eurostat, "At Risk of Poverty or Social exclusion in the EU28," News release, 4 November 2014. http://epp.eurostat.ec.europa.eu/cache/ITY_PUBLIC/3-04112014-BP/EN/3-04112014-BP-EN.PDF.

lies in the incentives to work for low-paid persons implied by the Latvian tax benefit system.

Recent research using micro-simulation methods[12] suggests that work incentives as measured by marginal effective tax rates (METR)[13] are particularly poor for the lowest-paid workers in Latvia. The mean METR for Latvia in 2013 was 32.2%, only slightly below the EU average (34.5%), but much higher than the average in Estonia (22.8%) and Lithuania (27.4%), despite a lower degree of income redistribution in Latvia as compared with these countries. However, in 2013, 94% of individuals who faced METRs in excess of 50% (generally regarded as a high level) belonged to the two bottom deciles of the distribution of equivalised disposable income.[14] This is different from many other European countries, where the distribution of high METRs is either more even across deciles or rises towards the top end of income distribution.[15]

The main reason for high METRs faced by the poorest population groups in Latvia is the design of means-tested benefits (GMI and housing benefits), which generates 100% METRs i.e. 100% withdrawal of benefits as earnings rise, for the recipients of these benefits. Figure 4 illustrates mean METRs by deciles of equivalised disposable income in Latvia and shows the contribution of taxes, benefits and social insurance contributions (SICs).

---

12 Anna Zasova and Anna Zdanovica, "Equity and Efficiency of the Latvian Tax-Benefit System," (2014) http://freepolicybriefs.org/2014/11/03/equity-and-efficiency-in-the-latvian-tax-benefit-system/.
13 The marginal effective tax rate is defined as the proportion of a small increase in earnings that is lost in tax and withdrawn benefits.
14 Equivalised disposable income is the total income of a household, after tax and other deductions, that is available for spending or saving, divided by the number of household members converted into equalised adults where household members are equalised or made equivalent by weighting each according to their age, using the modified OECD equivalence scale.
15 X. Jara and A. Tumino, "Tax-Benefit Systems, Income Distribution and Work Incentives in the European Union," *International Journal of Microsimulation*, International Microsimulation Association, 1, 6 (2013): 27–62.

Figure 4: The contribution of direct taxes, benefits and social insurance contributions to METRs in Latvia by deciles of equivalised disposable income in 2013

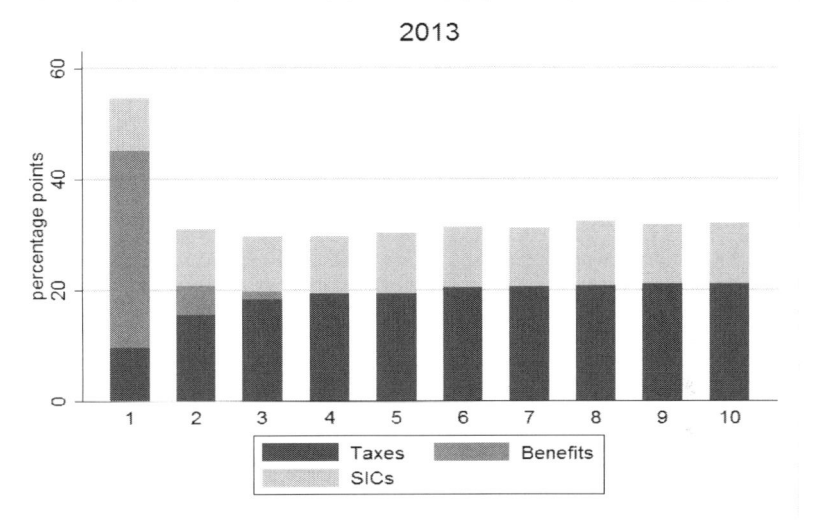

Source: Anna Zasova and Anna Zdanovica, "Equity and Efficiency of the Latvian Tax-Benefit System," (2014) (http://freepolicybriefs.org/2014/11/03/equity-and-efficiency-in-the-latvian-tax-benefit-system/.)

It can be seen that high METRs in the bottom deciles result mainly from the impact of benefits—i.e. the 100% withdrawal rate for means tested benefits. This effect disappears in the fourth decile. Because of basic tax allowances, the contribution of direct taxes is smaller in the bottom deciles, but then the contribution of taxes levels off, reflecting the Latvian flat tax rate.

Thus, Latvia is more unequal and has more poor people than most other EU countries, including its Baltic neighbours. There is a prevailing opinion that the poor are poor because they are lazy or drinkers. It is not widely understood that this state of affairs is policy induced and could be improved by appropriate policy actions. For example, incentives to work can be improved by introducing a tapering of the withdrawal of benefits as earnings grow above the minimum income thresholds,[16] which currently are extremely low. For example, the 2014 level of guaranteed minimum income was EUR 64 a month.

The Shadow Economy

According to the annual survey of the shadow economy in the Baltic states organised by SSE Rīga,[17] the Latvian shadow economy in 2013 represented 23.8% of GDP. Although down from the more than 30% estimates for 2009–2011, this is much higher than in Estonia (15.7%) or Lithuania (15.3%). The problem with a large and persistent shadow economy is not that it prevents a "level playing field" or that tax revenues are less than they would otherwise be, but that, as was argued in the Latvian Competitiveness Report,[18] the shadow economy creates disincentives for firms to invest in productivity improvements and grow. As a result, many Latvian enterprises are smaller and use more labour-intensive techniques than is optimal.

Why is the shadow economy in Latvia so large in relative terms? Why is it high as compared with Estonia and Lithuania? The standard answer is that the tax burden in Latvia is higher. The motivation for participating in the informal economy is typically expressed in terms of a balance between the gains from avoiding taxes and other regulations and expected costs associated with detection. Typical reasoning is as follows: "the informal sector arises when excessive taxes and regulations are imposed by a government that lack the capability to enforce compliance."[19] Typical conclusions are that high taxation encourages informal activity and that effective enforcement discourages it. However, this is

---

16 This has been advocated among other by the International Monetary Fund. See: International Monetary Fund, *Staff Report for the 2014 article IV consultation (2014)* https://www.imf.org/external/pubs/ft/scr/2014/cr14115.pd.
17 Tālis J. Putniņš and Arnis Sauka, *Shadow Economy Index for the Baltic Countries 2009–2013* (Rīga: Centre for Sustainable Business at the Stockholm School of Economics in Riga, 2014) http://www.sseriga.edu/files/content/sseriga_baltic_shadow_economy_index_2009_2013_eng.pdf.
18 Zane Cunska, Christian Ketels, Anders Paalzow and Alfs Vanags, *Latvia Competitiveness Report* (Rīga: Stockholm School of Economics in Riga, 2013) http://www.sseriga.edu/download.php?file=/files/news/lcr2013.pdf.
19 Norman Loayza, "The Economics of the Informal Sector: A Simple Model and Some Empirical Evidence from Latin America," *World Bank Policy Research Papers* WPS 1727 (1997), 1. http://wwwwds.worldbank.org/servlet/WDSContentServer/WDSP/IB/1997/02/01/000009265_3970619111006/Rendered/PDF/multi0page.pdf.

at odds with casual experience in European countries, where some of the highest taxed countries are also those with the lowest share of measured informal activity.[20] Moreover, the tax burden in Estonia and Lithuania is very similar to that in Latvia. The truth is that:

> "we do not know the exact motives, why people work in the shadow economy and what is their relation and feeling if a government undertakes reforms in order to bring them back into the official economy."[21]

It seems that simple economic arguments are not sufficient to explain international differences in informal activity. Anthropological evidence,[22] meanwhile, suggests that participation in the informal economy is frequently regarded as normal and even honourable.

An interesting development in the context of the shadow economy has been the micro-enterprise regime introduced in September 2010. This offers a reduced administrative burden and a simplified tax regime for enterprises with a turnover of less than EUR 100,000 a year. One aim of this initiative was to reduce incentives for enterprises to operate in the shadow economy. In part this has been successful, but at the same time the regime has created new disincentives for firms to grow. Thus, recent research[23] suggests that of the more than 33,000 registered microenterprise tax payers in Latvia in 2014, only 16% or around 5,600 are genuinely new enterprises. The others were economically active prior to registering as a microenterprise, and registered as microenterprises for tax optimisation purposes. At the same time, approximately one third fully or partly legalised their activities by moving them from the shadow economy to the official one.

---

20 This is not always the case. Thus, according to the latest Eurobarometer survey, the highest mean earnings from undeclared work among Baltic Sea countries were observed in Sweden, where the sum amounted to EUR 1346, as compared with EUR 478 in Latvia.
21 Friedrich Schneider, "Work in the Shadow: Some Facts," Johannes Kepler University of Linz Department of Economics Working Paper 1318 (2013), 16.
22 Klāvs Sedlenieks, "Cash in an Envelope: Corruption and Tax Avoidance as an Economic Strategy in Contemporary Riga," in Karl-Olov Arnstberg and Thomas Boren, eds., *Everyday Economy in Russia, Poland and Latvia* (Stockholm: Södertörns högskola, 2007), 25–69.
23 Juris Stinka and Dainis Bonda "Micro Enterprises Tax Payers in Latvia" SSE Riga EMBA thesis (2014). (http://www.sseriga.edu/en/research/student-research/page:4/).

The Higher Education System

For a country with very limited natural resources, human capital represents a key development resource. By many conventional indicators, the Latvian population is well educated. As indicated by enrolment and graduation rates, education attainment figures and the large number of higher education institutions, the education level has been growing over time. However, all is not well, especially in higher education. There are deep structural problems: for example, it is very common for students in Latvia to combine work with studies, hence they are absent from classes. This has a statistically significant negative effect on average grades, class attendance, and independent study time.[24] Additionally, Science Citation Index (SCI) data show that Latvian researchers are rather unsuccessful in international publications, and are significantly outperformed by Estonia and Lithuania. In January 2014, the research assessment exercise carried out by Technopolis[25] found that of 150 Latvian research institutions, 15 were strong international players; 33 were strong local players and the rest were evaluated as poor or average quality local players.

In the light of such evidence, there has been much talk of reform. Yet, although various reports and evaluations have been published, there has been little in the way of concrete progress. The key problem and the key issue is to open up Latvian higher education to outside competition, i.e. to outside lecturers and researchers. However, a combination of nationalist sentiments and the desire of university teachers to protect their own interests have ensured that restrictions on the language of instruction and language requirements for appointment as a full-time university teacher remain largely unreformed. For example, while is not mandatory for PhD candidates to write the thesis in the state language (Latvian), it is difficult get permission to write in, say, English. The result is that local lecturers continue to enjoy a cosy monopoly and much of Latvian scholarship remains closed to the rest of the world. As long as this is

---

24 Daunis Auers, Toms Rostoks and Kenneth Smith, "Flipping Burgers or Flipping Pages? Student Employment and Academic Attainment in Post-Soviet Latvia," *Communist and Post-Communist Studies*, 40, 4 (2007): 477–491.
25 Technopolis, *Innovation System Review and Research Assessment Exercise: Final Report: Latvia* (2014) http://izm.izm.gov.lv/upload_file/2014/Latvia-systems-review_2014.pdf.

unchanged, Latvian higher education will remain closed to quality scrutiny and competition from the outside world.

4. Conclusions

The Latvian Competitiveness Report notes that:

> "The persistence of the same problems over time points to the presence of a systemic failure in policy making. That is, failure exists at the level of political institutions and the implementation process of economic policy. There is in effect a classic time-inconsistency problem—policy makers can and do identify correct policies but the institutional mechanisms for commitment appear to be weak or missing."[26]

This time-inconsistency problem has been avoided to the extent that policy makers have been subject to external constraints. What to do now? Partly the answer is more rule-based policy making—the Fiscal Discipline Law adopted in 2013 to avoid the fiscal excesses experienced in the run-up to the crisis is an example of this.

However, not all policy can be made by rules. How to improve regular policy making? One option is to improve the accountability of elected politicians. By reverting to its 1922 constitution, Latvia reverted also to a party list electoral system rather than a constituency based one. Since 1991 there have been some minor reforms to the electoral system—for instance, the threshold for gaining party representation in parliament has been increased from 4% to 5% and candidates are now restricted to being nominated in just one regional list. Overall, however, the Latvian parliament remains one in which deputies, once elected, have little in the way of individual accountability to the electorate. Accountability could be improved by adopting a mixed constituency/list system as prevails in Ireland. This would tip the balance of power towards the electorate and away from the line ministries and the special interests they often represent.

---

26 Cunska, Ketels, Paalzow and Vanags, *Latvia Competitiveness Report*,135.

The Unbearable Myth of Convergence: Episodes in the Economic Development of Latvia

Aldis Purs, University of Washington

1. The "Grand Narratives" Question Revisited

One of the most frequently discussed dilemmas in writing a history of Latvia, particularly one that spans several centuries, is the distortions that are created if said history is an exercise in state- and/or nation-building. An independent state of Latvia has existed for less than 100 years in one, legalistic sense; and as a state with agency for less than 50 years. How do you include the historical experience of the region through the tsarist era or through Soviet and Nazi occupation? Too frequently the history before 18 November 1918 is discussed as the antecedent to the independent state. Likewise, the years of Nazi occupation and the decades of Soviet occupation become a historical pause from a norm. A similar, and perhaps more profound distortion revolves around writing the history of Latvia as the history of ethnic Latvians (and in the most egregious cases, as the history of ethnic Latvians that support an ethnic Latvian state). Even first-rate, nuanced approaches struggle with integrating the disparate ethnic communities and notable individuals into a consistent narrative.

If this is a serious obstacle, it is however, one that is frequently addressed and considered. A corollary to these tangents is how to weave the long, economic history of Latvia through empires and states into a comprehensive history that, borrowing from antiquated Marxist terms, addresses the relationship between the base (the economic system) and the superstructure (the cultural and political system). In a previous work, *Baltic Facades,* I touched very briefly upon the economic histories of Estonia, Latvia, and Lithuania with the broadest of brushstrokes. Here, however, I will limit myself to expanding on a few ideas about the history of economic development in the geographical area that is now Latvia.

2. The Never-Ending Quest for Convergence

In the chapter in *Baltic Facades* dealing with economic developments in Estonia, Latvia, and Lithuania, I stressed two key overarching ideas.[1] The first, and likely most important, idea was a reiteration of the economists' maxim that continuity and stability in economic policy are almost sacrosanct; throughout the 20th and 21st century Estonia, Latvia, and Lithuania have all lurched from one extreme to the other, mostly due to "extraneous circumstances". If nothing else, economic developments in all three countries should first and foremost be measured against a backdrop of near constant change and frequent ruin. I also tried to refute a common economic myth (the second idea) begun by the Estonian, Latvian, and Lithuanian *émigré* communities, that if not for Soviet occupation, Estonia, Latvia, and Lithuania would enjoy the same degree of economic development and affluence as Finland. This myth is deceptively simple: Finland, like Estonia, Latvia, and Lithuania, was an Imperial Russian Baltic Province that won its independence amidst the ashes of World War I and the Russian Revolution. Finland, like Estonia, Latvia, and Lithuania, was marked by rural inequities and poverty. Yet, after losing the Finno-Soviet War of 1939–1940, but maintaining its independence, it experienced a prolonged economic boom in the post-World War II world and rose to become one of the world's most developed, and affluent states. The logical inference behind this myth is that if Estonia, Latvia, and Lithuania had remained independent, they too would have equally prospered. This is highly suspect and doubtful, and it should be telling that, at least in the Latvian case, interwar politicians, activists, and commentators did not place Finland and Latvia on an equal footing. The sub-text to this myth regards Latvia's convergence with modern, industrial Western economies (either in a counter-factual past, if there had been no Soviet occupation, or sometime in the near or less near future now that occupation has been lifted). Here I will introduce a few episodes that explicate the idea of convergence and economic development in Latvia's historical experience, in the hope of provoking more debate.

By convergence, I do not intend to speak about the formal European Union concept of convergence, which took place for Latvia on 1 January 2014. The

---

[1] Aldis Purs, *Baltic Facades: Estonia, Latvia and Lithuania Since 1945* (London: Reaktion Books, 2012).

European Commission periodically published "Convergence Reports" that examined if Latvia met the criteria for the adoption of the Euro. These criteria included a host of economic conditions and a degree of legislative compatibility with EU laws that govern the use of the Euro. In this narrow, fiscal EU sense, Latvia has already converged and moved on from its "derogation" or term of exemption for the immediate use of the Euro that was applied after Latvia entered the European Union in May 2004. In this vein, other member states, such as Sweden, continue to have derogations, but are expected (and legally obliged) to join the Euro at some point. Instead, I intend to talk about the type of convergence recently expertly discussed by Morten Hansen, the Head of the Economics Department of the Stockholm School of Economics in Rīga, most frequently in his blog on the internet version of the weekly, *Ir*.

Hansen, who distils complex economic ideas and theories into simple and straightforward prose, has on several occasions examined the likelihood of Latvia's convergence with European Union standards. Hansen does not look at convergence in terms of use of a common currency, but in terms of a convergence of *wealth*. Or, in other words, if Latvia will "catch up" with the West, and if so, when. In 2011, close to the tail end of the economic downturn, Hansen addressed the issue through a detailed comparison of Latvia's GDP per capita relative to that of Greece and Portugal.[2] In short, Latvia's chances of convergence were slim. In 2013, Hansen revisited the convergence theme with a novel twist: to demonstrate the long odds of convergence,[3] he compared the GDP of countries in 1960 with that of 2013, and concluded that the best indicator of ranking highly in 2013 was ranking highly in 1960. In other words, there is very little convergence across the spectrum of countries, and Latvia will probably not be one of the few exceptions. Hansen uses GDP per capita as the gauge for countries, but any other set of indicators (from Big Mac Indexes to standards of living) reinforce the scale of the challenge inherent in making convergence happen.

---

2 Morten Hansen, "How Much Convergence to Expect?" *Ir*, 24 August 2011. http://www.ir.lv/2011/8/24/how-much-convergence-to-expect.
3 Morten Hansen, "Of Latvian Growth and Convergence," *Ir*, 23 July 2013. http://www.ir.lv/2013/7/23/of-latvian-growth-and-convergence.

Hansen also quotes the ominous summer 2013 warning from Latvia's President, Andris Berziņš, that Latvia needed to reach the European Union GDP average within 10 years or cease to exist politically. Hansen quickly dismissed Latvia's chances of meeting this bar. To do so, Latvia would need to grow 64% faster than the EU over ten years or, which meant that its annual economic growth would need to outstrip that of the EU as a whole by around 5% throughout that period. So, if the EU grows at 2%, Latvia would need to grow at 7%, a likely outcome in any given year or two, but very difficult to maintain over a decade.[4] Berziņš' statement likely says more about his poor grasp of economics and the survival of nations than anything else, but it does uncover the fundamental conundrum of convergence, and that is economic development strategy.

3. Latvia's Economic Development in Historical Perspective

With thoughts of Hansen's critique of the contemporary economic state of Latvia, Berziņš' dire warnings, and the myth of a Latvia robbed of Finnish-level prosperity dancing in my mind, I decided to return to development theory and Latvia's long historical performance to dig at the myth of convergence. The question of why some countries are wealthier than others has long fascinated historians, political scientists, economists, and politicians alike. For those that are poorer and/or weaker (they often go hand in hand), there is no universally agreed upon path forwards for development. Very broadly speaking, there are two schools of thought about development. The first, an evolutionary school, imagines that most societies develop along a path, and that some nations are simply further along. There is an end point and convergence is inevitable at some future date. Although this is a heavily bastardised and simplified description, and although few academics still stick closely to this view, it does have "popular legs." The reaction to this simplistic idea has been varied and multifaceted. Some theories pinpoint the relationship between wealthy and less wealthy states as the reason for said wealth or poverty. Others propose ways in which states can speed up the process of development, most commonly in

---

4   For some comparative balance, Spain and Italy may or may not rise to the EU average over the course of the next 10 years. iN 2014, Austria, Ireland, the Netherlands, Sweden, Denmark, Germany, Belgium, Finland, the United Kingdom and France were the only countries that meet Berziņš' high standard.

the form of state-sponsored and directed targeted development as opposed to the slow, meandering pace of an evolutionary path. Distillates of all of these theories on development can still be frequently parsed from contemporary politicians and economists. If there is one universally agreed upon idea about development, it is the most basic. Development occurs when a society produces surplus and reinvests that surplus into further increasing the productive capacity of society. The type of investment can be physical and labour intensive (the sweat of the brow or "sweat equity") or financial and technical intensive (capital and know-how). Returning to Latvia, we see both in its episodes of economic development. The abundance of the former and difficulties with the latter go far in explaining the myth of convergence.

The timeline for the economic development of Latvia dovetails with that of modern Latvia more generally. Conceptually, each starts with the emancipation of serfs in the Imperial Russian Baltic Provinces in the 1810s. At least theoretically, after the dissolution of serfdom, peasants and barons alike could function as independent economic actors. In practice, these changes did not begin to bear economic fruits until after a flurry of additional legislation in the 1840s and 1860s that allowed for the purchase of land and freer mobility. Agricultural development through the 19th century is a testament to the capabilities of physical, labour-intensive investment, and its shortcomings. Behind the dry statement that increases in productivity fuelled continuing investments in the sector lay a reality in which a peasant and his family had to work very long hours for six or seven days a week, coupled with near constant deprivation, in order to save sufficient money to purchase a farm. Additional work and the farm as collateral would then serve as the basis for purchasing livestock holdings and tools, and funding the construction of houses and barns. Over a generation, real but limited wealth accrued to some landed peasants. Similarly, some modernising barons invested (in crop and livestock choices, in the building of mills and agricultural services) in their properties, taking advantage of market forces to raise productivity and generate wealth. A slowly awakening cycle of supply and demand further encouraged this process and led to the rise of cartage services and a host of other corollary economic developments that diversified and variegated the local economy. Still, progress was painstakingly slow and susceptible to sudden reversals caused by market booms and busts, extraneous circumstances, and misfortunes such as failed harvests, death, dismemberment, and illness.[5]

Progress was slow and at a rate far below the demands of convergence, an idea not even entertained at the time. Development based on this kind of agricultural investment, the investment options available to most farmers and barons in the mid-19th century, could transform society from one generation to the next, but not lead to a massive economic transformation. Andrejs Plakans summarises the change well in his *A Concise History of the Baltic States*:

> "proprietorship changed incentives since now farmers had a very high probability of bequeathing improved farms to the next generation. A palpable return could be expected on expansion, improvement, and the adaptation of 'scientific' farming... with each decade after the mid-century, a new peasant subpopulation established itself in the Estland, Livland, and Kurland countryside—successful and relatively well-off farmers who by the century's end were being referred to as the 'grey barons.'"[6]

A continued brake on further economic development in the countryside was the "intractable problem" of the rural, landless population. Simply put, there were many more people that wanted land than land available. The countryside was split between large, landed estates of the nobility (many of whom now used this land to the best of their economic sense), small holdings of Latvian farmers, and a mass of the landless that sold their labour, sharecropped, and/or migrated to towns, cities and abroad. The scale of poverty among this last group could be stunning, as outlined in the fact-finding report of Senator N. A. Manasein, who toured the Baltic Provinces in 1881. It seemed inconceivable to logically expect that these peasants could generate the resources needed for the rudimentary first step of property acquisition (even if there was land to be sold) without a radical, and potentially revolutionary, break from the *status quo*. On the eve of World War I, substantial economic development and growth had changed the Latvian countryside, with a considerable number of "winners",

---

5   On the cyclical generation of wealth in peasant families, see, for example: Teodor Shanin, *The Roots of Otherness: Vol. 2 Russia 1905–1907 Russia's Turn of the Century* (New Haven: Yale University Press, 1986).

6   Andrejs Plakans, *A Concise History of the Baltic States* (Cambridge: Cambridge University Press, 2011), 220–221.

as well as an entrenched stratum of "losers". This alone is rather unremarkable and similar to agricultural communities across the world. Within this paradigm, there was no hope for, or anticipation of, convergence with the most advanced, modernised, and industrialised parts of the world. The crux centred on the lack of capital and know-how for investments into large-scale modern, industrial enterprises and utilities that could recast the region. Neither capital nor technical investment could be created in a hurry through an economic system overwhelmingly dominated by early stage market agriculture, particularly for a very small country with a small population (a small surplus per individual could not be multiplied across tens or hundreds of millions of similar individuals).

Throughout this same period, however, there were coterminous development projects that used massive amounts of capital and technical expertise. The modernisation of the port of Rīga, particularly the near-constant dredging of the Daugava River to ever-deeper depths, and the construction and improvement of sea walls and jetties was an early such, and almost continuous, project.[7] A second and related massive infrastructure project was the construction of the railroad system in the second half of the 19th century.[8] Both of these infrastructural improvements and the myriad corollary projects, from planning, to financing, to operations, to upkeep and improvements, were Imperial endeavours far outpacing the abilities and resources of the Baltic Provinces themselves. Although funds for port improvements often came from loans taken out by long distance merchants (loans that were never entirely paid in full due to the outbreak of World War I), the bulk of the costs were covered by Imperial coffers and from international loans and securities guaranteed by the tsarist state. Almost all of the foundations of the modern (meaning 19th and 20th century) commercial and industrial infrastructure of the Baltic Provinces and the types of industries developed were set as part of the larger Imperial plan of state sponsored industrialisation, more commonly referred to as the Witte System.[9]

---

7   See: Arvis Pope, *Rīgas osta deviņōs gadsimtos* (Rīga: Jumava, 2000), particularly Part Two, chapters 3 and 4; and Part Three in its entirety.
8   Lidija Malahovska, *Latvijas transporta vēsture: XIX gs. otrā puse—XX gs. sākums* (Rīga: LV Fonds, 1998).
9   Also, interestingly, this plan was one of the earliest and most aggressive plans for state intervention to "catch up" with a more industrial West. Theodore H. von Laue, *Sergei Witte and the Industrialization of Russia* (New York: Columbia University Press, 1969).

Fascinatingly, much of the later Soviet industrialisation of the Latvian Soviet Socialist Republic, such as the extension of transit rail routes to Liepāja and Ventspils, and the development of the port of Ventspils, were all anticipated in long-term 19th century Imperial Russian economic plans.

To say this is not to imply that the nature of these capital-heavy infrastructural investment projects was tailored to be beneficial to the local population, or that the local population had an appropriate say in their development, or that they should be thankful for this development; rather, it is to point out that the speed and scope of modernisation and industrialisation in Courland and Livland would have been impossible without the larger Imperial framework that provided access to capital and know-how. The creation of a proto-modernised industrial sector in the midst of an agricultural sea further affected all economic life. Many of the landless migrated to industrial concerns desperate for manpower.[10] By the outbreak of World War I, nearly one fifth of Rīga's population was employed in industry, an almost unheard of statistic for late, Imperial Russia. After St. Petersburg and Moscow, Rīga was the third largest industrial centre of the entire Russian empire, and was home to massive industrial enterprises such as the Russo-Baltic Wagon Factory.[11] Burgeoning cities and economies also needed cohorts of trained and educated bureaucrats, accountants, lawyers, doctors and engineers. Increasingly, the sons of landed Latvian farmers moved away from the countryside and into these professions in the city. Disaffection, of which there was as much in the city as in the countryside due to the Dickensian conditions of early industrialisation, also followed a modern, industrial, and Empire-wide trope with the rise of socialist thought. The decades from 1890–1914 may have witnessed the first baby steps towards convergence, or rather a small, limited closing of the gap with the most advanced parts of Europe.

The end of this economic development, however, was equally due to extraneous events. The local populations of Kurland and Livland played almost no part in the international stumbles and missteps that led to the outbreak of World

---

10 See: Erich Haberer, "Economic Modernization and Nationality in the Russian Baltic Provinces, 1850–1900," *Canadian Review of Studies in Nationalism*, 12, 1 (1985): 161–175.
11 See: Andres Kasekamp, *A History of the Baltic States*, (London: Palgrave MacMillan, 2010), 89.

War I, yet they suffered disproportionately nonetheless. Almost all of these provinces were at some point occupied by foreign armies during the course of the war (and Kurland for the great majority of the war), suffered severe civilian casualties, catastrophic casualties among inhabitants conscripted into the tsarist army, massive forced population displacement, an almost complete economic standstill, and the evacuation and/or destruction of most of the economic infrastructure created over the preceding 50 years.[12] Devastation along the stalled military front (for two and a half years), along the Daugava River was on par with the worst hit areas of any part of Europe. These were the foundations that a newly declared state, the Republic of Latvia, inherited. In terms of this chapter's inquiry, near total war created almost no economic growth and/or development and produced only a retraction in the economic circumstances of Latvia in the most catastrophic sense.

Building a National Economy: The Interwar Period

Independent statehood, declared in November 1918, achieved by 1920, and internationally recognised by 1921, was a radical break from the past. The Republic of Latvia was the first functioning modern, democratic political system on a state scale with an ethnic Latvian majority. The political accomplishments, challenges, and failures of this state in the interwar years are broadly known. The scale, magnitude, and impact of the complete economic transformation of the state, however, is less studied and more poorly understood. For all practical purposes heavy industrialisation (and its sizeable workforce) did not reemerge during the interwar years.[13] Raw materials were not available (they originated in now separate, often hostile, states), the industrial working class was decimated (by death and migration), and markets for goods were unclear. Equally importantly, there was little or no capital available for reconstruction. The industrial character of Rīga similarly collapsed. The number of people employed

---

12 See: Peter Gatrell, *A Whole Empire Walking: Refugees in Russia During the First World War* (Bloomington: Indiana University Press, 2005); and Vejas Liulevicius, *War Land on the Eastern Front: Culture, National Identity, and German Occupation in World War I* (Cambridge: Cambridge University Press, 2005).

13 Latvia's left wing cabinet of 1927–1928 tried desperately to negotiate the return of equipment and a resurrection of trade with the Soviet Union; but, despite a Treaty, neither goods nor trade arrived. See: Edgar Anderson, "The USSR Trades with Latvia: The Treaty of 1927," *Slavic Review*, 21, 2 (1962): 296–321.

in industry in Rīga dropped from a high of close to 20% before the war to less than 6% in the early 1920s. By the late 1930s, this percentage climbed back above 15%, but its nature was radically different. With a few notable exceptions, the large industrial concerns vanished and factories were small, poorly mechanised and even more poorly powered. In less than a decade, the former industrial metropole, Rīga, which towered over a fairly simple agricultural countryside, became an administrative, cultural, and commercial capital of an independent state dominated by the political interests of small holding, ethnic Latvian farmers. The Republic of Latvia built the economic foundations of its state on physical and labour-intensive strategies, and on the very limited local capital available and nurtured through the interwar years. If, in the late 19th century and early 20th century, the Baltic Provinces were transformed into the cutting edge of an industrial Russian Empire, the Republic of Latvia returned to an overwhelmingly agricultural economy. This step may have achieved a dream of many romantic nationalists that held to the powerful image of the land (the common Latvian refrain and longing for a little corner of land), but in terms of economic growth and development this dream was a significant obstacle. Convergence remained a lofty ideal and not a practical goal.

Agrarian reform is generally credited as the most important political and economic act of the democratic era. The near complete expropriation of land from the Baltic German nobility with no compensation was a supreme political act establishing a new political order and supposedly "righting a historical wrong." Politically it was perhaps a more acute move than economically, as in one legislative fell swoop, the state created an entire class of landholders invested in the continued existence of the state. Although some economists have questioned the economic sense of the nature of expropriation and the full shift to small holding agriculture, given the political climate of the times, little else seems possible. The economic development of agriculture after the reform followed a similar trajectory to the 19th century establishment of farms, but on a much larger scale and scope. If the earlier, dry economic sentence was "increases in productivity fuelled continuing investments in the sector," what that meant on the ground was again similar. Land recipients and their families worked long hours on six and seven-day workweeks and, again, they went without much to build up their farms. This was an even more complete transformation, because legislated Agrarian Reform gave land to so many, so quickly. In the 19th century land purchases started slowly and remained an economic path for a minority. Labour was abundant and cheap, and benefitted the lucky few who were able to purchase land. In the 1920s (and into the 1930s), most received land, and labour became scarce. Coupled with the great degree of war destruction, the conditions in the first years of the post Agrarian Reform countryside were marked by extreme poverty and want. The state was equally destitute and was almost incapable of providing much support, aid or capital investment to boost economic recovery.

If the state could offer little financial assistance, it helped with the limited resources available to it, state forests and tax deferrals. To encourage the hard work and industry of tens of thousands of farmers, the state offered lumber subsidies (for firewood and construction) and temporary tax deferrals. The loss of revenue may have handicapped the state in accruing immediate capital for investment, but it proved a successful medium and long-term plan. Within a few years, farmers had built and converted their smallholdings into market, agricultural producers. With the return of some funds to state coffers, the state was able to further develop the agricultural sector through programmes that encouraged the introduction of better breeds of livestock (particularly pigs and dairy cattle), and that provided some of the local infrastructure for food processing (dairy collection, churning facilities, and cold storage for butter and bacon). Tapping into this same vein of local initiative and industriousness, the state managed the reconstruction of roads and public buildings (schools, train stations, and markets) with local labour, capital and know-how.

The great obstacle to further development was how to provide the "large ticket items" of a modern state, those that required massive capital investment and detailed, technical knowledge. Latvia's dilemma was how to deliver this modern state to a citizenry that hoped for it, but could not immediately finance it. In other words, farmers could use their own (and their family's) labour, and do without seeming necessities to build a farm. The same approach, however, could not provide large-scale improvements in transportation, electrification, universal education beyond grade school, and modern health care.

For Latvia's economy, the ability to finance almost any project was a remarkably difficult task. There was little home-grown capital; most was lost during the war, and to some extent some Baltic German capital was lost through the expropriation of their estates, while the remaining was partially withheld as international legal challenges to said expropriation wound their way through the League of Nations. Furthermore, disgruntled Baltic Germans somewhat successfully lobbied the German economic world to withhold funds to Latvia over this same issue. The alternative, English capital (US investment was initially negligible, although US aid through the American Relief Agency was vital in the early years[14]) was mired in the Lazard Brothers scandal. Prior to World War I, the London branch of the investment firm, Lazard Brothers, loaned money to the Rīga Municipal government for the construction of a tram system. The tram system was dismantled and destroyed during the war, and the Rīga City Council of the independent Republic of Latvia refused to recognise that it was liable for the debt. Lazard Brothers replied by calling on British capital to avoid Latvia. The legal and negotiated wrangling between Rīga, Lazard Brothers, and the state dragged on for years and seriously restricted another source of capital for the new state. Furthermore, a general climate of corruption, and excessive legislation and regulation further limited Latvia's appeal to international capital. Even the age-old government resort of issuing bonds was frequently unsuccessful in Latvia. A government issued bond drive with a 4% return in 1920, for example, had only sold 50% of the bonds after eight years. Similarly, a considerable bond created in 1931 to finance road construction promised a 6% return, but only became partially viable when the government forced its employees to purchases through automatic paycheque deductions.[15] Essentially, the state's economic foundations rested mostly on state monopolies of flax, timber, and alcohol. Timber concessions were often parts of international business deals, while the expropriation of wealth from flax farmers was astounding. From 1919–1921, the government return on the international trade of the flax harvest

---

14 See: Aldis Purs, "'Weak and Half Starved Peoples' meet 'Vodka, Champagne, Gypsies and Drozhki': Relations between the Republic of Latvia and the USA from 1918 to 1940" in Daunis Auers, ed., *Latvia and the USA: From Captive Nation to Strategic Partner* (Rīga: Academic Press of the University of Latvia, 2008), 19–31.

15 See: Nicholas Balabkins and Arnolds Aizsilnieks, *Entrepreneur in a Small Country: A Case Study against the Background of the Latvian Economy, 1919–1940* (Hicksville, New York: Exposition Press, 1975), 38.

yielded a 75% profit and accounted for nearly 15% of all government revenue.[16] Returns from alcohol sales were a double-edged sword considering the multiple social costs of high rates of alcohol sales.

There was a brief moment in time, in 1927 and 1928, when state officials reflected on the accomplishments of reconstruction, understood that the national economy had moved from crisis, to recovery, to growth, and planned for a more ambitious future of economic development. Early plans and projects were floated that imagined large, intensive development projects. One scheme for the development of the left bank of the Daugava (around the Spilve airfield) imagined a network of canals and amelioration of land in anticipation of space for hundreds of factories, and port facilities for hundreds of ships and thousands of large boats.[17] A similarly grandiose plan that worked its way through the halls of the Department of Local Government imagined a plan to bring electricity to most of Latvia.[18] These projects were only in their early stages, and it is entirely unclear if they would have mustered political support or managed to find enough investment capital. Yet, they are precisely the types of projects that could have potentially led to economic transformation and moves towards convergence with the most modern and industrialised states of Europe. The worldwide Great Depression scuttled all of these plans.

Soon after the Latvian economy emerged from the Great Depression in late 1933 and early 1934, the authoritarian *coup* of Kārlis Ulmanis ended the democratic, political experiment. His regime moved Latvia into the authoritarian, statist model for politics, the economy, and culture so prevalent across much of East and Central Europe at the time. The regime's deft, domestic use of

---

16 Balabkins and Aizsilnieks, *Entrepreneur in a Small Country*, 39. The government monopoly on flax and the small amounts given to its farmers, who came largely from Latgale, proved an early, but not the only, source of conflict between Latgale and Latvia.
17 Pope, *Rīgas osta deviņōs gadsimtos*, 223.
18 Coincidentally, the earlier development of a mass electrical network in Finland, and the experience of adopting a new technology to transform an entire national economy, is often cited as one of the reasons why Finland was materially far ahead of the Baltic States in the 1920s and 1930s, and subsequently ready for a further economic boom after World War II. See the work of Timo Myllyntaus, such as: Timo Myllyntaus, *The Gatecrashing Apprentice: Industrialising Finland as an Adopter of New Technology* (Helsinki: Yliopistopaino, 1990); and Timo Myllyntaus, *Electrifying Finland: The Transfer of a New Technology into a Late Industrialising Economy*, (London: MacMillan, 1991).

propaganda (volumes of vague and misleading economic statistics that always pointed upward, and a relentless hammering home of the *vadonisprincips*— borrowed from the German *Führerprinzip* connoting infallibility of the supreme leader—and the benefits of a "renewed Latvia") a time of general stability, and the horrors that would follow, have left many to remember the Ulmanis years as a "golden era."[19] The record of the economic development of Latvia during these years, however, is not as flattering. In agriculture, the regime accelerated the small holding model that stressed butter and bacon production, much of it for export.

The development of the industrial and commercial sectors during the Ulmanis regime was defined by control and statism, not by transformative growth or convergence. The regime seemed to share nationalists' concern that foreigners and minorities "owned" too much of Latvia's economy. The regime's solution was to quietly assume control over most levers of economic control and create a state-owned and controlled economy in the name of ethnic Latvians. Foreigners and minorities lost control of much of the economy, but to the state and not to Latvians. The state's favoured tool was its control of the banking system. Using state controlled banks, the state bought out foreigners, and forced private companies into large, state controlled cartels. The Mussolini-inspired chamber system further controlled and managed relations between labour and business. This near total control, however, did not lead to greater investment in industry.[20]

Essentially, in economic investment terms the regime tackled only one massive, infrastructural project, the building of a hydro-electrical dam on the Daugava River. Building such a dam (as well as several grand canal projects) were projected in Imperial Russian economic plans, as well as during the 1920s. Preliminary topographical sketches were produced on several occasions, including by an American firm in 1932. The engineering consensus was to build

---

19 This view has been a mainstay of *émigré* memoirs and literature, although serous academics such as Arnolds Aizsilnieks seriously rebuffed these assertions. See: Arnolds Aizsilnieks, *Latvijas saimniecības vēsture, 1914–1945* (Stockholm: Daugava, 1968). The myth has, however, resurfaced in contemporary Latvia in, among others, Oļģerts Krastiņš. *Latvijas Saimniecības vēsturiskā pieredze. 1918–1940* (Rīga; Latvijas valsts agraras ekonomikas institutes, 2001).
20 Aizsilnieks, *Latvijas saimniecības vēsture*, 831.

a dam at Ķegums, but negotiations with French and German firms broke down. Ultimately, in 1936, the Ulmanis regime signed a contract with the Swedish firm Svenska Entreprenad A.B. and opted for foreign loans brokered by the Stockholm Enskilda Bank to be repaid by 1950. Several other Swedish firms, Diamantbergsborrnings A/B, Allmänna Svenska Elektriska A/B, and Karlstads Mekaniska Verkstads A/B, as well as the Swiss firm Von Rollsche Eisenwerke Giesserei Bern, and the German enterprises Maschinenfabrik Augsburg-Nürnberg A/G, and A/G Siemens also participated in the complex project.[21] Ultimately, the dam was expected to have four turbines that would provide much of the electrical demand of Rīga and several other cities and towns. For propaganda purposes, the regime touted the limited number of foreign workers, and/or capital, and trumpeted its early completion and low costs. In 1939, the regime used the beginning of electrical production as a great propaganda event, but ultimately the dam would not be completed until 1943, with considerable foreign involvement and sizeable cost over-runs.

The wartime history of the dam serves as a kind of metaphor for Latvia during this era. The Soviets and Nazis understood the value of the engineering feat (particularly to power wartime industry), but also worried about sabotage. Both occupying forces guarded the facility tightly, but also attempted to destroy it during retreat (for the Soviets in the summer of 1941, and for the Germans in 1944). The Germans were more successful in dismantling or destroying the generators and caused a flood that damaged low-lying streets and basements in distant Rīga. The Soviets were able, however, to eventually repair the dam and replace the turbines. Echoing the Lazard Brothers scandal about the repayment of a foreign loan, the Soviet Government refused to honour the majority of the loans from Sweden (only around 10% of the total was ever repaid). Ultimately, the dam, independent Latvia's one great public work, built to transform and electrify the country and power an industrial revival, was only completed during one occupation, significantly damaged by war, and left largely unpaid by another occupation.

---

21 See: Aizsilnieks, *Latvijas saimiecības vēsture,* 770–771; Arnolds Aizsilnieks, "Ķeguma spēkstacija" in A. Švābe, ed., *Latvju enciklopēdija* (Stockholm: Apgāds Trīs zvaigznes, 1952), 1180–1185; and Harijs Jaunzems, "Pamatakmens" in *Latvijas arhīvi,* 2 (1997): 34–35.

In short, the independence era witnessed radical, political, cultural, and economic transformations. These transformations were most impressive in terms of reconstruction following a nearly cataclysmic war, and the awakening of agency in the state's citizenry. The authoritarian regime stunted this agency, reinserted the primary role of the state in all things, and offered little by way of a transformative development plan to attempt convergence. The political choices of the day (limited by geopolitical realities) and the affinities of the regime pushed Latvia towards a kind of autarchic, agricultural state with limited import substitution programs and a small holding agricultural sector following a "Danish model" for bacon and butter exports. People's standards of living increased relative to their own previous experience, and relative to other lands of the former Russian Empire, but did not converge with Western Europe. Latvia simply did not have access to the capital needed for such a transformation.

Assimilation into Soviet Economic Space

Such capital and investment resources potentially arrived with occupation, but the nature of occupation determined investments and denied local agency or even input and involvement. Before this Soviet economic transformation, Latvia suffered through multiple occupations during World War II. Soviet occupation focused on absorbing Latvia into the Soviet Union and introducing all of its political, economic, and cultural norms, whereas Nazi occupation, despite occasional fantasising by a few key Nazis about what the post-war era might look like, was overwhelmingly focussed on two goals: mobilising all resources for the war effort, and the destruction of perceived threats to the Aryan race. The sum total of economic ruin brought about by World War II is almost incalculable considering the lost human capital (deportations, executions, the Holocaust, war deaths, war casualties and mass flight), physical destruction because of military action, frequent use of scorched earth tactics by each occupying army during retreats, and the exhaustion of almost all accrued economic reserves and capacity. The overall economic destruction of World War II likely surpassed that of World War I, and after the armistice, the national economy of an independent state of Latvia was not revived.

Soviet return and victory meant, among many other things, the continuation and complete integration of the Latvian economy into a larger Soviet, command economic whole dictated by five-year economic plans decided in Moscow.

From the first days, the amount of investment in reconstruction and new economic development was on a scale that even surpassed the era of tsarist industrialisation (as mentioned, the plan was often very similar), and which dwarfed anything that an independent state of Latvia could muster. The investments in transportation (roads, bridges, railroads, ports, harbours, airports), communications (telegraph and telephone), power (the repair of Ķegums and the construction of additional dams, coal power stations, the creation of an electrical grid), and industry (the retooling of abandoned and destroyed factories, and the wholesale creation of entirely new industrial sectors, many of which serviced the Soviet military) were unmatched in the history of Latvia in terms of their sheer economic transformative power. The crux, however, was that the transformation was a part of the larger economic whole of the Soviet Union, with either the complete disregard or actual denigration of local concerns and interests. Soviet industrialisation and modernisation, from its beginnings with the first ideas of "building socialism in one country," was a massive attempt to achieve economic and military convergence with the industrialised, capitalist West. This was seen first as a matter of survival, and then later, when Soviet economic power would surpass the West, as a weapon for political and international class victory. This project superseded and ignored the interests and well-being of individuals from the 1920s onwards, as well as the national economic interests of nations and occupied nation-states, Latvia included. Soviet economic success meant the death of an independent Latvian national economic basis. Latvia was awash in capital and technical investment, but its use was detrimental, problematic or irrelevant to the economic growth of a sovereign Latvia.

4. Conclusion: A New Chapter?

By the 1980s, the centrally controlled planned economy was collapsing under its own weight, inefficiencies, failings, and environmental degradations. Tight one-party political control was unable to contain popular dissatisfaction. In Latvia, this dissatisfaction led to the re-establishment of the independent Republic of Latvia in 1991.[22] Latvia moved rapidly towards a free market capitalist system based on the European mould and undertook a breakneck-paced race towards full membership in the European Union (for economic prosperity) and NATO (for security).[23] This rapid transformation involved great economic pain, dislocation, graft, and corruption, but also succeeded in placing Latvia within an economic system and union that seems to offer the best realistically possible solution to Latvia's essential economic dilemma: how to access capital and know-how needed to meet the needs, demands, and aspirations of its citizenry for a modern society, while preserving a considerable degree of political sovereignty.

Still, is there any likelihood that Latvia will meet President Andris Bērziņš' aforementioned ominous deadline and attain a level of GDP on a par with the EU average within 10 years? Ultimately, this is a moot question, deadline, and criterion. Convergence is certainly likely (if not almost upon us) across some sectors and sub-classes. Parts of Latvia already "feel" like Amsterdam, Frankfurt or Paris for the fortunate, as do parts of Greece, Portugal, Slovenia, and the Czech Republic. The economic challenge lies in addressing the great regional and class disparities in wealth and development that exist across Latvia and the majority of European Union member states that are below the average EU GDP (as well as within impoverished parts of those few states above the average EU GDP). To borrow a phrase, Latvia has wagered its economic development on the strength of the European Union. In the current international climate, rarely is the EU described as strong, and within it are also serious challenges and obstacles to Latvia's sovereignty. Nevertheless, among the realistic other options, there are no other viable alternatives to Latvia's age-old dilemma: how to access capital and expertise for development while maintaining some local control over those forces. The myth of convergence overshadows the possibility of real economic modernisation and transformation.

---

22 Academics and lay people alike have disagreed over a final evaluation of the Soviet era. Tendentious accounts, such as Modris Šmulders, *Who Owes Whom: Mutual Economic Accounts Between Latvia and the USSR, 1940–199,* (Rīga: 1990), and the dozens that glorify Soviet construction miss the obvious: a solid majority of the citizens of the newly independent state have repeatedly turned away from the Soviet economic model since 1993.

23 The nature of this transition has also spawned a huge—and still ongoing—academic debate.

The Roots of Radicalism:
Persistent Problems of Class and Ethnicity in Latvia's Politics

Matthew Kott, Uppsala University

1. Securitisation and Ethnification

Society in multicultural, multiethnic Latvia has a long history of social disparity and political injustice, dating back to early modern times at least.[1] Social—e.g., class—cleavages have often mirrored cultural and ethnic divisions, promoting the ethnification of social conflict. Particularly since the rise of competing ideologies, such as nationalism and socialism, in the 19th century, ethnified social conflicts have tended to become radicalised in response to securitising measures of the state.

Securitisation, as defined by Buzan, Wæver, and de Wilde, is the process by which a particular issue is politicised to such an extreme that it is presented by a societal actor as "an existential threat, requiring emergency measures and actions outside the normal bounds of political procedure".[2] Herein, I will argue that, since at least the end of the 19th century, the state that controlled the territory of present-day Latvia—regardless of regime—has tended to securitise ethnicities and ethnify social issues. This, in turn, has led to greater political radicalisation from the object of securitising policies, both deepening the conflict, rather than resolving it, and reinforcing the conflation of ethnic and social identities that hinder the consolidation of an open, pluralistic, and inclusive polity. Only when this tendency towards confrontation is sidestepped, has society in Latvia made significant steps towards equality, democracy, and integration.

2. The 19th-Century Background

The Baltic Provinces of the Russian Empire—Estland, Livland, and Courland—were brought under tsarist rule stepwise during the 18th century, culminating with the annexation of Courland in the last Partition of Poland in 1795. Like the

---

1 Serfdom came comparatively late to the territory of Latvia, becoming predominant only from the 16th century onwards.
2 Barry Buzan, Ole Wæver and Jaap de Wilde, *Security: A New Framework for Analysis* (Boulder: Lynne Rienner 1998), 23–24.

later Grand Duchy of Finland, they retained much of their legal particularism and cultural distinctness even after the conquest. These were feudal societies where a Baltic German minority (itself adept at absorbing elites arriving from other cultures) ruled despotically over a predominantly Latvian peasant class as aristocrats, state officials, clergy, and burghers. Social injustice of serfdom coupled with ethnic difference created a potentially explosive mix. Baltic German authors inspired by the Enlightenment were critical of the feudal practice of serfdom; nevertheless, having seen the class-violence unleashed by the French Revolution, they worried of the consequences of emancipating a peasantry unprepared for the responsibilities of freedom.[3] For his part, Garlieb Merkel, who championed the abolition of serfdom, conjured up a frightening vision of what could happen in the future, should the emancipation be resisted too long by the privileged classes: the result would be civil conflict, where the long-suffering Latvian nation would rise up in genocidal violence against all Germans in the land.[4] Merkel may not have been the first to ethnify the power relations between rulers and ruled in the Baltic Provinces, but his influence on the Latvian nationalist imaginary of the ethnified Baltic German overclass as social and political enemy has been salient. Furthermore, he may have inadvertently contributed to the securitisation of the serfdom question with his apocalyptic prophecies. That literate peasants—a result of successful proselytising by the Moravian Brethren in Livland—read Merkel's *Die Letten* prior to the uprising at Kauguri in 1802 is noteworthy, especially given the heavy-handed response by the authorities: the peasant revolt was put down using regular infantry and artillery.[5]

The developments of the 19th century brought a succession of modernising transformations to society. As result, there also arose new social disparities and tensions. When the abolition of serfdom arrived in the aftermath of the Napoleonic Wars (1817 in Courland and 1819 Livland),[6] it in many respects made the position of the peasantry worse. Whilst peasants gained personal

---

3   Pauls Daija, *Apgaismība un kultūrpārnese: Latviešu laicīgās literatūras tapšana* (Rīga: LU Literatūras, folkloras un mākslas institūts, 2013), 195–213.
4   Garlieb Merkel, *Die Letten* (Rīga: Rigna, 1924), 228–233.
5   Arveds Švābe, *Latvijas vēsture 1800–1914* (Stockholm: Daugava, 1958), 69.
6   For Latgale, then part of Vitebsk *guberniia* and subject to general Russian legislation, serfdom was abolished only in 1861.

freedom and legal personhood, the manor lords retained all rights to the land and legal powers to punish the peasants. As tenant farmers, the in-kind rents and *corvée* obligations to the manor forced the peasants into poverty, while the manor lords were absolved of any obligations towards their former serfs. This led to periodic peasant unrest, and prompted reforms in the late 1840s that monetised the rural economy with cash rents and mechanisms for peasants to acquire land. Modernisation began to change the countryside, with social differentiation and social mobility shaking up the socio-economic structure of the Latvian population, and new techniques and technologies affecting the relations between employers (manors and independent farmers) and agricultural labourers. Upwardly-mobile peasants were often co-opted into the Baltic German community, while the economically marginalised developed into a growing landless rural proletariat. These modernisation processes were described in early classics of modern Latvian literature, such as *Mērnieku laiki* ("The Time of the Surveyors", 1879) and *Līduma dūmos* ("In Smoke from the Assart", 1899).

Similar processes were taking place in the towns and cities, which were attracting free peasants in search of a better life. As elsewhere in Europe, industrialisation and urbanisation went hand in hand, contributing to the replacement of the Baltic German-dominated power structures of the pre-capitalist socio-economic order, e.g. the guilds and municipal corporations. Here, the Germanisation of the upwardly mobile and the proletarisation of the marginalised were even more pronounced than in rural areas.

These radical societal and economic shifts were accompanied by the arrival of new political ideas. All three major ideologies that shaped European policies in the 19th century—liberalism, nationalism, and socialism—affected society in the territory of Latvia. They not only informed the developing "National Awakening" of the ethnic Latvians,[7] but also affected the other national groups as well. Liberal ideals inspired some Baltic Germans to support the early initiatives of the urban Latvian civil society, while, by the close of the century, the growing self-confidence of the Latvians and pressures of Russification from the tsarist

---

7   Gints Apals, *Pēterburgas Avīzes: Latviešu pirmā saskare ar Eiropas politiskajām idejām* (Rīga: Zvaigzne ABC, 2011).

regime prompted the rise of a Baltic German ethnic nationalism.[8] The political development of the Russian, Jewish, and Polish communities also was affected by these ideologies, particularly nationalism and socialism. From the 1890s, socialism and the national liberationist ideal became increasingly intertwined for the Latvians and Jews. Although the proto-Marxist Latvian "New Current" (*Jaunā strāva*) was crushed by the tsarist secret police in 1897, the first Latvian social democratic organisation was founded in Rīga in 1899, about the time the *Bund* first spread to Jewish workers in Daugavpils. The same year, 1899, also marked major labour unrest in Rīga, where rioting workers skirmished with police, infantry, and Cossack units. After the string of uprisings in the neighbouring Polish–Lithuanian territories of the Empire in the mid-19th century, the tsarist authorities were prone to securitising unrest in the non-Russian provinces.

For a period in the 1850s and 1860s, liberalism offered a hope for evolutionary change and socio-political modernisation without the need for violent rebellion. Latvian political activists and their allies, inspired by Alexander II's reforms, appealed to the Russian state to reform Baltic institutions and erode entrenched Baltic German privilege inherited from feudal times. The response of Alexander III's government—the Manasein Inquiry—was opportunistic, implementing imperialistic reforms that strengthened Russian autocracy in the provinces, and implementing a programme of Russification that affected not only Baltic Germans, but the Latvians as well. Social problems like the question of agrarian reform became ethnified and securitised. Baltic Germans used their influence over the rural police to create an atmosphere of ethnic and social tension, portraying the Inquiry as the catalyst for an uprising.[9] Latvian opinion was also in danger of being radicalised: a group of Latvian officers associated with *Narodnaia vol'ia* was discovered in Rīga in 1882, and a further *narodnik* cell was found in Cesvaine the next year.[10] In the final report of the Inquiry, however, it was asserted that socialist, nihilist, and anarchist ideas were not

---

8   Anders Henriksson, *The Tsar's Loyal Germans: The Riga German Community: Social Change and the Nationality Question, 1855–1905* (Boulder: East European Monographs 1983), 59–61.
9   Švābe, *Latvijas vesture*, 437.
10 Švābe, *Latvijas vesture*, 432.

widely held amongst the peasantry at the time.[11] Nevertheless, from the 1880s onward, the increasing tensions resulting from accelerating modernisation, conflicting nationalist agendas, and reactionary, imperialist autocracy promoted a stepwise radicalisation of securitised ethnopolitics.

Table 1 presents a snapshot of the ethnic and social relations in the provinces of Livland and Courland circa 1900. According to this simplified schematic representation, political and economic power, as well as inherited privilege was concentrated in the hands of a relative few. Furthermore, the Baltic German community dominated these elites, adeptly co-opting elites from other ethnic backgrounds into its hegemonic system of cultural norms. At the other end of the scale, the economically vulnerable, disenfranchised classes arising from modernisation (the urban proletariat and the rural landless agricultural labourers) was comprised mainly of ethnic Latvians.[12] It is this combined precariat that, under the direction of a radicalised intelligentsia, would play a central role in the cycles of ethnified political violence at various key moments in the 20th century, particularly during the first two decades.

Table 1

Class/social group	Dominant community	Competing others (directions of social mobility)*
Aristocracy	Baltic Germans	Russians (↔), Poles (↔)
Clergy (mainly Lutheran)	Baltic Germans	Latvians (↑)
Upper middle class (bourgeoisie, gentry)	Baltic Germans	Latvians (↑, ↔), Russians
Lower middle class (professionals, artisans, landed peasantry)	Latvians	Baltic Germans (↓), Russians, Jews
Urban proletariat	Latvians	Russians and others from neighbouring provinces (↑)
Rural landless (ca. 3/5 rural population)[13]	Latvians	Lithuanians, Estonians, etc.

* where ↑ represents proportional growth within said social group; ↓ a tendency to declining proportion; and ↔ trends of assimilation by/of other communities within the same social group.

---

11 Švābe, *Latvijas vesture*, 439.
12 Kristīne Volfarte, *Rīgas Latviešu biedrība un latviešu nacionālā kustība no 1868. līdz 1905. gadam* (Rīga: LU Akadēmiskā apgāds, 2009), 71–90.
13 Švābe, *Latvijas vesture*, 549.

The rumblings of social and political unrest presaged by the rioting of 1899 came to a head in the revolutionary outburst of 1905. Arguably, the infrastructure of the working-class movement in Latvia developed prior to the Latvian national movement becoming a truly mass political phenomenon. Furthermore, revolutionary socialist ideas gained ground among educated and working class Latvians before anything resembling a liberal political order was achieved in tsarist Russia. As the national idea of the Latvians was still in the process of formation at this time when class and ethnic cleavages were still roughly congruent, the goals of socialism and nationalism for Latvians (and, to a certain extent, for Bundist Jews) became intimately intertwined. In the symbolic representation of Miroslav Hroch, this developmental path would look thus:

AB →IR →WCM →BC → BR → FN(?)[14]

This parses as the shift from the phase of an ideological elite movement (AB) to a mass national movement (BC) having been preceded by the Industrial Revolution (IR) and the development of the working-class movement (WCM). The "bourgeois revolution" (BR)—in Latvia's case, the founding of the liberal-democratic nation-state—comes only in 1918, while it has even been suggested that the Latvian nation was not fully formed (FN) until the end of the Soviet period,[15] if, indeed, this process has been completed yet at all.

3. Revolution and World War

Starting in the urban industrial centre of Rīga, the revolutionary violence of 1905 soon spilled out into the countryside. Revolutionaries from the cities and towns fanned the flames of revolt in rural areas. Not only the gentry, but also clergy, seen as the mouthpieces of the gentry's interests, were targeted, with many manors and parsonages being torched. Churches became instead the locus of revolutionary meetings. The Baltic German elites ethnified their image of the enemy, with Astaf von Trensehe-Roseneck's account of the brutality of the "Latvian Revolution"[16] strongly influencing the historical narrative within his

---

14 Cf. Miroslav Hroch, *Social Preconditions of National Revival in Europe: A Comparative Analysis of the Social Composition of Patriotic Groups among the Smaller European Nations* (New York: Columbia University Press, 2000), 27.
15 Cf. Detlefs Henings, "Nacionālā kustība un nacionālās valsts tapšana Latvijā: Pētījuma rezultāti," *Latvijas Vēstures Institūta Žurnāls*, 1 (1995), 74.
16 Astaf von Transehe-Roseneck, *Die lettische Revolution*, 2 vols. (Berlin: Reimer, 1906–8).

community.[17] At the same time, the aggrieved mass of rural landless—estimated by Aivars Stranga to number some half million—viewed the gentry as not only a social, but also a hateful, and hated ethnic Other.[18]

The events of 1905–1906 were marked by ethnified radicalisation on the part of the revolutionaries, and ethnified securitisation as the response. The Latvian revolutionary ideologue and future Bolshevik leader, Pēteris Stučka, publicly proclaimed that use of lethal force was now legitimate in the revolutionary struggle against the forces of tsarist autocracy.[19] A minority of ideologically motivated Latvian revolutionaries even felt that individual acts of political terror could be justified.[20] The response of the tsarist regime and the Baltic German *Selbstschutz* vigilantes was also violent and brutal, reminiscent of the discourse of terrorism/anti-terrorism familiar today. Once again, Cossacks were dispatched, courts martial prescribed the executions of over a thousand revolutionaries, and farmsteads of those supporting the revolution were burned in reprisal actions.[21] This reinforced a cycle of violence that left festering social and psychological wounds long after the uprising was crushed, producing mutually antagonistic memories that could be revived to justify repressions in future conflicts.[22] On both sides, competing narratives of ethnified violence and victimhood were nurtured and incorporated into the community's identity discourse. At the same time the social injustices and political inequalities that had been the root cause of the failed revolution remained unresolved. A number of radicalised Latvian revolutionaries gravitated to increasingly extreme ideological positions, whether these be the violent anarchists responsible for the bloody

---

17 Jānis Stradiņš, "Latvijas 1905. gada revolūcijas kaujinieki starptautiskā aspektā," in Jānis Bērziņš, ed., *1905. gads Latvijā: 100. Pētījumi un starptautiskās konferences materiāli, 2005. gada 11.–12. janvāris* (Rīga: Latvijas Vēstures institūta apgāds, 2006), 413.
18 Aivars Stranga, "Pārdomas par 1905. gada revolūciju," in Bērziņš, ed., *1905. gads Latvijā: 100*, 575.
19 Pēteris Stučka, *Politiska brīvība* (Berne, 1905), 50.
20 Švābe, *Latvijas vesture*, 601–602.
21 Mark R. Hatlie, *Riga at War: War and Wartime Experience in a Multi-Ethnic Metropolis* (Marburg:Herder-Institut, 2014), 29.
22 Detlefs Henings, "1905. gada revolūcija un 1919. gads," in Bērziņš, ed., *1905. gads Latvijā: 100*, 522–523. Cf. the deep societal rifts caused by the experience and memory of the Spanish Civil War.

Siege of Sidney Street in London in 1911,[23] or those, like Stučka, who became ardent Bolsheviks. Detlef Henning even suggests this heretofore understudied period between 1907 and 1914 be called the "quiet revolution".[24] One response from the Baltic German aristocracy was a plan to prevent future rural uprisings by inviting German colonists to settle in the Latvian countryside; in the end, some 15,000 arrived from Volhynia;[25] other sources mention around 20,000 German colonists in total. Some Baltic German landowners evicted Latvian tenant farmers to make room for the colonists, exacerbating Latvian land hunger and rural unemployment. Some colonists were dissatisfied and re-emigrated, while the tsarist authorities also raised obstacles: for example, a plan to deport large numbers of the restive local populations to Vologda Province failed to materialise.[26] At the same time, Russian nationalists sought to bring in 300,000 Russian colonists to Courland, while encouraging Latvian emigration to other parts of the Empire. Little Russian colonisation occurred, however, except in Latgale—which was nevertheless administratively part of Vitebsk *guberniia*.[27] Neither the Baltic German, nor the Russian nationalists' efforts to promote colonisation succeeded in significantly altering the perceived ethnic security imbalance in the Baltic Provinces.

The outbreak of World War I only exacerbated the persistent social problems and furthered the securitisation of attitudes towards the ethnic minorities of the non-Russian periphery of the Empire. The fragmentation of social life along ethnic divides continued apace in the run-up to the war, with even volunteer fire brigades being created for the different ethnic communities. These latter organisations also had the threatening potential to serve as nuclei for mobilising paramilitary organisations in the event of communal violence.[28] In 1914,

---

23 Filips Rufs, *Pa stāvu liesmu debesīs: Nenotveramā latviešu anarhista Pētera Māldera laiks un dzīve* (Rīga: Dienas grāmata, 2012). The Latvian *émigré* "Society for the Struggle of the Working Class" published one issue of the newspaper *Naids* (Hatred) in Manchester and Paris 1908; whereas the "Latvian Anarcho-Communists" published *Melnais Karogs* (Black Flag) in New York in 1911–1913.
24 Henings, "1905. gada revolūcija," 524.
25 Valerian Tornius, *Die Baltischen Provinzen* (Leipzig & Berlin: Teubner, 1915), 19.
26 Valdis Bērziņš, ed., *20. gadsimta Latvijas vēsture*, vol. 1 (Rīga: Latvijas Vēstures institūta apgāds, 2000), 408.
27 Bērziņš, ed., *20. gadsimta Latvijas vesture*, vol. 1, 410–411.
28 Hatlie, *Riga at War*, 26.

anti-German sentiment blossomed openly amongst Latvians and Russians, putting Baltic Germans on the defensive. A number of anti-German measures were implemented in the Baltic Provinces, culminating with the deportations of groups whose loyalty was in doubt: not only ethnic Germans (even those who were Russian subjects), but also many Jews were forcibly transferred to the Russian interior, away from the frontlines with Germany.[29]

The conflict was ethnified on other levels as well. When Rīga was in danger of falling to the German advance in 1915, the decision was made—at the request of Latvian groups—to allow the creation of ethnically Latvian units within the Russian Army.[30] The public appeal for patriotic recruits to volunteer had the headline, "Rally to the [ethnic] Latvian flags!" (*Pulcējaties zem latviešu karogiem!*),[31] a formulation which buttressed the national identity of the defenders, and implied resuming the struggle with the ancient enemy, the Germans. The war also created vast numbers of internally displaced persons from the western regions of Russia, a phenomenon the Peter Gatrell has aptly termed "a whole empire walking".[32] The relief committees for these refugees were organised with official sanction along ethnic lines, with the Latvian Central Committee for Providing Help to Refugees being created by the Ministry of Internal Affairs on 9 November 1915.[33] This organisation helped to consolidate a sense of common Latvian nationhood, as well as providing a forum for activists to hone their political skills and mobilise their national interests.[34] This decision to ethnify social solidarity in response to the refugee crisis by the tsarist government, thus served to hasten the eventual breakup of the empire.

The February Revolution was greeted in those Latvian territories not occupied by Germany without the explosion of revolutionary violence seen in 1905. One explanation offered for this was that the primary object of hatred, the Baltic

---

29 Hatlie, *Riga at War*, 163–178. On the deportation of the Jews of Courland: Andres Kasekamp, *A History of the Baltic States* (Basingstoke: Palgrave Macmillan, 2010), 94.
30 Hatlie, *Riga at War*, 232.
31 Valdis Bērziņš, *Latviešu strēlnieki Pirmajā pasaules karā (1915–1918)* (Rīga: LU Akadēmiskais apgāds, 2014), 9.
32 Peter Gatrell, *A Whole Empire Walking: Refugees in Russia during World War I* (Bloomington: Indiana University Press, 1999).
33 *Pravitel'stvennaia reviziia v Latyshskom tsentral'nom komitet po okazaniiu pomoshchi bezhentsam* (Petrograd: Stroitel', 1915), 5.
34 Hatlie, *Riga at War*, 238–240.

Germans, were largely absent from the political stage at this point, due to the aforementioned deportations.[35] Nevertheless, the underlying social issues from 1905 remained unresolved, and other societal problems had been exacerbated by the war and the central government's mishandling of the situation. Thus, the Latvian Social Democrats, by now thoroughly Bolshevised under the leadership of Stučka, were able to quickly gain control of most of the post-revolutionary power structures, old and new. They came to dominate city councils, the provincial assembly, district soviets, and the delegation to the Constituent Assembly. Andrew Ezergailis has described the Rīga City Council elections—the first truly free, universal, direct, and secret ballot elections in the history of Latvia—as being a worse outcome for liberal democracy than the 1848 elections in France that brought Napoleon III to power:[36] Of the 120 seats contested, the Latvian Bolshevik faction won 49 and an alliance of other revolutionary socialists won 18. On 31 July 1917, the Executive Committee of the Soviet of Workers, Soldiers, and Landless of Latvia—*Iskolat*—was created, essentially a Bolshevik dominated political coordinating body, if not a nascent government. One of *Iskolat*'s top priorities was the agrarian question, passing a decree on 16 August on the need to confiscate the (mainly Baltic German-owned) manors.[37] Even if the collapse of Russian military power and the occupation by German forces prevented the realisation of these aims, Latvian territory was one of the main strongholds of Bolshevism outside of Petrograd at this point.

In September 1917, Rīga finally fell to the German forces. By early 1918, all of present-day Latvia was under German control. Prior to this, much of western Latvia—i.e. Courland Province—had been ruled by Germany since 1915 as part of the semi-colonial *Ober Ost*. An attempt was made by the occupation authorities following the Treaty of Brest-Litovsk to create a Baltic Duchy with the German Emperor as its crowned head of state. In order to not repeat the mistakes of past rulers, it was proposed that the German regime intensively colonise the Baltic Provinces, thereby ensuring these lands remain firmly within

---

35 Hatlie, *Riga at War*, 241.
36 Andrievs Ezergailis, *Esejas par 1917. gadu* (Rīga: Zinātne, 1991), 10.
37 *Iskolata un tā prezīdija protokoli (1917.–1918.)* (Rīga: Zinātne, 1973), 11.

Germany's orbit forever.[38] Some of these initiatives foresaw the complete ethnic reconfiguration of Courland within fifty years, through a combination of colonisation by Germans, and the assimilation and expulsion of ethnic Latvians.[39] The ethnic composition of the population was thus highly securitised in *Ober Ost*,[40] just as it had increasingly been in the wartime Russian Empire. Nevertheless, just as Russian nationalist ambitions in the Baltic region collapsed along with the fall of the Romanov dynasty in 1917, German hopes of a renewed *Drang nach Osten* suffered a major blow with the dethroning of the Hohenzollerns in 1918.

4. Alternative National Futures

In the period from 1917 to 1920, political regimes—and political visions of the future—in Latvia were increasingly identified with a particular ethnic group. At the same time, there was a crisis of liberalism, which seemingly could not provide the solutions to the problems wracking wartime societies.[41] In 1919, the situation in Latvia, located in the "shatterzone of empires",[42] became engulfed in an internecine conflict that some—this author included—categorise as a civil war.[43]

In the spring of 1919 three competing visions of the future for Latvia arose, each with its own prospective government claiming the right to power. The last

---

38 Alexis von Engelhardt, *Die deutschen Ostseeprovinzen Rußlands: Ihre politische und wirtschaftliche Entwicklung* (Munich: Georg Müller, 1916), 149–152.
39 Vejas Liulevicius, *War Land on the Eastern Front: Culture, National Identity and German Occupation in World War I* (Cambridge: Cambridge University Press, 2000), 165.
40 The German authorities in Ober Ost also manipulated Belarusian nationalism in order to weaken Polish and Russian influences over territories conquered from Russia: Per Anders Rudling, *The Rise and Fall of Belarusian Nationalism 1906–1931* (Pittsburgh: University of Pittsburgh Press, 2015), 72–75.
41 Society in Latvia was in no way unique in this respect. For the more general European crisis of liberalism in the wake of World War I, see: Charles S. Maier, *Recasting Bourgeois Europe: Stabilization in France, Germany, and Italy in the Decade after World War I* (Princeton: Princeton University Press, 1988), 3–15.
42 Cf. Omer Bartov and Eric D. Weitz, eds., *Shatterzone of Empires: Coexistence and Violence in the German, Habsburg, Russian, and Ottoman Borderlands* (Bloomington: Indiana University Press, 2013).
43 Aldis Minins, "Latvia, 1918–1920: A Civil War?," *Journal of Baltic Studies* 46, 1 (2015): 49–63. Cf. Alexander V. Prusin, *The Lands Between: Conflict in the East European Borderlands, 1870–1992* (Oxford: Oxford University Press, 2010), 74–75.

of these to appear was the most backwards looking: on 16 April, with Baltic German units of the *Baltische Landeswehr* staged a *coup* that would seek to revive the project for a Baltic Duchy, controlled by conservative German aristocrats. In this, they were supported by the German *Freikorps* under the control of the Entente-appointed military commander of Liepāja, Rüdiger von der Goltz, previously active in the Finnish Civil War. Even though the schemes of *Landmarschall* Heinrich von Stryk lost some importance when the arch-conservative Latvian pastor, and author of the aforementioned *Līduma dūmos*, Andrievs Niedra, was appointed prime minister, this pro-German government was by no means progressive or democratic. Niedra's government agreed to broad cultural autonomy for Baltic Germans, German as co-official language, and a third of ministerial posts being earmarked for the Baltic German minority. In return, Niedra received assurances that the aristocracy would give up some of its privileges, and allow redistribution of some of the manor lands (with compensation) to the landless—albeit this category was to also include *Reich* Germans granted citizenship for fighting in Latvia against the Bolsheviks. Generally, the polity proposed by Niedra did little to remedy societal imbalances: the pre-revolutionary system of local government was reintroduced in the rural parishes, and elections to a legislative assembly (of which one-third of the seats would be reserved for national minorities, i.e. Baltic Germans) would employ a curia system, with electoral colleges based on both ethnic and social (e.g. property) criteria. The votes of the propertied classes weighed more than those of the landless and the proletariat, with the intent to prevent a takeover of the organs of power by Bolsheviks or other radicals. Despite its Latvian figurehead, the Niedra government was widely seen as representing reactionary Baltic German interests, and therefore enjoyed the support of only the most conservative minority of the ethnic Latvian population. Its survival was also dependent entirely on the force of German arms under the command of General von der Goltz.[44]

The main alternative that prompted the Baltic German *coup* and the creation of Niedra's administration was the Latvian Bolshevik regime headed by Stučka.

---

44 Valdis Blūzma, "Latvijas valstiskuma alternatīvas revolucionāro pārmaiņu laikmetā (1917–1920)," in Jānis Stradiņš, ed., *Latvieši un Latvija: Akadēmiskie raksti*, vol. 2 (Rīga: Latvijas Zinātņu akadēmija, 2013), 253–257.

A Soviet Latvian government claiming to be the successor of *Iskolat* was declared in December 1917. A Soviet Latvian army, at the core of which was Bolshevised "Red" Latvian Riflemen units, invaded with support from Soviet Russia. By 3 January 1919, Rīga fell to the Soviet forces, giving Stučka control over half of Latvia. He and his supporters began a programme of radical reforms that sought to fundamentally transform society as quickly as possible. Property was nationalised and redistributed, the bourgeoisie was declared class enemies and stripped of political and civil rights.[45] In the city of Rīga, this class war disproportionately pitted working-class Latvians against middle and upper-class Baltic Germans. The cabinet in Stučka's Bolshevik government was composed entirely of ethnic Latvians.[46] Thus, Red Terror in Rīga had a strong element of ethnified violence.[47] When the peasants refused to supply the city foodstuffs on the regime's terms, Stučka responded in March 1919 with a heavy-handed land nationalisation campaign in the countryside. Only when they felt that being made into "red serfs" to the Soviet manors (an early form of *sovkhoz*) was a betrayal of their demands for land redistribution did the majority in the countryside begin to turn against the Stučka government, despite revolutionary tribunals imposing Red Terror in rural areas against Latvians.[48]

The third alternative was the one offered by the liberal-democratic national government proclaimed on 18 November 1918. Initially, this claimant to statehood lacked the direct military backing that the other two enjoyed from von der Goltz's forces or Bolshevik Russia, respectively. Nevertheless, they had the sympathies of the Western *Entente* powers, who were interested in preventing both German and Soviet sympathisers from gaining a foothold the Baltic region. Although strongly identifying democracy with the need to grant the Latvian majority unprecedented control over the instruments of state, this government was not purely ethnocentric: in its proclamations, it addressed all inhabitants a citizens of Latvia, regardless of ethnicity, and included several non-Latvians in the

---

45 See: Jānis Šiliņš, *Padomju Latvija 1918–1919* (Rīga: Vēstures izpētes un popularizēšanas biedrība, 2013).
46 Cf. Rihards Treijs, *Latvijas Komunistiskā partija 1919. gadā* (Rīga: Liesma, 1968), 33.
47 Šiliņš, *Padomju Latvija*, 111. Cf. Hatlie, *Riga at War*, 197. Šiliņš (124) even goes so far as to say that the policies of Stučka's goverment exhibited 'characteristics of genocide.'
48 Šiliņš, *Padomju Latvija*, 128–131, 193–195.

cabinet of ministers under provisional prime minister Kārlis Ulmanis.[49] Based purely on ethnic criteria, the Russian-backed Stučka government was the most "Latvian" of all three in 1919; this, however, did not ensure it legitimacy in the long run. Even though the national-liberal forces were to emerge victorious from the civil war, the unresolved relationship between state and nation would eventually lead to the downfall of democracy after just fifteen years.

As in Finland, the civil war in Latvia unleashed a cycle of retributive terror. Here, however, the pattern of revolutionary and counter-revolutionary violence had not only a clear class, but also an ethnic aspect, with political terror targeting the ethnified Other.[50] Mirroring 1905 and its aftermath, the victims of the Red Terror, especially in Rīga, were mainly Baltic Germans (Baltic German = bourgeois); while those summarily executed as "Bolsheviks" in the White Terror after Baltic German forces retook the city in May 1919 were ethnic Latvians (Latvian = Bolshevik). Not only was the pattern of equating class, political, and ethnic groups replicated, a new precedent for securitisation was set, whereby certain ethnic groups are singled out as having collaborated with or seeking support from a particular political regime. As a result, when support for different, competing regimes is projected upon different ethnic communities, not only do ethnic relations become increasingly securitised, the chances of genocidal policies being implemented also grows substantially.

As things turned out, the government promoting the liberal-democratic model for Latvia came out victorious from the War of Independence.[51] Thanks to the fact that the more moderate social democrats sided with the Ulmanis provisional government, and came to be the largest single party (57 of 150 seats) in the elected Constituent Assembly, democratic Latvia was founded with a for

---

49 See, for example, the proclamation "Latvijas pilsoņiem!", reproduced in: *1918.–1920. gads Latvijas Republikas Pagaidu valdības sēžu protokolos, nolikumos, atmiņās* (Rīga: Latvijas Vēstnesis, 2013), 68. Initially, the Ulmanis Provisional government only included one Baltic German (Auditor General Eduard von Rosenberg), but in a reshuffle in July 1919, included two Baltic Germans (Justice Minister Edwin Magnus and Finance Minister Robert Erhardt) and a Jew (Auditor General Paul Mintz): *1918.–1920. gads*, 33, 35.

50 Cf. Juha Siltala, "Dissolution and Reintegration in Finland, 1914–1932: How Did a Disarmed Country Become Absorbed into Brutalization?", *Journal of Baltic Studies*, 46, 1 (2015), 27.

51 For a fuller discussion, see: Blūzma, "Latvijas valstiskuma alternatīvas", 225–260.

the time progressive, Weimar-style constitution. The second paragraph of the *Satversme* (Constitution) declared that sovereign power belonged to the "people of Latvia" (*Latvijas tauta*), thus raising the prospect of an inclusive, civic national identity open to all ethnicities. A proposed second part to the *Satversme* that would enshrine the democratic rights and freedoms of citizens was, however, not adopted, in part due to a difference of opinions between various socialist factions.

Latvian socialist politician and activist Kārlis Balodis (*Carl Ballod*) had already in late 1918 expressed the hope that the new Republic of Latvia would not only be independent and democratic, but also "anointed with the oil of social [justice]" (*sociālo eļļu svaidīto republiku*).[52] If this had indeed happened, then some of the later problems that afflicted society and politics in Latvia may have been mitigated, if not avoided completely. Yet the new Latvian state soon succumbed to nationalising tendencies, which, in turn, came to erode the legitimacy of the constitutional foundations upon which independent Latvia's statehood rested.

5. What Kind of State?

From the very beginning, there were debates about the nature of Latvian statehood: was it primarily to be a nation-state of, by, and for the ethnic Latvians, or was it—as stated in the original, laconic preamble to the *Satversme*—a manifestation of the sovereignty of the civic nation, the "people of Latvia"? After the Latvian government signed a peace treaty with Soviet Russia in 1920, the issue of the ethnic composition of Latvia became a matter of public debate. As Marina Germane demonstrates elsewhere in this volume, one of the main causes of this was the inflow of refugees form war-torn Russia, particularly Jews, claiming citizenship of independent Latvia. These Jewish refugees were viewed with suspicion on political, economic, and ethnic grounds. Aside from parliament, where wrangling over Jewish refugees' citizenship claims went on for years, one of the key battlegrounds for deciding the ethnic nature of the new nation-state was the newly created University of Latvia.

---

52 Kārlis Balodis, "Latvijas izveidošana: Individuālā un sociālā Latvija", *Ievads tautsaimniecībā un ekonomiskā politika* (Rīga: Drukātava, 2013), 525.

Officially founded in 1919, the University had, as in most European societies of the time, the tack of educating the coming elite of the state: its lawyers, doctors, engineers, and intellectuals. These elites were also to be loyal, and *national*: form an early stage, the ambition was to promote professors who could teach advanced subjects in Latvian. Those teachers who could not or would not were marginalised and eventually forced out of academia. This policy was particularly directed against Baltic Germans inherited from the Rīga Polytechnic Institute, from which the University was created; specially recruited foreign experts, such as the Swedish anatomist, Gaston Backman, were, however, given greater (albeit not permanent) dispensation to teach in German instead of Latvian. Herein is revealed the underlying paradox of the University's mission: science and scholarship are international phenomena, whilst universities are expected by governments to fulfil national agendas.[53] The internal contradictions this institutionalised served to make the University a hotbed of radicalism in the coming decades.

A further example of how social, ethnic and security issues were intertwined to create a policy that paved the way for future problems was the agrarian reform of 1920–22. Ostensibly this was a modernising and democratising reform, the aim of which was, on the one hand to satisfy the longstanding social problem of the rural landless, by nationalising, and then redistributing manorial lands as new smallholdings, with priority being given to veterans who had fought for Latvia's independence. Not only was this policy designed to completely undermine any residual appeal for communism amongst the agricultural labourers following their disenchantment with the overzealous experiments of the Stučka regime; it also intended to direct a fatal blow to the remaining feudal social, economic, and political power base of the Baltic German gentry.[54] Since the Baltic German leadership was viewed as having been disloyal to the aspirations of the national democratic Provisional Government during the struggle for independence, the terms of the land reform were intentionally harsh towards the great landowners: all manorial lands except for 50, sometimes 100 ha of

---

53 Per Bolin, *Between National and Academic Agendas: Ethnic Policies and National Disciplines at the University of Latvia, 1919–1940* (Huddinge: Södertörns högskola, 2012).
54 Arnolds Aizsilnieks, *Latvijas saimniecības vēsture 1914–1945* (Stockholm: Daugava, 1968), 234–235.

demesnes in direct proximity to the manor house were confiscated for the State Land Fund without compensation.

The land reform process was officially completed in 1937, and radically transformed Latvia to a country with a high level of owner-occupied smallholdings. At the time, the reform was generally declared a success, as it had kick-started the rural economy ravaged by war, and had seemingly satisfied the age-old land hunger of the Latvian peasantry. For the non-Latvian former elites, however, this was a major trauma. Baltic German representatives complained to the League of Nations that this policy infringed on the rights of national minorities in Latvia, but the calls for the repeal of the reform or the payment of compensation gained no international support. In some cases, considerations of *Realpolitik* led to the payment of compensation by the state to some non-Baltic German foreign citizens: for example, in an annex to a trade treaty from 1929, Latvia agreed to pay out over 5 million lats in compensation to Polish nationals whose holdings in Latvia had been confiscated.[55] The sense of rejection and alienation from a state that sought to not only deprive them of their former status, but also their economic livelihood caused lingering hostility amongst some Baltic Germans in Latvia. A minority chose to emigrate to Germany, where not an insignificant number of them joined the Nazi movement out of irredentist sentiment.[56] Of those who stayed, the majority accommodated themselves, at least at first.[57] Here, the role of the Baltic German liberal Paul Schiemann was pivotal.[58] Nevertheless, a younger generation of radicalised Baltic German activists including Erhard Kroeger eventually formulated a revanchist Baltic German radical nationalism that aligned itself with national socialism. In the 1930s, Kroeger and his peers were able to force the liberals like Schiemann from positions of influence, exposing the Baltic German community to pressures of Nazification. This set the community on a collision course with the increasingly nationalising state, and eventually to the mass exodus of the *Umsiedlung* in

---

55 Valdis Bērziņš, ed., *20. gadsimta Latvijas vēsture*, vol. 2 (Rīga: Latvijas Vēstures institūta apgāds, 2003), 394–395.
56 Michael Kellogg, *The Russian Roots of Nazism: White Émigrés and the Making of National Socialism, 1917–1945* (Cambridge: Cambridge University Press, 2005).
57 Bērziņš, ed., *20. gadsimta Latvijas vēsture*, vol. 2, 339–340.
58 On Schiemann, see: John Hiden, *Defender of Minorities: Paul Schiemann, 1876–1944* (London: Hurst, 2004).

1939, which Kroeger oversaw on behalf of Nazi Germany.[59] Arguably, had the agrarian reform been more open to Baltic German concerns and perceived as less of a punishment for past sins, sympathies for Nazi Germany may have gained less traction in Latvia, thereby reducing the communal tensions within this multicultural society. Instead, the Latvian political police felt obliged to keep tabs on the anti-government sentiment amongst its Baltic German citizens.[60]

Baltic Germans were not the only minority whose activities were viewed with deep existential suspicion by the young Latvian nation-state. Even the Belarusians, who were numerically small in number, but mainly concentrated in politically contested and economically marginalised border areas in the southeast, were the cause of a major security crisis. In 1925, a major trial of seven teachers from Belarusian schools, including the leading Belarusian national activist Kanstantyn (Kastus) Jezavitaŭ (Konstantīns Jezovitovs), was held in Daugavpils. The defendants stood accused of threatening the territorial integrity of the Latvia by having contacts with Belarusian nationalist groupings, as well as the Polish and Soviet governments, with the aim of separating the areas traditionally inhabited by Belarusians from Latvia. Among the evidence against them was a school map of "ethnographic Belarus" that included parts of Latgale. Even if the verdict was "not guilty", this case still offers clear proof of the securitising reflex of the Latvian state regarding minorities already from an early date.[61] Because of cultural ties to Soviet Belarus, this minority was persistently suspected by the political police of being susceptible to separatism

---

59 Raimonds Cerūzis, *Vācu faktors Latvijā (1918–1939): Politiskie un starpnacionālie aspekti* (Rīga: LU Akadēmiskais apgāds, 2004). For a thorough, albeit teleological study of Kroeger, see: Matthias Schröder, *Deutschbaltische SS-Führer und Andrej Vlasov 1942–1945: "Rußland kann nur von Russen besiegt warden": Erhard Kroeger, Friedrich Buchardt und die 'Russische Befreiungsarmee'* (Paderborn: Schöningh, 2001).
60 Inesis Feldmanis, "Latvijas interesēm kaitīgās vācbaltiešu organizāciju darbības novērošana un apkarošana," in Vija Kaņepe, ed., *Latvijas izlūkdienesti 1919.–1940.: 664 likteņi* (Rīga: LU žurnāla "Latvijas Vēsture" fonds, 2001), 169–189.
61 Ilga Apine, "Baltkrievi Latvijā," in Leo Dribins, ed., *Mazākumtautības Latvijā: Vēsture un tagadne* (Rīga: LU Filozofijas un socioloģijas institūts, 2007), 196–197.

and communist ideas.[62] Belarusian activists felt hostility from parts of the Latvian political elite.[63]

The generation of young men who had fought in the war of independence had ambitious hopes for their role in the building of the nation-state. Having put their lives on the line for the freedom of their country, they now expected to become the new elite that helped build the national state. Hence many of them took the opportunity to enter higher education, in hopes of a building a career. During the interwar period, Latvia had the highest number of university students *per capita* in Europe. The problem was, many of these were forced by economic necessity to pursue their studies only part-time; and even if they eventually completed their degrees, many found that the job opportunities and concomitant social mobility to which they felt entitled were simply not there. In both the public and private sectors, young graduates were frustrated by the fact that career paths were blocked by the older generation of established, pre-war elites—most of whom never had any patriotic military service. This included a disproportionate number of non-Latvians, whose social capital, regardless of upheavals and transformations, remained greater than that of many Latvian would-be *parvenus*. Furthermore, even at the university, many young Latvians felt aggrieved by the fact that they faced stiff competition for places with minority students who were often perceived as having better economic resources and educational preparation for higher education than themselves. Particularly irksome to the front generation was the arrival of a significant number of Jewish students with the return of wartime refugees to Latvia following the peace treaty in 1920. Student politics became radicalised, with calls for Latvian language testing (for minority background applicants), and even a *numerus clausus*. From the ranks of the nationalist students arose the first protofascist movement

---

62 Bērziņš, ed., *20. gadsimta Latvijas vēsture*, vol. 2, 364–6. On Jezavitaŭ's pro-Soviet contacts, see: Ēriks Jēkabsons, "Baltkrievu sabiedriski politiskā darbība Latvijā nacistiskās Vācijas okupācijas laikā 1941.–1945. Gadā," in Dzintars Ērglis, ed., *Totalitārie okupācijas režīmi Latvijā 1940.–1964. gadā: Latvijas Vēsturnieku komisijas 2003. gada pētījumi / Totalitarian Occupation Regimes in Latvia in 1940–1964: Research of the Commission of the Historians of Latvia 2003* (Rīga: Latvijas Vēstures institūta apgāds, 2004), 306. At the same time, the Soviets officially decried Jezavitaŭ as a "national fascist": J. Dolgijs [Ia. Ia. Douhi] (1934), *Baltkrievu nacionālfašisms Latvijā* (Minsk: Baltkrievijas Zinātņu akadēmijas izdevniecība, 1934).

63 Per Anders Rudling, *The Rise and Fall of Belarusian Nationalism*, 205.

in Latvia, *Latvju nacionālais klubs* (National Club of Latvians) whose activities included violent anti-Semitic attacks on Jewish students.[64] This organisation initially enjoyed tacit support from broad sections of the national leadership, and explicit support from more radical-conservative members of the old elites. It was shut down in 1925 following a bomb attack and a deadly altercation, both targeting the Social Democrats. The short period of the Club's activity became the legendary period of national unity in the Latvian far right, and remained a point of reference and inspiration for radical nationalists and fascists, many of whom had had their first political successes with the Club.[65] Out of this radicalised milieu of students and the frustrated, post-university precariat eventually arose the Latvian national socialist *Pērkonkrusts* (Thunder Cross) party—the longest-lived, largest, and most infamous fascist organisation in interwar Latvia. With its anti-Baltic German, but also anti-Semitic ideology, *Pērkonkrusts* helped shape the Latvian nationalist discourse, and also contributed to the Holocaust in Latvia during the war.

Radical nationalism was thus seen as the answer to social frustrations of key segments of both the Latvian and Baltic German communities. For other minorities, particularly Russians and Belarusians (as already mentioned), but also some Jews, the lack of solutions to social inequality led to a gravitation towards more radical leftist solutions. Even if significant numbers of working-class Latvians were also becoming more militant in their demands for change, the linkage of communism and even of the more radical left wing of the Latvian Social Democrats to sympathies with or outright support from the USSR contributed to a discourse that both securitised and ethnified socialism and the labour movement as a foreign threat.

Latvia, as a country dependent on exports of agricultural and forestry products and on imports of manufactured goods, was struck hard by the global economic crisis of the early 1930s; nevertheless, by 1933, the worst appeared to already be over.[66] In the end, it was the convergence of the aforementioned radical

---

64 Bolin, *Between National and Academic Agendas*, chapter 5.
65 Uldis Krēsliņš, *Aktīvais nacionālisms Latvijā 1922–1934* (Rīga: Latvijas vēstures institūta apgāds, 2005), 91–101.
66 Aizsilnieks, *Latvijas saimniecības vesture*, 582.

discourses—both from below, where the far right and the far left actively discredited the political establishment and liberal democracy—and from above, as the state embarked stepwise on a path towards ethnonationalism and securitisation of minorities and opposition—that led to end of parliamentary democracy and the chances for an inclusive, civic national identity.

On the night to 15 May 1934, then Prime Minister Kārlis Ulmanis and his supporters from the Peasants' Union and the Home Guard staged a *coup d'état*. Ostensibly, this was because radical Latvian nationalists—among them *Pērkonkrusts* and an ideologically ambiguous organisation of independence war veterans known as the Legion—were said to be planning a fascist *coup* themselves. Tellingly, however, Ulmanis ordered the arrests of not only known Latvian fascists, but also of the leadership of the Social Democrats.

The authoritarian Ulmanis regime was itself illiberal: political parties were banned, parliament dispersed, the Constitution suspended, and freedom of the press curtailed. It was also a nationalist and increasingly nationalising regime. The Ulmanist slogan, "A Latvian Latvia" was consciously very similar to "Latvia for Latvians" of *Pērkonkrusts*. Statist policies aimed at not only modernising and centralising the economic life of the country, it also sought to "Latvianise" whole branches of industry through the creation of state-backed trusts, thereby reducing what economic influence non-Latvians had retained until then. Even civil society was subjected to state capture: the newly-created Ministry of Social Affairs had functions of propaganda, oversight of nationalised organisations like the *mazpulki* (patterned on the American 4-H movement), and even took over the running of the Home Guard from the Ministry of Defence. As there was no state-bearing party under Ulmanis, membership in the Home Guard and its allied organisations became *de facto* proof of loyalty and hence a prerequisite for holding certain positions in the state. Over time, its function as a kind of deep state structure increased, with historian Ilgvars Butulis noting that the intention was to develop the Home Guard into an elite, privileged organisation for selecting the very best elements of the nation, with a central role in the future political life of the country, and a prominent role in the indoctrination of youth via the *mazpulki*[67]—suggesting a clear similarity with the cradle-to-grave

---

67 Ilgvars Butulis, *Sveiki, Aizsargi! Aizsargu organizācija Latvijas sabiedrības politiskajā dzīvē 1919.–1940. gadā* (Rīga: Jumava, 2011), 74–76.

deep state that Himmler was creating in Germany with the SS. Ulmanis and his government thus responded to economic crisis, social pressure, and radical threat (from left and right) by adopting elements of fascism; indeed, Jordan Kuck suggests that the regime Ulmanis created is best described as a manifestation of 'transnational fascism'.[68]

The watchword of this nationalist and nationalising ideology was "unity", suggesting a unified people rallying behind the paternal figure of the wise leader, Ulmanis. This ideology, while effective for certain groups, was less effective on others. It still failed to fully neutralise important economic problems, such as the persistence, albeit reduced, of an underclass of rural landless, or real falling wages for the working class and even civil servants.[69] Thus it could not fully neutralise the fascist threat from those who saw the Ulmanis regime as promoting a new cronyism. Nor could it stamp out the appeal of the radical left for members of the working class, as the autobiography of the National Communist Eduards Berklavs bears witness.[70]

This frustration with the ideology of "unity" intensified the scapegoating impulse of the state to securitise social issues and ethnify security. It became ever more difficult for minorities to serve in the armed forces or the Home Guard, at the same time as this was seen as proof of their questionable loyalty to the new "Latvian Latvia". Ethnically heterogeneous and economically marginalised Latgale—the internal Other—was seen as a security threat, the answer to which was to encourage internal colonisation by non-Latgalian ethnic Latvians to shore up the eastern borders of the country. Even numerically small minorities like the Finno-Ugric Livs were not immune from this securitising scrutiny: the political police suspected Estonia and Finland were promoting separatism amongst Finno-Ugric compatriots in Latvia, thereby threating national unity and territorial integrity.[71] Such attitudes could backfire, creating greater alienation of minorities from the new, "Latvian Latvia": the final Nazification of the Baltic German community took place under the Ulmanis regime.

---

68 Jordan Kuck, "Renewed Latvia: A Case Study of the Transnational Fascism Model," *Fascism* 2, 2 (2013): 183–204.
69 Aizsilnieks, *Latvijas saimniecības vesture*, 814, 820.
70 Eduards Berklavs, *Zināt un neaizmirst* (Rīga: Preses Nams, 1998).
71 Bērziņš, ed., *20. gadsimta Latvijas vēsture*, vol. 2, 608.

6. World War II and the Soviet Era

World War II brought with it not only the end of Latvia's independence, but also political regimes that actively promoted the fragmentation of society along class and ethnic lines.[72] A prelude to this was the *Umsiedlung* in late 1939, as Latvia's sovereignty was already overshadowed by the Molotov–Ribbentrop Pact and the treaty whereby the Soviet Union was allowed military bases in Latvia, ostensibly to protect the country's neutrality. The departure of the Baltic German community *en masse* as Nazi Germany's colonists for the newly conquered *Warthegau* in occupied Poland was greeted by the regime as the decisive destruction of remaining Baltic German socio-economic power. That practically an entire minority left the country after many centuries was seen as proof of their disloyalty (i.e. unwillingness to become Latvians), rather than as a testament to the failure to build a more inclusive society. Immediately thereafter, the regime introduced a new wave of Latvianising measures, such as a campaign for people with German-sounding surnames to adopt more 'Latvian' ones: a typical example was then Interior Minister Kornelijs Veitmanis, who adopted the new surname Veidnieks in early 1940.

Such identity politics did little to shore up what was left of Latvian sovereignty in a steadily worsening geopolitical situation. In the end, Latvia was occupied by the Soviet Union in June 1940 without official resistance, and those presiding over the loss of independence were not radical *putschists* or ethnic minority Fifth Columnists, but some of the very people who had helped create independent Latvia in the first place: President Kārlis Ulmanis and Minister of Defence General Jānis Balodis. Even the quislings who took over the interim government before the formal incorporation of Latvia into the USSR were well-connected ethnic Latvians with pro-Soviet sympathies, for example, the microbiologist Augusts Kirchenšteins and popular writer Vilis Lācis.

While the wartime regimes of Stalinist Communism and German Nazism had many differences, they both resulted in the radical reorganisation of social and ethnic power relations. Under Soviet rule, the working class and rural landless were to gain at the expense of the middle class and elites. Minorities that had

---

72 Cf. Björn M. Felder, *Lettland im Zweiten Weltkrieg: Zwischen sowjetischen und deutschen Besatzern 1940–1946* (Paderborn: Schöningh, 2009).

been marginalised under Ulmanis, such as Russians and Jews, also became more visible in the public sphere, particularly the state apparatus. Creating a sharp and rapid contrast to the Latvian nationalist regime that preceded it, this emphasised for many the "foreignness" of the Soviet system that was being imposed upon the country. This was reinforced by the wave of Stalinist political terror culminating with the mass deportations of 14 June 1941, which particularly targeted people of significance during the Ulmanis era, and their families. As such, 81% of those arrested or deported were Latvians. Urban elites were hit hardest, with one third of the 15,424 victims coming from Rīga alone. Farmers made up 23.5% of the total, with the majority of these being members of the Home Guard and their families. These figures may give the impression that the Soviet security apparatus was targeting Latvians on an ethnic basis; however, the statistics do not bear this out. Jews made up almost 12% of the victims, a figure completely out of proportion to their share of the total population at the time. This, as with the fact that ethnic Russians are underrepresented proportionately, can be explained by the socio-political, rather than the ethnic criteria of the operation against "anti-Soviet elements", which were not only defined as nationalists (including, for example, Zionists) but also politicians and civil servants, police and military personnel, key persons in civil society, and wealthier owners of property or businesses.[73] The deportation teams included significant numbers of locals (in Tukums District—1 in 4),[74] but deportee memoirs and social memory stress the "foreign" element, usually military personnel sent in from other parts of the USSR. According to the deportee memoirs and present-day social memory, in these traumatic meetings, the victims often saw the Orientalised oppressor as being "Russian". For their part, the newly arrived representatives of the Soviet authorities likely saw the Latvian populace as alien and riddled with disloyal elements that threatened the USSR from within.

---

73 Indulis Zālīte and Sindija Eglīte, "1941. gada 14. jūnija deportācijas struktūranalīze," in Ainārs Bambals et al., Aizvestie: 1941. gada 14. jūnijs (Rīga: Latvijas Valsts arhīvs, Nordik, 2001), 687–91; Jānis Riekstiņš, "1941. gada 14. jūnija deportācija Latvijā", in Bambals et al., 10–12. An example of a list of deportees from Rīga lists a Home Guard, several military officers, a Zionist, a social democrat, and two "former persons" (i.e. dispossessed bourgeoisie): Zane Baķe et al., Dokumenti liecina: Latvijas vēstures dokumentu izlase skolām 1939–1991 (Rīga: Latvijas Okupācijas muzejs, 1999), 80.
74 Report to the LKP CC on "Practical Work in [Tukums] District from 8 to 18 June 1941", reproduced in: Baķe et al., Dokumenti liecina, 82–4.

The ethnification and securitisation of social relations under the subsequent Nazi rule was near total. The Holocaust, whereby Jews were seen as an existential threat to the Germanic peoples, and therefore needed to be destroyed, was the most extreme aspect of this process. Other manifestations were the plans—known under the name *Generalplan Ost*—for Germanisation of the territory through colonisation with Germanic immigrants, assimilation of "racially valuable" (i.e. ethnic Latvians who expressed "Nordic" traits), and deportation of the rest (i.e. Latgalians and Slavs).

In a tragic turn of history, the Nazi period also marked a high point of Latvianisation in Latvia. Despite it being a major administrative centre of the Nazi-controlled *Reichskommissariat Ostland*, Rīga was in 1943 inhabited by proportionally more Latvians—79%—than at any other time in its history.[75] Some of the policies of the Ulmanis era, such as the eugenic rejuvenation of the Latvian nation, were reactivated under the Nazi occupation by the same persons who had spearheaded them before.[76] And when it came to the genocide that murdered half the Romani population—another example of securitising a minority instead of addressing real or perceived social marginalisation—it was local Latvian authorities, usually the police, who were the decisive actors deciding life or death—not the German SS.[77] In this way, there was both a continuity, and an intensification the ethnic securitisation mindset amongst Latvians who sought to use the structures of the state (even if not their own) for the perceived good of their nation.

In doing so, such Latvians became instruments of Nazi manipulations of public perception. This time around, volunteers to the Nazi-controlled *Selbstschutz* ("self-defence units") gave the Holocaust a Latvian face. So, too, did the tactical collaboration of prominent *Pērkonkrusts* activists—despite their anti-German sentiments—in activities that led to the murder of Jews by Latvians. Even if brave Latvians also helped save Jews in the Holocaust, the rift between these

---

75 Ilmārs Mežs, "Latvieši Rīgā", *Latvijas Vēstures Institūta Žurnāls*, 1 (1992): 136. Even the proportion of Germans in 1943 (3.7%), was actually lower than in 1935 (10%).
76 Felder, *Lettland im Zweiten Weltkrieg*, 275–97.
77 Matthew Kott, "The Fate of the Romani Minorities in Estonia, Latvia, and Lithuania during the Second World War: Problems and Perspectives for Romani Studies and Comparative Genocide Research," in: Inesis Feldmanis *et al.*, eds., *Latvijas vēstures un historiogrāfijas problēmas 1918–1990* (Rīga: Zinātne, 2015), 256.

two communities caused by vastly different experiences of the Nazi period in World War II has yet to be fully reconciled. To fully acknowledge the existential trauma of the Holocaust for the Jews, for example through compensation of the victims or their descendants, is all too often seen as a threat to the Latvian nation and state today.[78]

The post-war Soviet era was not homogenous, though some trends were consistent, even if they varied in intensity over the decades and depending on Communist Party leadership. More so than in 1940–41, the system—not only the elites, but also the lionised social group known as "workers"—was identified with a Russian language and culture that was seen as progressive *vis-à-vis* the more "junior" nationalities of the USSR. Particularly during the last decade of Stalinism, moulded from the Soviet tragedy and triumph of World War II, was there a stigmatisation of whole national groups based on allegations of collective collaboration with Nazism. While the Balts did not suffer the same fate as, for example, the Crimean Tatars, the mass deportations of March 1949 not only were essential to the collectivisation of agriculture, due to the ongoing nationalist guerrilla resistance and the Cold War fear of Western military intervention, there was also a strong element of ethnic securitisation: a quarter of the 44,271 deportees were in the category "nationalists" (as opposed to "*kulaks*"); furthermore, this time over 40,000 of the victims were of Latvian ethnicity.[79] These deportations struck a major blow to the Latvian self-identity—particularly cultivated during the Ulmanis era—of being a nation rooted in the farmsteads of the countryside.

The Soviet programme of development was one of modernisation, particularly industrialisation. These policies encouraged large-scale labour migration to help rebuild war ravaged Latvia in a new, Soviet mould. Particularly in the cities,

---

78 LETA, "Ebreju kopiena: Saeimas lēmums ir nozīmīgs solis vēsturiskā taisnīguma atjaunošanā", *Delfi.lv*, 25 February 2016, http://www.delfi.lv/news/national/politics/ebr eju-kopiena-saeimas-lemums-ir-nozimigs-solis-vesturiska-taisniguma-atjaunosana.d? id=47112441 (accessed 11 November 2016). Cf. Elita Veidemane, "Grūtups: Ebreju kompensāciju prasītāji—nekad vairs nenāciet!", *nra.lv*, 28 January 2011, http://nra.lv/lat vija/40319-grutups-ebreju-kompensaciju-prasitaji-nekad-vairs-nenaciet.htm (accessed 11 November 2016).
79 Andra Āboliņa et al., "1949. gada 25. marta deportācijas struktūranalīze," in: Andra Āboliņa et al., *Aizvestie: 1949. gada 25. marts*, vol. 1 (Rīga: Latvijas Valsts arhīvs, Nordik, 2007), 182, 188.

the new immigrants bolstered the role of Russian language and culture in everyday life, something that high-ranking Communist Party cadres posted in Latvia by Moscow saw as positive. William Prigge has characterised the two Second Secretaries of the Latvian Communist Party during the post-war Stalin era, Ivan Lebedev and Fedor Titov, as having been "Russian nationalists". Others, such as the Soviet Latvian communist Arvīds Pelše or Mikhail Suslov, who oversaw operations against Lithuanian nationalist guerrillas in 1946, are characterised by Prigge as "Marxist internationalists", who, nevertheless, being good Stalinists who had survived the Great Purges, viewed all Latvian nationalist tendencies with deep suspicion.[80]

The efforts to bring Latvia more in line with the rest of the USSR—through collectivisation, industrialisation, education reforms, and concomitant increase in the prominence of the Russian language—provoked a reaction from a number of Latvian communists who had lived in independent Latvia under Ulmanis. They wanted reform—communism, even—and modernisation, but not at the expense of losing their people's own identity in its native territory. A group of leading Latvian Communist Party members around Eduards Berklavs used the opportunity provided by the death of Stalin to try to modify the implementation of policies that would continue to erode the role of Latvian language and culture in the Soviet Socialist Republic, for example by suggesting that Party functionaries from outside Latvia must acquire a working knowledge of Latvian to keep their posts. These National Communists, as they were known, also hoped that more local Latvians would join the Party, so that the system could be co-opted into protecting, rather than further diluting Latvian culture and identity. Furthermore, it was hoped that the pace and form of industrialisation could be modified to better serve the needs of the local population, rather than catering primarily to recently arrived labour from elsewhere. The response from the central authorities in Moscow was harsh: when military and KGB officials in Rīga reported that Berklavs and his colleagues represented a "bourgeois nationalist" threat, they were eventually deposed by Khrushchev in 1960. Anti-nationalists led by

---

80 William D. Prigge, *Bearslayers: The Rise and Fall of the National Communists* (New York: Peter Lang, 2015), chapter 1.

Arvids Pelše took over in their stead, reducing the security threat but not answering the social and cultural concerns of the shrinking Latvian majority, whose loyalty to the Soviet regime remained in question.[81]

The 1960s and 1970s remain a gravely under-researched period of contemporary Latvian history. In recent years, some literature about everyday life in Soviet Latvia has appeared, but this—for example, the book on "our only yesterday" by Juris Pavlovičs[82]—is more aimed at a popular, rather than a scholarly audience.[83] Such works represent a reaction to the overwhelming focus heretofore on the war and Stalinism, particularly on terror and oppression. The generation that is in the prime of life today does not want to remember its childhood in Soviet times as what Vladimir Shlapentokh termed a "normal totalitarian society";[84] instead there is an entirely understandable need for sense-making and comfort. Hence Pavlovičs, with his focus on the everyday, portrays the years 1965 to 1975 as years of stability and "prosperity", a time when most Latvians accepted the welfare that living in the USSR offered them.[85]

Even if the processes of Russification continued—in 1971, seventeen Latvian communists, including Berklavs, famously wrote an open letter to Western European Communist Parties criticising this[86]—it can be argued that Soviet nationalities policy actually contributed to the final consolidation of Latvians as a nation. Ethnicity as a label in the post-war Soviet system was essentialised and fixed, passed on by heredity and recorded at birth in official documents—regardless of mother tongue or self-identification of individuals. At the same time the content of ethnicity was fluid, shaped by its interaction with the social engineering of Soviet system. As Detlef Henning provocatively asked: "Did not the social levelling measures, the psychological and political pressure of the Soviet

---

81 On the National Communists, see the contribution by Geoff Swain in this volume.
82 Juris Pavlovičs, *Padomju Latvijas ikdiena: Mūsu vienīgā vakardiena* (Rīga: Jumava, 2012).
83 A rare exception in the literature is: Daina Bleiere, *Eiropa āprus Eiropas...: Dzīve Latvijas PSR*, 2nd ed. (Rīga: LU Akadēmiskais apgāds, 2015). This scholarly monograph, however, still has as its main focus the political system and its ideological precepts.
84 Vladimir Shlapentokh, *A Normal Totalitarian Society: How the Soviet Union Functioned and How It Collapsed* (Armonk: M.E. Sharpe, 2001).
85 Pavlovičš, 80–114.
86 Cf. Baķe et al., 157.

annexation lasting 50 years, create the Latvian nation?"[87] In other words, by finally removing, albeit in a heavy-handed manner, most of the social cleavages between ethnic Latvians, a half century of Soviet Communism forged a more unified Latvian national community than had ever existed before.

Violeta Davoliūtė has written an account of how this national consolidation occurred in Lithuania, and how this recently unified national identity that gave Lithuanians the strength to take advantage of the weakening Soviet system and reclaim their independence.[88] It is expected that a study of the Latvian case would yield roughly similar conclusions. Indeed, the National Awakening of the *Atmoda* during the Gorbachev era was characterised by concerted social, cultural, political, and economic mobilisation on a scale not seen in Latvia before or since. At the same time, late Soviet Latvia was a deeply divided society, prompting a new round of mutual ethnification on both sides of the struggle for and against independence. Inhabitants of all backgrounds were pressured to choose sides between the Latvian-dominated pro-independence movement, and the predominantly Russophone pro-Soviet *Interfront*. Ethnic relations deteriorated and became securitised: minor scuffles between Latvians and Russians had started taking place again in the 1970s, but by the early 1980s increasingly radical groups appeared on by sides of the ethnic divide, with some sources suggesting that the KGB had fostered different antagonistic radical groups, to be activated in order to divide society along ethnic lines in the event of an attempted challenge to the central authorities.[89] Others have suggested that the KGB also had a role in creating the various grassroots movements that metamorphosed into the Popular Front and allied organisations working for independence.[90] Regardless of to what degree the Soviet authorities and the Communist Party thought they could control the Popular Front, developments

---

87 Detlefs Henings, "Nacionālā kustība un nacionālās valsts tapšana Latvijā", *Latvijas Vēstures Institūtā Žurnāls*, 1 (1995), 74.
88 Violeta Davoliūtė, *The Making and Breaking of Soviet Lithuania: Memory and Modernity in the Wake of War* (Abingdon: Routledge, 2014).
89 See, for instance: Pavlovičs, *Padomju Latvijas ikdiena*, 117–118.
90 The most elaborate attempt to uncover the security services behind anti-communist protest movements, not only in Latvia, but across the Warsaw Pact, is: Jerzy Targalski, "Rola służb specjalnych i ich agentury w pieriestrojce i demontażu komunizmu w Europie Sowieckiej", MS (Warsaw, 2010). Pages 172ff. deal with the period in Latvia from 1988. My thanks to Aleś Michalevič for generously sharing this source with me.

proved otherwise, and on 4 May 1990, the newly elected Supreme Soviet of the Latvian SSR declared the beginning of the transition to regained independence from the USSR.

7. 1991—A New Window of Opportunity?

As in 1918, in 1991 there was a window of opportunity to break decisively with the centuries-long pattern of ethnifying social conflicts and securitising minority issues. A step in the right direction was the reinstating of the original, pre-Ulmanis Constitution of 1922, thereby rejecting the "Latvian Latvia" national state model of Ulmanis for a more liberal alternative. Nevertheless, tensions between civic and ethnic nationalism have plagued post-Soviet Latvia's politics from the beginning.

The doctrine of state continuity with interwar Latvia made the question of citizenship acute. Descendants of citizens from before 1940 automatically became citizens of the re-emergent Latvia; Soviet-era migrants and their descendants did not, and would have to go through an initially very restrictive naturalisation process. When the USSR ceased to exist in December 1991, these people became stranded as "non-citizens". While legally logical, given the view that Latvia had been illegally occupied by the Soviet Union, and already had a body of citizens stemming from before 1940, there was also an aspect of securitisation here. By 1989, Latvians constituted just 52% of the population of the country. There was a fear that Soviet-era migrants would act as a brake on political reforms, whether it be strengthening the place of Latvian language and culture in official use, or in an orientation towards joining Euro-Atlantic bodies, rather than regional post-Soviet ones. By disenfranchising this group, they could not actively hinder the recreation of Latvia as a national state in the Euro-Atlantic sphere; furthermore, it was hoped that marginalisation would encourage many of them to leave for their kin states.

Instead, this exclusion of "Russian" non-citizens had several detrimental effects. Firstly, it contributed to their radicalisation: many felt cheated by the Latvians, opening the way for irredentist radical nationalism. It also gave Russia political leverage over what it called its discriminated "compatriots" in Latvia. In both these senses, it is clear that no lessons were learned from the mistakes made in dealing with the Baltic German minority during the interwar years. Finally, this restrictive citizenship policy, interpreted as exclusive nationalism, invited sharp criticisms from the OSCE, the EU, and NATO—the very Euro-Atlantic structures the post-Soviet Latvia's political elites were intent on joining in order to secure their geopolitical security. Later, when the government tried to adopt more pragmatic positions on citizenship, it prompted the rise of right-wing populist parties that have in turn acted as a brake on liberalisation of society and a deepening of liberal democratic values.[91]

Similarly, the ethnification of social problems has hindered the very development of a welfare state that would reduce ethnic grievances. Even though there is a long history of Latvian social democracy, continuing into exile in the West during the Cold War, in post-Soviet Latvia class and ethnic grievances have again been conflated. Leftist parties are viewed suspiciously by Latvian voters as being "Russian" and pro-Russia. Even the European economic crisis, which hit Latvia particularly hard during 2008–2010, did not open the door for post-ethnic leftist politics in Latvia. Since these "Russian" leftist parties have had perennial difficulty attracting Latvian members and voters, they become susceptible to the lure of Russian nationalism, particularly since the geopolitical resurgence of Russia under Vladimir Putin. Symptomatic of this was the leftist-identifying party "For Human Rights in a United Latvia", which includes communists who remained loyal to Moscow in 1991, renaming itself as the decidedly more ethnonationalist Latvian Russian Union in early 2014, just before Russia's annexation of Crimea.

The exodus of inhabitants after EU accession in 2004 exacerbated already negative demographic tendencies, prompting a discourse of impending national crisis. As a result, these social problems were again conflated with securitising a minority, albeit this time, it was sexual minorities that were singled out

---

91 See: David Galbreath, "The Politics of European Integration and Minority Rights in Estonia and Latvia," *Perspectives on European Politics and Society*, 4, 1 (2003), 35–53. Cf. Timofey Agarin, "Iz odnogo soiuza v drugoi: Zapadnaia nauka o baltiiskoi ethnopolitike v preddverii vstupleniia v ES," in: V.V. Poleshchuk and V.V. Stepanov, eds., *Ethnicheskaia politika v stranakh Baltii* (Moscow: Nauka, 2013), 258–93.

as a threat. Already in December 2005, the Constitution was amended to enshrine marriage as only being between a man and a woman.[92] Political homophobia has proven a mobilising force for radicals on both sides of the ethnic divide: the Rīga Pride parade in 2005 was attacked by both Latvian and Russian ultranationalists, and in 2014 a popular initiative was launched to demand a referendum of legislation banning "homosexual propaganda". The front figures for this campaign were the Latvian radical songwriter, Kaspars Dimiters, and the veteran National Bolshevik activist, Vladimir Linderman.

Marina Germane concluded a few years ago that "a political nation, which failed to materialise during the interwar republic, continues to be a highly-contested subject at the present."[93] This still holds true today. The tensions between civic and ethnic nationalism continued to be played out as society's problems are ethnified, and then securitised as existential issues. Typical of this is the rapid stepping up of ethnic tensions in the political discourse since 2010. After a period when ethnic relations appeared to be normalising—the economic crisis hit all inhabitants hard, creating a sense of commonality across the ethnic divide—the conflict was rekindled. Latvian nationalists in the government coalition suggested provocatively that, in order to save money in the state budget, the publicly-funded Russian language schools should go over to teaching in Latvian. This revived memories of the 2004 schools reform, resistance to which mobilised large segments of the Russian-speaking community. Even if the budget suggestion was never implemented, old networks of activists were revitalised, including Russian ultranationalists. The aforementioned Linderman was among a dedicated group of radicals who created the NGO *Za rodnoi iazyk!* (For the Mother Tongue!) that lobbied for a constitutional referendum on the question of making Russian co-official language in Latvia—a prospect that is an anathema for a great many Latvians, who still, decades after regaining independence, feel their small language is disadvantaged in the public sphere and that Russian speakers do not respect it. *Za rodnoi iazyk!* was able to collect enough signatures, triggering a referendum in February 2012.

---

92 *Latvijas Republikas Satversme*, §110.
93 Marina Germane, "A Nation in the Making? The Social Integration Process in Latvia since 1991", in: David J. Smith, David J. Galbreath, and Geoffrey Swain (eds), *From Recognition to Restoration: Latvia's History as a Nation-State* (Amsterdam: Rodopi, 2010), 128.

The referendum also acted as a catalyst for mobilising ethnic Latvian voters, who defeated the motion by a significant margin (non-citizens, as with other elections in Latvia, were not allowed to vote). One outcome, however, was that it contributed to the aforementioned radicalisation of the political parties aiming at the Russian-speaking electorate, since the radical nationalist *Za rodnoi iazyk!* gained political legitimacy from the referendum, and transformed itself into a political party.

It also served to reinforce the Latvian nationalists' discourse that, even as members of the EU and NATO, Latvia was still not guaranteed to be the national state of the Latvians. As a result, nationalist political circles proposed to amend the 1922 *Satversme* with a preamble that would reinforce the role of the Latvians in Latvia. This was finally achieved in 2014, with a text originally proposed by Egils Levits, a judge of the European Court of Justice. The text of this new preamble proclaims the Republic of Latvia to be the result of the Latvians' unwavering longing for a state throughout the centuries, and speaks of Latvians as the state-bearing nation. The purpose of the state is to guarantee the survival of the Latvian nation, its language, and culture for the centuries to come. Furthermore, loyalty to the state is proclaimed to also mean supporting Latvian as sole official language.[94] Even if, before its adoption, critics were assured that the text was simply declaratory and would have no binding legality, since it came into force, references to the preamble have appeared in legal opinions from ministry officials, on such issues as education policy and even on gender issues.[95] Already previously Latvia has been assessed an example of Sammy Smooha's model of an ethnic democracy.[96] In the run-up to EU ac-

---

94 For the full text of the preamble, see: "Latvijas Republikas Satversme", *likumi.lv*, http://likumi.lv/doc.php?id=57980 (accessed 11 November 2016).

95 An opinion issued by the National Alliance-controlled Ministry of Justice referred to the preamble in its reasoning for why Latvia should not ratify the Istanbul Convention, in a manner which even prompted sharp criticism from Levits: Liene Barisa-Sermule and Anete Bērtule, "Levits: Stambulas konvencijas analīzes sasaiste ar Satversmes preambulu—nekorekta pieeja (precizēts*)", *lsm.lv*, 10 May 2016, http://www.lsm.lv/lv/raksts/latvija/zinas/levits-stambulas-konvencijas-analizes-sasaiste-ar-satversmes-preambulu--nekorekta-pieeja-precizets.a182186/ (accessed 1 November 2016).

96 Graham Smith, "The Ethnic Democracy Thesis and the Citizenship Question in Estonia and Latvia," *Nationalities Papers*, 24, 2 (1996): 199–216.

cession this seemed less feasible; however, since the adoption of the constitutional preamble, the risk that Latvia develops more in this direction again is increasingly real.

8. Conclusion

In conclusion, since at least tsarist times the state has consistently failed to properly address and resolve persistent socio-economic disparities in Latvian society. Instead, Latvia has always had a multiethnic society where the congruence of social and ethnic cleavages has all too often led to the ethnification of socio-political conflicts, with mutually reinforced radicalisation and securitisation as a result.[97] On the one hand, inadequate responses from the state—whether too half-hearted, or too heavy-handed—have prompted minority radicalisation, as can be seen with the Latvian populace in 1905, the Baltic German community between the wars, or the post-Soviet community of Russian-speakers. On the other hand, the securitisation of minority issues led to increased radicalisation of state policy. In turn, this could further alienate the affected minorities from the state, resulting not in a resolution, or even containment, of the underlying socio-political problem, but instead fuelling further radicalisation on the part of targeted groups. This mutually-reinforcing dynamic can be illustrated with the following diagram:

Figure 1

```
         ethnification of
          social issues
            ↗      ↖
           ↙        ↘
 radicalisation of  ⟷  securitisation by
 political actors         the state
```

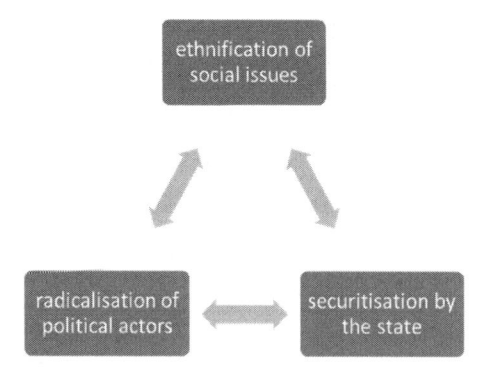

97 Cf. Gert von Pistohlkors, "Führende Schicht oder nationale Minderheit? Die Revolution von 1905/06 und die Kennzeichnung der deutschen Balten zwischen 1840 und 1906 in der zeitgenössischen deutsch-baltischen Geschichtsforschung," *Zeitschrift für Ostforschung*, 21, 4 (1972), 608.

Security is a real issue for Latvia today, particularly since Russia's annexation of Crimea has put in doubt adherence to the international legal order based on the Helsinki Accords. Nevertheless, securitisation of minorities is not the right way to go. Securitisation certainly did not work a century ago to quell the fervour of infamous Latvian terrorists like Peter the Painter;[98] nor, too, should one expect that similar approaches will work with those in Europe who are drawn to Islamist terrorism today.

Even if one considers political developments in Latvia currently to be heading in the wrong direction, there is a significant historical irony at work here. Radical solutions exploiting the socio-ethnic fault lines in society have been a constant undercurrent in political discourse, which at times even determined political acts. The radical responses of a securitising state contributed to creating the Latvian nation as it is today: the uprising of 1905 and its brutal suppression; the catastrophic experience of Bolshevism in 1919; the nationalising state of Ulmanis; Nazi racial policies that, however unintentionally, actually made Latvia more ethnically Latvian; and the system of Soviet repression that arguably completed the process of constructing the Latvian nation. All this has contributed to the consolidated narrative of nationhood enshrined in the current preamble to the *Satversme*. Unfortunately, the nation formed by these historical processes lacks the self-confidence to see its own potential for good, and for evil. Instead of being the sleeping tiger envisioned by Garlieb Merkel, potentially threatening others' unjust hegemony, it is now a nation constructed to view itself as constantly under threat. If history is any indicator, retaining this perspective will not lead to greater social justice or welfare for all the inhabitants of Latvia. Instead, a wise policy would be to work on solving persistent social problems by de-ethnifiying and de-securitising them, as a more inclusive and prosperous society is more likely to enjoy a higher level of human security.[99]

---

98 The most recent study of the life story of Peter the Painter is: Rufs, *Pa stāvu liesmu debesīs*.
99 Cf. Paul Goble, "Strategic Assessment: The Paradox of Baltic Security in 2016," *Eurasia Daily Monitor*, 13 (2016): 175, https://jamestown.org/program/strategic-assessment-paradox-baltic-security-2016/ (accessed 1 November 2016).

Index

A

Agriculture: 25, 91, 93, 136, 229, 265, 267, 268, 270, 271, 274, 276, 281, 283, 294, 298, 304

America (see United States)

Authoritarianism: 21, 33, 61, 69, 85, 91-105, 123, 124, 139, 150, 151, 152, 186, 202, 273, 276, 299,

B

Balodis, Jānis: 301

Baltic Germans: 17, 30, 34, 42, 43, 48, 49, 57, 58, 61, 66, 67, 71, 72, 74, 75, 76, 77, 81, 85, 86, 87, 94, 102, 103, 114, 145, 146, 270, 272, 280, 281, 282, 283, 284, 285, 286, 287, 288, 290, 291, 292, 294, 295, 296, 298, 300, 301, 303, 309, 312

Belarus: 289, 296-297,

Beria, Lavrentii: 108, 118, 119, 120, 121

Berklavs, Eduards: 109, 110, 111, 112, 113, 115, 117, 118, 300, 305

Bērziņš, Andris (President, 2011-2015): 25, 264, 278,

Bērziņš, Andris (Prime Minister, 2000-2002) : 192

Bolshevism: 13, 41, 44, 45, 47, 48, 49, 63, 74, 75, 78, 86, 127, 144, 145, 146, 285, 286, 288, 290, 291, 292, 313,

Bush, George H.W.: 155, 156, 158, 161, 165

C

Čakste, Jānis: 47

Citizens' Committees: 181,

Citizens' Congress: 181-183

Citizenship: 13, 15, 18, 19, 20-22, 48, 51, 52, 59, 60, 62-69, 80, 82, 84, 88, 89, 121, 127, 129, 144, 175-187, 199, 200, 246, 247, 276, 290, 293, 308-309

Communism (see also 'National Communism', 'Post-communism'): 31, 48, 73, 111, 112, 116, 119, 120, 123, 125, 126, 129, 130, 131, 132, 134, 135, 136, 145, 146, 149, 151, 164, 180, 181, 186, 189, 190, 193, 197, 228, 294, 297, 298, 300, 301, 304, 305, 306, 307, 308, 309,

Conference on Security and Cooperation in Europe (CSCE) – see Organisation for Security and Cooperation in Europe

Constitution: 14, 56, 59, 175, 176, 178, 179, 181, 182, 186, 192, 243, 259, 293, 299, 308, 310, 311, 312, 313

Council of Europe: 199

Council of the European Union: 213, 214, 216, 217,

Coup d'état (15 May 1934): 15, 69, 91, 93, 94, 97, 98, 100, 101, 103, 124, 132, 151, 273, 299

Courland: 37, 42, 266, 268, 269, 279, 280, 283, 286, 287, 288, 289

Crimea: 87, 195, 222, 304, 309, 313

D

Democracy / Democratisation: 12, 13, 14, 15, 21, 22, 23, 24, 27, 44, 46, 55, 57, 59, 67, 69, 74, 77, 78, 79, 85, 86, 89, 92, 97, 103, 123, 144, 145, 146, 151, 152, 160, 169, 170, 171, 173, 176, 177, 182, 186, 187, 189-203, 246, 247, 269, 270, 279, 284, 288, 290, 291, 292, 293, 294, 299, 309, 312

Denmark: 170, 223, 244, 252, 264, 276

Deportations: 12, 276, 287, 288, 302, 304,

Destalinisation: 124,

Dievturi: 15, 91, 94, 95-96, 100-105

Dombrovskis, Valdis: 192

E

Émigrés / Emigration: 25, 32, 33, 35, 37, 38, 39, 63, 71, 88, 96, 124, 138, 141, 143, 144, 146-154, 241, 262, 266, 269, 274, 286, 295.

Estonia: 19, 26, 60, 65, 75, 81, 82, 148, 155, 57, 158, 159, 160, 161, 162, 164, 170, 173, 175, 176, 177, 178, 179, 180, 181, 183, 184, 187, 243, 244, 252, 253, 254, 256, 257, 258, 261, 262, 300

European and Euro-Atlantic Integration: 20, 22, 72, 77, 87, 125, 161, 184, 185, 186, 187, 195, 205, 225, 243,

European Union: 11, 22, 24, 25, 26, 72, 85, 88, 205, 225, 244, 251, 262, 263, 264, 278

F

Fascism: 31, 104, 113, 297, 298, 299, 300,

Finland: 62, 156, 252, 262, 264, 273, 280, 290, 292, 300,

France: 18, 77, 155, 157, 158, 160, 161, 162, 163, 164, 165, 166, 168, 169, 170, 171, 172, 173, 252, 264, 275, 280, 288

G

Georgia: 214,

Germany: 12, 19, 31, 32, 40, 42, 43, 45, 48, 49, 72, 74, 75, 77, 86, 91, 92, 95, 97, 101, 102, 104, 113, 144, 157, 158, 160, 161, 163, 168, 169, 170, 200, 244, 252, 264, 272, 274, 275, 286, 287, 288, 289, 290, 291, 295, 296, 300, 301, 303

Godmanis, Ivars: 251

Gorbachev, Mikhail: 16, 18, 155, 158, 159, 160, 161, 162, 168, 169, 170, 171, 173, 307,

Gorbunovs, Anatolijs: 159, 160, 162,

H

Harmony Centre: 88, 194-195

Holocaust: 12, 276, 298, 303, 304

I

Iceland: 170, 252

Identity: 17, 20, 22, 24, 29, 50, 51, 53, 66, 71, 73, 79, 80, 82, 94, 97, 124, 137, 138, 142, 143, 144, 154, 207, 211, 212, 222, 223, 285, 287, 293, 299, 301, 304, 305, 307

Immigration / Immigrants: 12, 21, 22, 68, 107, 124, 135, 141, 175, 303, 305, 308

Industry / Industrialisation: 17, 25, 40, 42, 111, 112, 226, 229, 230, 231, 237, 238, 262, 267, 268, 269, 270, 271, 273, 274, 275, 277, 281, 284, 299, 305,

Integration of Society: 17, 22, 68, 69, 82, 84, 85, 89, 178, 261, 279

Italy: 97, 101, 104, 223, 252, 264,

J

Jews in Latvia: 12, 17, 42, 57, 59, 64, 65, 66, 67, 101, 102, 103, 104, 282, 283, 284, 287, 292, 293, 297, 298, 302, 303, 304

K

Kalnbērziņš, Jānis: 116, 117, 118, 120,

Kalvītis, Aigars: 197

Kazakhstan: 176,

Khrushchev, Nikita: 107, 108, 115, 116, 117, 118, 119, 120, 121, 135, 306

Kirhenšteins, Augusts: 62

Kohl, Helmut: 156, 161, 165, 169

Krūmiņš, Vilis: 108, 109, 110, 113, 115, 116, 117, 118, 119, 120, 121

Kviesis, Alberts: 94

L

Latgale: 46, 102, 136, 139, 273, 280, 286, 296, 300, 303

Latvian Legion: 114, 121, 138

Latvian Riflemen: 44, 45, 115, 291

Latvian Soviet Socialist Republic (LSSR): 16, 18, 130, 137, 150, 139, 307,

Legal Continuity of Latvia's Statehood: 11, 16, 18, 19, 20, 21, 88, 162-163, 168, 179, 180, 186, 243, 308

Lembergs, Aivars: 194, 243

Leninism: 17, 18, 33, 35, 36, 38, 110, 111, 113, 120

Liberalism: 56, 58, 74, 77, 82, 85, 87, 123, 146, 186, 190, 196, 281, 282, 284, 288, 289, 291-292, 295, 299, 308, 309

Livland: 37, 42, 75, 266, 268, 279, 280, 283,

Levits, Egils: 56, 311

Lithuania: 16, 17, 19, 65, 145, 148, 154, 155, 156, 157, 158, 159, 160, 161, 162, 163, 164, 165, 168, 169, 172, 173, 175, 180, 184, 186, 251, 252, 253, 254, 256, 257, 258, 261, 262, 282, 305, 307,

M

Merkel, Garlieb: 280, 313

Minorities: 13, 16, 17, 21, 34, 56, 57, 59, 60, 61, 62, 65, 66, 67, 68, 69, 70, 72, 76, 78, 79, 80, 81, 82, 83, 84, 88, 89, 92, 97, 102, 145, 146, 151, 161, 175, 176, 177, 186, 193, 197, 198, 199, 201, 246, 247, 274, 280, 286, 290, 296, 297, 299, 300, 301, 303, 308, 309, 312, 313

Mitterand, François: 19, 156, 158, 160, 161, 162, 165, 168, 169, 170, 171, 172, 173

Moldova: 21, 176, 178, 183, 187, 214,

Molotov, Viatcheslav: 163

Molotov-Ribbentrop Pact: 12, 86, 164, 165, 200, 301.

Mukhitdinov, Nuridin: 107, 111, 115, 116, 117, 120,

N

National Bolsheviks: 310

National Communism: 18, 107, 108, 112, 113, 115, 117, 121

National Council of Latvia: 47, 59, 60, 62, 64

National Partisans: 12, 114, 304, 305

Nationalism: 15, 16, 20, 21, 27, 30, 37, 45, 52, 55, 56, 57, 69, 70, 75, 77, 81, 84, 86, 87, 88, 89, 95, 96, 103, 105, 113, 115, 117, 129, 135, 144, 145, 146, 164, 177, 180, 182, 183, 186, 187, 190, 258, 270, 274, 279, 280, 281, 282, 283, 284, 286, 289, 293, 295, 296, 298, 299, 300, 302, 304, 305, 306, 308, 309, 310, 311, 313,

NATO: 11, 12, 21, 24, 26, 72, 87, 88, 161, 183, 184, 185, 186, 200, 201, 244, 246, 247, 278, 309, 311.

Nazi German occupation: 12, 14, 31, 123, 261, 275, 276, 301, 303, 304, 313,

Nazism: 15, 31, 73, 86, 87, 102, 104, 163, 200, 295, 296, 300, 301,

Niedra, Andrievs: 48, 49, 290,

Non-citizens: 20-22, 65-67, 199-200, 246, 247, 308-309, 311.

Nordic Countries: 25, 170, 200, 250, 303

Norway: 252

O

Organisation for Security and Cooperation in Europe (OSCE; formerly CSCE): 164, 169, 199, 309, 313

P

Pelše, Arvids: 114, 115, 117, 118, 120, 305, 306,

Pērkonkrusts: 15, 102, 103, 104, 298, 299, 303

Poland: 172, 252, 279, 301

Popular Front of Latvia: 11, 19, 21, 138, 177, 179, 180, 182, 185, 307, 308

Post-communism: 18, 55, 190, 192, 195, 202, 203, 225, 226, 227, 229, 230, 231, 234, 235, 236, 237, 238

Putin, Vladimir: 87, 194, 309

Putsch (USSR August 1991): 169, 170, 171, 185

R

Russia (see also Tsarist Russia): 19, 20, 21, 23, 26, 44, 57, 63, 65, 67, 75, 78, 86, 87, 88, 98, 144, 146, 170, 171, 173, 175, 176, 178, 183, 184, 185, 193, 194, 195, 196, 197, 199, 200, 201, 226, 229, 231, 233, 246, 288, 289, 291, 292, 293, 308, 309, 310, 313

Russian Revolution (1905): 56

Russian Revolution (February 1917): 57, 144, 262, 289

Russian Revolution (October 1917): 75, 78, 86, 262

Russian-speakers in Latvia: 17, 20, 21, 22, 34, 61, 62, 67, 107, 108, 109, 110, 111, 116, 117, 119, 121, 127, 129, 135, 137, 138, 139, 146, 164, 175,

176, 177, 178, 179, 181-187, 193-202, 282, 283, 286, 287, 298, 302, 305, 307, 308, 309, 310, 311, 312

Russification: 17, 74, 88, 119, 134, 164, 281, 282, 306

S

Saeima(Latvia's Parliament): 55, 56, 62, 71, 73, 104, 182, 195, 197, 201, 217, 218, 243, 245,

Satversme (see Constitution)

Scandinavia (see Nordic Countries)

Schiemann, Paul: 14, 61, 64, 67, 71-89, 295

Security: 13, 24, 27, 77, 81, 87, 88, 93, 99, 103, 130, 131, 162, 176, 187, 195, 199, 201, 207, 211, 212, 222, 223, 246, 247, 278, 279, 280, 282, 283, 285, 286, 289, 292, 294, 296, 298, 300, 303, 304, 306, 307, 308, 309, 310, 312, 313

Šķēle, Andris: 243

Skujenieks, Marģers: 14, 57, 58, 61, 63, 65, 66, 68, 69

Stalinism: 12, 18, 32, 86, 96, 110, 115, 120, 121, 124, 126, 130, 134, 135, 200, 301, 302, 304, 305, 306

Social Democracy: 47, 57, 61, 76, 193, 251, 282, 288, 292, 298, 299, 302, 309

Sovietisation: 17, 19, 132, 137

Soviet Occupation: 12, 19, 22, 25, 31, 38, 87, 96, 123, 129, 130, 142, 152, 159, 162, 164, 179, 180, 200, 261, 262, 275, 276, 277, 301, 308,

Soviet Union (see USSR):

Strēlnieki (see Latvian Riflemen)

Stučka, Pēteris: 41, 48, 285, 286, 288, 290, 291, 292, 294

Supreme Council of Latvia: 159, 160, 179, 181, 182, 183, 184

Suslov, Mikhail: 117, 120, 305

Sweden: 32, 156, 163, 223, 249, 251, 253, 257, 263, 264, 275, 294

T

Tsarist Russia: 21, 30, 35, 40, 41, 42, 43, 62, 64, 65, 74, 75, 92, 98, 262, 265, 268, 270, 274, 276, 279, 280, 282, 284, 286, 287

U

Ukraine (see also Crimea): 21, 23, 26, 87, 88, 111, 116, 178, 187, 193, 195, 201, 214

Ulmanis, Kārlis: 15, 17, 33, 48, 49, 51, 59, 69, 91, 92, 93, 94, 96, 97, 98, 99, 100, 101, 102, 103, 104, 115, 118, 124, 125, 128, 129, 130, 132, 134, 136, 139, 150, 151, 273, 274, 275, 292, 299, 300, 301, 302, 303, 304, 305, 308, 313

United States of America (USA): 16, 32, 63, 91, 120, 141, 144, 145, 146, 152, 155, 161, 162, 163, 165, 170, 172, 226, 237, 272, 274, 299

Union of Soviet Socialist Republics (USSR): 11, 17, 19, 26, 27, 32, 36, 38, 86, 102, 129, 130, 131, 135, 155, 156, 159, 160, 161, 162, 163, 166, 167, 168, 169, 170, 171, 172, 173, 180, 181, 184, 185, 190, 269, 276, 298, 301, 302, 303, 304, 305, 306, 308

United Kingdom: 26, 71, 88, 249, 252, 264

Ušakovs, Nils: 193

V

Valters, Miķelis: 14, 57, 58

Vīķe-Freiberga, Vaira: 24, 148, 235

W

World Bank: 199, 216, 244

World Health Organisation: 232, 233

World Trade Organisation: 244, 245

World War I: 15, 25, 31, 36, 38, 39, 40, 41, 45, 77, 78, 91, 92, 98, 124, 143, 144, 262, 266, 267, 268-269, 272, 276, 284, 286, 289

World War II: 22, 34, 38, 39, 72, 73, 79, 124, 129, 143, 147, 151, 153, 154, 179, 200, 262, 273, 276, 301, 304

Y

Yeltsin, Boris: 19, 171, 173, 176

Z

Zatlers, Valdis: 194, 202

SOVIET AND POST-SOVIET POLITICS AND SOCIETY

Edited by Dr. Andreas Umland

ISSN 1614-3515

1   Андреас Умланд (ред.)
    Воплощение Европейской
    конвенции по правам человека в
    России
    Философские, юридические и
    эмпирические исследования
    ISBN 3-89821-387-0

2   Christian Wipperfürth
    Russland – ein vertrauenswürdiger
    Partner?
    Grundlagen, Hintergründe und Praxis
    gegenwärtiger russischer Außenpolitik
    Mit einem Vorwort von Heinz Timmermann
    ISBN 3-89821-401-X

3   Manja Hussner
    Die Übernahme internationalen Rechts
    in die russische und deutsche
    Rechtsordnung
    Eine vergleichende Analyse zur
    Völkerrechtsfreundlichkeit der Verfassungen
    der Russländischen Föderation und der
    Bundesrepublik Deutschland
    Mit einem Vorwort von Rainer Arnold
    ISBN 3-89821-438-9

4   Matthew Tejada
    Bulgaria's Democratic Consolidation
    and the Kozloduy Nuclear Power Plant
    (KNPP)
    The Unattainability of Closure
    With a foreword by Richard J. Crampton
    ISBN 3-89821-439-7

5   Марк Григорьевич Меерович
    Квадратные метры, определяющие
    сознание
    Государственная жилищная политика в
    СССР. 1921 – 1941 гг
    ISBN 3-89821-474-5

6   Andrei P. Tsygankov, Pavel
    A. Tsygankov (Eds.)
    New Directions in Russian
    International Studies
    ISBN 3-89821-422-2

7   Марк Григорьевич Меерович
    Как власть народ к труду приучала
    Жилище в СССР – средство управления
    людьми. 1917 – 1941 гг.
    С предисловием Елены Осокиной
    ISBN 3-89821-495-8

8   David J. Galbreath
    Nation-Building and Minority Politics
    in Post-Socialist States
    Interests, Influence and Identities in Estonia
    and Latvia
    With a foreword by David J. Smith
    ISBN 3-89821-467-2

9   Алексей Юрьевич Безугольный
    Народы Кавказа в Вооруженных
    силах СССР в годы Великой
    Отечественной войны 1941-1945 гг.
    С предисловием Николая Бугая
    ISBN 3-89821-475-3

10 Вячеслав Лихачев и Владимир
    Прибыловский (ред.)
    Русское Национальное Единство,
    1990-2000. В 2-х томах
    ISBN 3-89821-523-7

11 Николай Бугай (ред.)
    Народы стран Балтии в условиях
    сталинизма (1940-е – 1950-е годы)
    Документированная история
    ISBN 3-89821-525-3

12 Ingmar Bredies (Hrsg.)
    Zur Anatomie der Orange Revolution
    in der Ukraine
    Wechsel des Eliteregimes oder Triumph des
    Parlamentarismus?
    ISBN 3-89821-524-5

13 Anastasia V. Mitrofanova
    The Politicization of Russian
    Orthodoxy
    Actors and Ideas
    With a foreword by William C. Gay
    ISBN 3-89821-481-8

14 Nathan D. Larson
Alexander Solzhenitsyn and the
Russo-Jewish Question
ISBN 3-89821-483-4

15 Guido Houben
Kulturpolitik und Ethnizität
Staatliche Kunstförderung im Russland der
neunziger Jahre
Mit einem Vorwort von Gert Weisskirchen
ISBN 3-89821-542-3

16 Leonid Luks
Der russische „Sonderweg"?
Aufsätze zur neuesten Geschichte Russlands
im europäischen Kontext
ISBN 3-89821-496-6

17 Евгений Мороз
История «Мёртвой воды» – от
страшной сказки к большой
политике
Политическое неоязычество в
постсоветской России
ISBN 3-89821-551-2

18 Александр Верховский и Галина
Кожевникова (ред.)
Этническая и религиозная
интолерантность в российских СМИ
Результаты мониторинга 2001-2004 гг.
ISBN 3-89821-569-5

19 Christian Ganzer
Sowjetisches Erbe und ukrainische
Nation
Das Museum der Geschichte des Zaporoger
Kosakentums auf der Insel Chortycja
Mit einem Vorwort von Frank Golczewski
ISBN 3-89821-504-0

20 Эльза-Баир Гучинова
Помнить нельзя забыть
Антропология депортационной травмы
калмыков
С предисловием Кэролайн Хамфри
ISBN 3-89821-506-7

21 Юлия Лидерман
Мотивы «проверки» и «испытания»
в постсоветской культуре
Советское прошлое в российском
кинематографе 1990-х годов
С предисловием Евгения Марголита
ISBN 3-89821-511-3

22 Tanya Lokshina, Ray Thomas, Mary
Mayer (Eds.)
The Imposition of a Fake Political
Settlement in the Northern Caucasus
The 2003 Chechen Presidential Election
ISBN 3-89821-436-2

23 Timothy McCajor Hall, Rosie Read
(Eds.)
Changes in the Heart of Europe
Recent Ethnographies of Czechs, Slovaks,
Roma, and Sorbs
With an afterword by Zdeněk Salzmann
ISBN 3-89821-606-3

24 Christian Autengruber
Die politischen Parteien in Bulgarien
und Rumänien
Eine vergleichende Analyse seit Beginn der
90er Jahre
Mit einem Vorwort von Dorothée de Nève
ISBN 3-89821-476-1

25 Annette Freyberg-Inan with Radu
Cristescu
The Ghosts in Our Classrooms, or:
John Dewey Meets Ceaușescu
The Promise and the Failures of Civic
Education in Romania
ISBN 3-89821-416-8

26 John B. Dunlop
The 2002 Dubrovka and 2004 Beslan
Hostage Crises
A Critique of Russian Counter-Terrorism
With a foreword by Donald N. Jensen
ISBN 3-89821-608-X

27 Peter Koller
Das touristische Potenzial von
Kam''janec'–Podil's'kyj
Eine fremdenverkehrsgeographische
Untersuchung der Zukunftsperspektiven und
Maßnahmenplanung zur
Destinationsentwicklung des „ukrainischen
Rothenburg"
Mit einem Vorwort von Kristiane Klemm
ISBN 3-89821-640-3

28 Françoise Daucé, Elisabeth Sieca-
Kozlowski (Eds.)
Dedovshchina in the Post-Soviet
Military
Hazing of Russian Army Conscripts in a
Comparative Perspective
With a foreword by Dale Herspring
ISBN 3-89821-616-0

29 Florian Strasser
    Zivilgesellschaftliche Einflüsse auf die
    Orange Revolution
    Die gewaltlose Massenbewegung und die
    ukrainische Wahlkrise 2004
    Mit einem Vorwort von Egbert Jahn
    ISBN 3-89821-648-9

30 Rebecca S. Katz
    The Georgian Regime Crisis of 2003-
    2004
    A Case Study in Post-Soviet Media
    Representation of Politics, Crime and
    Corruption
    ISBN 3-89821-413-3

31 Vladimir Kantor
    Willkür oder Freiheit
    Beiträge zur russischen Geschichtsphilosophie
    Ediert von Dagmar Herrmann sowie mit
    einem Vorwort versehen von Leonid Luks
    ISBN 3-89821-589-X

32 Laura A. Victoir
    The Russian Land Estate Today
    A Case Study of Cultural Politics in Post-
    Soviet Russia
    With a foreword by Priscilla Roosevelt
    ISBN 3-89821-426-5

33 Ivan Katchanovski
    Cleft Countries
    Regional Political Divisions and Cultures in
    Post-Soviet Ukraine and Moldova
    With a foreword by Francis Fukuyama
    ISBN 3-89821-558-X

34 Florian Mühlfried
    Postsowjetische Feiern
    Das Georgische Bankett im Wandel
    Mit einem Vorwort von Kevin Tuite
    ISBN 3-89821-601-2

35 Roger Griffin, Werner Loh, Andreas
    Umland (Eds.)
    Fascism Past and Present, West and
    East
    An International Debate on Concepts and
    Cases in the Comparative Study of the
    Extreme Right
    With an afterword by Walter Laqueur
    ISBN 3-89821-674-8

36 Sebastian Schlegel
    Der „Weiße Archipel"
    Sowjetische Atomstädte 1945-1991
    Mit einem Geleitwort von Thomas Bohn
    ISBN 3-89821-679-9

37 Vyacheslav Likhachev
    Political Anti-Semitism in Post-Soviet
    Russia
    Actors and Ideas in 1991-2003
    Edited and translated from Russian by Eugene
    Veklerov
    ISBN 3-89821-529-6

38 Josette Baer (Ed.)
    Preparing Liberty in Central Europe
    Political Texts from the Spring of Nations
    1848 to the Spring of Prague 1968
    With a foreword by Zdeněk V. David
    ISBN 3-89821-546-6

39 Михаил Лукьянов
    Российский консерватизм и
    реформа, 1907-1914
    С предисловием Марка Д. Стейнберга
    ISBN 3-89821-503-2

40 Nicola Melloni
    Market Without Economy
    The 1998 Russian Financial Crisis
    With a foreword by Eiji Furukawa
    ISBN 3-89821-407-9

41 Dmitrij Chmelnizki
    Die Architektur Stalins
    Bd. 1: Studien zu Ideologie und Stil
    Bd. 2: Bilddokumentation
    Mit einem Vorwort von Bruno Flierl
    ISBN 3-89821-515-6

42 Katja Yafimava
    Post-Soviet Russian-Belarussian
    Relationships
    The Role of Gas Transit Pipelines
    With a foreword by Jonathan P. Stern
    ISBN 3-89821-655-1

43 Boris Chavkin
    Verflechtungen der deutschen und
    russischen Zeitgeschichte
    Aufsätze und Archivfunde zu den
    Beziehungen Deutschlands und der
    Sowjetunion von 1917 bis 1991
    Ediert von Markus Edlinger sowie mit einem
    Vorwort versehen von Leonid Luks
    ISBN 3-89821-756-6

44   Anastasija Grynenko in
     Zusammenarbeit mit Claudia Dathe
     Die Terminologie des Gerichtswesens
     der Ukraine und Deutschlands im
     Vergleich
     Eine übersetzungswissenschaftliche Analyse
     juristischer Fachbegriffe im Deutschen,
     Ukrainischen und Russischen
     Mit einem Vorwort von Ulrich Hartmann
     ISBN 3-89821-691-8

45   Anton Burkov
     The Impact of the European
     Convention on Human Rights on
     Russian Law
     Legislation and Application in 1996-2006
     With a foreword by Françoise Hampson
     ISBN 978-3-89821-639-5

46   Stina Torjesen, Indra Overland (Eds.)
     International Election Observers in
     Post-Soviet Azerbaijan
     Geopolitical Pawns or Agents of Change?
     ISBN 978-3-89821-743-9

47   Taras Kuzio
     Ukraine – Crimea – Russia
     Triangle of Conflict
     ISBN 978-3-89821-761-3

48   Claudia Šabić
     "Ich erinnere mich nicht, aber L'viv!"
     Zur Funktion kultureller Faktoren für die
     Institutionalisierung und Entwicklung einer
     ukrainischen Region
     Mit einem Vorwort von Melanie Tatur
     ISBN 978-3-89821-752-1

49   Marlies Bilz
     Tatarstan in der Transformation
     Nationaler Diskurs und Politische Praxis
     1988-1994
     Mit einem Vorwort von Frank Golczewski
     ISBN 978-3-89821-722-4

50   Марлен Ларюэль (ред.)
     Современные интерпретации
     русского национализма
     ISBN 978-3-89821-795-8

51   Sonja Schüler
     Die ethnische Dimension der Armut
     Roma im postsozialistischen Rumänien
     Mit einem Vorwort von Anton Sterbling
     ISBN 978-3-89821-776-7

52   Галина Кожевникова
     Радикальный национализм в России
     и противодействие ему
     Сборник докладов Центра «Сова» за 2004-
     2007 гг.
     С предисловием Александра Верховского
     ISBN 978-3-89821-721-7

53   Галина Кожевникова и Владимир
     Прибыловский
     Российская власть в биографиях I
     Высшие должностные лица РФ в 2004 г.
     ISBN 978-3-89821-796-5

54   Галина Кожевникова и Владимир
     Прибыловский
     Российская власть в биографиях II
     Члены Правительства РФ в 2004 г.
     ISBN 978-3-89821-797-2

55   Галина Кожевникова и Владимир
     Прибыловский
     Российская власть в биографиях III
     Руководители федеральных служб и
     агентств РФ в 2004 г.
     ISBN 978-3-89821-798-9

56   Ileana Petroniu
     Privatisierung in
     Transformationsökonomien
     Determinanten der Restrukturierungs-
     Bereitschaft am Beispiel Polens, Rumäniens
     und der Ukraine
     Mit einem Vorwort von Rainer W. Schäfer
     ISBN 978-3-89821-790-3

57   Christian Wipperfürth
     Russland und seine GUS-Nachbarn
     Hintergründe, aktuelle Entwicklungen und
     Konflikte in einer ressourcenreichen Region
     ISBN 978-3-89821-801-6

58   Togzhan Kassenova
     From Antagonism to Partnership
     The Uneasy Path of the U.S.-Russian
     Cooperative Threat Reduction
     With a foreword by Christoph Bluth
     ISBN 978-3-89821-707-1

59   Alexander Höllwerth
     Das sakrale eurasische Imperium des
     Aleksandr Dugin
     Eine Diskursanalyse zum postsowjetischen
     russischen Rechtsextremismus
     Mit einem Vorwort von Dirk Uffelmann
     ISBN 978-3-89821-813-9

60 *Олег Рябов*
    «Россия-Матушка»
    Национализм, гендер и война в России XX века
    С предисловием Елены Гощило
    ISBN 978-3-89821-487-2

61 *Ivan Maistrenko*
    Borot'bism
    A Chapter in the History of the Ukrainian Revolution
    With a new introduction by Chris Ford
    Translated by George S. N. Luckyj with the assistance of Ivan L. Rudnytsky
    ISBN 978-3-89821-697-5

62 *Maryna Romanets*
    Anamorphosic Texts and Reconfigured Visions
    Improvised Traditions in Contemporary Ukrainian and Irish Literature
    ISBN 978-3-89821-576-3

63 *Paul D'Anieri and Taras Kuzio (Eds.)*
    Aspects of the Orange Revolution I
    Democratization and Elections in Post-Communist Ukraine
    ISBN 978-3-89821-698-2

64 *Bohdan Harasymiw in collaboration with Oleh S. Ilnytzkyj (Eds.)*
    Aspects of the Orange Revolution II
    Information and Manipulation Strategies in the 2004 Ukrainian Presidential Elections
    ISBN 978-3-89821-699-9

65 *Ingmar Bredies, Andreas Umland and Valentin Yakushik (Eds.)*
    Aspects of the Orange Revolution III
    The Context and Dynamics of the 2004 Ukrainian Presidential Elections
    ISBN 978-3-89821-803-0

66 *Ingmar Bredies, Andreas Umland and Valentin Yakushik (Eds.)*
    Aspects of the Orange Revolution IV
    Foreign Assistance and Civic Action in the 2004 Ukrainian Presidential Elections
    ISBN 978-3-89821-808-5

67 *Ingmar Bredies, Andreas Umland and Valentin Yakushik (Eds.)*
    Aspects of the Orange Revolution V
    Institutional Observation Reports on the 2004 Ukrainian Presidential Elections
    ISBN 978-3-89821-809-2

68 *Taras Kuzio (Ed.)*
    Aspects of the Orange Revolution VI
    Post-Communist Democratic Revolutions in Comparative Perspective
    ISBN 978-3-89821-820-7

69 *Tim Bohse*
    Autoritarismus statt Selbstverwaltung
    Die Transformation der kommunalen Politik in der Stadt Kaliningrad 1990-2005
    Mit einem Geleitwort von Stefan Troebst
    ISBN 978-3-89821-782-8

70 *David Rupp*
    Die Rußländische Föderation und die russischsprachige Minderheit in Lettland
    Eine Fallstudie zur Anwaltspolitik Moskaus gegenüber den russophonen Minderheiten im „Nahen Ausland" von 1991 bis 2002
    Mit einem Vorwort von Helmut Wagner
    ISBN 978-3-89821-778-1

71 *Taras Kuzio*
    Theoretical and Comparative Perspectives on Nationalism
    New Directions in Cross-Cultural and Post-Communist Studies
    With a foreword by Paul Robert Magocsi
    ISBN 978-3-89821-815-3

72 *Christine Teichmann*
    Die Hochschultransformation im heutigen Osteuropa
    Kontinuität und Wandel bei der Entwicklung des postkommunistischen Universitätswesens
    Mit einem Vorwort von Oskar Anweiler
    ISBN 978-3-89821-842-9

73 *Julia Kusznir*
    Der politische Einfluss von Wirtschaftseliten in russischen Regionen
    Eine Analyse am Beispiel der Erdöl- und Erdgasindustrie, 1992-2005
    Mit einem Vorwort von Wolfgang Eichwede
    ISBN 978-3-89821-821-4

74 *Alena Vysotskaya*
    Russland, Belarus und die EU-Osterweiterung
    Zur Minderheitenfrage und zum Problem der Freizügigkeit des Personenverkehrs
    Mit einem Vorwort von Katlijn Malfliet
    ISBN 978-3-89821-822-1

75 Heiko Pleines (Hrsg.)
    Corporate Governance in post-
    sozialistischen Volkswirtschaften
    ISBN 978-3-89821-766-8

76 Stefan Ihrig
    Wer sind die Moldawier?
    Rumänismus versus Moldowanismus in
    Historiographie und Schulbüchern der
    Republik Moldova, 1991-2006
    Mit einem Vorwort von Holm Sundhaussen
    ISBN 978-3-89821-466-7

77 Galina Kozhevnikova in collaboration
    with Alexander Verkhovsky and
    Eugene Veklerov
    Ultra-Nationalism and Hate Crimes in
    Contemporary Russia
    The 2004-2006 Annual Reports of Moscow's
    SOVA Center
    With a foreword by Stephen D. Shenfield
    ISBN 978-3-89821-868-9

78 Florian Küchler
    The Role of the European Union in
    Moldova's Transnistria Conflict
    With a foreword by Christopher Hill
    ISBN 978-3-89821-850-4

79 Bernd Rechel
    The Long Way Back to Europe
    Minority Protection in Bulgaria
    With a foreword by Richard Crampton
    ISBN 978-3-89821-863-4

80 Peter W. Rodgers
    Nation, Region and History in Post-
    Communist Transitions
    Identity Politics in Ukraine, 1991-2006
    With a foreword by Vera Tolz
    ISBN 978-3-89821-903-7

81 Stephanie Solywoda
    The Life and Work of
    Semen L. Frank
    A Study of Russian Religious Philosophy
    With a foreword by Philip Walters
    ISBN 978-3-89821-457-5

82 Vera Sokolova
    Cultural Politics of Ethnicity
    Discourses on Roma in Communist
    Czechoslovakia
    ISBN 978-3-89821-864-1

83 Natalya Shevchik Ketenci
    Kazakhstani Enterprises in Transition
    The Role of Historical Regional Development
    in Kazakhstan's Post-Soviet Economic
    Transformation
    ISBN 978-3-89821-831-3

84 Martin Malek, Anna Schor-
    Tschudnowskaja (Hrsg.)
    Europa im Tschetschenienkrieg
    Zwischen politischer Ohnmacht und
    Gleichgültigkeit
    Mit einem Vorwort von Lipchan Basajewa
    ISBN 978-3-89821-676-0

85 Stefan Meister
    Das postsowjetische Universitätswesen
    zwischen nationalem und
    internationalem Wandel
    Die Entwicklung der regionalen Hochschule
    in Russland als Gradmesser der
    Systemtransformation
    Mit einem Vorwort von Joan DeBardeleben
    ISBN 978-3-89821-891-7

86 Konstantin Sheiko in collaboration
    with Stephen Brown
    Nationalist Imaginings of the
    Russian Past
    Anatolii Fomenko and the Rise of Alternative
    History in Post-Communist Russia
    With a foreword by Donald Ostrowski
    ISBN 978-3-89821-915-0

87 Sabine Jenni
    Wie stark ist das „Einige Russland"?
    Zur Parteibindung der Eliten und zum
    Wahlerfolg der Machtpartei
    im Dezember 2007
    Mit einem Vorwort von Klaus Armingeon
    ISBN 978-3-89821-961-7

88 Thomas Borén
    Meeting-Places of Transformation
    Urban Identity, Spatial Representations and
    Local Politics in Post-Soviet St Petersburg
    ISBN 978-3-89821-739-2

89 Aygul Ashirova
    Stalinismus und Stalin-Kult in
    Zentralasien
    Turkmenistan 1924-1953
    Mit einem Vorwort von Leonid Luks
    ISBN 978-3-89821-987-7

90 Leonid Luks
    Freiheit oder imperiale Größe?
    Essays zu einem russischen Dilemma
    ISBN 978-3-8382-0011-8

91 Christopher Gilley
    The 'Change of Signposts' in the
    Ukrainian Emigration
    A Contribution to the History of
    Sovietophilism in the 1920s
    With a foreword by Frank Golczewski
    ISBN 978-3-89821-965-5

92 Philipp Casula, Jeronim Perovic
    (Eds.)
    Identities and Politics
    During the Putin Presidency
    The Discursive Foundations of Russia's
    Stability
    With a foreword by Heiko Haumann
    ISBN 978-3-8382-0015-6

93 Marcel Viëtor
    Europa und die Frage
    nach seinen Grenzen im Osten
    Zur Konstruktion ‚europäischer Identität' in
    Geschichte und Gegenwart
    Mit einem Vorwort von Albrecht Lehmann
    ISBN 978-3-8382-0045-3

94 Ben Hellman, Andrei Rogachevskii
    Filming the Unfilmable
    Casper Wrede's 'One Day in the Life
    of Ivan Denisovich'
    Second, Revised and Expanded Edition
    ISBN 978-3-8382-0044-6

95 Eva Fuchslocher
    Vaterland, Sprache, Glaube
    Orthodoxie und Nationenbildung
    am Beispiel Georgiens
    Mit einem Vorwort von Christina von Braun
    ISBN 978-3-89821-884-9

96 Vladimir Kantor
    Das Westlertum und der Weg
    Russlands
    Zur Entwicklung der russischen Literatur und
    Philosophie
    Ediert von Dagmar Herrmann
    Mit einem Beitrag von Nikolaus Lobkowicz
    ISBN 978-3-8382-0102-3

97 Kamran Musayev
    Die postsowjetische Transformation
    im Baltikum und Südkaukasus
    Eine vergleichende Untersuchung der
    politischen Entwicklung Lettlands und
    Aserbaidschans 1985-2009
    Mit einem Vorwort von Leonid Luks
    Ediert von Sandro Henschel
    ISBN 978-3-8382-0103-0

98 Tatiana Zhurzhenko
    Borderlands into Bordered Lands
    Geopolitics of Identity in Post-Soviet Ukraine
    With a foreword by Dieter Segert
    ISBN 978-3-8382-0042-2

99 Кирилл Галушко, Лидия Смола
    (ред.)
    Пределы падения – варианты
    украинского будущего
    Аналитико-прогностические исследования
    ISBN 978-3-8382-0148-1

100 Michael Minkenberg (ed.)
    Historical Legacies and the Radical
    Right in Post-Cold War Central and
    Eastern Europe
    With an afterword by Sabrina P. Ramet
    ISBN 978-3-8382-0124-5

101 David-Emil Wickström
    Rocking St. Petersburg
    Transcultural Flows and Identity Politics in
    the St. Petersburg Popular Music Scene
    With a foreword by Yngvar B. Steinholt
    Second, Revised and Expanded Edition
    ISBN 978-3-8382-0100-9

102 Eva Zabka
    Eine neue „Zeit der Wirren"?
    Der spät- und postsowjetische Systemwandel
    1985-2000 im Spiegel russischer
    gesellschaftspolitischer Diskurse
    Mit einem Vorwort von Margareta Mommsen
    ISBN 978-3-8382-0161-0

103 Ulrike Ziemer
    Ethnic Belonging, Gender and
    Cultural Practices
    Youth Identitites in Contemporary Russia
    With a foreword by Anoop Nayak
    ISBN 978-3-8382-0152-8

104 Ksenia Chepikova
‚Einiges Russland' - eine zweite KPdSU?
Aspekte der Identitätskonstruktion einer postsowjetischen „Partei der Macht"
Mit einem Vorwort von Torsten Oppelland
ISBN 978-3-8382-0311-9

105 Леонид Люкс
Западничество или евразийство? Демократия или идеократия?
Сборник статей об исторических дилеммах России
С предисловием Владимира Кантора
ISBN 978-3-8382-0211-2

106 Anna Dost
Das russische Verfassungsrecht auf dem Weg zum Föderalismus und zurück
Zum Konflikt von Rechtsnormen und -wirklichkeit in der Russländischen Föderation von 1991 bis 2009
Mit einem Vorwort von Alexander Blankenagel
ISBN 978-3-8382-0292-1

107 Philipp Herzog
Sozialistische Völkerfreundschaft, nationaler Widerstand oder harmloser Zeitvertreib?
Zur politischen Funktion der Volkskunst im sowjetischen Estland
Mit einem Vorwort von Andreas Kappeler
ISBN 978-3-8382-0216-7

108 Marlène Laruelle (ed.)
Russian Nationalism, Foreign Policy, and Identity Debates in Putin's Russia
New Ideological Patterns after the Orange Revolution
ISBN 978-3-8382-0325-6

109 Michail Logvinov
Russlands Kampf gegen den internationalen Terrorismus
Eine kritische Bestandsaufnahme des Bekämpfungsansatzes
Mit einem Geleitwort von Hans-Henning Schröder
und einem Vorwort von Eckhard Jesse
ISBN 978-3-8382-0329-4

110 John B. Dunlop
The Moscow Bombings of September 1999
Examinations of Russian Terrorist Attacks at the Onset of Vladimir Putin's Rule
Second, Revised and Expanded Edition
ISBN 978-3-8382-0388-1

111 Андрей А. Ковалёв
Свидетельство из-за кулис российской политики I
Можно ли делать добро из зла?
(Воспоминания и размышления о последних советских и первых послесоветских годах)
With a foreword by Peter Reddaway
ISBN 978-3-8382-0302-7

112 Андрей А. Ковалёв
Свидетельство из-за кулис российской политики II
Угроза для себя и окружающих
(Наблюдения и предостережения относительно происходящего после 2000 г.)
ISBN 978-3-8382-0303-4

113 Bernd Kappenberg
Zeichen setzen für Europa
Der Gebrauch europäischer lateinischer Sonderzeichen in der deutschen Öffentlichkeit
Mit einem Vorwort von Peter Schlobinski
ISBN 978-3-89821-749-1

114 Ivo Mijnssen
The Quest for an Ideal Youth in Putin's Russia I
Back to Our Future! History, Modernity, and Patriotism according to *Nashi*, 2005-2013
With a foreword by Jeronim Perović
Second, Revised and Expanded Edition
ISBN 978-3-8382-0368-3

115 Jussi Lassila
The Quest for an Ideal Youth in Putin's Russia II
The Search for Distinctive Conformism in the Political Communication of *Nashi*, 2005-2009
With a foreword by Kirill Postoutenko
Second, Revised and Expanded Edition
ISBN 978-3-8382-0415-4

116 Valerio Trabandt
Neue Nachbarn, gute Nachbarschaft?
Die EU als internationaler Akteur am Beispiel ihrer Demokratieförderung in Belarus und der Ukraine 2004-2009
Mit einem Vorwort von Jutta Joachim
ISBN 978-3-8382-0437-6

117 Fabian Pfeiffer
     Estlands Außen- und Sicherheitspolitik I
     Der estnische Atlantizismus nach der
     wiedererlangten Unabhängigkeit 1991-2004
     Mit einem Vorwort von Helmut Hubel
     ISBN 978-3-8382-0127-6

118 Jana Podßuweit
     Estlands Außen- und Sicherheitspolitik II
     Handlungsoptionen eines Kleinstaates im
     Rahmen seiner EU-Mitgliedschaft (2004-2008)
     Mit einem Vorwort von Helmut Hubel
     ISBN 978-3-8382-0440-6

119 Karin Pointner
     Estlands Außen- und Sicherheitspolitik III
     Eine gedächtnispolitische Analyse estnischer
     Entwicklungskooperation 2006-2010
     Mit einem Vorwort von Karin Liebhart
     ISBN 978-3-8382-0435-2

120 Ruslana Vovk
     Die Offenheit der ukrainischen
     Verfassung für das Völkerrecht und
     die europäische Integration
     Mit einem Vorwort von Alexander
     Blankenagel
     ISBN 978-3-8382-0481-9

121 Mykhaylo Banakh
     Die Relevanz der Zivilgesellschaft
     bei den postkommunistischen
     Transformationsprozessen in mittel-
     und osteuropäischen Ländern
     Das Beispiel der spät- und postsowjetischen
     Ukraine 1986-2009
     Mit einem Vorwort von Gerhard Simon
     ISBN 978-3-8382-0499-4

122 Michael Moser
     Language Policy and the Discourse on
     Languages in Ukraine under President
     Viktor Yanukovych (25 February
     2010–28 October 2012)
     ISBN 978-3-8382-0497-0 (Paperback edition)
     ISBN 978-3-8382-0507-6 (Hardcover edition)

123 Nicole Krome
     Russischer Netzwerkkapitalismus
     Restrukturierungsprozesse in der
     Russischen Föderation am Beispiel des
     Luftfahrtunternehmens "Aviastar"
     Mit einem Vorwort von Petra Stykow
     ISBN 978-3-8382-0534-2

124 David R. Marples
     'Our Glorious Past'
     Lukashenka's Belarus and
     the Great Patriotic War
     ISBN 978-3-8382-0574-8 (Paperback edition)
     ISBN 978-3-8382-0675-2 (Hardcover edition)

125 Ulf Walther
     Russlands "neuer Adel"
     Die Macht des Geheimdienstes von
     Gorbatschow bis Putin
     Mit einem Vorwort von Hans-Georg Wieck
     ISBN 978-3-8382-0584-7

126 Simon Geissbühler (Hrsg.)
     Kiew – Revolution 3.0
     Der Euromaidan 2013/14 und die
     Zukunftsperspektiven der Ukraine
     ISBN 978-3-8382-0581-6 (Paperback edition)
     ISBN 978-3-8382-0681-3 (Hardcover edition)

127 Andrey Makarychev
     Russia and the EU
     in a Multipolar World
     Discourses, Identities, Norms
     With a foreword by Klaus Segbers
     ISBN 978-3-8382-0629-5

128 Roland Scharff
     Kasachstan als postsowjetischer
     Wohlfahrtsstaat
     Die Transformation des sozialen
     Schutzsystems
     Mit einem Vorwort von Joachim Ahrens
     ISBN 978-3-8382-0622-6

129 Katja Grupp
     Bild Lücke Deutschland
     Kaliningrader Studierende sprechen über
     Deutschland
     Mit einem Vorwort von Martin Schulz
     ISBN 978-3-8382-0552-6

130 Konstantin Sheiko, Stephen Brown
     History as Therapy
     Alternative History and Nationalist
     Imaginings in Russia, 1991-2014
     ISBN 978-3-8382-0665-3

131 Elisa Kriza
     Alexander Solzhenitsyn: Cold War
     Icon, Gulag Author, Russian
     Nationalist?
     A Study of the Western Reception of his
     Literary Writings, Historical Interpretations,
     and Political Ideas
     With a foreword by Andrei Rogatchevski
     ISBN 978-3-8382-0589-2 (Paperback edition)
     ISBN 978-3-8382-0690-5 (Hardcover edition)

132 Serghei Golunov
The Elephant in the Room
Corruption and Cheating in Russian Universities
ISBN 978-3-8382-0570-0

133 Manja Hussner, Rainer Arnold (Hgg.)
Verfassungsgerichtsbarkeit in Zentralasien I
Sammlung von Verfassungstexten
ISBN 978-3-8382-0595-3

134 Nikolay Mitrokhin
Die "Russische Partei"
Die Bewegung der russischen Nationalisten in der UdSSR 1953-1985
Aus dem Russischen übertragen von einem Übersetzerteam unter der Leitung von Larisa Schippel
ISBN 978-3-8382-0024-8

135 Manja Hussner, Rainer Arnold (Hgg.)
Verfassungsgerichtsbarkeit in Zentralasien II
Sammlung von Verfassungstexten
ISBN 978-3-8382-0597-7

136 Manfred Zeller
Das sowjetische Fieber
Fußballfans im poststalinistischen Vielvölkerreich
Mit einem Vorwort von Nikolaus Katzer
ISBN 978-3-8382-0757-5

137 Kristin Schreiter
Stellung und Entwicklungspotential zivilgesellschaftlicher Gruppen in Russland
Menschenrechtsorganisationen im Vergleich
ISBN 978-3-8382-0673-8

138 David R. Marples, Frederick V. Mills (eds.)
Ukraine's Euromaidan
Analyses of a Civil Revolution
ISBN 978-3-8382-0660-8

139 Bernd Kappenberg
Setting Signs for Europe
Why Diacritics Matter for European Integration
With a foreword by Peter Schlobinski
ISBN 978-3-8382-0663-9

140 René Lenz
Internationalisierung, Kooperation und Transfer
Externe bildungspolitische Akteure in der Russischen Föderation
Mit einem Vorwort von Frank Ettrich
ISBN 978-3-8382-0751-3

141 Juri Plusnin, Yana Zausaeva, Natalia Zhidkevich, Artemy Pozanenko
Wandering Workers
Mores, Behavior, Way of Life, and Political Status of Domestic Russian Labor Migrants
Translated by Julia Kazantseva
ISBN 978-3-8382-0653-0

142 David J. Smith (ed.)
Latvia—A Work in Progress?
100 Years of State- and Nation-Building
ISBN 978-3-8382-0648-6

ibidem
Press

Laima, Rita

SKYLARKS AND REBELS

A Memoir about the Soviet Russian Occupation of Latvia, Life in a Totalitarian State, and Freedom

Skylarks and Rebels is a story about Latvia's fate in the 20th century as told by Rita Laima, a Latvian American who chose to leave behind the comforts of life in America to explore the land of her ancestors, Latvia, which in the 1980s languished behind the Soviet Iron Curtain. In writing about her own experiences in a totalitarian state, Soviet-occupied Latvia, Laima delves into her family's past to understand what happened to her fatherland and its people during and after World War II. She also pays tribute to some of Latvia's remarkable people of integrity who risked their lives to oppose the mindless ideology of the brutal and destructive Soviet state.

Rita Laima is a published writer, translator, and children's book illustrator. Born in the United States to the children of refugees who settled in New Jersey, Laima was raised biculturally, speaking Latvian at home. After studying art at Parsons School of Design in New York City, she traveled to Latvia in 1982 and lived there for 17 years. During that time, she experienced life under Soviet communism, the Soviet Union's efforts to russify her ancestral country, Latvia's National Awakening, and its long-awaited independence from the USSR in 1991.
Rita Laima currently lives in the Washington, DC area.

> "Rita Laima has written a unique memoir that explores the experiences of the Latvian exile community during the Soviet era and the situation of Latvians in their Soviet-occupied homeland in the 1980s, as well as during the first decade of independence beginning in 1991. [...] This memoir is not a nostalgic longing for the past but rather a truthful and sometimes harsh story about life in all its complexity and rich nuances, gleaned from the author's personal experience."
> **Mārtiņš Mintaurs, PhD, Assistant Professor at the Department of History and Philosophy, University of Latvia, Rīga**

€ 49,90, ISBN 978-3-8382-0854-1
502 Seiten, Paperback

ibidem.eu